Chinese Politics and Government

D0222804

Over the past two decades China's political reforms, open-door policy, dramatic economic growth, and increasingly assertive foreign policy have had an unprecedented regional and global impact. This introductory textbook provides students with a fundamental understanding of government and politics in China as well as the conceptual ability to explore the general patterns, impacts, and nature of continuities and changes in Chinese politics. Further, it equips students with analytical frameworks by which they can understand, analyze, and evaluate the major issues in Chinese politics, including:

- The basic methodologies and theoretical controversies in the study of Chinese politics.
- The major dimensions, structures, processes, functions, and characteristics of the Chinese political system, such as ideology, politics, law, society, economy, and foreign policy.
- The impact of power, ideology, and organization on different spheres of Chinese society.
- The structure, process, and factors in Chinese foreign policy making.
- Whether China is a "strategic partner" or "potential threat" to the United States.

By examining contending theoretical models in the study of Chinese politics, this book combines an essentialist approach that keeps focus on the fundamental, unique, and defining features of Chinese politics and government with other theoretical approaches or analytical models which reveal and explore the complexities inherent in the Chinese political system.

Extensively illustrated, the textbook includes maps, photographs, and diagrams, as well as providing questions for class discussions and suggestions for further reading. Written by an experienced academic with working knowledge of the Chinese government, this textbook will provide students with a comprehensive introduction to all aspects of Chinese politics.

Sujian Guo is Professor in the Department of Political Science and Director of the Center for U.S.–China Policy Studies at San Francisco State University, USA. Concurrently, he is a distinguished Professor of Fudan University, Associate Dean of the Fudan Institute for Advanced Study in Social Sciences, PRC, and Chair Professor at Zhejiang University, PRC.

Chinese Politics and Government

Power, ideology, and organization

Sujian Guo

Routledge
Taylor & Francis Group

LONDON AND NEW YORK

First published 2013
by Routledge
2 Park Square, Milton Park, Abingdon, Oxon OX14 4RN

Simultaneously published in the USA and Canada
by Routledge
711 Third Avenue, New York, NY 10017

*Routledge is an imprint of the Taylor & Francis Group,
an informa business*

British Library Cataloguing in Publication Data
A catalogue record for this book is available from the British Library

Library of Congress Cataloging in Publication Data
Guo, Sujian, 1957–
    Chinese politics and government: power, ideology and
    organization/Sujian Guo.
    p. cm.
    Includes bibliographical references and index.
    1. China—Politics and government. I. Title.
    JQ1510.G865 2012
    320.951—dc23   2012003057

ISBN: 978-0-415-55138-0 (hbk)
ISBN: 978-0-415-55139-7 (pbk)
ISBN: 978-0-203-10616-7 (ebk)

Typeset in Times New Roman
by Florence Production Ltd, Stoodleigh, Devon

Printed and bound in the United States of America by Publishers Graphics,
LLC on sustainably sourced paper.

Contents

Illustrations

Maps

Figures

Tables

Boxes

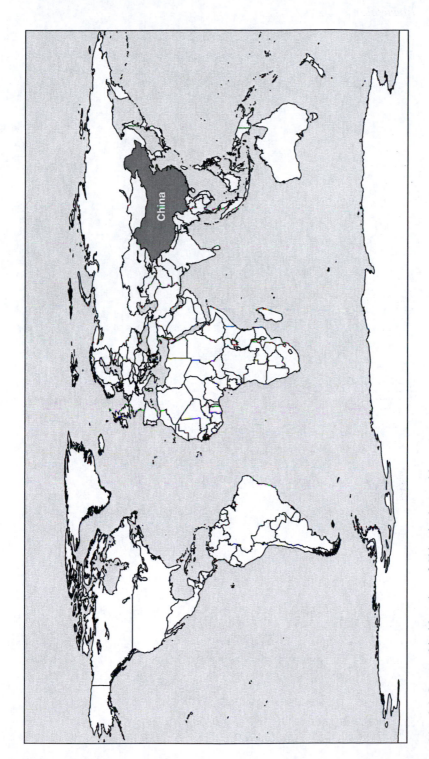

Map 0.1 Geographical location of China in the world.

Part I
Introducing Chinese politics

1 Chinese politics in comparative communist systems

Over the last two decades, China has gained prominence in the world economy and regional and global affairs. China's economic reforms, open-door policy, dramatic economic growth, and more assertive foreign policy have all had an unprecedented impact on the region and around the world, particularly on relations between China and the United States and other major world powers. Recent reactions to the rise of China by the U.S. Congress, the media, and the general public attest to a compelling need to enhance our understanding of what has happened and what is likely to happen in the years to come as well as to foster mutual understanding and goodwill between the two nations.

First, China's rising is beyond dispute, and it has enhanced its economic and military power tremendously in the past three decades. China is one of the largest countries, with a total land area of about 3.7 million square miles, slightly larger than that of the United States, and over 1.3 billion people, about 10 times more than that of the United States, one-fifth of the world population. The size itself proves its significance in world affairs. Moreover, after three decades of spectacular economic growth, with average growth rate of 10 percent for the past 30 years,[1] China has become the second largest economy in the world, and many predict that China will overtake the United States economically by the mid-twenty-first century, and some predict as early as 2030. Despite the real or potential conflicts, the United States and China also have significant common interests in many global issues (terrorism, nuclear proliferation, energy, environmental protection, financial and economic stability, and public health), regional security issues (nuclear crisis on the Korean peninsula and peace across the Taiwan Strait), and bilateral economic, business, and market benefits.[2]

Second, China is increasingly America's major trading nation, according to the U.S. Census Bureau, ranking number two, slightly behind Canada, with total trade of $456.8 billion, 14.3 percent of the total trade of the United States.[3] This provides many great opportunities for American companies and investors to do business with China. However, the U.S. trade deficit with China, $273 billions in 2010, is the largest in the world between any two countries.[4] Many Americans are concerned about the increasing job outsourcing to China and the job losses in the United States. China is now the largest creditor of the

U.S. Government. By November 2010, China owned $895 billion in U.S. Treasuries, 32 percent of the total $2.8 trillion outstanding.[5] However, many Americans are concerned that this might give China political leverage over U.S. fiscal policy, because, theoretically, China as the lender has the right to call in its loan. China is also the largest exporter and second largest importer of goods in the world. China's total trade in 2009 already surpassed $2.20 trillion, making China the world's second largest trading nation after the United States.[6] China may become the largest trading power within five years. China has become the world's largest recipient of foreign direct investment. Therefore, all figures tell us that it is in America's commercial interest to engage China, because China has a huge market, and at the same time is also one of the most dynamic economies in the world for over three decades (Box 1.1).

Third, China is a UN security council member and a major power in the world. Americans have been heavily involved in Asia at all levels: security, economic, political cultural, and even ideological. Americans were involved in the three wars in three decades in Asia, all of which confronted the Chinese communist military (Chinese civil war, Korean war, and Vietnam war), and

---

Box 1.1   The rise of China as an economic powerhouse

- China is the largest creditor nation in the world and owns approximately 20.8% of all foreign-owned U.S. Treasury securities.
- Chinese foreign exchange reserves have passed 2.65 trillion U.S. dollars, ranking first in the world.
- It is the largest recipient of foreign direct investment (over $100 billion in 2010), surpassing the U.S.
- China is also the largest exporter and second largest importer of goods in the world.
- China is the world's second largest consumer of oil.
- China has indeed become a world factory. China produces two-thirds of the world's photocopiers, 50% of DVD players, 70% of cement, 40% of socks, one-third of desktop computers, and 25% of mobile phones.
- Some predict, at its present rate, China will overtake the U.S. economy by 2025 while others project 2050, even predicting China will become a superpower to rival the US. China's economic boom and continued growth would definitely present the world a tremendous opportunity in businesses and sales.
- The UN hails China as the role model for the developing world— huge foreign currency reserves, huge trade surplus, emerging middle class, all the markings of an economy on the rise.

Americans can still feel the consequences of that involvement. It is in American interest to engage East Asia and remain a strong presence in the region. However, many Americans are concerned that a rising China might pose a challenge to U.S. foreign policy in the twenty-first century. Faced with a rising China, there has been an increase in wariness, fear, and suspicion from the world, particularly the United States. Many analysts have advised the U.S. government to adopt a new containment strategy to counterbalance the "China Threat."[7] In order to understand Chinese foreign policy behavior, we must understand the domestic politics and the context in which foreign policy and decisions are made.

This textbook is designed to provide a basic understanding of government and politics in China. The text will begin with a historical and cultural perspective in understanding the origins of China's politics and government, such as geographical and climate conditions as shaping forces of Chinese state making, political tradition, and political culture, and then focus on major dimensions of Chinese politics and government, such as ideology, politics, law, society, economy, and foreign policy. The basic themes, methodologies, and theoretical models for the study of Chinese politics will also be introduced at the beginning of the text. This text will help students develop their conceptual ability to analyze and explain the following general questions: What are the political implications of the relationship between the land and its people and how did the physical and climate conditions (the geographical context) influence the making of the state and the political culture in China? What factors have contributed to the rise of communism in China? What are the nature and characteristics of Chinese politics and government? What is the foundation that has continued to support and sustain the political regime? How has politics affected different spheres of Chinese society, economy, and law? Why has China opened itself to the outside world and embarked on reforms? What changes have taken place in the last decades? What has changed and what has not? What is the nature of the changes? In degree or in kind? What impact do these changes have on Chinese society? What are the dynamics and prospects for these changes? What is China's position and changing role in world affairs? Is China a "strategic partner" or "potential threat" to the United States? What foreign policy and strategy should the United States take toward a rising China in the twenty-first century? Is it the end or a continuation of Chinese communism? These are just some examples of the major questions students should learn to answer. More questions will be provided for discussion at the end of each chapter.

By examining contending theoretical models in the study of Chinese politics, this book *combines* an essentialist approach that keeps focus on the fundamental, unique, and defining features of Chinese politics and government that distinguishes it from others with theoretical approaches or analytical models wherever they fit in the analysis of major aspects of Chinese politics and government. This hybrid approach allows us to reveal and examine the complexity of political reality and context, adaptive, developmental, and institutional changes, operative features, and action means by the Chinese political leadership to maintain the fundamental and essential features of Chinese communist politics and government. This approach provides a conceptual framework in defining the Chinese political system and examining the essential characteristics, structures, processes, functions, and changes of the Chinese government and politics, and thus providing answers to some fundamental, basic, and general questions.

After this introductory chapter, we will study theoretical models employed by China scholars for studying Chinese politics (Chapter 2), and then begin to examine the geographical, historical, and cultural contexts of Chinese political development, major aspects, structures, processes, and functions of the Chinese political system, development, and changes, and assessment of the changes and their impact on the state of Chinese politics and government. The study will focus on the following central topics: land and people (Chapters 3–4), political development (Chapters 5–6), political ideology (Chapters 7–8), political institutions (Chapters 9–10), legal and legislative systems (Chapters 11–12), Chinese society (Chapters 13–14), political economy (Chapters 15–16), and foreign policy (Chapters 17–18). The selection of these topics reflects my assumptions about what is most important for American students to know about Chinese politics and government.

The geographical and climate conditions are essential in understanding the impact of environmental conditions on the agriculture and ways of living and thinking of the people who lived in early Chinese civilization, and thus on the making of the state, the political development, and the formation of political culture in China. The political culture has shaped the creation, maintenance, and development of particular types of state and the general patterns of political development dominated by power, ideology, and organization. Chinese civilization and Confucianism have been the cultural context in which political actions have taken place, and have been traditionally the dominant forces shaping political development in China. The political development from earlier times to the present has been characterized and complicated by the rise and fall of despotic, military, and Leninist authoritarianism, peasant uprisings, violence, war, revolution, and communism. The main locus, structure, and problems of Chinese politics and government are rarely known and experienced by American students.

Indeed, Chinese politics and government is new to many American students. China also has a constitution and other similar political institutions that look like those in the United States, such as congress, executive, courts, and political parties, but they are organized so differently and work in very different ways to achieve different ends that students cannot truly understand them without putting them in a comparative context. Therefore, we should not simply look at what they appear to be but focus on the nature of those institutions and their relationships, and not simply look how they have evolved historically, but focus on how they work from political science perspectives.

Most importantly, the textbook will provide students with an analytical framework against which they can observe, understand, interpret, and evaluate the most recent changes, development, and continuity of Chinese politics and government.

The study of Chinese politics in the subfield of comparative politics

Communist China has dramatically survived the collapse of communism in the Soviet bloc. What is the foundation that has continued to support and sustain the political regime? What are the nature, dynamics, and functions of the government in China? How different is it from a democratic regime? The answer to such questions requires comparison of different political systems that allows us to identify the most fundamental or essential features of this type of regime that distinguishes it from others, and explain what constitutes the very foundation of the regime. Therefore, we must place the study of Chinese politics and government in the subfield of comparative politics.

Then, what is comparative politics? According to Howard J. Wiarda, comparative politics involves the systematic study and comparison of the world's political systems, seeking to explain broad patterns, processes, and regularities among political systems. Comparative politics share the same logic of comparative social inquiry.[8] That is to say, Chinese political studies should seek to explain patterns and regularities of Chinese politics and government in a comparative context, not simply describe what has happened and what is happening in this country.

There are two general methodological approaches to political studies. One approach emphasizes the uniqueness of each country and rejects generalization and common regularities of every kind. The other seeks to explain common regularities or general patterns of development and generalize the experience of certain groups of nations or general historical laws. I belong to this group of scholars and believe that regularities in political life and human societies are very common, broad, and comparable, and thus cross-cultural patterns exist, and patterns of development and change can be generalized.

China is a communist country that shares many fundamental features in common with other communist countries despite all the variations among them due to different historical and cultural heritage, political leadership, social and economic contexts.[9] Therefore, it is logically necessary to put Chinese politics in a comparative context in order to have a comparative perspective of Chinese politics and understand its dynamic, functioning, and change. This comparative context is comparative communist systems which would allow us to distinguish it from other political systems, such as an authoritarian or democratic system. Then, the central question to begin with is: what are the commonalities of the communist system?

The communist party

In all communist countries, the government is controlled by a communist party that declares allegiance to Marxism–Leninism, proclaims itself as the vanguard of the working class, and represents the fundamental long-term interests of the people as a whole. In many of these countries, the party declares itself to be historically entitled to rule by the "democratic dictatorship of the proletariat." The communist party rests at the peak of the power structure, controls and dominates all sectors of state, and penetrates in every corner of society, with party branches as the party's basic cells established at all levels of government and within almost all political and public institutions.[10] Some communist states, such as East Germany, Czechoslovak Socialist Republic, China, and North Korea, may have some legally existent small parties, but they were or are all required to follow the leadership of the communist party under the constitution or by statute, and they were or are totally integrated into the communist party dominant political system to function as a consultative body or supporting role for the party and the government. There is the existence of party-led and state-sanctioned social organizations, such as trade unions, youth organizations, women's, teachers', writers', journalists' and other professional or industrial associations, which are also fully integrated into the political system, and are required to follow the leadership of the communist party, serve as a transmission belt or a link between the party and the society, to provide regime support to the leadership of the communist party, and promote social unity and stability.[11]

The party ideology

In all communist countries, the communist party and the state declare allegiance to a communist ideology or Marxism–Leninism as the guiding principle of the state, while the communist party claims to be the vanguard of the working class, represents the fundamental and long-term interest of the whole people and acts in accordance to objective and historical laws declaimed to be the truth. The party ideology is official, paramount, and formally codified into the constitution in all communist countries, and it serves as the guiding principles for the party–state policy and justifies the party's political actions and movements. However, the party ideology can be modified by the top party leaders according to their political needs, and under different circumstances. Those modifications are usually demonstrated in their speeches and writings, party conference documents, official textbooks, the press, and all other official pronouncements. The party ideology is also exclusive, in a sense that the party–state does not allow for other ideologies to exist and influence the general population. The communist party enjoys an almost full ideological monopoly and uses its official ideology to indoctrinate the general population and remold politics, society, law, economy, culture, and man. Therefore, the party, the state, and the ideology are totally intertwined, and the party's political power is intertwined with ideological power.[12]

The power structure

In all communist countries, the party and the state are completely intertwined, with the leadership of parallel organizations of the communist party, which is termed the "party–state" system. That is, party organizations are totally intertwined with state institutions in a kind of duplication at all levels from the top down. Party organizations play the key role in selecting the members of the legislature, the state administration, and the judiciary. The party's power covers all major political appointments, promotions, and dismissals. Party organizations reach decisions on all major state affairs, and state institutions led by party leaders and party organizations execute party decisions. Party leaders hold state office or leading positions in public organizations, as premier, ministers, state president, presidents of parliament and judiciary, chief directors of state-owned enterprises, generals and all officers in the military and police, etc. The existence of the party–state and the blending of the political and administrative functions is one of the distinctive characteristics of the communist system worldwide.[13]

The power structure in all communist countries is indivisible and totalistic in nature. Party–state power extends to every sphere of the country, such as politics, culture, education, religion, economy, and social life. Party–state power penetrates the whole society and influences every citizen. The party–state apparatus and police authorities of each region and workplace keep a household or residential registration account of every resident and employee for his or her entire life. Party–state power is not checked by law or legislative institutions because of the lack of an independent legislative and judicial system. Laws, government regulations, and court orders can be used to give formal, legal sanction to the prosecution of groups and individuals.[14]

Therefore, to sum up, a communist state can be defined as a form of government that is controlled by the communist party that declares allegiance to Marxism–Leninism as the guiding principles of the state and the whole nation, claims to have total representation of the people and total guidance of national goals, with parallel party organizations being completely intertwined with the state and public institutions. By definition, at the height of communism in the twentieth century, there were 16 communist states that shared similar characteristics of the political system as depicted above: the Soviet Union (now broken up into many independent states such as Russia, Belarus, Ukraine, Moldova, Georgia, Armenia, Azerbaijan, Kazakhstan, Uzbekistan, Turkmenistan, Kyrgyzstan, Tajikistan, Estonia, Latvia, and Lithuania), Poland, Czechoslovakia (now divided into Slovakia and the Czech Republic), Hungary, Bulgaria, East Germany (now part of Germany), Romania, Yugoslavia (now divided into Slovenia, Serbia, Montenegro, Kosovo, Macedonia, Croatia, Bosnia and Herzogovina), Albania, Mongolia, China, North Korea, Vietnam, Laos, Cambodia, and Cuba. However, some other countries that also declared themselves to be communist/socialist states and had a similar form of government were Grenada, Angola, Benin, Congo, Ethiopia (now divided into

Eritrea and Ethiopia), Mozambique, Somalia, and South Yemen (now part of Yemen)[15] (Map 1.1).

After the collapse of the communist regimes in the Soviet Union and Eastern European countries in the late 1990s, some countries, such as China, North Korea, Vietnam, Laos, and Cuba, have retained the essential characteristics of the communist system and thus remain communist states, although they have adopted different economic policies and market reforms

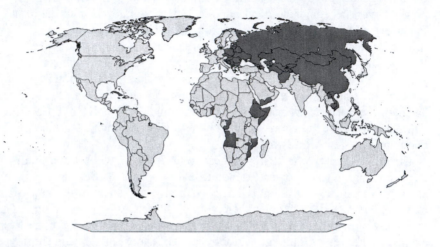

Map 1.1 Political map of communist states in the twentieth century.

Map of countries that declared themselves or were declared to be socialist states under the Marxist–Leninist or Maoist definition between 1979 and 1983.

Source: http://en.wikipedia.org/wiki/File:Communist_countries.svg.

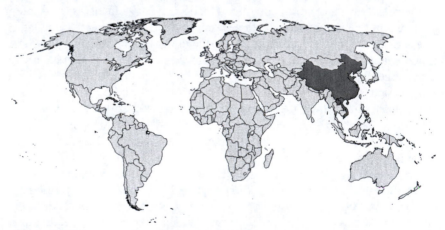

Map 1.2 Political map of communist states in the twenty-first century.

A map showing the current (2010) states with communist/socialist governments: China, North Korea, Vietnam, Laos, and Cuba.

Source: http://en.wikipedia.org/wiki/File:Communist_countries.svg.

to transition from the centrally planned command economy based on the Soviet model (Map 1.2).

To conclude, despite the variations of the party's official ideology from country to country, shaped by political leaders, such as Stalin, Tito, Mao, Kim Il-sung, and Deng, we can easily generalize from the variants of communism and identify common traits, characteristics, or regularities to the greatest degree. That is to say, China is a communist country that shares many fundamental features with other communist countries despite all the variations among them due to different historical and cultural heritage, political leadership, social and economic context. Therefore, political scientists can explain common regularities or general patterns of development and generalize the experience of certain groups of nations. Political scientists can put Chinese politics in a comparative context to understand its dynamics, function, and change.

Questions for discussion

1. Why do we study Chinese politics, and how should we study it from theoretical and methodological perspectives in political science?
2. What is a communist state in a comparative context? What are the distinct political features that differ from those of an authoritarian state, such as a dictatorship, military regime, or a monarch?
3. How can the Chinese communist state manage not only to survive but also to grow and enhance its strength in the grand failure of communism in the twentieth century?

Further reading

Stephen White, John Gardner, George Schopflin, and Tony Saich, *Communist and Postcommunist Political Systems: An Introduction* (Palgrave Macmillan, 1990).
Janos Kornai, *The Socialist System: The Political Economy of Communism* (Princeton: Princeton University Press, 1992).

2 Theoretical models for studying Chinese politics

Theories are important because political studies are not simply a summary of observation, facts, or data, but a means to uncover meaningful patterns in the data or in the empirical world and explain causal relationships among observed political phenomena, actions, and behaviors at individual, group, community, subnational, or national levels.[1] Moreover, theories are important in the study of Chinese politics because theories are analytical tools for understanding, explaining, and predicting political occurrence and help students think about problems or questions in the field come up with hunches, hypotheses or assumptions, develop arguments or theses that address questions, identify and justify variables or factors selected for an explanation of the political phenomena under study, and collect relevant data or evidence in support of arguments. Often, theoretical models, or approaches informed by or derived from theories, are as useful as theories in the analysis of politics; therefore, theories and models are treated as equally important in scientific research or empirical analysis of political phenomena.

Theories and models for studying Chinese politics and government have reflected different methods, assumptions, and emphases on different levels of unit in the analysis of China's political development as well as the subjects of study by different generations of China scholars in the changing political and economic environments in China in the decades since 1949. Therefore, the study of Chinese politics has been constrained by the accessibility of information and data as well as the changes in methodologies that are associated with the changing environment. The study of Chinese politics can be generally divided into two main periods: from the 1950s to the 1970s, when China was isolated from the world, and from the 1980s onward, when China was increasingly and gradually opening to the world with ongoing economic reforms carried out by the post-Mao leadership. We have witnessed the substantial transformation of Chinese political studies in the past 30 years due to changes in China and its rising status in the world as well as changes in our ways of conducting research.

As area studies specialists, we are no longer "isolated" from the larger disciplines of Political Science and International Relations but an integral part of them. A simple survey of the *Journal of Chinese Political Science* and other political science journals reveals that we have applied theories and methods from these larger disciplines to Chinese political studies and that we have sought to meet the standards of scientific research and theoretical relevance in the two disciplines. The scholarship we produce today has advanced far beyond the days of classic Sinology in the 1950s–1970s.[2] However, theoretical and methodological approaches in Chinese political studies are very diverse and very rich, and substantive issues in various Chinese contexts are being studied from a broader comparative perspective. Scholars and students in our field still vividly remember texts used in graduate school and innumerable papers published by first-rate comparativists such as Sydney Verba, Arendt Lijphart, David Collier, James Mahon, Giovanni Satori, Gary King, David Easton, and many others. All of them have had a great impact on how we study China and Chinese politics.[3]

In order to understand how Chinese politics has been studied, and help students develop consciousness about the application of theories in the study of Chinese politics, this textbook will provide a brief overview and introduction to the rich and diverse theories and models that seek to explain phenomena or aspects of phenomena, and their patterns in Chinese politics and government (see Figure 2.1). However, it is not the intention of this textbook to introduce

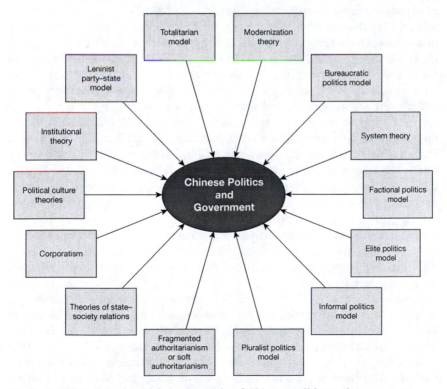

Figure 2.1 Theoretical models in the study of Chinese politics and government.

students to all of these or provide an exhaustive list of theories and models, but at least some popular ones that China scholars have employed in the analysis of Chinese politics: the totalitarian model, modernization theory or developmental model, bureaucratic politics model, system theory model, factional politics model, elite politics model, informal politics model, pluralist politics model, soft authoritarianism or fragmented authoritarianism, theories of state–society relations, corporatism, political culture theories, institutional theories, and the Leninist party–state.

The totalitarian model

The totalitarian model dominated the field of communist studies in the 1950s, and it was popular in the analysis of the essence and dynamics of Chinese politics and the power structure of government. The classical totalitarian model identified several key institutional features, such as an official ideology, a command economy, a party–state, and a wide-ranging control over virtually all areas of society.[4] However, the model was criticized as weak in reflecting change and political development influenced by socio-economic development in post-Mao China. Many of the features listed in the classical model have been considered no longer applicable to China since the early 1980s as a result of changes brought about by the reforms in post-Mao China. For example, the role of official ideology has become less restrictive, the economy has become more market oriented, society has become more pluralistic, etc.[5] Although many scholars no longer find the totalitarian model in its original form a useful framework for analyzing Chinese politics and government, some scholars have attempted to revisit the utility of the totalitarian model as a macro-model in defining the regime identity and assessing the nature of change in the political regime. They have attempted to establish that the totalitarian model has undeniable analytic utility in communist studies in general and China political studies in particular, and think that it should be amended rather than discarded totally. They have sought to reconstruct or refine the totalitarian model on more theoretical and comparative grounds so that it can be used to specify what existed before post-Mao China or to define the original point at which the change has occurred.[6] More recently, William E. Odom, for example, has plausibly argued that the classical totalitarian model captures the key features of Soviet rule, and that "in dismissing the totalitarian model, we lost the basis for measuring change."[7] According to Odom, none of those alternative models have fully replaced the classical totalitarian model and no one rivals its dominance. He has plausibly argued that "where they emphasize other things, they neglect central realities."[8] Even in recent years some distinguished scholars have not wholly discarded it. "The totalitarian model has far more analytical utility than its competitors (which is not to deny that the others have yielded insights)," because "the totalitarian model captures critical features of the system that tend to get pushed aside by other models."[9] Stephen E. Hanson argues that those alternative models to the totalitarian model leave us in no better position than the classical totalitarian model in identifying the conceptual continuity of the entire history of the Soviet or Chinese regime.[10] Donald W. Treadgold concurs: "whether all of these changes can still be accounted for within the analytical framework of totalitarianism is in dispute, but no other term has yet gained general acceptance as a substitute."[11]

Modernization theory

Modernization theory has been the result of the attempt to develop an alternative model for analyzing the communist systems and Chinese politics, and emphasizes the impact of socio-economic development brought about by the modernization process on political development and polity. This model derives from the evolutionary theories which assume a single and progressive line of development from backward and agrarian societies to modern and developed societies. The modernization model assumes that there is a causal link between socio-economic development and political change: a higher level of socio-economic development, a higher level of democracy. In other words, in the long run China as a communist state will develop into a competitive, pluralistic, and democratic political system that corresponds to their higher level of social and economic development.[12] However, many empirical studies have not found sufficient evidence to support the empirical relationship or causal link between socio-economic development and political regime change in China. As a matter of fact, many studies suggest that China, as well as some communist and authoritarian regimes with relatively high levels of socio-economic development, has low levels of political pluralism and freedom, despite the increasing plural socioeconomic changes, while other states, such as India, the Philippines, and many other less developed countries in the twentieth century, have successfully combined a liberal-democratic political system with relatively low levels of industrialization, urbanization, and per capita national income.[13]

The bureaucratic politics model

The bureaucratic politics model recognizes the dominant position of the communist party, the intertwined party–state apparatus, and the absence of competitive elections and oppositions. However, it assumes that politics takes place not between the communist party and other contenders for power as in the West but within the party and other bureaucratic organizations. The system can be seen as the hierarchically organized bureaucratic organizations with the top leadership standing in relation to other parts of the political system as much as the board of directors stands in relation to their administrative subordinates in a large Western corporation. Major bureaucratic interests and local party–state officials bargain and compete informally for political and economic resources, emphasizing the interest of their area or industry in their dealings with the top leadership or central authorities.[14] However, many studies question the assumption that bureaucratic behavior in the West and in the communist states must be necessarily comparable. As a matter of fact, there are few similarities in bureaucratic functioning and motivation in the East and West. Bureaucratic behavior and bargaining do not in themselves justify conceptualizing the political system as a whole as a giant bureaucracy, which would neglect the distinctive role of the communist party and its relationships with bureaucratic organizations as well as the special role of ideology in bureaucratic behavior, motivation, policy making, law making, and the remolding of society and man.[15] Therefore, the bureaucratic politics model cannot yield insights into the hard core of the party–state power structure and the influence of political ideology in shaping the dynamics, essence, and internal workings of contemporary Chinese politics.

System theory

The system theory has also been employed by scholars to analyze Chinese politics. According to this theory, demand, expectations, and support, which are termed as "input," are first turned to the political system and processed by government authorities within the political system, which are termed as "conversion process," and made into decisions, policies, and laws, which are termed as "output" for all members of society. These outputs, in turn, create reactions from society, which are termed as "feedback," which will then be again turned into demands, expectations, and support. The demand and support can be influenced by the "environment," which includes domestic and international dimensions and factors.[16] Some scholars have skillfully renovated this model and applied it to policy analysis of some important issues in Chinese politics, such as local politics and governance, policy implementation, regime legitimacy, and stability.[17] However, some studies criticize the utility of this model for studying Chinese politics and government. One of the major problems is the "conversion" black box of the Chinese political system in which the decision-making process is not transparent and unpredictable. The Party makes the decision based on its own ideology, norms, and political needs without being influenced by significant congressional and public debates, as political and public institutions, including news media, are controlled by the Party organizations and official media organizations. Although the news media in China today do reflect more different opinions, they usually have to do it in conformity with the Party's propaganda disciplines or they might be at risk of political sanctions by the Party organizations. Thus, scholars will have to rely on the published official documents based on their understanding and interpretation of the information.

The factional politics model

The factional politics model focuses on the power struggle among factional members within the ruling party leadership that are tied together based on personal loyalty of factional members to their factional leaders, their superior–subordinate relationship, and other historically rooted and political relationships in the power structure. Factions share different interpretations of the significance of emerging problems as well as perceptions of the changing environment and their policy preferences in the resolution of those problems. Factional leaders sometimes have to enter some alliances with other factional leaders to enhance their power, and accomplish their goals and policy preferences. However, there is a constant power struggle among factions for influence and personnel appointments, which results in certain policy outcomes.[18] However, many criticize the model as too simplistic as it ignores the influence of too many factors, such as ideological, societal, cultural, and even institutional constraints on the outcomes of the decision-making process. Owing to the lack of accurate and sufficient information about factions and intra-factional interaction, the outcomes of power struggle are usually analyzed afterwards rather than predicted.[19]

The elite politics model

The elite politics model is a new development of the factional politics model in more recent years, with renewed interests in studying the power relationships between top leaders and their dynamic interaction in shaping the power balance and decision making. Influenced by elite theory or power elite theory in social sciences, it provides a theoretical perspective in explaining "power transfer" between the Party's generational leadership, interaction "between different factional groups" within the party–state, "characteristics of China's political elites, and the balance of power among formal institutions as well as among factional groups."[20] Many scholars study elite politics by examining the elite in power and the new generation that is made up of technocrats who have largely turned away from ideological debates, concentrated their attention on concrete problems and their resolution in the country, and introduced rules and institutions for settling their differences in decision making.[21] Therefore, Chinese politics has become "more rational, normal and predictable."[22] However, this approach tends to neglect the constraints of the structural, institutional, and ideological context in which the elite interact with one another, and their interactions are largely a closed door. Therefore, the lack of accurate and sufficient information would result in guesses, speculations, and even misleading predictions.

The informal politics model

The informal politics model is another variant of the factional politics model. However, the informal politics model focuses on the relationships and impacts from outside the formal structures, institutions, and processes of the party–state, particularly the influence of "guanxi" (关系) networks or connections among individuals and groups based on mutual self-interests and patron–client relationships such as families, friends, work units, native places, etc., which seek reciprocal benefits and mutual interests for each other.[23] The patron provides protection and resources to the client while the client provides loyalty, support, and services to the patron. It seems that such relationships have played a prominent role in Chinese politics due to the influence of Confucian culture and tradition, and such activities have created informal rules of the game (潜规则) in Chinese politics that can be studied for a better understanding of the influence of those informal dimensions of the politics on decision-making processes and changes in China.[24] However, patron–client relationships exist in almost all cultures, and vary in degree of influence from country to country. Therefore, the informal politics model or the study of patron–client relationship alone cannot yield insights into the hard core of the party–state power structure and the influence of political ideology in shaping the dynamics, essence, and internal workings of contemporary Chinese politics.

The pluralist politics model

The pluralist politics model, unlike the elite politics model that focuses on the top level elite, focuses on the provincial and local governments as its analytical unit, and the relations between central and local levels of the party–state. They observe that market reform and decentralization have resulted in emerging "de facto federalism" for competition and negotiation in allocation of resources and power of decision making in China in recent years. Such collective bargaining, negotiation, and competition between central and local levels of the party–state have played an important role in policy formation and implementation.[25] "Thus, 'real' political activities are based on groups that share common sector interests, and these groups act through formal and informal political institutions."[26] However, the model overlooks the important role of the central government in defining and constraining the role of local governments and determining the structural and institutional parameters of group interests and activities, although local governments have enjoyed increasing autonomy in economic decision making in recent years. These institutional constraints include major personnel appointments and career advancement in the power structure of the party–state, the organizational principle of the Party "democratic centralism," the extent and scope of power delegation from the power center to local levels, the punishments of Party disciplines, and so forth.

Fragmented authoritarianism

Fragmented authoritarianism or soft authoritarianism is a concept used by some scholars to capture the nature of the Chinese political system. Like scholars who employ the pluralist politics model, these scholars have observed the considerable institutional changes, less cohesive decision-making processes, regional differences, weakening ability of central control, and expanded legal space for social organizations and individuals in China as a result of market reforms and decentralization in the past decades. The new developments have caused a fragmentation of the "core apparatus" of the Chinese state, but recognized that "the changes have not yet brought about a systemic transformation; to repeat, at its core, it is still a Soviet-Leninist state."[27] However, as one leading scholar of "fragmented authoritarianism" recognizes, this model is a "static model" and fails to explain the changes and forces that have produced changes in the 1990s and onward.[28] The utility of the concept is compatible with the pluralist politics model in the study of Chinese politics, but it is less conceptualized and theorized, often loosely used by everyone, either scholars or journalists, to describe the Chinese communist regime in post-Mao China whenever they observe that the party–state has maintained power while its control has been relaxed, and is less pervasive and intrusive. However, the major problem of this model is to confuse two different political regimes—it cannot distinguish a communist regime from a regular authoritarian regime, and fails to capture the defining features of the Chinese political system.

State–society relations

Many scholars have focused on state–society relations in their analysis and explanation of Chinese politics and changes in recent years, and, therefore, the study of state–society relations has been recognized as a model of studying Chinese politics. This model is also compatible with the pluralist politics model, but it has a particular focus on the interaction between the state and the society.[29] In other words, scholars interpret changes, both causes and consequences, in Chinese politics as an outcome of interactions between the state and the society.[30] One of the major research issues in the study of state–society relations is "whether the post-Mao economic reforms are producing a significant change in the relative power of state–society relations."[31] Many political scientists who study China have observed the changes in Chinese society, and their impact on institutional changes and policy making, and therefore they believe that the study of state–society relations should provide a good understanding of Chinese politics.[32] However, how to interpret the changes in state–society relations is a challenge for scholars. For some, the Chinese state has been weakening, and even retreated from society or taken over by society characterized as a "societal taken over" or a fundamental change in state–society relations,[33] while others contend that a strong state and weak society remain unchanged, and a task facing the reformers is to develop a strong society and weak state. However, neither side seems to recognize the fact or a central reality in China, that the Party has actually and effectively controlled the state and society, and the interaction between them during the post-Mao transformation. The fact is that the party–state apparatus in post-Mao China has been highly institutionalized and strengthened compared with Mao's China while the party has redefined the role of the state, and its relations with society to allow society to play a greater role in economic reform and modernization.

Corporatism

Corporatism has recently become popular among scholars in their study of state–society relations. The concept is well theorized and informed by other disciplines within social sciences. Particularly since the late 1970s, corporatism has become a paradigm, a social science approach, a way of studying political systems and policy issues. The term "corporatism" has been widely used by social scientists to analyze modern labor relations, the relations of interest groups to the state, to parliaments, and to one another, the social security and social welfare legislation in which labor and state are involved, and the relations between policy making and public affairs. Corporatism refers to a set of beliefs held by people who value those institutions and practices and seek to bring them about. These institutions and practices involve a system of interest representation or a kind of state–society relationship in which the constituent units are organized and structured into functionally differentiated categories, and their relations are controlled and regulated by law or the predominant social norms, and their interactions are incorporated into the formal structures of the state, monitored and guided by the state in modern society or similar political authority in traditional society.[34]

Modern corporatism may take a variety of forms in different countries, ranging from "social-group-oriented" corporatism in its pluralist forms, "social-control-oriented" corporatism in its authoritarian statist forms, and neo-corporatism in its modern liberal-pluralistic and managed capitalistic forms. Different forms of corporatism suggest that corporatism tends to grow out of the history and culture of the society, out of political and ideological battle, out of crises and economic requirements, or out of the bureaucratization of the modern state and the need to link labor and capital together for coordinated national development.[35]

Some scholars have investigated the applicability of this analytical model in studying the social changes and state–society relations in China.[36] However, corporatism based on the division between capital and labor or state and society relations may not reflect the reality in China, because China is not a representative democracy, and societal interests independent of the state are not allowed to exist as social organizations, including newly emerging business associations. NGOs are integrated into the party–state, and interest allocation and coordination are controlled and manipulated by the party–state to facilitate its policy goals and regime legitimation. Social organizations still serve as the "transmission belt" for the party, and now as the means to strengthen the governance capacity of the party–state, not the other way around.[37] Social relations and social conflicts are structured, controlled, dominated, and determined by the party–state power, the Chinese communist tradition of "unit politics," and the institutional and political context despite the changes that have been brought about by the economic reforms since 1978. The changes have not fundamentally altered the above-mentioned structure, tradition, and context.

Political culture theories

Political culture theories provide a cultural lens for studying Chinese politics. Political culture is a particular distribution of political beliefs, attitudes, values, feelings, and socio-psychological orientations that structure political behavior both at individual and collective levels and shape the social context in which political action takes place. Thus, Chinese politics cannot be understood without reference to its political culture. However, as one leading authority on the subject points out, "within the academic discipline of political science political culture has lost status over the past generation as not conducive to the development of empirical political theory."[38] Efforts have been made by scholars to revisit and resurrect the utility of political culture approaches to the study of Chinese politics. People act, react, and interact to seek goods and values "in terms of the circumstances and limitations they find themselves in. Among these circumstances are those pertaining to the culture—the informal institutions, customs, and beliefs prevalent in the society in which they live. Cultural analysis details and sometimes explains these institutions, customs and beliefs, allowing political analysis to go beyond the banality that people generally act to foster their material, psychological, or moral good."[39]

However, the study of political culture has limitations in conceptualizing and explaining Chinese politics, although it does shape and constrain the circumstances and contexts in which political actions take place. Culture changes over time, so does political culture. As another leading authority on China contends, "Culture, if defined carefully, is always incoherent rather than unified. Deductions from one strand of a culture will not necessarily lead to the same conclusion as those from another. So culture cannot be used in determinist causal arguments, but it limits the alternative ways in which people conceive their options or preferences."[40]

Institutional theory

Institutions are social, political, economic, and cultural structures, customs, practices, and mechanisms of social cooperation, order, and governance that determine the rules of games that shape and constrain the behavior of individuals and organizations. Institutions are manifest in both *formal* organizations and *informal* social order and organization.[41] Some scholars treat institutions as "actors" making choices based on some "collective" interests, preferences, goals, alternatives, and expectations. Therefore, they are interested in the analysis of the strategic interactions and choices between principals and agents both constrained by the changing institutional environment, and what factors and how these factors contribute to the changes.[42] The institutional theory has been a popular approach to the study of Chinese politics. Scholars who take this approach have focused on the role of institutions in the shaping of economic, social, and political change in China, as well as the institutional environment and its implications for policy-making processes, social interaction, and economic transaction.[43]

Although actors make choices based on a calculus of individual or collective interests within the existing institutional constraints, such an institutional focus simply treats Chinese political institutions and actors within the institutions acting upon the same assumptions on the rationality, preferences, and goals, and thus in the same political logic as that under a Western democratic polity. Therefore, this approach often runs into a classificatory problem or "conceptual stretching" and "conceptual distorting,"[44] and confuses Chinese political institutions with other modern states with similar features— and fails to distinguish a communist regime from a democratic regime, and cannot capture the defining features of the Chinese political system, the government, and the politics.

Which model is optimal?

All the models of communist politics we have considered have their merits and shortcomings. But which one is optimal? Models by their very nature are used to picture social reality and simplify many aspects of a political system in order to capture the most important and distinctive features. According to Huntington, a most important political scientist, a macro-model for a political regime must at least (1) capture the defining features of critical importance; (2) offer a basis for comparison with other systems; and (3) account for change.[45] Now, which model do you think is optimal for the study of communist states and Chinese politics?

While I acknowledge the important insights and contributions of these theoretical models and approaches to the understanding of Chinese politics and government in one way or another, I think none of these theoretical approaches or models can provide us with a macro-analytical model that meets the above criteria for studying Chinese politics. Each model may capture one dimension of the empirical world of China, but tends to take the traits of the parts to characterize the whole or fails to capture the essence and central reality of Chinese politics and government while explaining the dynamics of changes that have taken place in communist China. Inspired by the ideas of Huntington's macro-model, and my understanding of Chinese politics and government based on my personal and professional experience and background in China—every scholar's understanding is based on knowledge, experience, and observation—I think a good macro-analytical model should not only capture the defining features of the Chinese political system, politics, and government, which can be theoretically and practically depicted and placed in a comparative context with other communist systems in the world either before the collapse of communism in the Soviet block or also in the post-communist era, but also provide a conceptual and theoretical framework for defining the point of departure (what China was or where it comes from), reflecting changes and continuities (what China is), and assessing the nature of changes against the point of departure to determine the extent to which the changes have taken place, a change in kind or in degree (where China is now). The macro-analytical model this textbook will adopt is the *Leninist party–state*, which would serve the threefold research purposes: define the point of departure, account for the changes, and assess the nature of changes.

However, from the methodological perspective, this textbook will *combine* an essentialist approach that keeps focus on the fundamental, unique, and defining features of Chinese politics and government that distinguish it from others *with* other theoretical approaches or analytical models wherever they fit in the analysis of major aspects of Chinese politics and government throughout the text. This hybrid approach allows us to reveal and examine the complexity of political reality and context, adaptive, developmental and institutional changes, operative features, and action means by the Chinese political leadership to maintain the fundamental core or essential features of the government and politics. This approach provides a conceptual framework in defining the Chinese political system and examining the essential characteristics, structures, processes, functions, changes of the Chinese government and politics.

The Leninist party–state

To answer the question of what kind of system it is, many people no longer use concepts like "Marxist–Leninist" or "Leninist,"[46] and have argued that post-Mao China's political system is no longer Leninist as the Communist Party of China (CPC) is no longer "Leninist." Some have argued that the CPC is a capitalist party as it carries out capitalist market reforms and, consequently, is no longer a communist party, while many others have found alternative terms to describe the political system in post-Mao China as a "corporatist state," "fragmented or decentralized authoritarianism," and so forth.[47] However, all these conceptualizations can neither capture the defining core features of the Chinese political system and central reality of post-Mao Chinese politics nor offer a basis for comparison with other communist systems. In fact, the Chinese political system as the Leninist party–state in post-Mao China has been further institutionalized and strengthened under Deng Xiaoping, and continued by Jiang Zemin and Hu Jintao both politically and ideologically,[48] as compared to Mao's China during the Cultural Revolution when the Party organizations and the party–state institutions were under serious attack, even dismantled and replaced by various "revolutionary committees" composed of workers, peasants, and soldiers. "It was and remains true today that much of what Stalin said about the Party as political organization still accurately describes the CPC in terms of contemporary political theory and practice."[49]

The aforementioned discussion begs the questions: What is a "Leninist political system?" What kind of party is "Leninist" as defined and practiced by Lenin himself and Stalin? What is the fundamental core of a "Leninist Party–state" that is distinguishable from other political regimes? The answers to these questions are essentially definitional and conceptual. We will summarize the key definitional properties in Tables 2.1 and 2.2. Students should refer to the actual examples of communist states as Leninist party states in Chapter 1 of this textbook.

However, the communist state has a number of operative features or action means which the Leninist party state usually uses to achieve and maintain the aforementioned three fundamental and core features. These action means, and operative methods include use of mass mobilization, mass violence, state terror (police), control over the state, information and media, education, culture, economy, means of production, military force, and weapons. Unlike this type of regime, authoritarian regimes not only depend to a considerable extent on a variety of social forces such as the monarchy, the church, the army, or business, but also leave whole areas of life untouched by official influence

Table 2.1 A "Leninist" political system and a "Leninist" party

What's a "Leninist political system?"	Simply put, it is a party–state political system that is created and led by a Leninist party, which dominates, controls and integrates the state as a party–state establishment and as its instrument to carry out its visions, long-term and immediate goals, political actions, and policies.
What kind of party is "Leninist" as defined and practiced by Lenin himself and Stalin?	A party that is "Leninist" declares itself as the vanguard of the working class, and thereby representative of the whole nation, armed with advanced knowledge of the laws and totality of the historical development process, theory of socialist revolution and construction, and thus in a position to lead its historical mission to achieve the "complete victory of socialism."
	The party claims possession of the instrument of "the dictatorship of the proletariat," extends its political leadership to every political organization, and dominates every sector of the state.
	The party exercises the organizational principle of "democratic centralism" under which the minority submits to the majority, the inferior submits to the superior, and the whole party submits to the central party committee (ultimately the Politburo).
	The party seeks to indoctrinate its members as well as the citizens under its rule with its political ideology, and uses or modifies its political ideology according to concrete or changing circumstances to justify its political leadership and political action.[50]

Table 2.2 The fundamental hard core of a "Leninist party–state"

A Philosophical absolutism and utopian goals are the first distinctive features of the Leninist party–state. The Party claims to be the possessor of absolute and universal truth, in command of historical destiny of human society, to claim a total representation of the entire nation and total guidance of the national goals, and therefore to be in the position of completing its course. Unlike the Leninist party–state, authoritarian regimes are rarely inspired by a utopian goal or barely have an exclusive truth claim as the important source of legitimacy.

B An official, pervasive, and exclusive ideology, which is the second core feature of the Leninist party-state in all communist countries, serves as another important legitimate source of the regime and the basis for a new political and social system and a new socialist man. Unlike this type of regime, authoritarian regimes seek only to control human behavior mainly through denying individuals civil and political rights such as participation in political life or the exercise of free speech, whereas the Leninist party–state aims not only to remold behavior but also to do so through the transformation of human nature, the exercise of extensive thought control, and the interference into personal beliefs and their political attitudes.

C A party–state apparatus is the third core feature of this type of regime. A highly hierarchical and centralized single elitist party is completely intertwined with the state, with an array of party organizational structures that supplement state institutions from the top right down to the bottom, forming a set of party–state apparatus and replacing to a large extent the governmental functions. While a single official party may also exist in some authoritarian regimes, the party in authoritarian regimes generally does not have the political and ideological vanguard status reserved only for the Leninist party, and an authoritarian single party may have to compete with the state, military, private organizations, and societal forces rather than penetrating and dominating them.

---

and control, and leave in place existing allocations of wealth, status, social values, and other resources, in particular, with a relatively strong private property sector as their socioeconomic basis.

For analytical purposes, philosophical absolutism (A), official ideology (B) and the party–state (C) are defined as the essential characteristics of the Leninist party–state political system that can be merged into the fundamental level.[51] Various action means and operative methods (D, E, F . . .) that the party–state employs to achieve and maintain the above essential characteristics can be defined as the operative characteristics that can be singled out into the operative level. The most important is distinguishing the "essential components" of the Leninist party–state from the "operative" features, since only the "essential components" account for the origins, the dynamics, and the essence of the Leninist party–state, while the operative features such as "actions means" or "operative mechanisms" largely account for its functioning and changes. Also, an assessment of the significance of changing features of a regime is critically contingent upon what can be considered the essential components of the Leninist party–state, which should be distinguished from

Table 2.3 A model of the Leninist party–state in comparative analysis

Category	Types	Essential components	Operative components
Primary category	Model I	A B C	
Secondary categories	Model II	A B C	D E F G
	Model III	A B C	H I J K

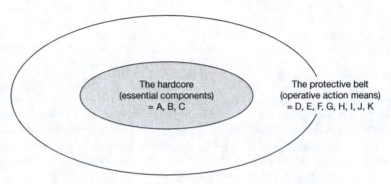

Figure 2.2 Lakatos's research program and the function of dynamic core in relation to action means.

those more tactical methods and operative mechanisms that are subject to change and fluctuation over time.[52] "The essential components" are decisive for determining the nature of the regime, whereas the fluctuations and selective use of methods and mechanisms do not affect the basic character of the regime, so long as they are within a certain scope.[53] Now, if these identified essential and nonessential (or operative) components are put together, a model of the Leninist party–state can be illustrated, as in Table 2.3.[54]

In Table 2.3 A, B, and C refer to a set of genetic attributes or essential components: philosophical absolutism, ideological monopoly, party–state. D E F G H I J K refer to a set of developmental attributes or operative components and features, such as action means, methods, and mechanisms.

The function of the dynamic core or fundamental level in relation to the action means or operative level is similar to the function of the "hard core" and "protective belt" suggested by Lakatos's research programs in Figure 2.2.

The Chinese Leninist party–state

Figure 2.2 suggests an illustrative profile of the defining features of a Leninist party–state, which deserves a more detailed elaboration in the Chinese context. After the communist takeover in 1949, Chinese communists largely duplicated the "Leninist party–state" government of the formerly Soviet Union. In what follows, we will take China as an actual case for elaboration, and define the Chinese Leninist party–state.

1. Philosophical absolutism and inevitable goals constitute the first fundamental part in the syndrome of traits of Chinese Leninist party–state political system. The Chinese communist regime claims to possess absolute and universal truth, to be in command of objective historical laws and historical destiny of human society, and therefore to be in the position of completing its course. It claims its ideological sources in Marxism–Leninism, which constitutes a universal formula for mankind toward an inevitable goal, and for the necessary development of all human society, from slavery through feudalism and capitalism to communism. Marx's historical materialism and dialectic materialism[55] supply the philosophical basis for the party's declaration of universal truths and inevitable goals. Historical materialism and dialectic materialism are used by the Chinese communist regime, as in all communist states, to explain universal phenomena of human society and general laws of social development and, moreover, to guide the development of all disciplines of the social sciences, such as political science, economics, sociology, history, law, anthropology, ethics, and aesthetics.

    The Leninist party–state pursues the twin goals of Utopia and modernization: the ultimate goal of the communist society and the immediate goal of modernization. The difference between Mao's regime and the post-Mao regime is that the former attempted to achieve the ultimate goal at an early stage of communist development whereas the latter recognizes the impossibility of the ultimate goal at an early stage and shifts its policy focus to the immediate goal and aims at preserving the ultimate goal by achieving the immediate goal. Modernization has been the goal of all modernizers, but in communist countries they are seen as "immediate goals." The achievement of modernization is merely seen as the means to the end of a better world, in our case, to achieve the long-term, ultimate goal of communism. Mao's regime pursued rapid industrialization and hoped to catch up with the Western powers within 15 years. But Mao's industrialization was within the framework of the Leninist party–state, and it was pursued as the means to maintain the monopolistic power of the Chinese Communist Party (CCP) and achieve the "great expectation" of communism.

    Post-Mao China "relaxes" the urgency of the achievement of Utopia and attempts to achieve "socialist modernization" by using market-economy methods and mechanisms for the purpose of paving a way for the future goal. Either more or less Utopian goal serves the same function of a political ideology used by the communist leaders to mobilize support and inspire the people to political action. According to Lowenthal, the twin goals of "utopia and modernity"[56] are intertwined but produce recurrent conflicts over certain policy issues and the communist regimes repeatedly try to undo the "ideologically undesirable by-products of economic development and spontaneous social change"[57] as we have observed since Deng's reforms and opening.

2. The second defining core feature of the Chinese Leninist party–state is the official, exclusive, and paramount ideology which serves to justify the CPC's political goals and actions, the basis for public policy and for a new type of society and man. Official ideology is crucial for the communist state to maintain its legitimacy to control the whole society and plays a decisive role in the process of development, since the Leninist party–state is neither able to eradicate the old society altogether nor fully to realize the new one, as it is unable to overcome those natural basic forms emerging directly and constantly either from the nature of man or from nature itself.

Communist ideology falls into the category of the unconstrained vision.[58] This vision assumes that man is capable of encompassing the world completely, in practice as well as in theory, that man can rise above matter, in action as well as in thought, and that the world and social life are perfectible and transformable because human nature is perfectible and transformable. Communist revolution and socialist construction are the only correct path of changing the old order, building socialism towards the ideal society of communism.

Ideological propaganda and communist moral education pervade society, in the attempt to convince the population of the infallibility of the party and the necessity of the measures to be taken, denying any moral and spiritual authority independent of the party or against the party doctrine. Individual conscience and attitude are subjugated to party ideological norms. Independent theoretical thinking and creation are constrained by party ideology and must follow party policy lines, and especially be subject to the personal interpretation of the paramount leader or the top political leaders. One might have some latitude for personal thinking in specific cases within the basic party policy line. Many of the ideological doctrines, including Mao's or Deng's personal thought, are taboos in academic research. Ideologization of socio-cultural life is a constant daily work of the party, frequently resulting in political, cultural, and ideological campaigns. Monopoly over the interpretation of doctrine has become the lifeline in policy making and policy change. "Mao Zedong Thought," "Deng Xiaoping Theory," Jiang Zemin's "Three Represents," and Hu Jintao's "Scientific Outlook on Development" are officially codified into the Chinese Constitution as the application of the universal truth of Marxism–Leninism in China's concrete conditions. "Thought" or "Theory" is viewed as the interpreter of "ism," through which the universal truth of Marxism–Leninism is applied into specific policy and practice in a particular time and place.[59] The interpretation of doctrine provides a basis for the Leninist party–state rule and policy changes, and prescribes for it a theoretical guidance and direction.

The party's ultimate goal or end-goal of communism, the universal truths of Marxism–Leninism, the "Four Cardinal Principles," the principle of "Democratic Centralism," thoughts and theories of top leaders, socialist public ownership of major means of production and exchange, and so forth, constitute the body of fundamental principles or core components of Chinese communist ideology. The body of these fundamental principles, universal truths, and official norms involves a small number of core elements that define the regime identity and play a key role in unifying it. These core components must be sustained to maintain regime identity, legitimize the party leadership and its proclaimed historical mission to "build socialism," "realize communism," and justify the necessity of the transformation of society and man.

3. The third defining core feature of the Chinese Leninist party–state is the special role of the CPC in the power structure. A highly hierarchical and centralized Communist Party is totally bureaucratized, completely intertwined with the state and replaces to a large extent the governmental functions. The real sovereign is the party, not the state. The party machine functions as the "hub" of the political system,[60] while the state serves as an instrument of party rule and functions as an administrative and bureaucratic apparatus for the party. The party, overriding the traditional concept of "the total state,"[61] carries out politics not restricted to the legal framework of the state, and in fact employs the state as a tool to realize its long-term goals and intermediate policy goals. The party power overrides the state power.

Under the leadership of the CPC, the structure and function of the party and the state are combined into one—the party–state, in which the party is the core of leadership, exercises highly centralized and unified leadership, and dominates the policy-making process. The CPC, as the governing party, in the political system, unlike its counterparts in the United States or in any Western European democracies, is statized and institutionalized, and acts like an institution of state power, in large part performing the functions of the state. The party is in effect a power center which exercises control over the state. The bureaucratization of party power has also been duplicated on lower levels. Party organizations penetrate all sectors of the state and almost every corner of society. The government and other state institutions are actually the executive and administrative bodies of the party. An overlapping institutional system exists from top to bottom in the hierarchy—the party leading bodies or leading groups exist at all levels of government institutions and "mass organizations." The party leaders simultaneously hold positions in government institutions or "mass organizations." One could hold several positions. All important powers are in the hands of party leaders. The party exercises "democratic centralism" by which every party member has to abide. So the party totally dominates the policy-making process within these institutions and organizations. The party–state relations have the following institutional features: (1) the overlapping and convergence of party and state leadership; (2) the overlapping and convergence of party organizations and state institutions; (3) party ideology becomes the governing ideology of the state; (4) party's organizational principle of "democratic centralism" becomes the guiding principle of the state leadership.

The legislature is a political tool used to preserve, maintain, and protect the ruling power of the Leninist party–state. In theory, deputies of the People's Congress, members of the Standing Committee of the People's Congress, and the leaders of the state are to be elected. However, in practice, they are not elected but selected by an official slate prepared in advance by the leaders themselves. Everything is already decided in advance before the opening of sessions, including the topics for discussion, the agenda, legislative proposals, the slate of the appointment of personnel affairs, and so on. The deputies actually do not have any substantial or real power in the decision-making process and serve as a "voting machine." The People's Congress is not a legislative body that initiates and independently decides on legislation. Its primary function is to enact the legislation or supply the final legitimation for the party decisions sent to it by the executive administrations or the party policy-making bodies. The legal system is not independent of party power and serves as an instrument of maintaining and protecting party rule. The Communist Party puts itself above the Constitution and the legal system, and dominates the process of law making and of law implementation. Laws and the legal system are a means of power and serve as a means of controlling the population, legalizing the ruling order and policy changes, and legitimizing the existing dictatorial rule.

The CPC's organizational principle of "democratic centralism" is a crucial aspect of the Chinese Communist political system. This principle is the foundation and backbone of the exercise of power. More importantly, this principle is extended to and strictly applied in governmental operations and other social, political, and cultural areas. This principle is largely ignored in post-Mao China study. So critical is its role in the exercise of power that one can not really understand the operation of the Leninist party–state without considering the key characteristics. The strict party discipline, the loyalty to the ideological program, the obedience to the will of the leadership and the decision of the party organization, and the acceptance of the party's interest above individual interests and rights, and so forth, are all carried out in the name of "democratic centralism." No wonder that "democratic centralism" is officially prescribed by the CPC as the "fundamental system" of Chinese government.

To conclude, the aforementioned three defining features of Chinese Leninist party–state serve as reference points which can be used to examine what has changed or what has not between now and then, and to explain what features of the Leninist party–state "syndrome" the regime can lose and still be "Leninist," or what degree of ideological, political, legal, social, and economic changes can occur and still leave the old regime's identity essentially unaffected. Philosophic absolutism, official ideology and the party–state are the most fundamental core features that account for the origins, dynamics, and essence of the Chinese political system while the action means or operative features account for its functioning. The fundamental features or hard core must always be there for the Chinese communist state to sustain regime identity; otherwise, it would have been transformed into something else. But the operative features are subject to change, as methods and mechanisms are always employed selectively and in varying degrees at different phases of history and in different situations. Therefore, change at the operative level will not have a decisive effect on the nature of a totalitarian regime and it will only reflect a difference in degree, not one in kind.

In other words, the operative features serve as its "protective belt" or a life belt, keeping the "hard core" afloat on an ocean of anomalies. As long as this belt can be adjusted, the communist regime is in no danger of sinking. A change in the operative features is not equal to a change of regime because it affects the elements not fundamental to the regime. For example, more resort to law by a regime does not necessarily mean that a society has transformed into one of the "rule of law." That is to say, if the changes in post-Stalin Soviet Union or post-Mao China aim at preserving the substance of Leninist party–state power or the core of the political system, the regime remains fundamentally unchanged and, by definition, "Leninist," in spite of all the changes or in however modified forms,

We have conceptually as well as graphically illustrated the model of the Leninist party–state by clearly defining and distinguishing the hard core features from other operative features and thus have established the criteria for assessing the change in a Leninist party state regime. The model provides reference points which can be used to define what constitutes the beginning and the end of a Leninist party–state regime in theoretical and comparative terms, to examine what has changed or what has not between now and then, to specify the precise point in a historical process of change at which the old regime ceases to exist or a new regime comes into being, and to explain what degree of change can occur and still leave the old regime's identity essentially unaffected. Moreover, the model places Chinese politics in a comparative context of communist states, and, thus, in the larger framework of comparative politics. The model can both enable us to observe, explain, and predict regime change in general and enrich our understanding of specific cases in particular.

Finally, there may be a need to combine one theoretical model with others in the analysis of a particular aspect and changing relationships in Chinese politics and government. The Leninist party–state model can go hand in hand with any of those analytical models in the study of Chinese politics and government when a combination is considered necessary. For example, when we analyze social change in China, we can utilize the theories of state–society relations to examine social changes, to determine what has changed and what has not changed, and to what degree such changes have affected the hard core of the Leninist party state, also to determine if a fundamental change of political regime has occurred or not in China. In this way, we should be able to capture, examine, and evaluate both the hard core and changes that might affect the hard core, and determine the nature of change, in degree or in kind.

Questions for discussion

1.   Why are theories and models important in the study of politics? Which theoretical model is more useful for studying Chinese politics and government?
2.   What is a Leninist party–state? What would constitute the "hard core" of a Leninist party–state that distinguishes itself from a regular authoritarian regime? What might be the operative features of a Leninist party–state? What is the relationship between the hard core and the operative features of a political regime? What is the distinction between a generic change and a developmental change? How useful is this distinction in the study of regime change?

Further reading

Barrett McCormick, *Political Reform in Post-Mao China: Democracy and Bureaucracy in a Leninist State* (Berkeley, University of California Press, 1990).

Bruce Dickson, *Democratization in China and Taiwan: The Adaptability of Leninist Parties* (New York: Oxford University Press, 1997).

Jonathan Unger, ed., *The Nature of Chinese Politics: From Mao to Jiang* (Armonk, New York: M. E. Sharpe, 2002).

Part II
Land and people

3 Shaping forces of Chinese state-making, political culture, and political tradition

To gain insight into the patterns of Chinese political development and China's political system, we need to look the natural forces that have shaped the making of the Chinese state in ancient times, and Chinese culture, history, and political tradition ever since. A fundamental factor in understanding China, particularly the making of the state, how power is ultimately ascertained, and its political implications for evolution, is the physical geography and climate conditions in China by which Chinese civilization came into being. This is not a geography class, but a country's topography and climate conditions have a great influence on the development of its society and culture in many ways, such as the locations where people live, ways of survival, lifestyles, and agriculture, and thus on the making of the state. Therefore, as students of political science, we are not interested in geography per se, but in its implications for political and economic development.

Geographical and climate influence on state-making and political culture

Students of Chinese politics often ask the question why China has had a long tradition of despotic government for thousands of years. In other words, what forces have shaped the making of the Chinese state, culture, history, and political tradition that endure into modern times? Students may look at the ideas of Chinese thought that created such a form of government, or explore the Chinese historical tradition and collectivistic culture that may shape the creation, development, and maintenance of such a government. But, the question is not answered. Which came first, the chicken or the egg? People make history, but they do so in a given natural condition—the physical, geographical, and climate environment in which man survives has a fundamental influence on his/her ways of living and thinking.[1] Therefore, one begs the question: what kind of natural conditions that people inhabit have shaped the creation of those ideas, historical tradition, and culture from the very beginning of Chinese civilization?

Chinese civilization originated in the Yellow River valley (Huang He 黄河), the second longest river in China. Originating in the Bayan Har

Mountains in Qinghai Province in western China, it flows through nine provinces of China and empties into the Bohai Sea, a gulf of the Yellow Sea, near today's Tianjin. The Yellow River is called "the cradle of Chinese civilization" (see the large dark tinted area in Map 3.1). But frequent devastating flooding since ancient times has also earned it the unenviable name "China's Sorrow." It has flooded 1,593 times in the last 3,000–4,000 years, while its main course has changed 12 times, with at least five large-scale changes in course from 602 BCE to the present day. These changes in course are due to the large amount of loess carried by the river and continuously deposited along the bottom of the river's channel. This sedimentation causes a natural dam to slowly accrue. Eventually, the enormous amount of water has to find a new way to the sea, causing flooding and creating a new valley. Flooding was unpredictable, causing death, famine, and difficulties for agriculture.[2]

China's land is largely hilly and mountainous, with an estimated 11 percent arable land area (Map 3.2).[3] Other studies suggest an estimated 15 percent of arable land in 2002. Per capita arable land is only one-tenth of a hectare, equivalent to the size of a moderate suburban home lot in the United States.

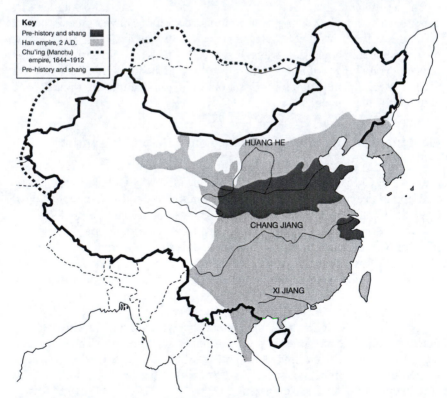

Map 3.1 Historical borders of China in four periods.

Source: Courtesy of Asia for Educators http://afe.easia.columbia.edu/china/geog/m_Hist.htm.

This means there is a small portion of the land that is suitable for cultivation and for good production.[4] However, the Loess Plateau region (Huangtu Plateau 黄土高原) of the Yellow River is where the "cradle of Chinese civilization" originated. Therefore, understanding the physical conditions that people of the Loess Plateau inhabited is essential in understanding the relationship between land and people, and the relationship between people and government. The Loess Plateau covers an area of some 640,000 km[2] in the upper and middle of China's Yellow River and China proper. Loess is the name for the silty sediment that has been deposited by wind storms on the plateau over the ages. Loess is a highly erosion-prone soil that is susceptible to the forces of wind and water; in fact, the soil of this region has been called "the most highly erodible soil on earth."[5] The Loess Plateau and its dusty soil cover almost all of Shanxi, Shaanxi, and Gansu, Ningxia, Henan, and parts of other regions.[6] It is the world's largest deposit of loess, approximately the size of France, designated by the large tinted area in Map 3.3.[7]

It is essential to understand the impact of topographical conditions on agriculture and the ways of living of people who lived there in early civilization. In ancient times, the Loess Plateau was highly fertile and easy to

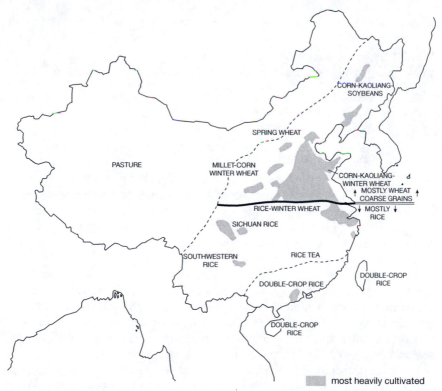

Map 3.2 Areas of China's arable land.

Source: Courtesy of Asia for Educators, http://afe.easia.columbia.edu/china/geog/M_agr.htm.

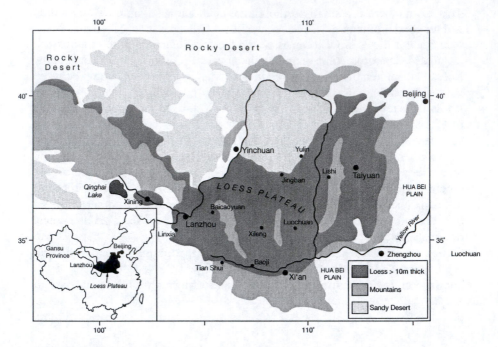

Map 3.3 Geomorphic regions of the Loess Plateau[8]

Source: Xin-min Meng and Edward Derbyshire, "Landslides and Their Control in the Chinese Loess Plateau: Models and Case Studies From Gansu Province, China," in Julian G. Maund and Malcom Eddleston eds., *Geohazards in Engineering Geology*, (London: Geological Society Engineering Geology Special Publication No. 15, 1998), p. 141.

farm, which contributed to the agriculture and thus the development of early Chinese civilization around the Loess Plateau.[9] However, its silty sediment is also noted as being among the most erosion-prone soils known on earth, as it is more easily blown and washed away than any other type of soil.[10] It reportedly receives, carries, and deposits downstream 30 times the sediment of the Nile River and 98 times the sediment of the Mississippi, with 90 percent of its sediment deriving from the Loess Plateau Region.[11] It is reported that 1,600 million tons of loess is absorbed by the Yellow River annually, causing the riverbed to rise by more than 10 centimeters every year and exceeding the land elevation on its banks by more than 10 meters in certain areas.[12] Therefore, this dust-swollen river is notorious for bursting its banks and flooding the nearby countryside, destroying crops and taking human lives.[13]

However, in addition to the impact of such a massive and unprecedented sediment load, the region's climate also had a great impact on the physical environment that people inhabited. Although the Plateau has annual rainfall amounting to only average of 20–55 centimeters (8–22 inches) a year, up to

40 percent of this annual precipitation has been known to fall during a single storm in the summer.[14] These violent stormy downpours for the most part occur in the three months between July and September, contributing anywhere from 24 percent to 100 percent of the total annual sediment load into the Yellow River.[15] Rainwater washes away loess easily, and makes its way into the river, which then rapidly overflows, causing flooding that destroys crops and takes human lives. Another recent study by a group of Chinese scholars has revealed the historical climate change, i.e., dry–wet patterns in the regions of Shaanxi, Gansu, and Ningxia, and confirmed the results of other studies on drought and flood disasters that happened alternately. The study concludes that these climate change patterns have had profound impacts on topographical conditions where people lived and on the formation and development of the socio-economic system,[16] with far-reaching political implications for the making of the Chinese state and the type of government since ancient times. "From earliest times Chinese administrators in this most ancient part of China have had to construct dikes to keep it within its channel,"[17] but it has frequently failed, resulting in serious flooding and "Yellow Sorrow."

As a result of limited arable land for food production, agriculture was pushed up onto steeper slopes on the mountains, and water shortage was thus a major problem. See Figure 3.1 for photos of agricultural terracing typical of China's Loess Plateau.

A famous classic Chinese text, *Intrigues of the Warring States* (*Zhan Guo Ce* 战国策), presents a dialogue between a king and his subjects about the water supply, and illustrates well the futility of division in a hydraulic society, and how manipulation of the water supply in ancient China could allow for dominance of one state over the other. West Zhou held immense power over Eastern Zhou just by controlling the water supply. Here is the translation:

> Eastern Chou wished to plant rice but Western Chou would not allow water to flow through. Eastern Chou was troubled about it. Su-tzu spoke to the Prince of Eastern Chou and said: "Your servant asks permission to make Western Chou let the water through, May I?" So he went, had an interview

Figure 3.1 Agricultural terracing.
Source: From left to right: photos courtesy of John B. Gates, Till Niermann, and Xu Peishe.

with the prince of Western Chou, and said: "Your Highness's policy is mistaken. Not to let water through now is to enrich Eastern Chou. Now its people are all sowing wheat; they sow nothing else. If your Highness wishes to do them harm the best plan is to let water through at once so as to injure what they are sowing. If you let water through, Eastern Chou will be sure to sow rice again. When they have sown rice deprive them of it again. If you do that you can make the people of Eastern Chou look up at once to Western Chou and receive commands from Your Highness." The Price of Western Cho said: "Good." He thereupon released the water. Su-tzu also got money from both the states.[18]

With Chinese civilization extending to a larger area after the Han dynasty (206 BCE to 220 CE), the geographical environment in other regions was more amenable for living and farming. However, the relationship between land and people has continued to be a basic unsolved problem. In most Chinese regions, in addition to the limited land area for food production, the climate conditions intensify the problem of food production. The climate of China is dominated by the southeast monsoon, which sets the distinctive pattern of wet summers and dry winters across the land, divided by a series of high and rugged mountain ranges—two intersecting southwest-to-northeast ranges and three parallel mountain chains protruding from west to east toward the Pacific[19] (Map 3.4). This natural landscape is ordered in three tiers, ranging from mountains to floodplains and lowlands, which are the smallest and the most populous. Rivers have their origins high in the mountains of western China and then flow east to the sea, running through several tiers of mountains, hills, and then into the basins.[20] Overall, the northwest is dry while the southeast is lush. In the summer, the monsoons push over the belt of mountains, providing moderate summer rains in the northwest, while the rains pour over eastern and southern China causing serious flooding.[21] Rainfall reaches most of southeast and central China in the spring and summer, usually in successive stormy downpours. If the downpours from the rainy season are not channeled into reservoirs, they may cause serious flooding, and then a serious water shortage may result in the dry season. However, usually successive downpours are often not controllable and cause serious flooding in China's two major rivers, the Yellow and the Yangtze, and their tributaries, where 90 percent of the population live and work.[22] The North China plain, the most populous part of the region, always faces a serious threat of flooding by the Yellow River. The Yangtze River, joined by a great network of tributaries, carries an enormous volume of water and silt into the China Sea. During the rainy season in the Yangtze basin and less mountainous regions when the water levels rise and the tributaries burst their banks, there are often disastrous floods that wash away crops and housing.[23]

China has been plagued by this basic problem of limited arable land with frequent flooding and droughts since ancient times. As one study has shown, between 206 BCE and 1911 CE, in the space of 2000 years, there were 1,621

Map 3.4 High and rugged mountain ranges.
Source: Courtesy of Asia for Educators, http://afe.easia.columbia.edu/china/geog/M_Mt.htm

floods and 1,392 droughts, which brought endless sorrow to the Chinese people.[24] From 108 BCE to 1911 CE, China experienced 1,828 famines, or one per year.[25] Yu the Great, the legendary founder of the first dynasty, Xia (2070–1600 BCE), controlled the waters (大禹治水) during a period of heavy flooding, and is remembered and honored by Chinese people with the appellation "the Great" for his hydraulic functioning as the ruler who effectively managed the waters and controlled the flood. With his successful leadership and water control, Yu emerged from being a tribal leader to king of a nation of nine provinces (Jiuzhou 九州), with power and domination over the land.[26] According to another study, from 1766 BCE to 1937 CE, there were 5,258 recorded natural disasters, averaging one every six months.[27] These natural features of China's landscape and climate inevitably necessitate large-scale human intervention for survival, if the forces of nature are to be kept at bay. Therefore, the functions of government involved what John Fairbank described as the control of "the land, the manpower, and the water supply"[28] for this society, which is noted as "hydraulic."

What then is a "hydraulic society?" It refers to a society dependent on water control and large-scale irrigation or a "hydraulic" system to bring the floods and droughts under control, from which emerged a despotic form of government—a despotic state. According to an eminent professor of Chinese history, Karl A. Wittfogel, unlike the feudalism of Europe in which the monarch was checked and restrained by other forces, such as the church, the nobles, and other competing organizations, a "hydraulic society" breeds a "total state" or "Oriental despotism" which is an absolutistic or despotic, highly centralized bureaucratic state.[29] Such a strong state, ruled absolutely by a despotic emperor who represented the common unity of all, had the power and capacity to mobilize manpower and resources to construct "hydraulic systems," such as dredging rivers, building channels, dams, and reservoirs, which relied upon the capacity of the state for the division of labor, organizational planning, appropriation, transportation, and distribution on a large scale, and the requirement of peasants for corvée labor (compulsory and unpaid mass labor) to build a massive irrigation system including dams, canals, reservoirs, aqueducts, etc., to bring the floods and droughts under control and enable the land to be cultivated for food production, because the construction and management of such large-scale water control and massive irrigation went beyond the capacity of unorganized individuals, any other organizations, communities, or groups. The concept of Oriental despotism is also closely related to Karl Marx's concept of an "Asiatic mode of production," in which irrigation and water control were the basis of agricultural production, society, and government in ancient civilizations emerging from river valleys, such as China, India, and Egypt.[30] Although such concepts, particularly "Orientalism," could be controversial, they provide a useful starting point for understanding the state formation and evolution in societies like China.[31]

So it is evident that geographical and climatic conditions have remarkable impacts on the making of a despotic state, with its political tradition enduring for thousands of years into modern times and shaping the collectivistic culture, history, and political development of China. Inhabitants of such physical conditions tend to look to a strong government that would be capable of coordinating and mobilizing resources for massive hydraulic systems to control floods and channel water reservoirs during the rainy season and save water for living and farming during the drought season, providing security and preventing turmoil, and protecting people's basic need for living and farming, which fosters collective values and norms among people who consider those seeking self-interest are selfish and damaging and those sacrificing self-interest are noble and glorious. This shaped and led to the development of the Chinese collective-oriented culture and national character. Submission to collective norms and authorities has always been glorified in Chinese traditional culture and history, and such norms, values, and cultural orientation toward authority have persisted to the present and have profoundly shaped the political behavior and attitudes of citizens toward their government and authority in contemporary China as well as their norms and perceptions of the relationships between individual interests and collective interests, and broadly between individuality and collectivity.

The harsh physical conditions also led to another Chinese character trait that breeds a despotic culture that supports a despotic state. That is, the trait of superstition and worship of idols, which can be traced to the origin of the Chinese hydraulic society. More than 2,000 years of hydraulic agriculture created an autarky economy, that is, "those living on a mountain live off the mountain, those living near the water live off the water," with good farming highly dependent on good weather. People felt powerless before nature. People had blind faith in blessings and safeguards from heaven, ancestry, or other supernatural powers. Farmers were at the mercy of the weather, dependent upon Heaven's gifts of sun and rain. Thus, the ecology influenced their culture in many ways.[32] The traditions of idol worship have been handed down from generation to generation since ancient times, and helped to reinforce the despotic culture and support a despotic power, as worship of idols was transformed into worship of the emperor and worship of state, which has been deeply seated in the Chinese psychological structure and national character and provided voluntary and enthusiastic mass support for the despotic state and later political actions of nationalist leaders, Sun Yat-sen and Chiang kai-chek, and communist leaders, such as Mao Zedong, and the performance of the communist state under Mao's leadership.

Although many schools in Chinese traditional thought, such as Legalism (法家), Daoism (道家), Confucianism (儒家), emerged in early Chinese civilization, Confucianism, a system of moral, social, and political thought which promoted collective social norms and ethnic codes of social behavior, became the most influential ideology that has had the greatest influence on Chinese history and political tradition. As a collectivistic based value system that supported a despotic emperor based on a centralized bureaucratic state, it was easily accepted by the population and adopted by imperial despotic rulers as the governing philosophy and official doctrine of the state to indoctrinate people and government officials since the Han Dynasty (汉朝206 BCE) regardless of dynastic changes since then (for a brief chronology of Chinese dynasties, see Table 3.1). In short, natural forces of physical conditions have shaped the form of Chinese government and culture into modern times. We will study Confucianism in the next chapter to provide students with a cultural perspective in understanding Chinese history and the form of government that has evolved since ancient times. Keeping this in mind, we will continue to examine Chinese history and understand how the relationship between land and people has influenced dynastic change throughout Chinese history and the traditional political system.

The traditional Chinese political system

Over thousands of years, the traditional Chinese political system has developed a "super-stabilized structure" (超稳定结构), despite repeated dynastic changes, with a set of coherent features of a despotic state that for most of the time is distinguishable from Western monarchies based on feudalism.

Table 3.1 Timeline of Chinese dynasties

Dynasty	Date
Xia	2205–1766 BCE
Shang	1766–1122 BCE
Zhou	1122–1221 BCE
Spring and Autumn Period	770–476 BCE
Warring States Period	475–221 BCE
Qin	221–206 BCE
Han	206 BCE to 220 CE
Three Kingdoms	220–80
Western Jin	265–316
Eastern Jin	317–439
Southern and Northern Dynasties	386–589
Sui	589–618
Tang	618–906
Five Dynasties and Ten Kingdoms	907–60
Liao	907–1125
North Song	960–1126
Xixia	990–1127
Southern Song	1127–1279
Jin	1115–1234
Yuan	1279–1368
Ming	1368–1644
Qing	1644–1911

Source: Xinhua News Service, Table of Chinese Dynasties. http://202.84.17.11/english/China-abc/.

Chinese political development has characterized the traditional Chinese political system as a despotic state with the Emperor who rules absolutely without facing significant challenges from local and social forces. A despotic monarch relied on a highly centralized bureaucratic state. The emperor is the "Son of Heaven" (天子) with the "Mandate of Heaven" (天命)—a divine mandate to rule the earth, chosen for his virtue and kept in office for his virtue. Therefore, the emperor is the "ruler of all under heaven" and no limits could be placed on imperial power. In contrast to the West, no significant hereditary nobility since the Han dynasty has existed that could challenge the authority of the central ruler, the Emperor. A hereditary nobility often limited the power of the central ruler, since nobility carried a prestige and authority of its own, as in Western Europe where kings fought for centuries to curb the power of the nobles. China also lacked another feature of the early modern West, an independent urban middle class or bourgeoisie who challenged the government's authority and placed a check on the government.[33]

Confucianism was the governing philosophy of the state for centuries regardless of dynastic changes. Confucianism had several core features that were particularly conducive to the imperial central bureaucratic state and welcomed by the despotic emperor as we have discussed previously. Therefore, mastery of the Confucian classics and ideology was most important for recruitment and promotion through the official hierarchy within the ranks of the imperial bureaucracy. The bureaucratic elite (the Mandarins) at central, regional, and local levels were recruited through imperial examinations by virtue of imperial degrees *zhuanyuan* (状元), *juren* (举人), and *xiucai* (秀才), equivalent to doctoral, master, and bachelor's degrees in the West. National civil service examinations were given at county, provincial, and central levels on state ideology Confucianism and literary classics. To be eligible for the higher levels, a candidate must first pass the lower exams, with the attrition rate increasing at each level: 10 percent would pass the county level exam, but only 2–3 percent would pass the provincial and central levels. As a result, ideological centralization and Confucian indoctrination by the state bound officials and scholars to the state and the emperor rather than making them independent of it.[34]

This system was characterized by "rule of man" (人治), "rule by law" (法制), or "rule by morality" (道德治国), rather than "rule of law" (法治), though law or a dynastic code was used to regulate and govern social relationships and the relationships between political institutions. Society was controlled by scholar–gentry–officialdom at all levels. Official positions were gained by education and indoctrination of Confucianism, and these positions often brought with them the means to obtain land; owning land in turn brought with it the resources to study for the official examinations. Given the close relationship between education, official position, and land or wealth, Chinese people were highly aware of the importance of education. Scholars, officials, and local gentry formed a special group of trained people who were entrusted with power and prestige in managing local affairs, implementing imperial order and policy, maintaining social order, administering justice, and managing the economy.[35]

China's ancient dynasties rose and fell, but the structure and form of government and centralized ideology remained essentially unchanged over thousands of years till the Nationalist Revolution in 1911 ended the last dynasty, Qing (清朝). Each of the historical dynasties followed a pattern of development known as the "dynastic circle:" (1) establishment of a new "virtuous and benevolent" imperial rule; (2) an era of intellectual revival and economic prosperity; (3) a period of corruption, misrule, or tyrannical rule (if the empire were corrupted, the emperor and officialdom did not take good care of the hydraulic water system, the system decayed, and flooding was out of control); (4) the occurrence of uncontrolled natural disasters such as floods and/or droughts; and (5) overthrow of the old dynasty by peasant rebellion or failure to resist invasions from the Mongol Khans, the Manchus, or other military tribes from the northwest.[36] Therefore, it is essential to understand the characteristics and political impacts of a "hydraulic" society on Chinese state-building, the formation of political culture, and the patterns of social,

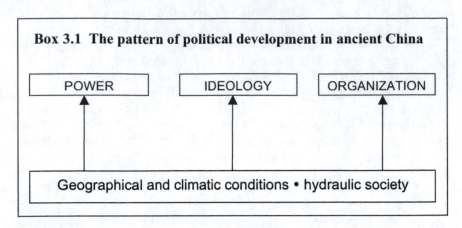

Box 3.1 The pattern of political development in ancient China

| POWER | IDEOLOGY | ORGANIZATION |

Geographical and climatic conditions • hydraulic society

economic, and political development in ancient China. Such a pattern was dominated by despotic power, Confucian ideology, and centralized bureaucratic state organization, which has endured to modern times and is even in China today (see Box 3.1 for illustration).

Questions for discussion

1. Why did China have a long tradition of despotic government for thousands of years? In other words, what forces have shaped the making of the Chinese state, culture, history, and political tradition that endure into modern times?
2. Discuss the political implications of the relationship between the land and its people and how physical and climate conditions have influenced "the making of the despotic state" and "the collectivistic political culture" in China.

Further reading

Karl A. Wittfogel, *Oriental Despotism: A Comparative Study of Total Power* (New Haven, Yale University Press, 1957).

John King Fairbank, *The United States and China* (New York: Viking Press, 1962).

John M. Laflen, Junliang Tian and Chi-Hua Huang, eds., *Soil Erosion and Dryland Farming* (Florida: CRC Press, 2000).

Hong Jiang, *The Ordos Plateau of China: An Endangered Environment* (New York: United Nations UP, 1999).

4 Traditional Chinese culture and Confucianism

Different groups of people have different kinds of inherent traits of culture, which may change over time. Political culture refers to the political characteristics of a particular human group, reflecting a particular distribution of political attitudes, values, feelings, and socio-psychological orientations. Political culture, or, broadly defined, culture, is the *context* in which political action takes place. Therefore, politics and political change are usefully understood in terms of their cultural context.

We have provided a historical perspective of understanding the making of the Chinese state and its long tradition. We now turn to Chinese culture as an avenue to arrive at an understanding of the political development in modern China and Chinese politics and government today.

Wittfogel's description of the origins and the major features of a hydraulic society is helpful in understanding the origins of Chinese communism, but not sufficient if we do not look at the cultural traits of China that furnish the fertile soil that has supported the emergence and development of communism as a political ideology, a political movement and a political system in modern China, and the effective functioning of the Chinese communist state.

Chinese traditional political culture and political history have always extolled the primacy of the state and the collectivity while minimizing individual rights and autonomy, which is quite different from the Western tradition of human rights based on individual rights, and they continue to influence the Chinese communists and provide the cultural base for Chinese official norms and popular mentality. Such a collectivistic culture is largely and fundamentally attributed to the Confucian traditions.

However, there have been some important schools of thought in traditional Chinese culture, such as Confucianism, Legalism, Daoism, and Buddhism. But Confucianism is the high culture of the elite and the only school of thought that became the governing ideology of the imperial state in China for 2,000 years, while Taosim and Buddhism have played a role in shaping traditional pop culture and art. Legalism was the governing ideology of the Qin Dynasty (秦朝), lasting only from 221 to 206 BCE after the death of the Qin emperor Qin Shi Huangdi. Confucianism was soon revived as the official ideology during the Han Dynasty and retained its official position throughout imperial China.

Confucianism (儒家)

Confucianism, Legalism, Daoism, and Buddhism are key elements of traditional Chinese culture. However, whereas Confucianism played a dominant role in shaping the political culture as it was the governing ideology of the state, and the "high culture" of the ruling elite, Daoism and Buddhism are popular religions and ideologies, or the "pop culture" of common people in daily life. Legalism also had a lingering and enduring influence in the practices of traditional polity in imperial China.

Confucianism came to dominate Chinese thought after 200 BCE and was China's orthodox ideology for over 2,000 years before the 1911 revolution regardless of dynastic changes. Although Communist China, founded in 1949, has instituted radical changes in all aspects of society, many of the Confucian ideas still remain influential as part of China's political culture.

Who is the founding father of Confucianism? Confucius (*Kong Qiu*, or *Kong Fuzi, Kongzi*; *Fuzi* or *zi* are honorific titles meaning Master or Teacher) was the founding father of Confucianism. He lived from 551 to 479 BCE. His family was descended from the Shang aristocracy (Shang was a state in east China). His teachings were edited by his pupils into a collection of his works known as *The Analects*.[1]

According to Peter R. Moody, the starting point of his idea is the concept of ritual (*li* 礼), which was used by Confucius to encompass the way human beings properly behave toward each other and toward nature. Ritual is the outward expression of human feelings. For example, Mencius (*Mengzi*; one of the most important Confucian scholars, who lived about 372–289 BCE) described that primitive people had no funerals. When their parents died, they would simply throw the bodies into a ditch. But passing by the place a few days later, they would feel inner sorrow at the sight of the bodies decaying and being eaten by animals. Hence, funeral ceremonies evolved. The ritual both expresses and channels our natural feelings. Ritual gives our feelings form. Ritual meets the obligations of status differences while preserving human feelings and dignity.[2]

But most fundamentally, ritual is the outward expression of the human virtue (*ren* 仁), which refers to the benevolence, kindness, or goodness human beings owe to each other and the character we share in common with each other as part of humankind. Virtue, according to Confucius, can be cultivated by study. As a Confucian passage says, we are born good, but our good nature can be corrupted by forces in the world. Therefore, man's good nature needs to be developed through study and cultivation, in a constant struggle against forces in the world that erode it. A true gentlemen or nobleman (*junzi* 君子) is one who has cultivated his character through education and behaves in accordance with ritual (*li*) and virtue (*ren*). Only such a person can be entrusted with authority over others. Moreover, cultivation is not only personal growth, because our personal growth in its turn is to be used for improving the world in which we live.[3]

Therefore, the Confucian doctrine has justified moral elitism, ideological centralization, and ideological indoctrination. Centuries-long indoctrination and Confucian education have given the central ruler (the state) the prestige and power to impose its values and ideologies on the population and suppress dissent.[4] It was the emperor who represented and defined the virtues, and later the communist party leadership. As people have to fight constantly against the forces that erode them, people need to be educated and indoctrinated by the ruling elite or the party to maintain the "virtues" or "goodness" of man and transform society. Confucian doctrines are highly supportive of communist doctrines, although they were under attack during political campaigns in Mao's China to justify political actions under Mao's leadership and to establish the absolute truth and paramount status of the communist ideology and Mao Zedong Thought, but its influence was hidden, penetrating and everlasting, because its doctrines have been embedded in traditional Chinese culture and influenced the mentality of both the elite and scholars.

First, Confucianism is a collectivistic-based value system which embraces a set of ethnic codes of behavior designed to regulate the relationships between ruler and subject, father and son, friend and neighbor, husband and wife, and brother and brother. These codes require individuals to behave according to rituals and social status. These codes emphasize conformity and de-emphasize individuality. Individuals are born into and belong to a collective, and thus are subordinated to the collective. Observation of these social codes would promote collective social norms which constitute the foundation on which social harmony rests.[5]

Second, Confucianism emphasizes the importance of personal cultivation of a moral or virtuous individual both at the collective level and at the individual level. Self-cultivation promotes "a government by goodness" and improves human relationships that are well structured and regulated.[6] As such, Confucianism is a collectivistic and totalistic philosophy that is intended to control and regulate both public and private life, and even remold people's thoughts and characters. Such a tradition that emphasizes moral education has persisted down to the present and still inspires the Communist Party of China (CPC) leaders to carry out moral and ideological education.[7]

Third, Confucianism is authoritarian in nature. This orthodox ideology emphasizes the paramount need for accepting and obeying the established social order and the centralized power of the emperor based on the doctrine of "the Mandate of Heaven." According to the Analects of Confucius, "a ruler is like wind, and the people are like grass. When the wind blows, the grass always bends."[8] The emperor is the "Son of Heaven" with a divine mandate to rule the earth. Thus, a challenge to the emperor's "Mandate of Heaven" was considered disobedient and deviant, and must be punished. When the emperor was overthrown, it was considered as the loss of the "Mandate of Heaven." However, when the challenge to the emperor failed, the emperor retained his "Mandate of Heaven."[9] Therefore, for centuries Confucianism was praised by emperors and fully institutionalized as the governing ideology or philosophy of the state to which all social members are required to conform.

Fourth, Confucianism is an elitist model of government. The duty and privilege of rule can only be accorded to those with intelligence and education, because "government by goodness" can only be promoted through study and learning by those who have a superior intellect and moral standard. As Mencius says, those who work with their hands feed those who work with their brains; those who work with their brains rule those who work with their hands (an attitude that is still popular among Chinese intellectuals). Therefore, for centuries the ruling class is constituted by "Confucian scholar–gentry–officialdom" regardless of dynastic changes over time.[10]

Of all the characteristics of Confucianism, one stands out as serving the best interest of imperial rulers or communist leaders. The ideological centralization, indoctrination, and self-cultivation for both individual and collective improvement and perfection allowed the ruler to "establish total control over 'the life of the mind' or 'thought control.'"[11] As such Confucianism is culturally "totalistic" in nature. It is here that Lifton's theories and terms "totalism" and "thought reform" can be used for us to understand the practices of both the Chinese traditional rulers and the communist regime, and explain why Chinese people could accept such practices and why Chinese intellectuals helped the regime to develop thought control programs in the practices of education and culture. Lifton's book *Thought Reform and the Psychology of Totalism: A Study of "Brainwashing" in China* studied "thought reform" or the "brainwashing" methods and techniques to exercise thought control or mind control in Mao's China. These methods and techniques were used to change people's minds: the control of information and communication, the manipulation of experiences that appear spontaneous but in fact were planned and orchestrated; the world is viewed as black and white and the members are constantly exhorted to conform to the ideology of the collective and strive for perfection. Confessions of sins, as defined by the collective, are to be made either to a personal monitor or publicly to the collective. The collective's doctrine or ideology is considered to be the ultimate Truth, beyond all questioning or dispute. The collective interprets or uses words and phrases in new ways so that often the outside world does not understand. Indoctrination of individuals by the collective–personal experience is subordinated to the collective doctrine, and any contrary experiences must be denied or reinterpreted to fit the ideology of the collective. The collective has the power to decide who has the right to exist and who does not.[12] Mao skillfully employed and manipulated all these techniques in all political campaigns and ideological movements that targeted a "class enemy" or groups of scapegoats in society in order to accomplish his political goals or ideological ideals about the new state and the new society in China. However, Daoism and Buddhism have never played such a role in China, because their doctrines do not serve the purposes of imperial rule and communist revolution.

Legalism (法家)

Legalism emerged as a school of thought out of "hundreds of schools" during the Warring States Period when Yan, Zhao, Qi, Chu, Han, Wei, and Qin fought for dominance. Legalist thought was applied by Shang Yang (商鞅) during his reform, notably called Shang Yang Reform (商鞅变法), to turn the relatively weak state of Qin into the most powerful state that eventually defeated all its powerful rivals and unified China through the reform measures.

First, the Shang Yang Reform strengthened the central authority through a centralized bureaucratic state under which 31 counties were created, and each was administered by a centrally appointed magistrate who reported directly to the central ruler.

Second, it emphasized hard and fast laws to govern, and advocated rewards and punishments as the "two handles" by which to contain undesirable behavior and encourage desirable behavior as defined by the central ruler.

Third, it abolished the hereditary privileges of the nobility and encouraged farming and fighting for the country. Rank and position were given to those who excelled in military victory.

Fourth, it strengthened state control over society and family by establishing a system of group-sharing of guilt and punishment. Group responsibility was decreed not only within each family but also among units of 5–10 families, and everyone within each unit was collectively responsible for any individual's wrongdoing. Those who failed to report lawbreakers would receive severe punishments.

Fifth, it strengthened agricultural production in order to build strong military power for the state of Qin to defeat all rival states. It abolished the "nine-square system" (a section of land was divided into nine portions) and allowed commoners to buy and sell land, making land private and stimulating farm enterprise and new land cultivation for food production. It built dams, reservoirs, canals, and irrigation networks to provide a water supply for agriculture.[13]

Another prominent Warring States legalist thinker was Han Feizi (韩非子). He synthesized the ideas of three legalist traditions: laws (法), methods/tactics (术), and authority (势). First, tradition emphasizes the "laws" by which the ruler can promote desired behavior by rewarding well those who follow the law and contains undesirable behavior by severely punishing those who disobey the law. Second, tradition emphasizes the ruling "methods/tactics" by which the ruler can maintain his authority, govern his subjects, and cope with the deceit and treachery in politics, which is like a battlefield in which morals and ethics do not exist. Third, tradition emphasizes the "authority" by which the ruler should expand and concentrate the power in his hands and stand above all: the power of the ruler is transcendent, and hence limitless and unquestionable. These principles of legalism are the foundation of human society and social order.[14]

However, Legalism was a utilitarian political thought that did not address higher questions like the nature and purpose of politics, man, and life; in particular, it did not provide moral codes for governing and regulating social behavior. Legalism also gained a bad reputation from the practice of Qin Shihuang Di's "burning of the books and burying of the scholars" (焚书坑儒), by which legalism gained the ruling position while all other schools of thought were suppressed. Therefore, it did not meet the political needs of the imperial ruler who heavily relied on the efficient function of a centralized bureaucratic state and a morally self-disciplined ruling elite and bureaucrats. Although rulers used some legalist ideas and methods to a certain degree in the practical operation of ruling, they adopted Confucianism as the governing ideology of the imperial state, and indoctrinated officials and people with its doctrines. However, in Mao's China, legalist ideas were used by Mao and his supporters in political and ideological campaigns to suppress different voices and purge the ranks within or outside the polity, particularly during the Cultural Revolution. After Mao's death, China began the reform and open up, and the government has downplayed legalism but revived Confucianism.

Daoism (道家)

Daoism, which flourished among the common people, was the school most different from Confucianism.[15] Daoism (Taoism) means "way:" the way of things, the inherent principle of things, the Way things are, or the Way of Heaven, the moral social order of the universe. Daoism derives from two Chinese thinkers: *Laozi* (who lived around 600–500 BCE, with his life overlapping that of Confucius) and *Zhuangzi* (who lived about the same time as Mencius). Politically, Daoism emphasizes the idea of "nonaction" or "inaction" (wu wei无为)—similar to the idea of *laissez-faire*, and advises the government for "rule by nonaction" (无为而治). The worst rulers are those the people hate, while the second worst are those they praise. The best are those the people never notice at all. All things are accomplished but the people seem to have done it themselves.[16] Politically, "rule by nonaction" means that the government should not take unnecessary action and interference in the operation of government, allowing lower level government and local communities to run by themselves in political, economic, and financial spheres.[17] There are some clear distinctions between Daoism and Confucianism.

First, Daoism advocates the idea that least government is best government and the philosophical tradition emphasizes spontaneous, natural social order without a government, whereas Confucianism advocates strong but wise government, and ideological centralization and indoctrination.

Second, Daoism is an individualistic-based value system that emphasizes the freedom of individuals, whereas Confucianism is a collectivist-based value system that emphasizes and glorifies collective interests over individual rights.

Third, Daoism advocates independent human relationships and observation of the natural social order in order to achieve human happiness, whereas Confucianism promotes the idea that human relationships should be interactive and structured in order to create a harmonious society under enlightened rulers.

Fourth, Daoism was never institutionalized as the governing ideology but remains a popular cultural tradition and practical ideology of ordinary people, whereas Confucianism was highly institutionalized as the governing ideology of the state and the criteria for recruitment of government officials through a system of imperial examinations for 2,000 years in China.

However, intellectually, some neo-Confucian scholars in the eleventh and twelfth centuries, such as Chu Hsi (朱熹), attempted to synthesize Confucianism, Daoism, and even Buddhism, and incorporate elements of all three traditions in their philosophical synthesis.[18] Such philosophical synthesis actually began as early as in the Han dynasty when Confucian orthodoxy then "had not only absorbed but also sustained elements of other schools of thought in its grand synthesis."[19] While Taosim and Buddhism have played a primary role in shaping traditional pop culture and art, Confucianism is the only school of thought that became the governing ideology of the state, and fully institutionalized by imperial rulers, because mastery of Confucian classics was the primary criterion in imperial examinations for the recruitment of mandarins (bureaucrats) in imperial China.

Confucianism as the dominant force shaping Chinese political culture

Confucianism is the major philosophical base for traditional Chinese culture and political history. "Confucianism (like Platonism) contains the inclination to establish total control over the life of the mind."[20] The dominant feature of Confucianism is essentially hostile to individualism and the autonomy of the individual, and it is requested that the individual should make self-sacrifice for the state, the highest ideal of citizenship.[21] Social relations are illustrated in hierarchical sets, such as the emperor and his subjects, father–son, husband–wife, which are defined in terms of the obligations and duties between them, and no conception of individual rights exists in the sense that is known in the West. The individual is subsumed in these relations in a familial and paternal hierarchy. The emperor is responsible to "Heaven" to maintain this bond. So in traditional China, individuals are not equal and independent, and society is not equal and free, but structured in a hierarchical order to maintain harmony.[22]

Confucianism is in and of itself a collectivistic-based value system. Confucianism recognizes the existence of individual interests in society, but it views them as belonging not to the individual but to the group—family, clan, kinship, or community. In the Confucian view, man is born into society and cannot prosper alone; the individual depends on the harmony and strength of the collective entity. The individual must cultivate himself, not for himself, but for the welfare of family and community.[23]

As Louis Henkin further elaborated, in traditional Chinese culture, the ideal was not individual liberty and equality but order and harmony, not individual independence but selflessness and cooperation, not the freedom of individual conscience but conformity to orthodox doctrine, which permeated all individual behavior.[24] According to Confucianism, the nature of man is originally good, changeable, and improvable. Man is capable of giving up evil and returning to good, through self-cultivation and improvement.

So "the individual is exhorted to engage in moral self-cultivation and improvement," according to established moral standards, and hence to seek moral perfection in terms of conformity to cultural norms, but not according to the uniqueness of each individual, because "the improvement of the individual is not the purpose of society." The purpose of society is to maintain the harmony of hierarchical social and political order. "The emperor is father of the people," and the holder of absolute truth or virtues. He has paternal authority, and sees to it that harmony and order are maintained.[25]

Thus a strong state is a necessary and desirable instrument to assure harmony and order. In order to fulfill this task, the state monopolizes power and authority on a national basis, without any authorized or organized counter-force to check or challenge the central authority, because traditional Chinese culture always favors the state, inhibits the growth of a civil society, and depresses individual rights.

Furthermore, Chinese culture is collective orientated, in which the individual is always seen as merely a disciplined element of collectivity, and the interests of the collective are always assumed to take primacy over those of the individual. Depressing self-interest and glorifying self-sacrifice for the collective is the ideal of traditional Chinese morality, because self-identity of individuals is seen as deriving from his or her relationships with collective entities, such as households, clans, kinship organizations, neighborhoods, communities, or the state, of which the state is paramount and represents the highest interest.

When any possible conflicts occur among them, state interest is given primacy over collective entities and the individual, then the interests of these collective entities take precedence over those of the individual. The individual should be ready to make sacrifices without hesitation for the state and the collectives. The individual is not seen as independent but as inseparable from the collective entities to which he or she belongs. The individual's relationship to the state and the collectivity is one of dependency, not one based on individual rights. So there is no place for individual rights; if any, they are "granted" by the collective, and could be "reasonably" deprived by the state and the collective. This is in contrast to cultures in which it is believed that each human being has a unique and precious soul, and thus each individual deserves respect and has certain inalienable rights, based on the inherent worth of human life.

Chinese collectivistic culture was ingrained into society and the psychological orientation of the Chinese before the communist revolution. Such political culture has not only contributed to the rise of communism in modern China but also shaped the practice of the communist regime. After the communist takeover of power, traditional Chinese culture and values including Confucianism were in fact not destroyed, but, instead, carried to the extreme in a new name—communism. Communism is not a new collective immortality for China but the old one with a new name in the Chinese context.

If traditional Chinese culture is hostile to individualism and does not provide fertile ground for the development of individual rights, norms, and systems, the communist revolution and socialist practice in modern China have not brought these to modern China either. The hostility toward individualism and the extolization and prioritizing of the state and collectivity are not only totally preserved but also greatly strengthened in the name of revolutionary claims, the party's paramount goals, class interest, and the whole interest of the state and collectivity, which has resulted in the systematic control of the party–state power and ideological power over "the life of the mind." Only Deng's market reform and open policy began to bring to China Western concepts and norms of individual rights. However, Deng and the post-Deng leadership have waged a constant struggle against the "capitalist" or "bourgeois" influences and tendencies within the party and in the society on all the fronts of ideological, intellectual, cultural, and political construction of "Socialism with Chinese Characteristics," which will be discussed in depth in Chapters 7 and 8.

Questions for discussion

1. How does traditional Chinese culture differ from Western culture in terms of the relations between individual and society, and society and state?
2. What are the political implications of traditional Chinese culture for the rise of communism and later political transformation in China?
3. Chinese political development has demonstrated a pattern dominated by power, ideology, and organization. What are the nature and characteristics of power, ideology, and organization in traditional China?

Further reading

Robert J. Lifton, *Thought Reform and the Psychology of Totalitarianism: A Study of Brainwashing in China* (New York: W. W. Norton & Company, 1961).

R. Randle Edwards, Louis Henkin, Andrew J. Nathan, *Human Rights in Contemporary China* (New York: Columbia University Press, 1986).

Thomas Sowell, *A Conflict of Visions: Ideological Origins of Political Struggles* (New York: William Morrow and Company Inc., 1987).

Part III
Political development

5   The collapse of the imperial state and the communist road to power

The fundamental question in this chapter is why the Chinese people chose communism in the twentieth century. The Chinese imperial state, Qing Dynasty, in the second half of the nineteenth century, suffered a rapid decline due to internal rebellions and external invasions, encroachment, and colonization, and failed to respond effectively and successfully to foreign invasions and divisions. This had a major effect on Chinese political development in the twentieth century that was later known as "a century of revolution,"[1] from nationalistic revolution, militant warlordism, military dictatorship, war, communist peasant revolution, to the creation of the communist state in China. At the turn of the twentieth century, China made a sharp turn from failed reformation to revolutionary ideological totalism, which led to the rise of communism in modern China.

Foreign invasions and divisions of China from the mid-nineteenth century

China faced a serious challenge from Western powers beginning in the mid-nineteenth century, marking the beginning of foreign invasion and colonization by European imperialists, which had a tremendous impact on political development in modern China. Two Opium Wars between China and Britain brought disastrous military defeat for China, and weakened the Qing dynasty. Prohibition of the opium trade in China and the burning of opium was the incident that sparked off the first Opium War (1840–42) between the Qing Dynasty and the British empire, resulting in China's military defeat. Unequal and humiliating treaties were signed. The Qing dynasty was forced to sign the Treaty of Nanking in 1842, agreeing to lease Hong Kong, open five ports to British vessels, and a war indemnity (millions of pounds in silver) to Britain. Extraterritoriality, by which foreigners were not subject to Chinese law, was also imposed upon China. The Second Opium War (1857–60) saw another disastrous defeat for China, and the subsequent signing of the humiliating Treaty of Tianjin in 1860. By this treaty, the Yangtze ports were open to warships, Kowloon was leased, and customs administration was surrendered to the British.[2]

China in the late nineteenth century and the early twentieth century faced more serious challenges and humiliation both from the West and the East. First, China was defeated in the Sino-Japanese War (1894–95). With the subsequent signing of the Treaty of Shimonoseki (1896), Taiwan and Korea were colonized by Japan, and China was asked to pay a huge war indemnity. Then China was forced to make more humiliating concessions to Western powers from 1895 to 1902, and foreign powers were dividing China into "spheres of influence" and claimed exclusive trading rights to certain areas: France, Yunnan, Gungxi, Guangdong; Russia, some areas of Northern China; Germany, Shandong; Britain, Yangtze delta. The New Territories were leased until 1997. Foreign countries established more extraterritorial zones across China in which they enjoyed extraterritoriality or diplomatic immunity to Chinese law. China's sovereignty was declining, which led to nationalistic fervor and hatred toward foreigners who practiced in China.[3]

Table 5.1 Foreign invasions and divisions before the 1911 nationalist revolution

The Opium War (1840–42)
  Treaty of Nanking (Nanjing)
  Hong Kong was leased
  Five ports were opened to British residence and foreign trade
  British extraterritoriality (exemption from Chinese laws)
  A large war indemnity (silver in million).

The Second Opium War (1857–60)
Treaty of Tientsin (Tienjin)
  Yangtze Ports were open for the British warship
  Kowloon was released
  Customs administration was surrendered to the British

Sino-Japanese War (1894–95)
Treaty of Shimonoseki
  Taiwan was colonized by Japan
  Korea was lost to be controlled and colonized by Japan
  War indemnity

More concessions, treaties, and divisions of the sphere of influence by foreign powers (1895–1902)
  France: Yunnan, Gungxi, Guangdong
  Russia: some areas of Northern China
  Germany: Shandong
  Britain: Yangtze delta; New Territories leased until 1997

Sacking of Peking by the Eight Power Allied Forces (1901)
  Demolition of forts at the southern border
  Foreign occupation of select areas
  Arms import banned
  Prohibition of anti-foreign societies
  Indemnity
  Customs and salt taxes

The Boxer Uprising (义和拳运动) that emerged in the late nineteenth century (1898–1901) in response to foreign invaders sparked off another major foreign invasion by Eight Power Allied Forces (八国联军) in 1900. The Sacking of Peking, the capital of imperial China, by the united armies of the eight foreign powers brought about another major disastrous and humiliating defeat for China: demolition of forts at the southern border; foreign occupation of select areas; arms importation banned; prohibition of anti-foreign societies; indemnity; surrender of administration of customs and salt taxes to foreign powers.[4] China's sovereignty was further undermined. All these led to "collective trauma" and "historical dislocation" of the Chinese people, who sought changes and solutions in response to the challenges.

China's response: towards ideological totalism

Robert J. Lifton, in his work "Death and History," attempts to explain the ideological origin of totalitarianism: a people who suffered from the fear of death terror and the loss of collective immortality after experiencing a historical trauma, tried to recreate a collective sense of immortality by the destruction of old culture and civilization, which gave rise to ideological totalism, which then led to victimization and the violence of totalitarianism.[5] Lifton, through his exploration of the human collective psycho-historical dislocation, has found explanations for the deeper causes and performance of totalitarianism. The history of modern China—the rise of communism—has provided empirical evidence to support this theory.

The history of modern China from 1840 to 1945 is one of foreign invasions and divisions—from the first Opium War in 1840, through the second Opium War, the Sino-Japanese War in 1894, the aggression of the united armies of the eight nations in 1900, the Japanese military occupation in northeast China in the 1930s, to the Japanese full-scale aggression (1937–45)—a history of more than 500 treaties of national sovereign betrayal and humiliation,[6] which had a devastating impact on China and caused destructive consequences on Chinese cultural psychology. It was in the atmosphere of ferment and feelings of anger, humiliation, psychological trauma, and disillusionment that a half century of revolution, turmoil, violence, and radical political actions took form, which led China toward the creation of a communist state guided by ideological totalism—Marxism–Leninism: from the 1911 nationalist uprising, the May Fourth Movement in 1919, the rising of communist movements with the founding of the Communist Party of China in 1921, the nationalist revolution from 1924–27, the protracted civil war between the communist military and the nationalist government from 1927–49, with a ceasefire and uneasy alliance between the nationalist government and the communist military during the Japanese invasion in 1937–45. With the surrender of Japan in 1945, the two forces renewed their military conflict and fought a full-scale national civil war for three years from 1946 to 1949, with the nationalist military being defeated and the communist government being created, thereby China began a radical social transformation and a complete nation-state rebuilding to create a new state, new society, and new culture under the communist leadership guided by ideological totalism. For studies of modern Chinese history and historical accounts of the communist revolution, students are advised to refer to Further reading and online review essays.[7]

After experiencing almost 100 years of historical traumas and national calamities caused by foreign aggression and oppression since the middle of the nineteenth century, the Chinese people suffered from a "fear of death terror" as described by Robert J. Lifton—a fear that China was about to be dismembered from the nation-state community of the world, and suffered from total disillusionment with traditional culture and values, so that the traditional collective sense of immortality was shattered.

Confronting such a historical trauma, many of China's younger generation of scholars, with lofty ideals and reforming ideas, from Kang Youwei, Liang Qichao, Tang Chitong, Zhang Taiyan, and Yan Fu to Sun Yat-sen, began to question Chinese tradition and civilization and searched for ways of transforming society, recreating a new culture and a new sense of collective immortality, and building a powerful country.[8] However, all their reform and revolutionary efforts failed to create a new society, a new state, and a new culture that would meet the demands for progressive changes towards a new China.

Most Chinese intellectuals agreed, though there existed opposing views on many of the issues, that the Chinese had to learn from the West in order to break the vicious circle, as they finally realized that traditional culture passed on for generations, including Confucianism, would not provide a way for "making their own country prosperous and building up their military power" (富国强兵).

While earlier reformers of the Tongzhi Restoration (同治中兴1864–90) sought to introduce Western science and technology to China, later reformers realized that China needed to introduce not only Western science and technology but also new ideas and institutions to reform Chinese culture, society, and politics, particularly to change Chinese imperial rule to a constitutional monarchy. However, their reform effort that became known as the Hundred Day Reform (百日维新1889) was thwarted by the Empress Dowager Ci Xi, who put the Emperor, who supported the reform, under house arrest and many of reformers were arrested and killed.[9]

The failure of their reform plans made it clear to the other radical group of Chinese intellectuals led by Dr. Sun Yat-sun that the imperial system was the root of all problems, and must be overthrown to create a constitutional democracy based on checks and balances and the rule of law. The revolution in 1911 ended the last dynasty in Chinese history, and created a government called the "Republic of China." However, the government had no effective control and authority over the territory, and the country fell into the hands of warlords. "The so called 'revolution of 1911' had changed nothing significant in the Chinese character."[10]

With total disillusionment in their own tradition and civilization, Chinese intellectuals began to look for a total vision of social transformation, deconstruction, and reconstruction. The Russian "October Revolution" in 1917, also known as the Bolshevik Revolution, and the successful creation of the Soviet Union brought to China a new hope, a new model, and a new vision: land redistribution among peasants, nationalization of all banks and private businesses, confiscation of private bank accounts, seizing of church properties, foreign forces were driven out, all foreign debts were repudiated, factories were controlled by the Soviets, wages were increased and fixed at higher rates, and a shorter working day (eight hours) was introduced. The great changes that took place in China's neighboring state offered Chinese intellectuals a total vision of social reconstruction and transformation.

It was in such a domestic and international context that the May Fourth Movement took place in China in 1919. The movement marked the introduction into China of various new ideologies, among which Marxism–Leninism was the most appealing to radical scholars and students who sought radical social transformation. The movement was initiated by faculty and students and then spread throughout China and involved people from all walks of life. The May Fourth Movement was considered as the greatest cultural and ideological upheaval, as it launched an unprecedented attack on every aspect of Chinese traditional culture and values, which took the Chinese people in a totally new direction. In its broad sense, the May Fourth Movement was really a "psycho-historical dislocation"—on one hand, it was comprehensive self-questioning and self-criticizing of its own traditional culture and psychology, "an attempt to redefine China's culture as a valid part of the modern world",[11] and, on the other hand, it was a search for a way of recreating a new culture, a new life, a new writing style, a new art, a new education, and a new way of thinking.

The May Fourth Movement was the turning point in the history of modern China. Many fundamental problems, particularly those deep-seated cultural and ideological problems in contemporary China, can be traced back to it.

Table 5.2 China's response to foreign invasions

The Taiping Heaven (太平天国) (1850–64)

Failed reform efforts at self-strengthening and learning from the West
    The Tongzhi Restoration (1864–90)
    The 100-Days Reform (1898)

The Boxer Uprising (1899–1901)
    The Nationalist Revolution (1911)
    The Qing Dynasty collapsed
    The 1911 revolution failed to create a central government and China disintegrated into warlordism
    The May Fourth Movement (1919)
    The Founding of the Communist Party of China (1921)
    The Northern Expedition (1924–27)
    The founding of the Nationalist Party-controlled Government (1927)

At that time, however, choices did exist in China, if we follow the logic chain of Lifton's theory, either turning to a "new life-giving vision," or to a type of "ideological totalism." As a result, it turned out to be on the four-step sequence from historical dislocation to ideological totalism, from which China ushered in a new epoch of revolutions, and total reconstruction and transformation. This is the far-reaching implication of the May Fourth Movement for China. The May Fourth Movement never developed into something like the Enlightenment or Renaissance in Western countries, because the two popular concepts of "democracy" and "science" in the May Fourth Movement were submissive to the central tasks of "national salvation" and "revolution."

In a more significant sense, the May Fourth Movement, which was led by faculty and the educated youth of Beijing, many of whom advocated a "New Culture Movement" (新文化运动) after the collapse of the Qing Dynasty, was an attempt to transform man, or, to be more exact, to transform Chinese people by remolding their basic spirit and basic attitude, remaking their cultural psychology, and creating a unifying ideology in order to transform society. This totalistic ideological trend, which was brought up by the brightest and the most radical "May Fourth educated youth" had a widespread and profound political influence throughout China—a strong tendency toward "ideological totalism." The May Fourth Movement was considered as the seedbed of revolutionary leaders, such as Chen Duxiu, Li Dazhao, and Mao Zedong, who founded the Communist Party of China. In this sense, the May Fourth Movement was a significant turning point and took the Chinese people in the direction of "ideological totalism"—a total vision of social destruction, reconstruction, and transformation for a Utopian goal, which called for strong political leadership and mass mobilization in China.

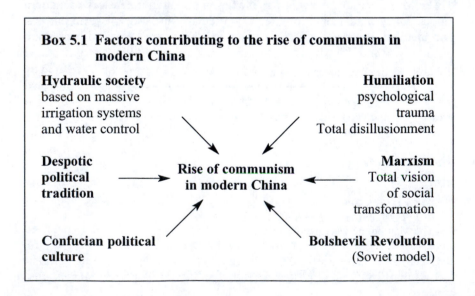

Box 5.1 Factors contributing to the rise of communism in modern China

Hydraulic society based on massive irrigation systems and water control

Humiliation psychological trauma Total disillusionment

Despotic political tradition

Rise of communism in modern China

Marxism Total vision of social transformation

Confucian political culture

Bolshevik Revolution (Soviet model)

By then, some basic internal and external factors and conditions had accumulated powerful forces to move Chinese intellectuals and the social classes toward psychological and cultural radicalism, ideological and political totalism (Box 5.1). Students should also take into account the political and cultural traditions described in Chapters 1–2 to think about the causal factors and how the traditional factors (internal) joined forces with modern factors (external), eventually contributing to the rise of communism in modern China.

The rise of communism: from ideological totalism to political totalism

No one would be able to take the Chinese people to the shore of "ideological totalism" until the Communist Party of China was created in 1921. The Leninist party, supported by the Soviet Union, arose at the historical moment and followed the successful model of the first communist state in Russia; it claimed to have a historical mission to remold the Chinese people's basic values and cultural psychology, and the universal truth of changing society and recreating a new society. Many educated young people inspired by the vision and ideals joined the communist party. The fledging communist party sought support and guidance from the Soviet Union, while Dr. Sun Yat-sen's nationalist party, Kuomintang (KMT), also sought military support from the Soviet Union to create its own army. Both parties were advised to join forces to establish a military academy fully supported by the Soviet Union, and both party leaders agreed. This military academy, which was known as the Whampoa Military Academy (黄埔军校), was officially created in 1924 in Guangzhou, with Chiang Kai-shek appointed as the first commandant. After years of military training and preparation of armaments, the KMT army, led by Chiang Kai-shek, joined by the forces of the CPC, launched the Northern Expedition (北伐) (1926–28), a military campaign to destroy the local warlords in central, eastern, and northern China and unify China under one government led by the KMT. However, there was a split between the KMT and the CPC in 1927, and all communist party members were purged, arrested, or killed by Chiang Kai-shek. Thus was born a nationally unified central government led by Chiang Kai-shek and the KMT while the CPC was forced to go underground in urban areas. Its remaining troops went to the Jinggangshan Mountains (井冈山), in the border region between Jiangxi and Hunan provinces of China, which became known as the cradle of the Chinese communist revolution and the birthplace of the Red Army (later renamed the People's Liberation Army in the full-scale civil war when the communist army launched the military campaigns to defeat the KMT military in 1946–49).[12] Map 5.1 shows the geographical location of Jiangxi province in China.

In the Jinggangshan Mountains the remaining troops of the CPC, led by Mao Zedong and Zhu De, joined forces to create a base area for guerrilla warfare, the first Soviet government of peasants and workers, and the first communist-led troop, called "Red First Regiment of the Chinese Workers' and Peasants'

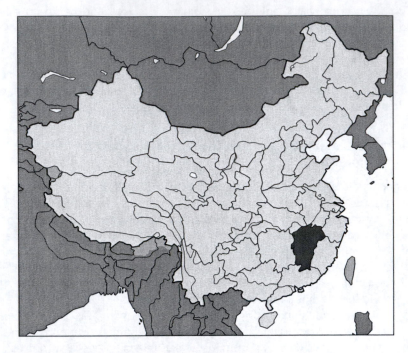

Map 5.1 The geographical location of Jiangxi province.
Source: http://en.wikipedia.org/wiki/File:China_Jiangxi.svg.

Red Army" (中国工农红军红一方面军) or the Central Red Army(中央红军). Mao developed his theories of rural-based communist revolution, guerilla warfare, and Soviet-type government in the Jinggangshan Mountains. As the Red Army grew, the KMT launched a series of military encirclement campaigns to attack the communist military forces, and eventually forced the Red Army out of the region in 1934. However, the Red Army was not wiped out and began the historical Long March (长征), and reportedly traversed many provinces, some 12,500 kilometers (8,000 miles) in 370 days,[13] from the south to the north and west, and eventually arrived in Shaanxi province and created another base there (Map 5.2).

The Red Army regrouped and united with troops from the 2nd and 3rd regiments of the Red Army (红二, 红四方面军) and various other communist armies. The new communist headquarters was established in Yanan (延安), northern Shaanxi, and the rural base areas gradually expanded to remote areas of provinces neighboring Shaanxi, such as Gansu and Ningxia, where the KMT forces did not reach. Yanan became the center of the Chinese communist revolution from 1936 to 1948 prior to the communist victory in China.[14] Map 5.3 shows the geographical location of Shaanxi province.

Politically, Yanan became a revolutionary holy land where Chinese communists sought to practice and realize their idealized vision of communist

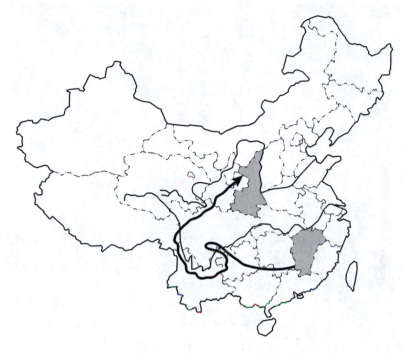

Map 5.2 The Long March of the Red Army from Jiangxi to Shaanxi.

new man, new life, new culture, new social organizations, and new government in the new red capital, the Shaan-Gan-Ning Soviet (陕甘宁边区苏维埃政府), covering areas of the provinces of Shaanxi, Gansu, and Ningxia. Yanan symbolized a utopian ideal for many Chinese people who pursued an ideal of a total reconstruction of Chinese social and political life that would be totally different from the past and from the rest of China under the rule of the KMT government. Yanan's communist practice also attracted many prominent Western journalists including Edgar Snow and Anna Louise Strong, who came to Yenan to interview Mao Zedong and other important communist leaders, such as Zhou Enlai and Liu Shaoqi. Yenan, as it then became known to the Western world, even hosted the United States Army Observation Group that was sent to Yanan to establish official ties with the communist party for possible cooperation against the Japanese.[15]

The Yanan practice also symbolizes the beginning of the "systematic remolding of human minds"[16] in the communist revolution and the socialist construction in later years after the founding of the People's Republic of China (PRC). Yanan's communist practices, such as the Yanan Rectification Movement (延安整风运动), ideological and political campaigns, criticism and self-criticism, brainwashing indoctrination, political purges to purify the ranks, mass mobilization via "mass line" (群众路线), etc., had an important and

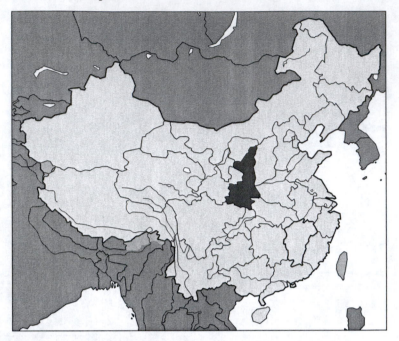

Map 5.3 The geographical location of Shaanxi province.
Source: http://en.wikipedia.org/wiki/File:China_Shaanxi.svg

enduring impact on the later political development after the CPC created the People's Republic of China. "Yanan Spirit" (延安精神) reflects the communist revolutionary tradition developed during the 13 years of communist practice, and all generations of the CPC leadership, from Mao to Deng, from Jiang to Hu, have continued to emphasize the importance of the "Yanan Spirit" in party ideological and organizational work as well as the ideological and political education at universities in the twentieth and twenty-first centuries.

It was in Yanan, where Mao studied lessons of the early Chinese communist revolution, that Mao further developed his thoughts on the philosophy of revolutionary struggle, his theories of revolutionary bases and guerilla warfare, mass line and mass mobilization, united front strategy and tactics, and tasks and goals of the Chinese communist revolution. Mao Zedong wrote a number of important works during the Yanan era, such as "Problems of Strategy in China's Revolutionary War," "On Guerilla Warfare," "Basic Tactics," "On Practice," "On Contradictions," "For the Mobilization of All the Nation's Forces for Victory in the War of Resistance," "On Protracted War," "Dialectical Materialism," "The May Fourth Movement," "The Orientation of the Youth Movement," "The Chinese Revolution and the Chinese Communist Party," "On New Democracy," "On Coalition Government," etc.[17] These works provided a theoretical basis for guiding the

Chinese communist revolution. His status as political, military, and ideological leader of the CPC was fully established during the Yanan period. His thoughts, "Mao Zedong Thought," were escalated to the level of Marxism–Leninism, codified into the party constitution, and became the guidelines for the Chinese communist revolution.

The communist party benefited from a valuable time of peace in Yanan, particularly after the Xi'an Incident in 1936,[18] when Chiang Kai-shek was forced to form the Second United Front with the CPC against the Japanese full-scale invasion in China. The Red Army was reorganized and renamed as the Eighth Route Army and the New Fourth Army of the National Revolutionary Army of the Republic of China to fight against the Japanese from 1937 to 1945. However, the communist armies were actually controlled by the CPC, though they were nominally designated as military units of the nationalist military. During these years, the CPC persevered and strengthened its influence both militarily and politically in fighting a guerilla war and organizing political campaigns against the Japanese invasion and occupation of China. The communist party's political programs and military resistance campaigns won over support from the Chinese people for its cause, particularly

Table 5.3 Major events of the Chinese communist revolution 1921–49

The founding of the CPC in 1921.

The split between the CPC and the KMT in 1927; in the same year, the KMT achieved national unification and established its Nationalist government without the CPC.

Mao Zedong advocated that the Chinese communist revolution should focus on the revolutionary potential of the peasantry due to the nature of agrarian society rather than on the urban proletariat as prescribed by orthodox Marxism-Leninism. Mao turned the local peasants into a politicized guerrilla force, the Red Army, from a several hundred local peasant guerrilla force to about 10,000 Red Army troops by the winter of 1927–28, and to 100,000 by 1934, threatening the Nationalist government. Nationalist government launched a series of military campaigns against the communist Red Army led by Mao Zedong, 1927–31.

The Long March of the Red Army began in October 1934 after the deadly defeat by Nationalist forces, set out on some 12,500 kilometers through 11 provinces, 18 mountain ranges, and 24 rivers in southwest and northwest China. Some 8,000 survivors of the original troop, joined by 22,000 from other areas, arrived in Shaanxi province in October 1935. The CPS set up its headquarters at Yanan, where the communist movement grew rapidly for the next 10 years. Contributing to this growth was a combination of internal and external circumstances, of which aggression by the Japanese was perhaps one of the most significant.

Japanese military stationed in Manchus (northeastern China) in 1931 and launched a full scale military invasion in 1937.

Chiang Kai-shek was forced to join a united front with the CPC to fight against the Japanese.

1937–45, eight-year anti-Japanese war and the communist growth during the war.

1946–49, three-year civil war and the KMT lost the battle and moved to Taiwan.

---

educated youth from the urban areas under KMT rule and peasants in vast inland rural areas. The size of the communist forces almost doubled to a total of 600,000 soldiers in 1945, which laid down a strong military base for victory over the KMT in the second civil war from 1946 to 1949.[19]

The CPC-led military was supported by the Soviet Union while the KMT government was recognized as the legitimate government of China; its military was largely supported by the United States. The two forces fought two protracted civil wars (国共内战) from 1927–37 and from 1945–49, except when the nationalist party and the communist party formed a united front to fight against the Japanese invasion from 1937 to 1945.

The civil war represented a full-scale ideological confrontation between the Western-supported Nationalist government led by the KMT and the Soviet-supported communist revolution led by the CPC, which eventually resulted in the communist victory in 1949.[20] After experiencing its ups and downs, the CPC's vision of future society and ideological appeal eventually prevailed over other ideological schemes along with the successful communist revolution, and finally became the official ideology of the PRC after the communist takeover of power in 1949.

The ideological battle was also fought within the communists, from all the levels of the top leaders to the rank and file soldiers and revolutionary participants, from the Soviet regime created in Ruijin (瑞金) from the late 1920s to early 1930s, then Yanan Rectification Movement, to a series of nationwide political and ideological movements after the new state was created in China. Those dissenting from Mao's ideological line were brutally purged in order to create a unifying ideological power of political leaders from Mao's time to the present.

After the communists attained power, communist ideology served as a means of controlling society and mobilizing the population, legitimizing current political and economic policies and arrangements, and enhancing group loyalty and cohesiveness. More importantly, communist ideology was entrusted with a mission to create "a new type of man."

In order to achieve all these purposes, the party ideologue resorted to "ideological totalism," through ideological propaganda and education, officially provided action series and preferences for every social member in nearly every aspect of social life, successive political campaigns of victimization and mass violence, and monopoly over ideology and mass media.

Drawing on the cultural legacy of Chinese traditional culture and the ideological tradition of the Russian October Revolution and Leninism–Stalinism, communist ideology declared that individualism was an obstacle in building socialism and creating socialist man. Individualism, human liberties, and rights were labeled as bourgeois concepts, seen as restraints on or challenges to the power and authority of the party and the state, and in the end treated as a threat to the goal of creating a new and socialist country. Collectivism and self-sacrifice were glorified as major principles of socialism and as a model for the "socialist new man."

The interests of the state, the collective, and the party are paramount; the individual is required to be selfless in sacrificing for the collective, the state and the party. Whenever individual and collective interests come into conflict, the individual interest should be subordinate to the higher interests of party, class, and nation, because the individual is an element of the collective, and individual interest is a short-term and partial one while collective interests are long-term and complete ones; and the party and state represent the fundamental and higher interest of both the collective and the individual. Such collective ideas are constantly propagated mainly through officially manipulated socialization, such as kindergartens, education, workplace, media, and successive political and mass campaigns, etc.

However, one of the sharpest differences from collectivism in the Chinese tradition brought about by the communist regime is the redefinition of the collective identity and the self-identity of the individual. With the establishment of the PRC in 1949, the authority of traditional collective entities, such as household, kinship, etc. was deliberately attacked, among which the family was one of the first institutions targeted for destruction. In place of the authority of traditional collective entities, "new units" of collective identity were introduced into society through successive nationwide communization movements (1953–59), such as "the Movement of Socialist Transformation," "Nationalization of the Means of Production," "the Collectivization of Agriculture," "the Great Leap Forward." The party began to impose its authority upon the Chinese people by simply relying on these established institutions of a collective nature, which were administratively and politically binding and much more easily controlled than those of traditional society.

Moreover, the communist regime went beyond placing individuals in established collective institutions by forcing the population into a system of class classification by giving everybody a "class" label according to the status of the head of the household at the time the PRC was established, and later to one's attitudes and thoughts. "Victimization" and "mass violence," as Lifton posited in his research, which had started from the early Red Army revolution to the Yanan communist government, now applied to the whole society. A party doctrine, "in class society there is no human nature above classes" provides a theoretical basis for the victimization and the transformation of man.

Owners of land and private enterprises, rich peasantry, counter-revolutionaries, rightists, etc., were classified into the "five black categories," as the enemy of the people, and became objects of proletarian dictatorship. Mass violence, in the name of the class, backed up by state power, began to get involved with the political victimization campaigns, such as "Anti-Three-Evils" and "Anti-Five-Evils," "Suppression of Counterrevolutionaries," "Anti-Rightists," and "Socialist Education," etc.

From the 1960s class labeling became an increasingly important element in every individual's life. Those who were fortunate enough to be classed among the "five red categories" could hope for a better future, while those in the "five black categories" were designated as "bad elements" and the enemy of the people, had no future at all, and were under frequent attack by mass violence. Those not in the "five black categories" were supposed to follow the party closely and participate actively in political campaigns; otherwise they would also become victims, because the self-identity of the individual was derived from both class classification and political attitudes. Nobody could go between, either friends or enemies, red or black. Those who were not for the party's policy or were away from collective, or those who claimed the protection of their individual liberties and rights were seen as selfish or self-centered and displaying social deviance, or worse, as anti-party, counter-socialist, and counter-revolutionary, which were grave offenses, punishable by a jail sentence or even death.

Such "ideology totalism" of the class classification and ideological line struggle was derived and transformed from Marxian class categories and the theory of class struggle of Mao Zedong, which had played a leading role in the CPC's struggle for state power, and was proclaimed as the working class's revolutionary weapon in the struggle for overthrowing the exploitative system and the building of communism. However, this weapon of struggle had not only pointed to the "class enemy" in the communist revolution, but also targeted and attacked the "people" or purified the ranks of communist party members, in particular the individual and individual rights.

The "class struggle" was also applied to the areas within the party, apart from the whole society, for the purpose of the intra-party power struggle among the leadership, which usually led to successive political purges and political campaigns, periodically on a large scale, both within and outside the party. All this was done in the name of collective norms such as the people, the state, the party, among which the CPC put itself above all in the name of the leadership of the "proletarian revolution" and the highest representative of the "working class" and other laboring classes. The "class struggle" provided a direct theoretical source and legitimacy for "ideological totalism" and "victimization" under Mao's regime.

Questions for discussion

1. What are the origins and the dynamics of Chinese communism? Under what conditions did communism arise and develop? In other words, what key factors would explain the rise of communism in the Chinese context?
2. How did factors such as the hydraulic society, political tradition of "oriental despotism," Confucian culture, a century of foreign invasions and historical trauma, the influence of the Russian communist revolution, Marxist-Leninist ideological totalism, and the May Fourth Movement, contribute to the rise of communism in modern China?

Further reading

Chow Tse-tung, *The May Fourth Movement: Intellectual Revolution in Modern China.* (Cambridge: Harvard University Press, 1960).

Robert Jay Lifton, *Thought Reform and the Psychology of Totalism: A Study of "Brainwashing" in China* (New York: W.W. Norton and Company, 1961).

Franz Schurmann, *Ideology and Organization in Communist China* (Berkeley: University of California Press, 1968).

Benjamin I. Schwartz, *Communism and China: Ideology in Flux* (Cambridge: Harvard University Press, 1968).

Benjamin Schwartz, *Chinese Communism and the Rise of Mao* (Cambridge: Harvard University Press, 1951).

Mark Selden, *The Yenan Way in Revolutionary China* (Cambridge: Harvard University Press, 1971).

Suzanne Pepper, *Civil War in China: The Political Struggle, 1945–1949* (Berkeley: University of California Press, 1978).

6 The making of the new communist state and the post-Mao transition

Since the Communist Party of China took over power in 1949, China has been under communist rule for over 60 years. This major development can be divided into two distinct historical eras: (1) the making of the new communist state from 1949 to 1976, and (2) the post-Mao transition from 1978 to the present day. Each era is characterized by different goals and ideological justifications, different central tasks and adjusted action means to achieve them, different leadership styles, and changes of continuity in Chinese politics and government. Each era can be further divided into several epochs. This chapter provides a brief overview of each historical era of the developments of the Mao era, during which the new communist state, new economy, and new society were established through radical social transformation and political campaigns, and of the post-Mao era, during which pragmatic economic reform was implemented to transition from centrally planned command economy under Deng Xiaoping and his successors. For studies of modern Chinese history and detailed historical accounts of the historical events, students are advised to refer to the Further reading list and online review essays.[1]

Radical social transformation 1949–76

1949–53: In 1949, the Chinese Communist Party (CPC) defeated the KMT and gained control over the country. A new era began in China. One of the most important issues facing the CPC centered on the making of the new state. The CPC's immediate goal was the founding of the People's Republic of China (PRC), creating a "new democracy," known as a "socialist democratic dictatorship," with the CPC as the ruling party. The central task was to consolidate the power of the CPC and suppress "counter-revolutionary" forces, with authority extending all over China, create a party–state regime modeled on the Soviet Union, reorganize the administration, and most urgently restore financial stability, social order, and the economy which had been seriously damaged during the civil war and the protracted war against the Japanese invasion. These were serious challenges facing the CPC in the early years of the new regime, and it responded remarkably well, through the leadership's confidence, determination, unity, talented organizational skills, enthusiastic popular support, Soviet aid, and, last but not least, individual sacrifices.[2]

Several million peasant soldiers discarded their uniforms and became the cadres or functionaries of the newly created government, with party committees being established as the body of leadership in every sector of the government at all levels, and the party secretary being the first-hand figure in the party–state institutions of the new state. Various committees and conferences were set up at national and local levels to incorporate these pro-communist and patriotic intellectuals and noncommunist elite figures into the formal and informal structure of the communist state, where they discussed issues of political consultation, education, science, economy, taxation, trade, labor, law, health, etc., and provided suggestions to the CPC government for their resolution. New laws were passed to regulate the trade unions, mass organizations, economy, political and social life.[3]

Chinese social life was reorganized into various party-led mass organizations that educated and indoctrinated the people with communist ideals and values, as well as Mao Zedong Thought in rural and urban areas. The "Campaign on Eradication of Illiteracy" (扫除文盲运动) was launched in 1950 as part of the ideological indoctrination effort to educate people who were illiterate and exposed them to the new communist ideology and practices. Training courses were politically and ideologically based, and simply used political slogans and quotations of Mao's speech as course materials. When illiterate people began to learn how to read and write, they went through the ideological brain-washing process. The "Suppression of Counterrevolutionaries" (镇压反革命运动) was launched in 1950–52, targeting and eradicating "local tyrants" (地方恶霸), "historical counterrevolutionaries" (历史反革命), the KMT underground forces, agents and their collaborators on mainland China. The campaign was carried out through mass mobilization in which urban residents and rural peasants were mobilized to attack the "class enemy" in struggle sessions as propaganda efforts and many of them were executed after the mass struggle sessions. The "Three Anti and Five Anti Movement" (三反五反运动) was launched in 1951–52, with the former (the three antis are corruption, waste, and bureaucracy) starting in 1951 and targeting those party and government officials who were corrupted by evil capitalist forces. The latter campaign (the five antis are bribery, theft of state property, tax evasion, cheating on government contracts, and stealing state economic information) began in 1952, targeting those wealthy capitalists who disobeyed the economic orders of the government or violated the new laws passed by the new regime. All these campaigns involved harsher punishments, torture, public humiliation, and public execution.[4]

The new CPC government also implemented a nationwide land reform as promised during the communist revolution. Lands of former landlords were confiscated and redistributed equally to landless peasants, those who did not have sufficient land, and the landlords themselves who now had to till the land for a living. As a result, the land reform equalized the wealth gap in rural areas. However, some landlords were tortured and executed during and after the mass campaign and struggle meetings organized by local CPC work teams, as they were found guilty of committing crimes or having incurred "blood debts" (血债) before the communist liberation in 1949.[5] The CPC radical agrarian reform policies enjoyed wide support from the Chinese peasants.

Internationally, the Soviet Union and other communist countries in Eastern Europe were quick to recognize the new government and establish diplomatic relationships with the PRC, and a growing number of Western countries began to recognize the PRC, despite the hostility of the United States and the U.S.-led UN trade embargo. The Korean War, to the surprise of many Western countries, actually had positive effects on the consolidation of the new communist state, the mobilization of the masses to participate in postwar reconstruction and restore prewar production, the unification of the Chinese people under a strong centralized government with strong support for the "anti-American and anti-imperialism" movement, the effective administration of the war economy, and thus the strengthening in confidence and the legitimacy of the new regime.

1953–56: The year 1953 marked a new phase of the radical social transformation, known as "Transition to Socialism." The central task was to implement a new socialist economic system through socialist transformation and nationalization of major industries and "China's First Five-Year Plan," creating a Soviet-type centrally planned socialist economy, and building a state-owned industrial economy with an emphasis on mass construction and heavy industry, mainly relying upon Soviet technology and material support, particularly for several hundred new large industrial projects, infrastructures, the production of coal, electricity, steel, iron, planned industrial renovation and massive hydraulic construction. The implementation of the First Five-Year Plan was largely successful, and thus boosted the confidence and determination of Mao and his colleagues to launch more ambitious industrial development plans and an agricultural transformation movement.[6]

The socialist transformation also began in rural areas during this period, encouraging peasant households to form "mutual aid teams" (互助组) and other collective farming organizations. The agricultural collectivization was actually pushed through gradually and voluntarily during the early period of socialist transformation, establishing various collective forms such as "mutual aid teams," "elementary agricultural cooperatives" (初级合作社), and "higher co-operatives" (高级合作社). However, in 1956, the party's policy shifted to organize all peasants into agricultural cooperatives. By the end of 1956, 98 percent of farm households had joined various forms of collective farming.[7] With the development of collective farming, the party was able to implement political and ideological campaigns more effectively to bring about radical social changes in rural areas by organizing peasants into mass organizations and to participate in political study meetings and educational sessions. Major political developments included the centralization of party and government administration and the institutionalization of party–state power.

1957–66: In late 1956 and early 1957, the party implemented a new policy, called "let one hundred flowers blossom and one hundred schools contend" (百花齐放, 百家争鸣) to promote free discussions on socialist construction and party policies, invite criticisms and proposals from intellectuals for the party's work and policies, and encourage different schools and forms of literature and arts. Intellectuals and non-Communist Party members were encouraged by the party's "double-hundred policy" (双百方针)to begin criticizing the pitfalls of the party's work, inefficient bureaucratic routines, the harshness of the past campaigns, the ignorance of uneducated cadres, and wrongheaded policies. However, criticisms began to shift toward Mao and challenge the party dictatorship, which was considered by the party to be unhealthy; the harmful criticisms were a threat to the legitimacy of the party ruling, which catalyzed the "Anti-Rightist Movement" (反右运动) in 1957. Many intellectuals, students, dissidents, artists, and even party officials who voiced their different opinions were purged and even prosecuted during the crackdown.[8]

The year 1958 ushered in a new phase in the full-scale experimentation of Mao's utopian ideals by launching a nationwide movement of the "Great Leap Forward" (大跃进), which encompassed collectivization and industrialization in parallel: the "nationwide agricultural collectivization movement" (全国农业集体化) that established people's communes (人民公社) throughout China's rural areas, and the socialist industrialization that relied on mass mobilization for "the nationwide iron and steel production campaign" (全民大炼钢铁运动). The party–state employed revolutionary means and political campaigns in an attempt to accomplish the goals of rapid industrialization to catch up with the United States and the United Kingdom and create new social and economic institutions to manage the party's programs. The experiment resulted in grand failure and a setback for Mao in political support from his colleagues, which led to his determination to drive forward and launch a nationwide and unprecedented massive political movement—the "Cultural Revolution" in 1966.[9]

The initial success of the Chinese socialist transformation led Mao to believe that China's transition to communism could be accomplished earlier than he had expected. The Great Leap Forward was a major attempt by Mao and his colleagues to accomplish the economic and technical development of the country at a faster pace and with greater results, "to catch up with Britain and America within 15 years," which was based on Mao's belief that it was achievable if domestic resources could be fully utilized, the peasantry and mass organizations could be fully mobilized, and the people could be ideologically aroused. To accomplish such an ambitious goal, the Great Leap Forward created new socio-economic and political organizations in the countryside, the People's Communes, which were placed under the control of local governments. Each commune was placed in control of all the means of production and operated as the sole accounting unit; it was subdivided into production brigades (concurrent with traditional villages) and then production teams. Each commune had administration, local security, militia organizations, small-scale local industry, schools, nurseries, communal kitchens, etc. Each commune was responsible for such major public projects as roads, irrigation works, reservoirs, and hydroelectric dams, which were seen as integral parts of the party's plan for an ideal new society. By the fall of 1958, some 23,500 communes were incorporated from some 750,000 agricultural cooperatives, each averaging 5,000 households, or 22,000 people. By the early 1960s, an estimated 74,000 communes had been established.[10]

To accomplish the goal of rapid industrialization, the party mobilized the masses to build backyard iron and steel furnaces in every commune, every town, and every urban neighborhood all over the country in addition to major investments in large-, medium-, and small-scale steel plants. Workers, peasants, students, doctors, artists, soldiers, cadres, and people from all walks of life were mobilized and participated enthusiastically in the movement without knowledge or special training. More than 100 million peasants shifted from grain to steel production. People brought their pans, pots, and any metals they could find for the furnaces and felled trees to fuel the furnaces. Despite the increasing production of iron and steel, the iron and steel produced were of low quality and virtually useless.[11]

The result was astonishing and disastrous, largely due to unrealistic targets, hubris, corruption, and poor accounting, and approximately 16–40 million Chinese died in a famine between 1959 and 1962, which was largely attributable to unrealistic and fanciful economic goals.[12] A more recent publication by a Chinese journalist, which is banned in mainland China, is widely considered to provide the most comprehensive account of the great famine, and a record of the 36 million Chinese who died of hunger, based on official achieves.[13] Some scholars called it the "Great Leap Famine."[14] The disastrous effects of the Great Leap Forward provoked the leadership to rethink the method of industrialization and collectivization, and adopt some more pragmatic economic policy and adjustment measures in the early 1960s. Mao suffered a major setback in political support for his utopian economic policy, and decided to step aside to let the moderate leader Liu Shaoqi take charge of running the economy, recovering production, and coping with the difficult situation. Liu implemented policies that allowed peasants to cultivate private plots in the backyard of their homes and sell produce to farmers' markets; he decentralized economics decision-making and planning to economic organizations below the level of communes, restored material incentives to peasants and collective farming, and carried out more realistic economic planning and programs.[15]

1966–76: In the mid-1960s, however, Mao believed that creeping "capitalist" and anti-socialist tendencies were developing as a result of such economic policy and corrupting the cadres and masses with bourgeois thought. Mao launched another campaign the "socialist education movement" (社会主义教育运动) in 1963 to purify the ranks and clean up politics, the economy, organizations, and ideology, which was also called "four cleanups" (四清运动) to purge corrupted elements from the party and government. At the same time, Liu and his allies attempted to block Mao's effort to arrest the so-called "capitalist trend." Mao believed that restoring ideological purity and purging those who were not supportive of his policies was necessary, and the only way to achieve these goals was to mobilize the masses for the "class struggle" against those "capitalist roaders" ("those in power taking the capitalist road") within the party–state and remove them from power. This massive and fervent political movement was called the "Great Proletariat Cultural Revolution" (无产阶级文化大革命) from 1966–76, during which Mao initiated a more radical transformation in all aspects of society by using moral and political campaigns to transform China into a pure communist society. China under Mao developed a radical pattern, characterized by utopian zeal, top-down mass mobilization, constant political and ideological campaigns, fervent class struggles, in an attempt to bring about a total transformation of Chinese society into a new socialist society and a total remolding of the Chinese people into the new socialist man.[16]

The "Cultural Revolution" was the highest point of communist fervor in China's radical social transformation. Students formed Mao's "Red Guard" and attacked the "Four Olds" (old ideas, old culture, old customs, and old habits) and the "capitalist roaders." Workers, peasants, soldiers, and people

Table 6.1 Major developments in Mao's China

1949–53, the founding of the communist government, the Korean war, the suppression of the anti-revolutionary campaign, "Three Anti and Five Anti Campaign" and the land reform, for the purpose of consolidating the communist new regime

1953–56, the socialist transformation movement and nationalization of major industries. The period of officially designated "Transition to Socialism" corresponded to China's First Five-Year Plan (1953–57). Major political developments included the centralization of party and government administration and the institutionalization of the party-state power modeled on the former Soviet Union

1957–59, the party implemented a new policy, called "let one hundred flowers blossom and one hundred schools contend" and then launched the "Anti-Rightist Movement" in 1957. This was followed by the "Great Leap Forward" campaign in 1958, aiming to accomplish the economic and technical development of the country at a faster pace and with greater results. Politically, anti-right campaigns to silence the dissident voices and establish the party's unchallengeable authority and infallibility

1959–62, three-year economic crisis took millions of lives: "natural" or "man-made" disasters?

1962–65, economic policy readjustment, four-clean-ups campaign, and socialist education campaign

1966–76, the Cultural Revolution was another major political campaign—Mao and the CPC intended to purify the party and transform the society and the Chinese people to create the "new socialist man" and a "new socialist state"

from all walks of life, in all age groups, were deeply involved in the movement and profoundly influenced by it. Chinese intellectuals and most party and state officials were attacked and removed from their positions, in places where emerged the ruling power of the "revolutionary committees" in all provinces, municipalities and autonomous regions. All work units, from factories to schools, from urban streets to rural communes, also formed their own revolutionary committees to run the administration.[17] The "revolutionary committees" consisted of workers, peasants, soldiers and leftist cadres who directed the "Cultural Revolution" and took over the administration of the government and the economy. Mao and his close allies (the "Gang of Four") adopted ultra-leftist economic policy based on utopian morality and political incentives and attacked those policies that emphasized production and industrialization in more pragmatic ways as "capitalistic" and "revisionist." As a result, the economy was on the brink of collapse at the end of the Cultural Revolution (Table 6.1).[18]

Pragmatic reform and economic transition in the post-Mao era

The post-Mao era began with the death of Mao Zedong in 1976, and the arrest of Mao's close allies during the Cultural Revolution, the "Gang of Four." Ironically their arrest was conducted under the leadership of Hua Guofeng, who was the successor hand picked by Mao Zedong. Hua had been appointed Chairman of the CPC, Premier of the state Council, and President of the Central Military Commission. He was pressurized and supported by the CPC senior veterans to arrest the "Gang of Four" and end the leftist policy of the Cultural Revolution.

However, Hua was not a reform-minded leader, but committed to maintain "whatever" Mao had said and done—which was later known as the "what-everist faction" in the very early stages of post-Mao reform. In the meantime, the "pragmatic faction" of the top leadership emerged, led by Chen Yun, a senior veteran, vice chairman of the CPC and vice premier of the State Council, who was reform minded, and joined forces with Deng Xiaoping, who had been under attack as the "capitalist roader" during the Cultural Revolution, and then later resurrected politically to resume his position as vice premier and vice chairman. Both had strong personal and authority bases in the military, the party, and the government due to their long history of positions of leadership during the communist revolution and socialist construction. In the late 1970s, a power and ideological struggle as well as a policy debate within the top party leadership broke out between the two factions, and resulted in the removal of Hua and his supporters from official positions in the early 1980s, though some of them were retained in some nominal positions.[19]

From the late 1970s to early 1980s, some major changes were made, which were called "readjustment, reform, correction, and improvement." While the

CPC retained its commitment to Marxism, Leninism, and Mao Zedong Thought, formally claimed its firm adherence to the "Four Basic Principles,"[20] and continued political and ideological campaigns against efforts that deviated from the party line as the "bourgeois liberalization". The party leadership began to repudiate Mao's "class struggle" theory and refocused its central task as economic development, rehabilitated millions of cadres, intellectuals, and people from all walks of life who had been purged and prosecuted during the series of political movements from the 1950s to the 1970s. It relinquished some dogmas of Stalinist and Maoist ideologies and models, and modified them under the slogan "practice is the sole criterion of truth," encouraged material incentives and a market role in production, gradually opened the door to the outside world, abandoned the people's communes and started decollectivization in rural areas. The CPC reinstitutionalized and strengthened the party–state organizations and apparatus that were smashed during the Cultural Revolution, re-established the party–state legal systems and legislative systems, restored churches and temples that were damaged, and so forth.[21]

However, after the defeat of the "whateverist factions," for the majority of the 1980s, a divide between Chen Yun and Deng Xiaoping emerged and shaped policy making and implementation, with Deng Xiaoping gradually prevailing. Deng Xiaoping eventually became the paramount leader of the CPC, and dominated the party–state policy line into the 1990s, with his influence enduring today, as he is labeled the "Chief Architect of China's Reform and Open Door Policy."[22]

To start with, the elite in China were short of a comprehensive plan or consensus on the pace, content, and direction of economic reform and, therefore, reforms largely proceeded in a step-by-step or stop-and-go manner. Partial reform without a long-term goal and a comprehensive plan were the key features of Chinese reform in transition from state socialism. Reforms are considered partial if economic reforms are introduced without significant political reform, or if economic reforms are carried out in an incremental dual-track fashion without complete abandonment of the old economic system. The transition process in China has demonstrated such a partial, phased, and gradualist pattern in contrast to the comprehensive, shock-therapist, and radical approach of formerly communist countries in Eastern Europe and Russia. In China, the reform often started where possible and the reform pace and direction have been shaped by a decade of long disagreement, debate, and balance between reformers and conservatives.

After Mao's followers had been purged, and, particularly, the fall of Hua Guofeng's "whateverist" factions, the reformers took control of the entire party–state apparatus in the early 1980s. They were led by a group of veteran party leaders who had been the principal victims of the Cultural Revolution. But the differences between the moderate and liberal wings of the reform movement became evident in the late 1970s. As Harry Harding points out, "the tensions between these two groups should not be characterized as a struggle between those who favor reform and those who oppose it."[23] They all agreed on the necessity of reforms that could improve the economic performance of the Chinese socialist economic system, promote China's economic modernization, and raise standards of living for the Chinese people. However, they disagreed on the content, scope and pace, and extent of reforms. More conservative leaders or moderate reformers, such as Chen Yun and Peng Zhen, were cautious and skeptical about dramatic departures from the planned economy and party–state political system that were the legacy of the Soviet model that China had imitated under Mao or the Maoist style of political economy. More liberal leaders or radical reformers, such as Hu Yaobang and Zhao Ziyang, entertained bolder reform measures that would make a radical departure from the traditional political economy of state socialism and launch China in the direction of a market economy.[24] Deng Xiaoping often played the role of balancer between the two groups, resulting in a dual-track, phased, and gradualist pattern of transition. Harry Harding provides the best picture of the division between these two groups.

First, the moderate reformers proposed making the market an important supplementary mechanism for the allocation of resources and the determination of prices, with the operation of the market restricted to agricultural goods and inessential economic sectors, industries, or areas, launching China in the direction of a planned commodity economy. Chen Yun, the chief spokesman for moderate reform, treated the Chinese economy like a bird in a cage and likened the economy to a bird and the plan to a cage: "If the cage is too small, the bird will die; but if there is no cage at all, the bird will fly away, unrestrained." In contrast, the radical reformers favored a central role for the market in the economy, with the development of markets for almost all factors of production, including capital, labor, and industrial machinery, launching China in the direction of a market economy.

Second, the moderate reformers favored a slow, gradual, and experimental approach to reforms, with lengthy periods of readjustment during which the imbalances generated by reform could be repaired. They wished to maintain stringent administrative control over certain important aspects of the economy, especially investment and foreign exchange, and feared that a rapid relaxation of controls over the economy would create severe disequilibrium in the management of the Chinese economy. The radical reformers, in contrast, favored a more rapid and comprehensive structural reform to quickly remove the inefficiencies and rigidities of the traditional economic system. They were willing to take risks for the sake of economic efficiency, even if the result was a temporary disequilibrium in the economy. This debate was especially severe when the party was drafting a proposal for the reform of the urban economy in 1984. At that time, Chen Yun suggested structural reform over a period of 30 years, while Hu Yaobang insisted on completing the process in three to five years. Whenever reform created serious imbalances, the moderate reformers wanted to slow the process and take administrative measures to correct it.

Third, the moderate reformers insisted on maintaining the basic principles of socialism prescribed by Marx, Lenin, and Stalin (the planned economy, public ownership of the means of production, and distribution according to labor), therefore preserving administrative guidance from the planning agencies, limiting the development of private and other nonpublic sectors, and controlling the exchange of land and labor in the marketplace. The radical reformers, in contrast, tended to provide a much less restrictive definition of socialism than their moderate counterparts, excluding the planned economy from the list of principles of socialism and recasting the principle of public ownership more flexibly, so as to allow for the existence of a diversified ownership structure while maintaining the dominant position of public ownership.[25]

The tensions between these two groups and the interaction of their reform strategies have caused alternate periods of "advance" and "retreat" since China's reforms, because compromises between these groups must be reached before major policy changes could occur. The constant political bargaining and occasional shifts in political alignments among the supporters of different factions gave China's economic reforms an incremental nature, and the appearance of "two steps forward and one step backward."[26] The cyclical pattern was reinforced by Deng Xiaoping, who, in an effort to balance between these two groups, supported both the periods of advance and retrenchment proposed by both radical and moderate groups.[27] "The fact that he also actively accommodated the concerns of the conservatives would put him close, if not sometimes in, the middle of the central plan-market spectrum throughout the 1978–90 period."[28] Whenever reforms generated problems such as inflation, inequality, runaway investment, reckless expenditure, or the outbreak of a dissident movement, the moderate reformers would blame their radical colleagues, try to limit the extent of reform and economic liberalization, and call for a slowdown in the pace of reform, a tightening of administrative control over the economy, a remedial measure to restore equilibrium, a crackdown against dissidence and crime, and a periodic campaign against unorthodox ideas in economics, politics, literature, and art. The radical reformers would be forced to defend reforms against critics, find an appropriate theoretical interpretation for their reform measures, and make a concession to the retrenchment launched by the moderate reformers, which actually reinforced the cyclical character of the Chinese reform. Almost all major party documents and policies reflected a compromise between the two groups on policy making.[29]

For example, the Central Party Committee decision on urban economic reform in 1984 reflected a compromise between the two groups on the relationship between plan and market, which continue to reassert planning as a basic characteristic of a socialist economy while calling for a reduction of mandatory planning. A dual-price system was introduced to achieve the balance between plan and market. "The partial liberalization and partial decentralization character of the 1984 enterprise was to the liking of both the conservative and the liberal reformers."[30] The reforms in the areas of state enterprises, financial industries, monetary policy, foreign trade, and so forth have also been incremental and experimental. Reforms would begin with some experimentation practices before they were more widely adopted over time. The open-door policy was characterized by a gradual opening up to the world, from the establishment of four "special economic zones" (SEZs) in Guangdong and Fujian in 1979, through the designation of 14 coastal cities as open cities for foreign investment in 1984, and the development strategy of "great international cycle" (*guoji da xunhuan*) for coastal areas in 1988, to the opening up of inland western areas in 1997. It took about two decades to expand the same open-door policy to all regions of the country. Such a gradualist approach was actually a compromise resulting from the continuous debate between the two groups on the nature and speed of socialist reform; it was a policy designed to confine foreign influence to officially designated areas while the open-door policy could be maintained and its benefits could be expanded gradually.

As a result, the Chinese reformers, in general, have implemented reforms in stages, beginning with the easier and less controversial reforms and proceeding with more complex and less popular reforms after the success of the initial reforms had created enough political support and momentum for further reforms. The entire process of post-Mao China's economic transition has been incremental and experimental in nature. Reform programs have been adopted and implemented in selected pilot sectors, areas, cities, or enterprises before being undertaken on a wider basis. Those that succeeded would be adopted on a wider basis while those that failed would be abandoned or modified.[31]

That is how reform and opening up in China have expanded gradually: an initial step of reform begins in rural areas before spreading to urban areas; it starts the opening policy with establishing SEZs, which is followed by a gradual expansion to the coastal regions, before spreading the same economic policies to the inland Western regions; it starts with the village and township economies, individual household economies, private economies and joint-venture economies before undertaking major reforms in the state-owned economic sector, particularly corporatization of state-owned enterprises through shareholding reform; it starts with microeconomic reform based on expanding the autonomous powers of enterprise management and production through profit retention and responsibility contracting systems before launching macroeconomic reforms, including price, planning, finance, banking, and so forth.[32] "Herein lies the primary reason for the slow, gradual, incremental and evolutionary nature of China's economic reform: the existence of two competing economic programs. The resulting economic policies drew upon both programs."[33] Therefore, the entire process of reform and opening has been shaped and determined by the tensions between moderate and radical reformers and the interaction of their reform strategies.

Deng Xiaoping eventually established his supreme leadership position in the late 1980s, claiming to be "the core of the second generation leadership" and hand-picked Jiang Zemin as the core of the third generation leadership, and Hu Jintao as the fourth generation leadership. In the spring of 1997, Deng Xiaoping passed away. However, Deng's arrangement of power succession as aforementioned has been maintained without facing any significant challenges.

Jiang presided over the party politburo as the General Secretary of the CPC from 1989 to 2002, as President of PRC from 1993 to 2003, and as Chairman of the Central Military Commission from 1989 to 2004. During his tenure, supported by Deng Xiaoping and other elders, Jiang became the paramount leader in the 1990s, till 2002, when Hu Jintao took it over. Under his leadership, China pursued more liberal economic reforms and achieved rapid economic growth. However, the single-minded pursuit of GDP growth also left behind serious social, political, environmental problems. His legacy, labeled as the theory of "Three Represents," was codified into the CPC Constitution, alongside Marxism–Leninism, Mao Zedong Thought, and Deng Xiaoping Theory at the 16th CPC Congress in 2002, and was then written into the PRC Constitution.

When Hu Jintao came to the power in 2002, and assumed full authority in the party, the state, and the military two years later, the party under his leadership began to modify some of the previous policies, with more focus on balanced and sustainable development, social equity, public governance, and people-based policies, etc., which was categorized under the new slogans called "Scientific Outlook on Development" and "Harmonious Society." We will discuss these ideas of the new party ideological doctrines in Chapter 7. Table 6.2 offers a summary of major developments in the post-Mao era. Table 6.3 categorizes the political and economic systems in China.

Table 6.2 Major developments in the post-Mao era (1977–2012)

1976–78, Mao's death in 1976 and the arrest of Mao's close allies; Hua Guofeng's leadership as Mao's successor
1978–89, power transition from Hua Guofeng to reform-minded leaders, Hu Yaobang and Zhao Ziyang, guided by elderly revolutionaries; rehabilitation, de-Maoism, anti-bourgeoisie campaigns, economic reforms, administrative rationalization, and 1989 crisis
1989–91, full backlash in reform and opening policy
1992–97, Deng's push for further economic marketization and opening up to the world; Jiang Zemin consolidated his power with Deng Xiaoping's full backup
1997–2002, Deng's death, Jiang's follow-up of Deng's political and economic policies; Jiang's "Three Represents" was codified into the constitution
2002–12, Hu Jintao managed "collective leadership" and coped with the influence of Jiang Zemin; Hu's "Scientific Outlook on Development" and "Harmonious Society" was codified into the constitution

Table 6.3 Transition of political and economic systems in China

Years	Political system	Power	Economic system
1949–53	Leninist party–state in consultation with 7 "democratic parties"	CPC under Mao	Consolidation of power and control over mainland; land reform; Korean war; and moderate social and economic policies
1953–56	Leninist party–state	CPC under Mao	Lower level collectivization; socialist transformation campaigns; First Five-Year Plan modeled on the Soviet command economy
1957–60	Leninist party–state	CPC under Mao	The Great Leap Forward; People's Communes; catch-up industrialization
1961–65	Leninist party–state	CPC under Mao	Readjustment and recovery period; corrective measures and re-organization of communes; decentralization
1966–76	Leninist party–state	CPC under Mao	Cultural Revolution; moral and political incentives
1978–89	Leninist party–state in consultation with "democratic parties"	CPC under Deng/ elders	Economic reforms and open-door policy in experimental and gradualist manner; dual track price; increasing the role of market mechanisms while reducing government planning and direct control
1989–92	Leninist party–state in consultation with "democratic parties"	CPC under Deng/ Jiang	Period of Readjustment
1992–2004	Leninist party–state in consultation with "democratic parties"	CPC under Jiang	Market socialism: "socialist market economy with the Chinese characteristics"
2004–12	Leninist party–state in consultation with "democratic parties"	CPC under Hu	Market socialism: "socialist market economy with the Chinese characteristics"

Questions for discussion

1. In which ways and to what degree does the new communist state confirm to the doctrine and the total vision of social transformation of Marxism?

2. What are the goals of the new communist state, politically, economically, and socially, and what are the main action means by which the CPC attempts to accomplish the goals? What were the successes and failures of the CPC radical "socialist transformation" under Mao's leadership?

Further reading

A. Doak Barnett, *Communist China: The Early Years, 1949–55* (New York: Frederick A. Praeger, 1964).

Vivienne Shue, *Peasant China in Transition: The Dynamics of Development Toward Socialism, 1949–1956* (Berkeley: University of California Press, 1980).

Roderick MacFarquhar, *The Origins of the Cultural Revolution, 2: The Great Leap Forward, 1958–1960* (New York: Columbia University Press, 1983).

Maurice Meisner, *Marxism, Maoism, and Utopianism: Eight Essays* (Madison: University of Wisconsin Press, 1982).

Part IV
Political ideology

7 Marxism–Leninism and Chinese political ideology

Political ideology has played a crucially important role in the politics of all communist regimes. It serves to justify communist revolution, political actions, and the Leninist party–state institutions, mobilize political and ideological movements, provide official explanations to some basic questions of human society, criticize capitalist society, and offer an outlook on an ideal society. China is such a political regime that relies on a codified system of political ideology derived from Marxism–Leninism, which guides the actions of the communist political elite, justifies the party's monopoly on truth, virtues, and power, establishes the party's moral superiority in defining and creating the new socialist moral order, and legitimizes its proclaimed historical mission to "build socialism" and "realize communism."

Chinese communist revolution and practice have demonstrated the important role of political ideology in the creation, development, and maintenance of the communist political system. The ideas embedded in the Chinese political system can be found in the framers of communist ideology—Marx, Lenin, Stalin, and Mao Zedong. The doctrines are modified to a certain degree to fit the party's political needs and market reforms in post-Mao China under the governments led by party leaders, such as Deng Xiaping, Jiang Zemin, and Hu Jintao. Therefore, Chinese official ideology encompasses all these ideas, and we need to understand each of these components in order to understand the Chinese ideology that provides legitimacy for the communist party's rule, its political actions and changes, and the essence of the political regime in post-Mao China.

Marxism

Marxism is a body of ideological doctrines developed by Karl Marx (1818–83). Marx's thought was based upon a synthesis of German philosophy, English classical political economics, and French social and political theory. This is known as the "three theoretical components" of Marxist thought and has been most often used as a framework for integrating his comprehensive thoughts in a meaningful manner.[1] No one can really understand Marx's theory fully without understanding all these constituent components at the same time. Marx

Figure 7.1 Poster from 1971 which states: "Long live the great Marxism–Leninism–Mao Zedong Thought".

Source: Courtesy of The International Institute of Social History / Stefan R. Landsberger Collection, www.chineseposters.net.

actually attempted to combine Hegel and Feuerbach and created his "historical materialism" and "dialectical materialism" which laid down the foundation for his political and economic theories (Box 7.1).[2]

Political philosophy

Marx's *historical materialism* reflected his materialist conception of man and history, which attempted to address three fundamental questions: Which matters most in human history, man's ideas or productive activity? Who makes history? How is history made?

The key to the first question was the idea that "man's productive activity" was the essential element in an understanding of man and his history. In other words, it was essential to begin with the material conditions of his production in order to understand man and his history. Most important, by acting on the external world and changing it, man at the same time changed his own nature—"alienation of labor"—what he created worked against himself. Thus Marx's concept of human nature was not a static one, like many previous political thinkers. This dialectic self-creation through labor was the primary factor in history, while ideas and concepts—either political, philosophical, or religious—through which men interpreted this activity were secondary. History

---

Box 7.1 Political philosophy

1. Intellectual sources and components of Marxist political philosophy: Hegel's dialectic and idealism and Feuerbach's materialism.
2. Marx's synthesis: attempted to combine Hegel and Feuerbach and created his "historical materialism" and "dialectical materialism" which laid down the foundation for his political and economic theories.
   - Marx's *historical materialism* reflected his materialist conception of man and history, which attempted to address three fundamental questions: Which matters most in human history, man's ideas or productive activity? Who makes history? How is history made?
   - Marx's *dialectic materialism* dealt with the relation between the consciousness of men and their social being and addressed the relationship of the base to the superstructure.

   Legal/political superstructure—forms of social consciousness

   $\uparrow$

   relations of production (economic base) ← forces of production.

---

was not the result of accident, nor simply a product of material conditions, nor was it shaped by the acts of great men or supernatural powers.[3] This is where Marx differs from Hegel.

The key to the second question is the idea that history was the creation of laboring men, their interaction with nature, and it was subject to observable laws. History did nothing; it did not fight battles. It was men, laboring men, who did all this, who possessed things and fought battles. It was not "history" which used men as a means of achieving its own ends. History was nothing but the activity of men in pursuit of their ends.[4] This is where Marx differs from Hegel.

The key to the third question is the idea that "men make their own history, but they do not make it just as they please; they do not make it under circumstances chosen by themselves, but under circumstances directly encountered, given, and transmitted from the past."[5] This suggests that the creation of history is human activity itself and it cannot be isolated from a given context.[6] This is where Marx differs from Hegel.

Marx's *dialectic materialism* dealt with the relation between the consciousness of men and their social being and addressed the causal relationship between the two. In contrast to Hegel, Marx contended that it was not the consciousness of men that determined their being, but, on the contrary, their social being that determined their consciousness. Therefore, for Marx, ideas were of secondary importance in the understanding of society. For example, the rights of man as proclaimed in the French Revolution and the Constitution of the United States were not eternal truths about the nature of man, but could be fully understood only if viewed in the context of demands by new commercial classes for the end of feudal restrictions and for free competition in economic affairs.[7]

Marx's most detailed account of his "dialectic materialism" was contained in the Preface to the *Critique of Political Economy*. According to Marx, in the social production of their life, men entered into definite relations that were indispensable and independent of their will, relations of production which corresponded to a definite state of development of their material productive forces. The sum total of these relations of production constituted the economic structure of society, the real foundation, on which rose a legal and political superstructure and to which corresponded definite forms of social consciousness, such as ideologies, religions, and social norms. The mode of production of material life conditioned the social, political, and intellectual life process in general. At a certain stage of their development, the material productive forces of a society came in conflict with the existing relations of production, or—in a legal expression for the same thing—with the property relations within which they had been at work hitherto. In other words, these relations turned into the fetters of development of the material productive forces. Then an epoch of social revolution began.[8] This is the passage that Marx used to describe the relationship of the base to the superstructure, and the one that has been probably most cited either by his supporters to provide a theoretical justification for social revolution or by his opponents to question the validity of Marx's theory—"economic determinism"[9] (Figure 7.2).

Political economy

Marx criticized the classical economists, in particular Adam Smith and David Ricardo, on two main grounds: first, they did not view the economic system as one of interacting forces, that is, they took the laws of capitalism to be unchangeable and could not explain the origins of the system they were describing; and, second, they took a one-sided view of man simply as a cog in the economic wheel and did not consider him "as a human being."[10]

Marx's economic theory is embedded in the materialist conception of history in that Marx aims to analyze the relations of production and

---

Box 7.2 Political economy

1. Intellectual sources of Marxist political economy: Adam Smith, David Ricardo, and others
2. Theory of surplus-value
3. Political implications

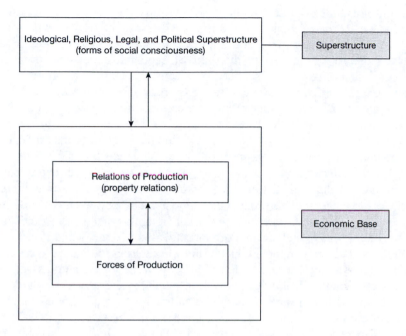

Figure 7.2 The relationship between the economic base and superstructure.

corresponding material productive forces in bourgeois society—to lay bare the economic law of modern society, as he wrote in the Preface to *Capital*. More than half the first volume of *Capital* is an application of the materialist conception of history to British capitalism in his day.[11]

The middle of the nineteenth century witnessed the rise of the "marginalist" school of economics in Western Europe and America, which tended to look at the capitalist market system as given, to construct models concentrating on private property, profit, and the free market, particularly on prices. To Marx, these models seemed superficial, in the sense that they were only a description of phenomena lying on the surface of capitalist society without an analysis of the mode of production that gave rise to these phenomena.[12]

Marx's most important "discovery" in economics, according to Engels, was the "theory of surplus-value." To Marx, the labor theory of value, which was part of a longer tradition of the classical economists, in particular Adam Smith and David Richard, seemed to involve the puzzle that in the exchange of capital and labor the wages of the laborer had a smaller exchange-value than the exchange-value of the commodity he produced.[13]

Marx accounted for this phenomenon of profit by means of his theory of surplus-value. Marx made a distinction between *constant capital* and *variable capital* to explain the production of surplus value under capitalism. Constant capital was the tangible part of capital, which was represented by the means of production, by the raw material, auxiliary material, and instruments of labor, and did not undergo any quantitative alteration of value in the process of production. Variable capital was the intangible part of capital, which was represented by labor power, and did undergo an alteration of value in the process of production. It was this part of capital that not only produced the equivalent of its own value, but also produced an excess, a surplus-value, which might itself vary, more or less, according to the circumstances.[14]

Simply put, if the exchange-value of a commodity equaled the amount of labor incorporated in it, the exchange-value of a day's labor must be equal to its product, i.e., the wages of the laborer would be the same as his product. In other words, surplus-value was the profit the owner made. It was the difference between the value of a product and the wage the worker received. The essential point was that the capitalist got the worker to work longer than was merely sufficient to embody in his product the value of his labor power. For example, if the value of the labor power of the worker (roughly what it cost to keep him and his family alive and capable of working) was $10 a day and if he could embody $10 of value in the product of his work during four hours: then, if he worked eight hours, the second half of his day would yield a surplus-value—in this case another $10, which was "exploited" by the capitalist who hired him. The variation in surplus-value was called the "rate of surplus-value" or "rate of exploitation" around which the struggle between capitalists and workers centered. Workers could not receive fair wages because the capitalists were constantly trying to maximize the rate of surplus-value by either extending the hours of labor, or making the labor more intensive or more productive. In capitalism, this production of a surplus was concealed by the free market bargain by the capitalists and workers who seemed to be merely exchanging equivalents.[15]

The theory of surplus-value had implications for the long-term future of capitalism. This was described in the famous passage at the end of Volume One of *Capital*: "Along with the constantly diminishing number of the magnates of capital, who usurp and monopolize all advantages of this process of transformation, grows the mass of misery, oppression, slavery, degradation, exploitation; but with this too grows the revolt of the working class . . . The monopoly of capital becomes a fetter upon the mode of production, which has sprung up and flourished along with, and under it. Centralization of the means of production and socialization of labor at last reach a point where they become incompatible with their capitalist integument. This integument is burst asunder. The knell of capitalist private property sounds. The expropriators are expropriated."[16]

Political theory

Marx's political theory (Box 7.3) starts from the human self-alienation and ends with "full human emancipation." The human self-alienation was caused by the separation of man from man, his production from the means of production, alienated labor, and more fundamentally by the deleterious

---

Box 7.3 Political theory

1. The starting and ending points of Marx's political theory
2. Communist revolution
3. Communist society

---

effects of private property. Communism was viewed as the true solution to the alienation of man from man, and man from nature. This is communism as the complete and conscious return of man himself as a social, i.e., human, being. Communism as completed naturalism is humanism and as completed humanism is naturalism. It is the genuine solution of the antagonism between man and nature and between man and man. It is the true solution of the struggle between existence and essence, between objectification and self-affirmation, between freedom and necessity, between individual and species.[17]

The central institution of capitalist society and the main target of Marx's political theory was the State. He emphasized the State as an instrument of class domination. This view is most clearly expressed in *The Communist Manifesto*: "Political power, properly so called, is merely the organized power of one class for oppressing another . . . The executive of the modern state is but a committee for managing the affairs of the whole bourgeoisie."[18] Marx traced the origin of the State, together with other social institutions and classes, to the division of labor: the state was opposed to the real interests of all members of society because it constituted an illusory sense of community serving as a screen for the real struggles waged by classes against each other. All previous revolutions had simply replaced one form of state by another more suited to the changing mode of production. And the form of state that went along with capitalism—capitalist democracy—was no exception. Although democracy held that it was open to everyone to emancipate himself by becoming a bourgeois, by definition not everyone could do so and the inevitable result was the exploitation of one group in society by another. Therefore, the fundamental solution was the proletarian revolution, or communist revolution, which would be the first revolution in human history to introduce a nonantagonistic mode of production.[19]

After a successful proletarian revolution there would be a period of transition which he occasionally referred to as "the dictatorship of the proletariat." The proletariat would assume state power aiming to eliminate the old relations of production based upon class antagonism and protected by the coercive instruments of the state. It would replace these old relations with the new relations that would both place the means of production under public control and pave the way for the abolition of class distinctions leading to a classless society.[20] However, according to Marx, this newly born society would still "in every respect, economically, morally, and intellectually, be stamped with the birthmarks of the old society from whose womb it emerges."[21] In the phase of transition from capitalism to communism—between capitalist and communist societies—unjust differences and inequality in wealth still persist, as the "bourgeois right" (private property right of individuals) still exists, which continues to generate inequality and injustice, although the major means of production are then transformed and converted into the common property of the whole society, which is controlled and dominated by the state. The defects of distribution also persist, as the distribution of goods is still conducted "according to the amount of labor performed." These defects are inevitable in the first phase, as it has just emerged from capitalist society.[22] Therefore, only after a considerable period of time could full communism—a higher phase of communism—be attained. This has been used by Deng and the post-Deng leadership to justify their departure from Mao's economic policy to market reform and an open-door policy that has allowed capitalist elements to develop to a controllable degree and market mechanisms to coordinate the allocation of resources that are dominated by the state.

In communism, the distribution of public goods is conducted according to the principle "To each according to his needs, from each according to his ability,"[23] because at that point private property, as the fundamental source of all the social evils, would be eliminated; the division of labor would be eliminated; the "three big differences" between classes, between urban and rural areas, and between intellectual work and physical work would be eliminated; the exploitation, class conflicts, injustice, and all other social evils would be wiped out. The political result of the abolition of the division of labor in communist society was the "withering away" of the State. Communism would no longer need the typical components of the State—bureaucracy, a standing army, and a professional judicature. Governmental functions would be transformed into "the mere administration of things."[24] Marx highly praised the practices of the "Paris Commune"[25]—all officials were elected by universal suffrage and their tenure was to be revocable at any time; all officials were paid the same wages as workmen; the standing army was replaced by the armed people; and so on.[26] Therefore, according to Marx, there are three stages to achieve the ideal society: Proletarian or Communist Revolution, "the Dictatorship of the Proletariat", and Communism.

Marx's ideas are a comprehensive and profound theoretical system encompassing political philosophy, political economics, and political theory. Marx's thought is an attempt to give a "total vision" and "total account" of the entire human history of the whole world, and thus provides a blueprint for communist revolution and building a new state and society in China. However, the ideas of Marx were revised and even distorted to meet the political need of communist revolution and the politics in communist practices in China where the Communist Party of China (CPC) has kept the ideology alive and modified it to fit its political needs and policy changes.

Leninism

Lenin made at least two major contributions to Marxism: the theory of imperialism (*Imperialism, the Highest Stage of Capitalism*) and the theory of the state and revolution (*The State and Revolution*). Lenin's theory of imperialism and theory of state and revolution probably had the greatest political implications, first for the Russian Bolshevik Revolution and later for the Chinese communist revolution in the twentieth century. Lenin's theory of imperialism describes the political conditions for communist revolution and provides justification for the communist revolution in less developed countries. A better understanding of Lenin's theory of imperialism requires special attention to Marx's conception of conflict and idea of global capitalism, which had great influence on Lenin, the most prominent imperialist writer in the twentieth century.[27]

Marx's conception of conflict was based upon socioeconomic classes. Class conflict tended to intensify rather than minimize the interest conflicts, since the most fundamental of these interest conflicts between classes involved the "mode of production" and the "social relations of production" which conditioned the social, political, and economic life process in general and the class conflict in particular. Class conflict was the driving force of social-historical development, from primitive communism, through feudalism and capitalism, to communism, which was defined in terms of modes of production and class relations—"the history of all hitherto existing society is the history of class struggle."[28] Modern capitalist society was divided up into two antagonistic conflicting classes—the bourgeoisie and the proletariat—formed by their relationships with the mode of production and the social relation of production. The capitalist mode of production became an obstacle to the further development of the power of production, so that the replacement of one mode by another was made possible by the productive superiority of the new one. The new mode grew within the old, but ultimately this growth required a change in social and political institutions to develop to its fullest potential. The conflict between the two major classes in capitalist society was the driving force of political change, and ultimately would lead to communist revolution. Marx's conception of conflict had a direct impact on Lenin in his analysis of international conflict and imperialist wars in the late nineteenth and early twentieth century.[29]

According to Marx, capitalism was not a domestic-oriented production process, but rather a worldwide dynamic and expansive economic process, and it would eventually incorporate the entire world through overseas expansion. Therefore, communist revolution would eventually spread all over the world and bring communist modes of production to the world. A classless communist society would eliminate international conflict. Marx's idea of global capitalism and communism also had great influence on Lenin in his development of the idea of imperialism as a part or a stage of capitalism, which made inevitable the international capitalist competition for the global redistribution of resources and territories.[30]

Lenin accepted Marx's idea that capitalism was not a domestic-oriented production process, but rather a worldwide dynamic and expansive economic process. However, Lenin further advanced that capitalism was developing a new stage—"the monopoly stage." Imperialism was the monopoly stage of capitalism, in which the concentration of capital and the formation of international capitalist monopolies intensified the interstate conflict over colonies and overseas markets. The conflict between capitalists and working classes in both capitalist and colonial nations was combined with the conflict among the major capitalist states, and between the imperialist powers and the subordinate states, reflecting an inherent feature of the capitalist world system.[31]

Imperialist states would inevitably end up in conflict and war because territorial division of the whole world among the greatest capitalist powers is completed, but latecomers to the imperialist states would demand territorial redivision. The contradiction between the scarcity of resources and territories on the one side and the expansionist motivation of international capitalist monopolies on the other will inevitably give rise to competition for and conflict over resources and territory, ultimately leading to imperialist war. War among the imperialist states would prepare the political conditions for communist revolution and allow the breakthrough of communist revolution in some less developed capitalist countries. This modifies the prediction of Karl Marx that communist revolution would first occur in Western industrialized countries, and justifies the communist revolution in Russia, a less developed country and other less developed countries. The elimination of all capitalist states was the essential precondition to establishing communist states and to abolishing international conflict. The only way to eliminate conflict or abolish war was to eliminate the capitalist system itself.[32]

Leninism has been used in the Marxist tradition, and to serve the purpose of political movements in less developed countries to arouse people to political action and provide a rationale and strategic guidance for that action. The first communist state was created based on the doctrines of Leninism, which provides strategic guidelines for making communist revolution and creating party–state institutions in China in the twentieth century.

Mao Zedong thought

Mao Zedong is the founding father of the communist state in China. Mao Zedong's thought has been often referred to as "Maoism" by Western writers, but is not a term the Chinese themselves use: it is always "Mao Zedong Thought." "Thought" refers to practical ideology, if using Schurmann's categorization of ideology, while "-ism" means pure ideology or universal truth. One common Chinese definition of Mao's thought is that it is the "application of the universal truths of Marxism–Leninism to the concrete practice of the Chinese socialist revolution and construction." In other words, thought is the universal truth of Marxism–Leninism selectively applied to the concrete practice of the Chinese revolution and construction. Therefore, Mao Zedong Thought has two ideological components: (1) commitment to the general or universal truths of Marxism–Leninism; and (2) improvement on or modification of some elements of Marxism–Leninism in order for the Chinese communists to apply the "-ism" to the concrete practice of the Chinese revolution and construction.[33] We must keep this relationship between "-ism" and "thought" in mind when we study the ideological modifications in post-Mao China in order to understand and evaluate the nature and the magnitude of change in the Chinese ideology.

Mao's most important philosophical works are two essays: "On Contradiction" and "On Practice." Contradiction is present in matter itself, and thus reflected in the ideas. Matter always develops through a dialectical contradiction: "The interdependence of the contradictory aspects present in all things and the struggle between these aspects determine the life of things and push their development forward. There is nothing that does not contain contradiction; without contradiction nothing would exist," Mao said.[34] Furthermore, each contradiction ("class struggle," then the contradiction holding between relations of production and the concrete development of forces of production) expresses itself in a series of other contradictions, some dominant, others not. "There are many contradictions in the process of development of a complex thing, and one of them is necessarily the principal contradiction whose existence and development determine or influence the existence and development of the other contradictions."[35] Thus, the principal contradiction should be tackled with priority when trying to make the basic contradiction "solidify." His basic stand on contradiction is founded on Marxist epistemology. Policy making and measures should be taken to focus on the solution of the basic, principal contradictions. When the principal contradictions are resolved, the party should have a "work focus shift," or a "policy shift"—e.g. the shift from revolutionary tasks to socialist construction, or the shift to the "class struggle." "Practice" connects "contradiction" with "class struggle" in the following way: inside a mode of production, there are three realms where practice functions: economic production, scientific experimentation, and class struggle.[36] The three of them deal with matter in its various forms. Thus, in each of these realms (economic, scientific, and political practice), contradictions (principle and secondary) must be identified, explored, and put to function to achieve the communist goal.[37]

In the post-revolution period, Mao argues that class struggle continues even if the proletariat has already overthrown the bourgeoisie, and there are capitalist restorationist elements within the Communist Party itself. This idea became the party's theoretical guideline with regard to: how to continue the socialist revolution after the communist takeover of power, how to create a socialist society, and how to achieve the communist goals. Various contradictions in socialist society will have to be addressed by what is termed "constant revolution under the proletariat dictatorship," which justifies constant political campaigns and mass mobilization to purify the revolutionary ranks and educate the masses to build a "New Socialist China" and defeat "imperialism" and all class enemies that attempt to overturn the socialist state in China.[38] Mao's thought includes the following major points.

1. Mao emphasizes the crucial role of peasantry in the communist revolutionary movement in an agrarian society such as China and appeals to peasant grievances in creating revolutionary bases in rural areas and developing a peasant revolution guided by a proletarian worldview and a highly disciplined and professional communist party. The poor peasants are the friendly class and driving force of the Chinese revolution, allied with the proletariat but accepting proletariat leadership through the CPC.[39] Therefore, contrary to the Russian October Revolution, the Chinese revolution must follow the path: "encircle the cities from the rural areas and then capture them."

2. Mao emphasizes that "practice is the criteria for measuring truths," and opposes the "bookishness" or "book worship" of Marxism–Leninism, and thus provides justification for a communist revolution with Chinese characteristics. According to Mao, theory by itself means nothing unless it is properly applied, and proper application requires detailed knowledge of local conditions as well as good political judgment. Marxism is not a dogma but a guide to action. Theory is necessary in order to give direction to practice, but theory is tested and corrected by practice. We need to study to understand the world, but we learn to make revolution by making revolution, not by reading books about it.[40]

3. Mao emphasizes the importance of "mass line" in the Chinese communist revolution and construction, and the "vanguard" party must always keep close links with the "masses" because the masses are the real driving forces of history and the revolutionary movement and because "policy comes from the masses and goes back to the masses." The vanguard party must follow the "mass line," go to the masses, mobilize the masses, investigate and discover what problems there are, and solve the problems.[41] Therefore, either during the revolutionary war or after the communist takeover of power, either in political campaigns or in economic construction, and either in preventing theft or in attacking criminals, the CPC always relies heavily on mass mobilization as a means to achieve its policy goals, although the CPC has never rejected using any means to achieve its ends.

4. Mao emphasizes "class struggle" as the dynamics of social development in building socialism—"class struggle takes command." Class struggle became the dominant theme of Mao's thought in the last two decades of his life. Mao believed that class struggle continued under socialism,[42] because, according to Marx, socialism as a newly born society would still "in every respect, economically, morally, and intellectually, be stamped with the birthmarks of the old society from whose womb it emerges."[43] Mao argued that this newly born society "produces capitalism and capitalist ideas every moment every day, and they are corrupting our

revolutionary team, our minds, and our cadres and masses." Therefore, the class struggle could end only after a considerable period when full communism would be attained. Political campaigns thus became a major means to prevent the "vanguard" from corruption and clean up the filth and mire left over from the old society—"the old ideas, customs, habits, traditions." Communist revolution is to institute radical social change and create "a new type of man" and "new type of society" by transforming society and human nature.

5.   Mao emphasizes the "heavy industry priority strategy" in industrialization and complete public ownership in the economic system. Mao was impetuous in bringing about the transformation of rural cooperatives into "People's Communes" and of urban collectives into "the whole people ownership" and in pursuing "larger in size and a higher degree of public ownership" (*yidaergong*一大二公) than the cooperatives and collectives.

Mao Zedong Thought continues to be the guiding ideology of the CPC. However, there have been some ideological modifications in the post-Mao reform during which the Chinese leaders have adjusted the "safety belt" of its political ideology by modifying some doctrines to adapt to the practical needs of market reforms in post-Mao China. These modifications include Deng Xiaoping's "socialist preliminary stage" (translated as "socialist primary stage"), "socialism with Chinese characteristics," and "socialist market economy;" Jiang Zemin's "Three Represents"; and Hu Jintao's "Harmonious Society," and "Scientific Outlook of Development." Such modifications mainly serve to justify economic reforms and an open-door policy under the leadership of these Chinese leaders, without fundamentally abandoning the CPC's ideological and political core. These modifications will be studied and evaluated in Chapter 8 to determine if the CPC's ideology still matters or not, and to what extent it continues to serve its political purposes and policy goals.

Ideological modifications in post-Mao China

Deng Xiaoping Theory represents a collective effort by the post-Mao leaders to modify some doctrines of Mao Zedong for the purposes of economic reform and modernization. Since the Third Plenum of the Eleventh Central Committee in December 1978, there has been a "Shift in Focus" (重心转移) away from Mao's "class struggle" to "economic development." Mao's grand strategy of the "great leap forward" into communist society has been replaced by a gradualist, practical approach to the goals of modernization and communist ideal society, and such an ideological change is conceptualized as the "Socialist preliminary stage" at which China's primary goal, as a less developed country, is to build an economic material base for communism, modernize its economy, and build a prosperous and strong socialism. In preliminary socialism, all means, including capitalist elements and market institutions, should be employed to fulfill the goals of economic modernization. However, the communist party must maintain its leadership and socialist direction, and retain the predominant position of public ownership in the economy to keep state control over the commanding heights of the national economy and its socialist direction. At the 17th CPC National Congress in 2007 it was declared that the CPC is the only political force in China that can lead China toward a bright future and build China into a "well-off, democratic, civilized and harmonious modern nation."

Paralleling this modification of Chinese official ideology are the two ideological concepts—"socialism with Chinese characteristics" and "socialist market economy"—which allow "capitalist elements" and noncommunist ideas to extend into subjects once considered "forbidden zones" and justify those

Figure 7.3 Four generations of communist leaders in China: (a) Mao Zedong.
(b) Deng Xiaoping; (c) Jiang Zemin; (d) Hu Jintao.

Source: www.gov.cn/test/2007–11/12/content_802099.htm.

reform policies and methods once considered "capitalist" or "bourgeoisie" in Mao's China. "Socialism with Chinese characteristics," according to the CPC official interpretation, is the application of the basic principles and values of socialism prescribed by Marxism and Leninism in the Chinese context to build a socialism that has unique Chinese characteristics and develop its own road toward the end goal of communism. It has been proclaimed that the CPC has provided correct answers to a series of key questions as regards to China's path of socialism, its historical periods, fundamental tasks, and steps to accomplish them in China, and has thus successfully found a correct path for China to build socialism with Chinese characteristics. These characteristics include a socialist market economy based on a mixed ownership structure with public ownership in the dominant position, a socialist political system based on the communist party leadership, multiparty cooperation and consultation, and the People's Congress and a socialist core value system based on Chinese culture with Marxism and Leninism as its fundamental guidelines.

Jiang Zemin was hand picked by Deng Xiaoping as the successor to his leadership of the "second generation" and became the "core of the third generation," serving as General Secretary of the CPC from 1989 to 2002, as President of the PRC from 1993 to 2003, and as Chairman of the Central Military Commission of China from 1989 to 2004. With the waning influence of Deng Xiaoping and the Eight Elders due to old age, Jiang became the "paramount leader" in the 1990s. His contribution to Marxist doctrine is called the theory of the "Three Represents" (三个代表), which has been written into both party and state constitutions, alongside Marxism–Leninism, Mao Zedong Thought, and Deng Xiaoping Theory, at the 16th CPC Congress in 2002.[44]

"Three Represents" was an attempt to adapt to the changing situations after two decades of economic reforms, with a pluralistic society and rising new riches in China. The formal statement of the theory was made by Jiang Zemin at the 16th CPC Congress, November 2002:

> Reviewing the course of struggle and the basic experience over the past 80 years and looking ahead to the arduous tasks and bright future in the new century, our Party should continue to stand in the forefront of the times and lead the people in marching toward victory. In a word, the Party must always represent the requirements of the development of China's advanced productive forces, the orientation of the development of China's advanced culture, and the fundamental interests of the overwhelming majority of the people in China.

The official statement of the ideology stipulates that the CPC is representative of advanced social productive forces, advanced culture, and the interests of the overwhelming majority. The ideology declares that the Communist Party represents the majority of the people as opposed to its old image of a vanguard party of the proletariat. To a certain degree it legitimized the inclusion of members of the business class, i.e. capitalists, into the party. It has been criticized as a political legacy project by leader Jiang Zemin, with the main purpose being to equate him with former leaders Mao Zedong and Deng Xiaoping, who each had their ideological vision enshrined in the party constitution. However, since taking power, Hu Jintao has gradually moved to take on the "Scientific Development" concept as the guiding ideology, while "Three Represents" continues to be used in official documents and programs.[45]

Hu Jintao is the current supreme leader of the CPC. He was also hand picked and designated by Deng Xiaoping in his political arrangement to succeed Jiang Zemin as the top leader of the Fourth Generation, aiming to ensure a smooth transition of power from the third-generation leadership to the fourth-generation leadership. Hu succeeded Jiang as General Secretary of the CPC in 2002, President of the People's Republic of China in 2003, and then Chairman of the Central Military Commission in 2004. Hu also leads the three leading small groups on national security, foreign policy, and Taiwan issues—three key decision-making bodies under the CPC Politburo.

Hu's contribution to the guiding ideology of Marxism in China is put forward as "Scientific Outlook on Development" (*kexue fazhan guan*科学发展观), promoting sustainable socioeconomic development (*kechixuxing de shehui jingjin fazhan*可持续性的社会经济发展), strengthening the governing capacity of the governing party (*zhizhengdang de zhizheng nengli*执政党的执政能力), creating a "harmonious society" (*hexie shehui*和谐社会) domestically, and seeking a "peaceful development" (*heping fazhan*和平发展) internationally. The concept seeks integrated solutions to tackle China's daunting domestic problems and foreign policy challenges facing China. The scientific development doctrine was also written into both party and state constitutions in 2007 and 2008, respectively. The concept is considered a major advance in the CPC guiding ideology and an important contribution to Marxism–Leninism, Mao Zedong Thought, Deng Xiaoping Theory, and Jiang Zemin's "Three Represents."

Since early 2000, Deng Xiaoping and Jiang Zemin's single-minded pursuit of economic growth along with socioeconomic policies that neglect the social wellbeing of those left behind in the rapid economic growth began to backfire and increase public unrest and instability. The "Scientific development" concept aims to correct the previous growth policies and seek a new ideological orientation and campaign to shift the focus from mere "economic growth" to "balanced" and "sustainable" socioeconomic development in order to create a "harmonious society." Subsequently, the CPC under Hu Jintao launched a new nationwide ideological campaign calling for the building of "a harmonious society," and a new nationwide educational campaign for "building the governing party" and "fighting corruption" to cope with social discontent.

The concept of "a harmonious society" represents the value orientation of the fourth generation of CPC leaders, and has been considered a major advance in the CPC's theory building. The concept first appeared vaguely in Jiang Zemin's Report to the 16th Party Congress of the CPC in 2002 which mentioned "social harmony" as one of the six goals of "building a well-off society," which was the immediate goal proposed by Deng Xiaoping for China. In the 4th Plenary Session of the 16th CPC Party Congress held on September 16 through 19, 2004, "building a socialist harmonious society" was officially introduced for the first time. It was set as one of the five governing capabilities the CPC intends to strengthen.[46] In February 19, 2005, Hu Jintao expounded upon this new concept in a speech delivered to the CPC Central Party School. The Sixth Plenum of the 16th CPC Central Committee was held in Beijing from October 8 through 11, 2006, to discuss the building of the harmonious society and adopted *The Decision on a Number of Important Issues Regarding the Building of a Socialist Harmonious Society*.[47] It states that social harmony is the intrinsic nature of the socialism with Chinese characteristics. To build a harmonious socialist society was the intrinsic demand of constructing a socialist modernized country which is prosperous, strong, democratic, civilized, and harmonious. Along with rapid economic development, there exist many contradictions, problems, conflicts, which have affected social harmony and political stability. While the party must continue to focus on economic development, it must put the building of a harmonious socialist society in a more prominent place and make great efforts to increase harmonious factors and reduce disharmonious factors to boost social harmony. A harmonious society should be full of vigor, and it should be a stable and orderly society in which humans live in harmony with nature, promote social equity and justice, foster a culture of harmony, improve public administration, enhance creativity of the society, pursue the road of common prosperity, and push forward coordinated development of social, economic, political, and cultural construction with the emphasis on issues people care about most and issues that concern their most immediate and practical interests.[48]

The 17th CPC Congress has quickly elevated the "new thinking" to parallel importance with Mao Zedong Thought, Deng Xiaoping Theory, and Jiang Zemin's "Three Represents." The 17th CPC Congress subsequently added this new tenet into the CPC's party constitution in 2007.[49] The emphasis on social harmony and stability represents a break away from the era of political campaign and class struggle and a transition from a revolutionary party to a governing party. In this sense, the party is increasingly interested in enhancing its governing capacity and in searching for new sources of political legitimacy. In its revolutionary past, the CPC relied heavily on ideology and leaders' personality cults as sources of political legitimacy. However, with the demise of communist ideology and the passing away of charismatic strong men such as Mao and Deng, the new generation of CPC leaders has to base their political legitimacy on their achievement and on their ability to promote economic growth and efficiency. The problem is that a single-minded pursuit of economic growth and an achievement-based legitimacy are inherently deficient in their moral and philosophical foundation, and are being over-shadowed by social and economic injustice, income and regional disparities, and environmental disasters.[50] The classical trade-off between efficiency and equity has become a serious challenge to the CPC.[51] Chinese leaders have quickly realized that efficiency without equity is unsustainable. But theoretically, instead of emulating the Western model of a welfare state, they have turned their attention to the traditional Confucian idea of a *Datong* society.[52]

The question remains if these ideological modifications in post-Mao China have fundamentally changed the CPC's ideology and the nature of political regime. With the so-called "demise" of Mao Zedong Thought and communist beliefs in post-Mao China, and a "focus shift" from the class struggle to economic modernization and market reform, can we still call it a "communist state?" We will tackle this question in Chapter 8.

Questions for discussion

1. What is Marxism–Leninism? How does the "-ism" provide moral justification and a blueprint for the communist revolution in China? How did Mao Zedong modify the doctrine and apply it in the Chinese context?
2. What is the relationship between the "-ism" and the "thoughts" of political leaders? Can an ideology (such as Liberalism or Marxism, Capitalism or Communism) evolve and modify itself over time but still retain its hard core unchanged? Have the ideological modifications in post-Mao China fundamentally changed the CPC ideology and the nature of the Leninist party–state?

Further reading

Angus Walker, *Marx: His Theory and Its Context* (Winchester, MA: Unwin Hyman Inc., 1979).

Vladimir Ilyich Lenin, *Imperialism, the Highest Stage of Capitalism* (New York: International Publishers, 1977).

Feng Chen, *Economic Transition and Political Legitimacy in Post-Mao China: Ideology and Reform* (New York: State University of New York Press, 1995).

Maurice Meisner, *Mao's China and After* (New York: Free Press, 1999).

8 Ideological modifications in post-Mao China

Post-Mao economic reforms and pragmatism have led many analysts to declare that the communist ideology is no longer relevant in post-Mao China. It seems to them that market reform has led towards de-ideologization. Indeed, many Chinese are now open to market change and engaging in money making. Also, greater openness to the outside world has brought in some new ideas, concepts, and values which have clashed with old ideological claims. These new ideas, concepts, and values have in many ways undermined the official ideology and threatened the base of party legitimacy. Moreover, there is more freedom of expression and more open talk about the "shortcomings" of the communist regime, as long as critics avoid crossing the party line and ideological taboos, and as long as such voices are strictly individual and do not aspire to organized support or collective action.[1]

Therefore, to many China analysts, post-Mao political ideology is downplayed and treated only at face value on the assumption that post-Mao Chinese leaders no longer believe in the ideology they advocate and rely more on pragmatic considerations and nonideological resources for solutions to the problems they have confronted.[2] Some other analysts have concluded that the communist ideology is no longer relevant to Chinese society, given the technocratic nature of the top leadership and their commitment to reform. Communism is dead. No one truly believes it.[3]

However, what has changed in China lends no support to the above conclusion, as we will discuss later. The fact that fewer people believe in the "official ideology," the so-called "faith crisis," only suggests an "ideological weakening" at the mass level, rather than a fundamental change at the regime level. We must evaluate the significance and nature of the change to determine if any fundamental change has occurred at the regime level.

To do so, an analytic framework is needed. We need to distinguish a change of "regime identity" or "official ideology" from a change of "popular" or "mass" ideology. In other words, ideology is defined as a system of beliefs which can be classified into two levels: the fundamental level (core beliefs) and the operative level (action principles). Accordingly, ideological changes may occur at both levels. The change of party goals or party identity indicates a fundamental change of core beliefs or change at the fundamental level.

A change at the operative level does not suggest a substitution of the final goal or a change of core beliefs. A communist party in a Western society can still be identified as "communist" even though it only gets 1 percent of the votes or no votes in an election or not many people really believe in their ideology. The reason is simple: the party does not lose its "identity" as long as it commits itself to the hard core or, fundamental principles, of its political ideology, regardless of how many people believe it or not, because it is a change at the mass level. This is just the equivalent of saying: "you are a liar because you lie or intend to cheat people despite the fact that few or fewer people believe you or buy what you say." No matter how far the party doctrine distorts reality, no matter how distressing the "faith crisis" is, the Chinese communist regime has not abandoned its ideological absolutism and commitment, as we will discuss later, but has continued to appeal to them, act upon them, and impose them upon the Chinese people, since the regime identifies itself with ideological absolutism, fundamental principles, and goals. The CPC is still claiming to be in possession of absolute and universal truth and therefore in the position of fulfilling its historical destiny—communism—through the "primary phase" of socialism to the "advanced phase" of socialism. Therefore, it is the Communist Party alone that possesses the universal truth and represents the fundamental interest of the people. Thus it is the party alone that has the right and the duty to guide and govern the society in order to achieve China's historical destiny.

Nevertheless, party doctrine can be modified to adapt to changing conditions without breaking faith with its fundamental principles and norms. As the post-Mao party leadership has declared, "Mao Zedong thought" and "Deng Xiaoping theory" are the application of the universal truths of Marxism–Leninism to the concrete practice of the Chinese revolution and construction of China's specific objective conditions. Therefore, "thought" or "theory" has two ideological components: commitment to the general or universal truths of Marxism–Leninism and modification of some elements of Marxism–Leninism in order for the Chinese communists to apply the -ism to the concrete practice of the Chinese revolution and construction. In fact, "thought" or "theory" has been adapted in accordance with changes in the specific conditions, and applied selectively and accordingly throughout communist political history in China. However, modification does not suggest discarding the fundamental principles and norms, but renovation within the same basic framework or "adherence to and development of Marxism" as repeatedly emphasized by the post-Mao leadership. It is not surprising that the regime has never thought to relinquish its commitment to the basic principles of Marxist and Maoist doctrines, though the post-Mao regime has cautiously modified some of Mao's doctrines through the official interpretation of Mao's doctrines. Therefore, modification of the official doctrine does not lend support to the assertion that post-Mao Chinese leaders no longer believe in the ideology they advocate, or that post-Mao political ideology is downplayed and treated only at face value.

While pragmatism and rationalism are features of post-Mao leadership style, we should not neglect the central realities of the Chinese political system and the fundamental character of its political elites. Some recent studies have presented a contending view in the evaluation of the political role of post-Mao communist ideology and offered a compelling illustration of how communist ideology still matters in post-Mao China.[4]

The two contending views in assessing the post-Mao political ideology beg the following questions: What are the core components of communist ideology? Is the ideology of the post-Mao regime fundamentally different from Mao's regime or is it in one continuous line with Mao's? To what degree have such core components changed so that the post-Mao regime is no longer communism? The answers to these questions require certain theoretical criteria or reference points against which to assess ideological change in post-Mao China and serious reconsideration of the change supported by empirical evidence.

In what follows, we will specify the major components of communist ideology to establish a theoretical framework against which to assess the political role of post-Mao ideology and the nature of the post-Mao change, and examine four major aspects of the post-Mao regime's theory and practice: two levels of communist ideology, communist twin-goal culture, the "four cardinal principles," and monopoly of mass communications. This chapter will provide empirical evidence to establish the argument that the communist ideology matters in post-Mao China, and that the post-Mao regime and Mao's regime have come down in one continuous line both in theory and in practice, and that the two regimes have no fundamental difference in terms of the political role of communist ideology and many aspects of the communist party–state practice.

Two levels of communist ideology

Ideology has been defined as "ideas which help to legitimate a dominant political power";[5] "the link between theory and action";[6] "sets of ideas by which men posit, explain and justify ends and means of organized action"; and "a set of ideas with a discursive framework which guides and/or justifies policies and actions, derived from certain values and doctrinal assumptions about the nature and dynamics of history."[7] According to Gordon White, "Ideology has played a crucially important role in the politics of state socialism or communist regimes. Such systems are 'ideocratic'—they rely on an explicit and codified system of political ideas derived from Marxism–Leninism which guides the actions of the political elite in the hegemonic Communist Party, justifies the party's monopoly on power, and legitimizes its proclaimed historical mission to 'build socialism.'"[8]

In China the political role of ideology reached high intensity during the periods of Maoist mass mobilization. However, as doctrinal ideas, communist ideology has been employed by the post-Mao leadership to guide and justify policy change and implementation. China's official ideology has more cohesive values which have shaped the thinking and mentality of the Chinese political leadership, and less coherent ideas which, nonetheless, do not counter the fundamental principles and norms, but represent ideological renovations within the same framework.[9] The framework of communist ideology is frequently classified by political scientists into two components: Seliger's "fundamental" and "operative" ideology,[10] Moore's "ideology of ends" and "ideology of means,"[11] Schurmann's "pure" and "practical" ideology,[12] and Lowenthal's "utopia versus development."[13] The former refer to universal truth, philosophical absolutism, and communist end-goal at the fundamental level, while the latter refer to practical ideas, policy preferences, and action means at the operative level.

According to Lowenthal, the conflict between the reality and the goal that confronted all communist states in the process of modernization was "development versus utopia" or "modernity versus utopia." With the advent of "mature industrialization," a communist state had to adapt itself to certain institutional changes (such as material incentives, managerial autonomy, specialization, and income differentials), all of which conflict with its fundamental ideological goals. The twin goals of "utopia and modernity" are intertwined but produce recurrent conflicts over certain policy issues, and the communist party–state regimes repeatedly try to undo the "ideologically undesirable by-products of economic development and spontaneous social change."[14]

Political leaders in the former Soviet Union and Eastern Europe experienced such a goal conflict as these countries moved toward more mature industrialized societies. China, today, is facing the same goal conflict in the marketization of its economy. However, goal conflict does not necessarily prove the post-Mao regime's abdication of the ultimate goal or suggest that the "fundamental goal" is being replaced by a "developmental goal" or "utopia" is being replaced by "modernity." In contrast, the reality in post-Mao China suggests that there has been coexistence of the two goals—the ultimate goal of communism and the intermediate goal of modernization. The post-Mao regime has attempted to balance the two goals to meet the needs of the regime's policy change and legitimacy. To do so, the post-Mao regime has become more tolerant of ideological change at the operative level while at the same time continuing to commit itself to its ultimate goal and those ideological elements at the fundamental level. The empirical evidence explored in this chapter will demonstrate that the most significant change has occurred at the operative level rather than at the fundamental level. Therefore, the terminology of "fundamental" and "operative" ideology is useful for analytic purpose. This framework can be illustrated in Figure 8.1.

The fundamental level refers to the body of fundamental principles or core components of the CPC's ideology, such as Marxism–Leninism and Mao Zedong Thought, the leadership of the Communist Party, the Socialist Road, the Dictatorship of the Proletariat, which are established as the "Four Cardinal Principles," and other "universal truths" or Utopian visions of an ideal society,

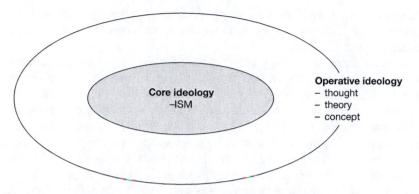

Figure 8.1 Two levels of ideology: fundamental and operative.

such as the end-goal of communism, the ultimate elimination of class, the major tenets of historical materialism and dialectic materialism, the transformation of human nature, democratic centralism, socialist public ownership, and the historical mission of the proletariat. The body of these fundamental principles and universal truths involves a small number of core elements that define regime identity and play a key role in unifying it. The fundamental components determine the CPC's final goal, legitimate the CPC's leading role, define the parameters of social and political life, conceptualize the social and political order desired by the CPC, and provide an ontological framework or a worldview to evaluate everything from policies to human behavior. These fundamental components are rigid, dogmatic, and impermeable to argument and evidence, and they tend to resist any significant change, for such change will ultimately change the regime identity and therefore the nature of the system.[15] As Daniel Bell noted, "dogmas such as dialectic materialism, historical materialism, the superiority of collective property, and the nature of scientific communism" serve as the doctrinal core of communist ideology. "The central fact is not any specific theoretical formulation *but the basic demand for belief in the Party* itself. It is not the creed but the insistence on the infallibility of the interpreters that becomes the necessary mechanism of social control."[16] Thus, the crucial feature of communist ideology is that party direction is essential in all fields of work.

The operative level designates sets of political ideas and theories put forward by political elites to guide, justify, and interpret their current tasks, intermediate goals or policy goals, concrete policies, policy choices, and actions within a given historical context, such as the goal of industrialization or moderniza-tion, theories of "Socialist Primary Phase," "Socialism with Chinese Characteristics," and "Socialist Market Economy." The intermediate goal and these theories serve to justify current measures as necessary for China, because China's socialism was created in the historical context of an underdeveloped society. Concepts such as "leasing," "shareholding," "private property," "coexistence of multiple ownership economic sectors," and "individual interests" are thus interpreted as applicable to the economy at the "primary phase of socialism."

Both fundamental ideology and operative ideology serve their own functions. Although there is some overlap between the two levels, each is sufficiently distinguishable for analytic purposes. For instance, the theoretical distinction between the two levels or two dimensions of communist ideology is important when one attempts to understand how and why two communist leaders, such as Deng Xiaoping and Chen Yun, who share common ideological allegiance, are often in conflict with each other in their policy preferences and choices. While they are committed to the same "pure" or "fundamental" principles, they may disagree on many points at the operative level of ideology, which could in turn produce different concrete policy choices. In fact, most controversies among the Chinese political elites tend to occur in the field of operative ideology regarding how to guide party policies, and relate more to the specific political and economic issues confronting them.[17]

The distinction of communist ideology into two levels serves as a theoretical framework against which to distinguish between fundamental and operative changes in post-Mao ideology as well as to assess the nature of post-Mao change. Therefore, we are not primarily concerned with how loyal political leaders are to their professed ideology but more concerned with the functional role and political use of ideology in guiding and justifying their political action and policy preferences.

Communist twin-goal culture

The key aspect to be examined in this section is the communist goal: Have the components of the communist goal changed under the post-Mao regime? The communist goal can be analytically divided into two major components: the "ultimate goal" at the highest stage of communism and the "intermediate goal" at the primary stage of socialism as officially prescribed by the CPC for China. Anthony Wallace's twin-goal culture serves as a sound starting point from which to examine the components of the communist goal. Anthony Wallace identifies two components of any revolutionary ideology as "goal culture" and "transfer culture."[18] An ideology's goal culture is its image of the ultimate Utopia, its idealized contrast to the present, while an ideology's transfer culture, on the other hand, provides the norms that guide policy formation: it specifies what steps the leadership must take or justifies the steps the leadership does take to move toward the goal culture.[19]

As Johnson concurs, economic modernization is an intermediate goal of policies adopted in the service of an ideological "transfer culture," an integral part of necessary measures for moving society toward a utopian goal culture.[20] "The communist goal culture does not aim at a 'modernized society,' but the task of transfer culture is to overcome China's economic backwardness as it seeks both to prepare the society for the goal culture and to maintain the society in the here and now."[21] It does not matter whether or not the intermediate goals specified by the transfer culture are in fact rational steps toward the goal culture—for example, whether forced industrialization under Mao or controlled marketization under Deng actually has anything to do with achieving a classless society. What matters is that these intermediate goals are justified and vigorously pursued in the direction, scope, and ways defined and dictated by the party ideology, and they are pursued in the name of a Utopia that serves as a legitimate source of the political regime.[22]

Communist ideology does not rise in opposition to industrialization or modernization but mandates a strong commitment to industrialization and economic development, since a truly classless Communist society is believed to represent the highest stage of economic development in human history.[23] Stalinist industrialization was the attempt to achieve the "highest stage" within the shortest period of time. Maoist industrialization was another type of attempt to achieve this goal rather than reject it. Maoist industrialization was based on the idea that

> the CPC will lead the people of the whole country in surmounting all difficulties and undertaking large-scale construction in the economic and cultural spheres to eliminate the poverty and ignorance inherited from the old China and improve the material and cultural life of the people step by step."[24]

Mao anticipated that, economically, China would achieve four modernizations—industry, agriculture, science and technology, and national defense; socially, the whole country would be transformed into "a unitary system of whole people's ownership" (total collectivization of production and social life); and politically, Mao hoped for "a situation in which we have both unity of will and liveliness, that is, both centralism and democracy, both discipline and freedom."[25]

Therefore, the post-Mao regime's commitment to the goal of economic modernization is not something new or any deviation from the communist ideology and goal, which is unfortunately misinterpreted by many China observers, analysts, and scholars. China's economic modernization is the transfer goal or intermediate goal that the CPC pursues to achieve the ultimate goal of communism. Mao's regime made a strong commitment to industrialization, though its industrialization drive relied upon mass mobilization and irrational economic policies rather than on the methods of the post-Mao regime. The post-Mao regime's commitment to modernization does not contradict its commitment to the ultimate goal of the communist ideology.

The post-Mao regime openly declares its commitment to the end goal of communism and its intermediate goal of economic modernization as preparing society for achieving the end goal. Therefore, the post-Mao leadership is still conditioned by its "ideological" system in which all important policies require an ideological justification.[26] As a Leninist one-party system, it requires a theoretical basis for all major policies to sustain the system's legitimacy. "Ideas held by top leaders and key policy makers are important for policy change and innovation," and " 'ideas from above' perform a significant function of forming and redefining political discourse and ideology in which new policy proposals can emerge."[27] For instance, to justify a particular policy option, a given leader has to present such a policy agenda in an acceptable ideological and theoretical framework in order to achieve a leadership consensus and communicate it to the party rank and file. In fact, general ideological statements made in party congresses and conferences are frequently the points of departure for more specific economic strategies and tactics. While Chinese reformist leaders might want to modify some of the ideological orthodoxy to meet the practical needs of economic modernization, they still commit themselves to Marxism–Leninism and Mao Zedong Thought and tend to undertake ideological modifications within such a framework.

To meet the needs of legitimizing the party leadership and justifying its reform policy without abdicating the commitment to the party's ultimate goal and utopian visions of an ideal future, as Alan R. Kluver observes, the post-Mao regime invents an important notion—the "Primary Phase of Socialism," and "inserts a new historical stage into the evolutionary progression of communism."[28] This is actually a new doctrine of the post-Mao regime, which asserts that "the full implementation of socialism is to be accomplished through distinct stages, and that each stage is to be accomplished by certain special policies. None of the stages can be skipped or altered, because certain historical processes have to occur at each stage."[29]

By arguing that there are distinct stages in the implementation of socialism and that each stage has its own historical goals and missions, the legitimacy of the early policies of the CPC under Mao's regime, such as the nationalization of private industry, is maintained and the post-Mao reform measures are not seen as contradictory to the early policies, only as fulfilling a different historical mission. By clearly demarcating a historical phase for the current reforms, the regime ensures that its policies are not seen to undermine the ultimate goal—a fully communist society.[30]

The central task of the "primary stage of socialism" is therefore defined as socialist economic construction or modernization, thus necessitating some measures that are not consistent with the ideological orthodoxy. That is to say, the CPC has to achieve this intermediate goal before it can proceed to the next stage. The post-Mao party line at this intermediate phase is summarized as the formula of "one center, two basic points" (一个中心，两个基本点): the one central task is to develop the productive forces and the two basic points are to uphold the Four Cardinal Principles (四项基本原则) as well as the reform and open-door policy.[31] Therefore, the CPC is leading the Chinese people to build "Socialism with Chinese Characteristics" (中国特色的社会主义), which

> is the product of the integration of the fundamental tenets of Marxism with the modernization drive in China and it is scientific socialism rooted in

the realities of present-day China. It provides the ideological basis that serves to unite all the party comrades and all the people in their thinking and their action. It is the great banner guiding our cause forward.[32]

Jiang Zemin has continued to uphold Marxism–Leninism and Mao's thought as the core of the party's ideology during the earlier revolution and attempts to justify the earlier policies under Mao's regime as the inevitability of the historical progression. "The old economic structure has its historical origins and has played an important and positive role. With changing conditions, however, it has come to correspond less and less to the requirements of the modernization program."[33] Moreover, Jiang's speech also reclaimed the absoluteness of communist ideology and reaffirmed the inevitability of socialism, even in other countries. His statement about the party's continued possession of the "absolute truth" is so crucial for our understanding and so important for our discussion that it deserves a long quote (Box 8.1).

Box 8.1 Quotation from Jiang Zemin

Socialism is a completely new system in the history of mankind. It is bound to replace capitalism—that is the general trend of social and historical development. Any new social system, as it is born, consolidated and developed, inevitably follows a zigzag course of struggles and sacrifices, of victories and defeats. Communists and the people in general will surely be tempered in this process and draw lessons from it, pushing socialism in the right direction.[34]

Jiang's Political Report to the 14th National Congress of the CPC admitted that socialism had suffered a temporary setback in the Soviet Union and Eastern Europe, but it declared that the ultimate progression of history would inevitably bring those nations back to socialism.[35] Socialism was declared as the only road for the Chinese people toward the communist future of common prosperity, and therefore only the CPC leadership could guarantee the socialist direction of China. China's task was to continue to uphold and advance socialism until the realization of the ultimate communist goal: "The ultimate goal of building socialism with the Chinese characteristics is to realize Communism, and therefore the promotion of socialist and communist morality is necessary for the whole society."[36] At a national conference on the campaign of studying Deng Xiaoping Theory held in Beijing in July 1998, Jiang asked the whole party to guard against a one-sided understanding of Deng's thought and the spirit of the fifteenth party congress. He reiterated the philosophical absolutism of the CPC in command of the absolute truth and historical destiny (Box 8.2).

> **Box 8.2 Quotation from Jiang Zemin**
>
> Taking the socialist road is the inevitable outcome of Chinese history and the correct choice of the Chinese people of all nationalities. Any attempt to abandon socialism or take the capitalist road is completely wrong and fundamentally infeasible. . . . Our reform is absolutely not to engage in capitalism, but is the self-perfection of the socialist system and the need of consolidating and developing socialism. Anything that might jeopardize socialism and the fundamental interest of our people must not be tolerated and must not be allowed to spread unchecked at any time and under any circumstances.[37]

He further illustrated the basic spirit of the 15th party congress and emphasized that the predominance of public ownership and the coexistence of multiple economic sectors constituted two sides of socialism with Chinese characteristics at the "primary socialist phase." The shareholding system is not a single form but one form of many to realize public ownership. Jiang asked the party and state cadres at all levels not to take a one-sided view of it—not to prescribe one solution for diverse problems (*yidaoqie*一刀切) or rush headlong into mass action (*yihongershang*一哄而上). The policy for state-owned enterprises (SOEs) to "hold the big and let the small go" (*zhuada fangxiao*) is to restructure and develop SOEs. "Let the small go" is to "invigorate them" (*fanghuo*), not to give them away or abandon them. There are many ways to "let the small go," such as reorganization, cooperatives, incorporation, leasing, contract, shareholding cooperatives, and sell-off. Sell-off, however, is only one form of many, and the policy is not to sell all the small state enterprises or simply give them away. A one-sided understanding of the policy leads to mistakes in action. The same is also true with political reform, which is not the equivalent of the multiparty system, bicameral houses, and separation of powers.[38]

Hu Jintao reiterated adherence to the same fundamental principles at the 5th Plenary of the 17th National Party Congress in 2010, and then Wu Bangguo, No. 2 figure of the Politburo Standing Committee and Chairman of the NPC Standing Committee, made a statement at the 4th Plenary of the 11th People's Congress in 2011, which reiterated "Five Nos" (*wudebugao*五个不搞): "We have made a solemn declaration that we will not employ a system of multiple parties holding office in rotation; diversify our guiding thought; separate executive, legislative and judicial powers; use a bicameral or federal system; or carry out privatisation."[39] The party calls for the "unification of thoughts of the whole party and the whole society based on the Five Nos" (以"五个不搞"统一全党全社会的思想). In short, since 1979, the 11th, 12th, 13th, 14th, 15th, 16th, and 17th party congresses have continued to uphold the party's ideological commitment, which suggests that the CPC has never abdicated its ultimate goal and the fundamental principles.

Although the post-Mao regime has become less attentive than in Mao's era to utopian visions of an ideal future, CPC ideology still officially retains many utopian elements as stipulated in the CPC constitution and reflected in the leaders' speeches. Moreover, many current practices still continue to follow the Maoist or Stalinist style and remain utopian in character: such as ultimate goals, ideological education, campaigns of "socialist spiritual civilization," ideological campaigns of learning from Lei Feng and other exemplary individuals and groups, mobilizing the whole party and the whole nation from above to campaign for certain policy goals, certain urgent tasks in the fields of politics, economics, and culture, campaigns to crack down on smuggling and criminals, re-education programs, mobilizing "the whole party and the whole people of the nation" to campaign for an annual economic growth rate or a five-year plan of economic growth, or the campaign for modernization, etc. Many of these Maoist "mobilization" mechanisms and practices have remained unchanged. The major function of re-education programs or re-education camps has remained in use, which is to remold human thought and behavior, which is particularly utopian in character.

In most recent years, inspired by "singing red songs" (唱红歌) in Chongqing, the re-education institutions and jails around the country have begun to introduce this practice to prisoners, such as red songs, red book, red movies, red dairies, red lectures, and red workshops, in an attempt to transform and remold the prisoners to be "new men" with "red culture," i.e., the Maoist communist ideology, It was reported that the Ministry of Justice held a conference on "Introducing Red Culture into Prisons" in Chongqing, on March 27, 2011, to promote the practice around the country.[40] The post-Mao regime, as in Mao's era, continues to remold human thought and behavior through the pedagogical education system and compulsory re-education programs governed by statute and the regulations of the government administration. This has been a typical political tradition of communist states and a prominent feature of the post-Mao regime.

The "Four Cardinal Principles"

The "Four Cardinal Principles," which were laid down by Deng Xiaoping, are the most fundamental aspect of the post-Mao regime's continuity of Mao's communist principles. The post-Mao leadership continues to hold Mao Zedong Thought as a "valuable spiritual asset of our party" and as "the integration of Marxist–Leninist universal truth with the realities of the Chinese Revolution."[41] Although the post-Mao political doctrine differs from Maoist orthodoxy in some respects of the political content at the operative level, it is indeed not something new at the fundamental level. It has come down in one continuous line from Maoist ideological orthodoxy. The post-Mao regime has attempted to resurrect the political tradition and political theory of the mid-1950s and base the political doctrine of the post-Mao regime on the "Four Cardinal Principles," proclaimed as defining the core elements of the post-Mao regime:

Marxism–Leninism and Mao Zedong Thought, the socialist road, the dictatorship of the proletariat, and the leadership of the Communist Party. These fundamental principles claim the CPC itself in possession of universal truth and assert the necessity for a ruling ideological orthodoxy as the guiding principle of China's socialist revolution and construction. It is in this fundamental sense that we are able to distinguish between a communist regime and an authoritarian dictatorship rather than in the sense of how many "pragmatic" elements are in the post-Mao ideological doctrine.

Deng Xiaoping urged the whole party and the whole people to counter-balance the influence of "bourgeois liberalization" and adhere to the "Four Cardinal Principles." He emphasized: "in order to realize the Four Moderniza-tions in China, we must, in the fields of ideology and politics, uphold the "Four Cardinal Principles." This is a fundamental prerequisite to the realization of the Four Modernizations."[42] There is no denying that the "Four Cardinal Principles" have fundamentally prescribed the direction, scope, content, and limits of the post-Mao reform from Jiang Zemin to Hu Jintao.

The political campaign, a defining feature of a communist regime, has always been employed as a means to achieve their goals. Although the post-Mao regime has repeatedly proclaimed their intention not to wage any further political campaigns in the course of constructing a socialist society, political campaigns have been widely and recurrently used in post-Mao China to educate the public about the official norms and current political line of the post-Mao regime.

For instance, the first campaign in the post-Mao era to eradicate "three type persons," the remnants of the Gang of Four; the "thought emancipation movement" in 1979–81; "anti-bourgeois liberalization" in 1981 and 1986–87; "anti-spiritual pollution" in 1983–84; "anti-imperialist peaceful evolution" in 1989–91; the "socialist spiritual civilization campaign" in 1987–98; the post-June 4 re-education campaigns on Chinese students; a series of "party rectification campaigns" under the post-Mao regime; and a series of "theoretical study movements" of Marxism–Leninism, Mao Zedong Thought, and Deng Xiaoping's Theory in both the 1980s and the 1990s. In 2010, Hu Jitao elevated the nationwide ideological campaign on "scientific development" and the "anti-three-vulgarities" campaign (*fan san su yundong*反三俗运动) to the same level as Mao's ideological campaign and Deng's "anti-spiritual pollution" to conduct brainwashing to transform and unify the thoughts of all party members and Chinese people in conformity with the party line and unify public opinion in accordance with the party propaganda orientation.[43] The 17th Central Committee of the CPC closed its sixth plenary session on October 18, 2011 and approved a decision to adopt new national cultural development guidelines to reform China's cultural system, start off a new upsurge in socialist cultural construction and development, and promote socialist core values and incorporate them into national education, cultural and ethical progress, and Party building.[44]

All have been conducted essentially as political and ideological campaigns and on a nationwide scale, although the measures that have been used are more moderate than those of earlier times under Mao's regime.[45] No one can deny this fact, which is actually consistent with the classical definition of communism as a political regime of mass mobilization. A comparison of political and ideological campaigns before and after 1978 is usefully illustrated in Table 8.1.

Political control over the social science curricula is justified by the principle of so-called "party nature" (*dangxing* 党性) of social science research and implemented in a traditional top-down manner throughout the whole higher education system. The principle of the university party committee strengthening control over all social science research has been repeatedly emphasized on the grounds that all such research falls into the category of party theoretical

Table 8.1 Political and ideological campaigns before and after 1978

Year	Campaigns	Targets	Characteristics
1950–78	Land reform, suppression of counterrevolutionaries, three-anti campaign, five-anti campaign, thought reform of intellectuals, agricultural cooperatives, socialist reform of private enterprises, anti-rightist, party rectification, great leap forward, people's communes, four cleanups, socialist education, cultural revolution	Landowners, rich peasants, counterrevolutionaries, former employees of the Nationalist government, former businessmen, former members of "democratic parties," intellectuals, cadres, "rightists," "capitalist-road-takers," and anyone suspected of disloyalty or opposition to Mao Zedong	high intensity, high penetration, on a nationwide scale, relying upon mass terror. In each of these campaigns, there were certain groups or classes designated to be the target of struggle
1980–2011	Four major anti-spiritual-pollution and anti-bourgeois campaigns, party rectification, constant socialist spiritual civilization movements, periodic crackdown on illegal publications, religions, campaigns against pop Falun Qigong, and "anti-three-vulgarities"	Intellectuals, dissidents, journalists, cadres, and anyone advocating "bourgeois liberalization" or espousing "Westernization"	low intensity, low penetration, but still on a nationwide scale, relying upon state terror. In each of these campaigns, there are many target individuals to be persecuted, arrested, or purged

work. Universities have assigned faculty as "political instructors" (*zhengzhi fudaoyuan*政治辅导员). The university party committees have continued to emphasize the purpose of education as training and molding "successors to the socialist cause." All elective courses should be strictly monitored to ensure they fit into the basic framework of Marxism, and they should not be seen as a free marketplace of ideas.[46]

Therefore, education in humanities and social sciences is seen as political education as well as training professional talents and "successors for the socialist cause," with all faculty being required to take responsibility for the political orientation of their students. One of the most recent re-education programs since the 1990s includes the introduction of Deng Xiaoping Theory and Jiang Zemin's "Three Represents" (*sange daibiao* 三个代表) into university curricula and university textbooks in an attempt to "conform the thought of university students to Deng Xiaoping Theory and the Party's basic line."[47]

All the evidence has suggested that there have been systematic attempts by the post-Mao regime to indoctrinate the general population, through the education system and the mass media, about the official ideology, with the "Four Cardinal Principles" as the core doctrinal components and the corner-stone of the post-Mao regime. The compilation of a paramount leader's ideas and speeches into textbooks and curricula is another typical Maoist style practice as well as the general practice of all communist regimes. The post-Mao regime has been committed to doing so on a nationwide scale, through pervasive ideological and political education work, organized through small study groups in workplaces and residential areas, or political study groups in schools, and daily "pedagogical" propaganda on mass media. These measures have continued to be a central political reality rather than treated by the CPC only at "face value" or can be simply denied by referring to economic changes and achievements of the post-Mao reforms. They serve to unify the communist regime identity and play a crucial political role in the post-Mao regime's political discourse in the service of its intermediate and ultimate goals.

Monopoly and uniformity of mass communication

The post-Mao regime has never abdicated its control over the mass media and still requires press uniformity and public opinion uniformity, though the number of newspapers, magazines, TV stations, and radio stations has greatly increased, with more diversity than in Mao's era. The monopoly of mass communications is a necessary characteristic of communist regimes. This has been recognized by almost all writers on the subject. Hannah Arendt, Carl Friedrich, Zbigniew Brzezinski, Michael Curtis, George Kennan, Ernest Menze, Juan Linz, and a host of others have described how such a monopoly attempts to get an entire society to think along the lines required by the party's ideology, ultimately for the transformation of man and society.[48] Such a monopolistic control is exercised by the Central Propaganda Department (CPD), both at central and local levels, which includes all functional bureaus and offices that are responsible for almost every aspect of media function, such as news reports, programs, and domestic and overseas propaganda. This department also oversees and provides policy guidelines for theoretical research, academic development, higher education, cultural education, literature and art, political and ideological work, and professional education.

Moreover, the party–state media includes but goes far beyond the functions of the authoritarian media, which are not "pedagogical" in nature but their primary aim is to eliminate criticism or dissent that can lead to serious opposition to the regime.[49] The "pedagogical" function of communist media is manifested in the requirement that the mass media reflect the party line and policy in their news reports, carry out political and ideological education guidelines and tasks prescribed by the Central Propaganda Department of the CPC, commit to the "Four Cardinal Principles," and propagandize around the central task of the current leadership.

To help understand the post-Mao change with respect to the party's ideological control, it will be useful to introduce Brantly Womack's three levels of ideological discourse: politics, policy, and private opinion. According to Womack, politics refers to the public realm of political discourse, overtly political questions, and ideological orthodoxy, in which open challenge and debate are still prohibited in China. Policy refers to expert discourse and the public discussion of concrete problems, solutions, and policies, which have been increasingly allowed but not without limit, some being restricted to internal circulation (*neibu tongxun* 内部通讯) and others being selected to appear in the press. Private opinion refers to the realm of private concerns, conversations, and opinions which, as long as they do not attempt to become public or political, are largely left alone in the post-Mao era.[50]

The important role of the communist mass media in China is to propagandize the "Four Cardinal Principles" and to sing the "leitmotif" prescribed by the Central Propaganda Department of the CPC. The Party Central Committee has constantly held national conferences on propaganda work and national conferences of propaganda chiefs, continued its commitment to communist ways of thinking, and required the mass media, journalists, and cultural personages to hold Deng's banner on high, grasp the party's basic line firmly, closely unite around the Party Central Committee with Jiang Zemin and then Hu Jintao as the leading core, uphold the correct direction of public opinion, and sing the "leitmotif" of patriotism, collectivism, and socialism. In his visit to the *People's Daily* in 1996 Jiang Zemin urged the press to "uphold the correct direction of public opinion, maintain and promote social stability, and mobilize all positive factors" (Box. 8.3).

The Central Propaganda Department of the CPC laid down six specific propaganda disciplines for the media to follow in 1994 and such directives remain effective in party propaganda work today (Box. 8.4).

To establish the press as a "work team" with a strong sense of "party nature," "propaganda discipline," and "correct press style," the Central Propaganda Department has continuously held a series of seminars for the directors and

Box 8.3 Party guidelines for the correct direction of public opinion

1. The press must be guided by the Party's basic theory, basic line, and basic guideline, and keep politics, ideology, and action in conformity with the Party Central Committee.
2. The press must firmly keep to the standpoint of the Party, adhere to principle, and take a clear-cut stand on what to promote and what to oppose on cardinal issues of right and wrong.
3. The press must adhere to the party's guideline with stress on propaganda by positive examples, sing the praises of people's great achievements, and conduct the correct supervision of public opinion that should help the party and the state to improve work and the style of leadership, solve problems, enhance unity, and safeguard stability.
4. The press must sing the leitmotif, hold patriotism, collectivism and socialism on high, and use best things to arm, direct and mold the people.[51]

Box 8.4 Six propaganda disciplines for the media

1. Provide help [to the party] and do not add trouble.
2. Sing the *leitmotif* and do not make cacophonous sounds.
3. Emphasize "social effects" and do not be lured by profit.
4. Observe orders in propaganda and do not go your own way.
5. Focus your energy on major party policies and do not dissipate your energy.
6. Materialize your goals and do not fool around with superficial effects.[52]

editors of provincial-level party newspapers, night editions of papers, radio stations, and television stations. However, the propaganda department leaders have also recognized that the art and technique of propaganda have become critically important for "upholding the correct direction of public opinion" in the press. Party propaganda departments have set up some more specific guidelines for the press to follow: the first is to stress the typical example in propaganda. In the past few years, several dozen "advanced examples" (xianjin dianxing 先进典型) have been established and propagandized to "influence and lead the whole social life." The second is to direct "popular subjects" (*redian huati* 热点话题) correctly. The "correct direction" means that the press must have a clear-cut departure point, not for the purpose of pursuing "stirring effects" (*hongdong xiaoyin* 轰动效应), not to stir the nation's attention, but for the purpose of helping the party and government to solve problems. The "correct direction" also means that the media must pay attention to the "conjunction point" (*jiehedian* 结合点), which is the conjunction of the "central work" of the party–state and the focal concerns of the "masses." The third is to conduct supervision of public opinion correctly. The "correct supervision" should be beneficial to improving the party and government's work, solving problems, maintaining stability, focusing on the party's central work, and listening to the masses. The targets of media supervision are such things as "unhealthy tendencies in industries," "regional protectionism," "corruption phenomena," "environmental pollution," "weakening of social and moral norms," "fake commodities," "violations of planned birth control," and "violations of law by law enforcement officers." Therefore, "China's media is still an arm of the state and public opinion supervision must take place under the larger umbrella of Party supervision and guidance."[53] The post-Mao regime's greater attention to propaganda art and technique does give the media some flexibility in news reporting of the above affairs, which mostly involves those issues in policy discourse or the "operative level." But such "flexibility" does not support the argument for "ideology decline," or suggest a fundamental change in post-Mao ideology, or categorize the post-Mao communist regime as less communist, irrelevant or declining.

The post-Mao regime has also periodically cracked down on the media, unofficial publications, indecent publications, and writings advocating "bourgeois liberalization" or "serious political mistakes" to purify the media. The books or magazines that are found to stray or are inappropriate will not be distributed. The party propaganda departments in all parts of the country have often rectified the media and publication industry in order to meet the requirement of "strengthening macro-control over the industry of the press and publication." The Party Central Propaganda Department and the Press and Publication Bureau of the State Council set up a joint leading group responsible for "the rectification of undisciplined and unchecked publications."[54] Since then the same leading group has issued several new regulations for the international internet, press and publication industries, and civil organizations, and many more newspapers and journals, including some major Chinese literature journals, and some popular regional newspapers have been ordered to shut down.

To tighten the party's control over the media, the Central Propaganda Department has asked the party propaganda departments in all parts of the country to set up examination groups to censor local publications and discover problems in local news reports and propaganda. The local party propaganda departments have been asked to be more strict in handling "negative reports" and to reduce the number of "negative reports" in the mass media.[55] The censorship at all levels of government and party propaganda departments keeps newspapers, periodicals, television stations, and film studios under firm party control. The censors are so nervous that they are banning things that are quite apolitical.

In response to the rapid expansion of China's internet and internet publications in the 1990s, the post-Mao regime has imposed new controls on both domestic internet users and foreign providers of information. In early 1996 Chinese central government issued two new sets of regulations designed to ensure the authority of national ministries over internet information, establish central planning and standard setting of international computer networking, and maintain informational boundaries between China and the rest of the world.[56] All networks are subject to administration and monitoring by the Information Office of the State Council, the Ministry of Posts and Telecommunications, the Ministry of Electronics Industries, the State Education Commission, and the Ministry of Public Security. The new regulations prohibit Chinese business organizations from obtaining economic information directly from foreign vendors. Instead, foreign news agencies must disseminate business and financial news through China's state-owned Xinhua News Agency. Legal action under China's criminal law could be taken against foreign journalists who report economic information that is considered harmful to national interests.

Moreover, all internet server owners are required to register with the local police within 30 days and sign an agreement promising not to use the computer networks for activities that might "damage the state, hinder public order, or harm national security" and promising to make the information available for investigation if they are under suspicion of wrongdoing. Internet accounts found guilty of the above activities would be suspended. Electronic publications must be produced by an approved publishing agency and assigned a six-digit number and, if imported, they must be approved by the Press and Publications Bureau before they can be put on internet sites. Authorities have also installed software to filter out information from overseas internet sites known to disseminate antigovernment information and pornography. This control also includes "keyword" searches covering all internet-related activities and personal emails. If a keyword defined by the internet authority as inappropriate was found in your email, the email would be blocked and would not be delivered.[57] Websites that publish any inappropriate or politically sensitive news or comments are blocked or removed. While blogging has been a high-growth activity in China, the government crackdown on dissenting internet voices has continued in recent years.[58] All this is to ensure party–state censorship over news reports of domestic and foreign events generated by foreigners and to give the official media organizations a monopoly over mass communication industries.[59]

The post-Mao leadership has continued to adhere to the principle of conformity in the media and public opinion, and to restrict, monitor, and control the contents and sources of information accessible to the general population, and stress the "pedagogical" and "educational" role of the media in educating, transforming, and perfecting human nature to mold socialist citizens. This is a most typical communist practice in modern times and should be recognized as hard evidence for the continuity of communist ideological practice of the post-Mao regime.

To conclude, all the evidence has suggested that the post-Mao leadership continues its commitment to Marxism–Leninism and Mao Zedong Thought, though some modifications have been made in inheriting the ideological orthodoxy. Post-Mao leadership declares that Deng's theory and Mao's thought have come down in one continuous line, with no fundamental difference. Establishing a paramount leader's ideas as the supreme, all-embracing authority in a polity has been a prominent feature of any communist state, having been recognized as the typical Maoist or Stalinist style of politics. Deng did it, Jiang did it, and so did Hu at a time of transition into the post-Deng era. Although fewer Chinese people believe the regime's communist ideology and practice, this does not suggest any fundamental ideological change at the regime level. In spite of incoherence among the components of the regime's ideology or inconsistency between the regime's ideology and related practice, the post-Mao regime has never abandoned the "hard core" of their inevitable goals, fundamental principles and norms, but only made adjustments to the action means of achieving them.

Questions for discussion

1. How can two levels of communist ideology and communist twin-goal culture serve as a conceptual framework by which we can observe, interpret, and explain the nature of ideological changes in a communist state, such as China, Vietnam, and North Korea?
2. Why must the CPC leadership maintain the "Four Cardinal Principles," ideological campaigns, and monopoly on propaganda and mass communication? How do the principles and the action means work together to maintain regime identity and legitimation? Does the post-Mao regime follow the same route and CPC traditions that were followed under Mao that combine ideological and political powers to accomplish its purposes and modify the governing ideology according to the changing context?

Further reading

Terry Eagleton, *Ideology—An Introduction* (London: Verso, 1991).

Martin Seliger, *Ideology and Politics* (New York: The Free Press, 1976).

Chalmers Johnson, ed., *Change in Communist Systems* (Stanford, CA: Stanford University Press, 1970).

Wei-wei Zhang, *Ideology and Economic Reform under Deng Xiaoping 1978–1993* (London and New York: Kegan Paul International, 1996).

Alan R. Kluver, *Legitimating the Chinese Economic Reforms: A Rhetoric of Myth and Orthodoxy* (New York: State University of New York Press, 1996).

Part V
Political institutions

9 The party–state structure of Chinese government

American students are taught about their political systems with reference to four relationships: relationships among the executive, legislative, and judiciary branches of government; relationships between the federal government and state and local governments; relationships between political parties and the government; and relationships between civilian and military authority. These relationships are governed and regulated by a system of checks and balances that are prescribed by the Constitution. However, when they study the Chinese political system, students might find many superficial similarities but fail to understand the profound differences.[1] Indeed, China also has a constitution and other similar political institutions that look like those of the United States, such as congress, executive, courts, and political parties, but they are organized differently and work in very different ways to achieve different ends. Therefore, we should not simply look at what they appear to be but focus on the nature, the guiding ideology and principles, and inner workings of those institutions and their power relationships.

The Communist Party of China (CPC) followed the Marxist and Leninist principles to create a "vanguard party," modeled on the Leninist party in the former Soviet Union during the Chinese communist revolution. After the communist takeover of power, the making of the Chinese communist state was modeled on the former Soviet Union, which is called the "party–state." The party is the power center in Chinese politics both in Mao's China and in post-Mao China. The party–state has been maintained and developed according to the so-called "Four Cardinal Principles" (四项基本原则) in post-Mao China: the adherence to Marxism–Leninism and Mao Zedong Thought, the leadership of the CPC, the socialist system, and the dictatorship of the proletariat.[2] In the Chinese party–state, the party stands at the top of the power structure pyramid, and assumes total representation of the nation and total guidance of national goals. The party has recently been defined as not only the vanguard of the working class but also the vanguard of the Chinese people, and the entire nation. "In this way, the party's claims to political representation became, in a sense, more totalizing, and one may well ask whether or not this effort of inclusion was more or less totalitarian. Nevertheless, it was, arguably, more 'Leninist'."[3] The party commands, controls, integrates, and completely intertwines with all sectors of the state: the government (the executive), congress (the legislative), courts (the judiciary), political consultative conference, the military, mass organizations, and all other political organizations and institutions, from top to bottom. The party–state accurately captures the nature and function of China's political structure and political reality.

The CPC is the Leninist vanguard party

The CPC has since its very birth been a Leninist party, declaiming itself as the "vanguard of the proletariat and all working classes" and following the principle of "democratic centralism" of the Leninist organizational line. As a result of this very nature, the CPC leadership not only requires the whole party to be subject unconditionally to its leadership but also requires the state, the military, society, and individuals to be subject to the party's will, leadership, and policy.

The post-Mao regime has continued to follow Bolshevik lines or the Maoist style in its organization, though it has taken some measures to rationalize the organizational line and decision making. The new policy of "cadre four modernization" (*ganbu sihua*干部四化)[4] or the "Three Represents" (*sange daibiao*三个代表)[5] in post-Mao China has not really changed the very nature of its organizational line. The current organizational line can be traced to the same origins as the Leninist or Maoist line in the following three major respects:

1. The party is conceived as a professional "revolutionary vanguard of the proletariat," an elitist party acting as the enlightened trustee of all the working classes and acting on behalf of the entire society. The CPC under the post-Mao regime continues to claim to be the "revolutionary vanguard" of all the working classes and social change. As Jiang Zemin declared, "our party is the Marxist–Leninist party standing at the forefront of the times and leading in the direction of the future. Our party will lead the people towards the full prosperity of the nation in the twenty-first century."[6] In a major speech in 2001, "Uphold the Four Cardinal Principles," Jiang describes the principle of party leadership as follows:

    > Maintaining the leadership of the CPC means maintaining the political leadership of the CPC over major state policy and overall work. It means maintaining absolute leadership of the CPC over state apparatuses, including the army and other facets of the people's democratic dictatorship. It means adhering to the principle of the party managing the cadres, maintaining the leadership of the party over the field of ideology and maintaining the leadership of the party over multi-party cooperation.[7]

    The "vanguard" status of the CPC is the keystone of the party and its ideological power, which little resembles the political party in Western democracy or the elite single party in the authoritarian regime. The "Three Represents" is the most recent formulation of the party's vanguard status at the 16th Party Congress in 2002. This official statement stipulates that the Communist Party of China is representative to advanced social productive forces, advanced culture, and the fundamental interests of Chinese people of all ethnic groups. The total representation of the nation and total guidance of national goals are codified into the Constitution: "under the guidance of Marxism–Leninism, Mao Zedong Thought, Deng Xiaoping Theory and the important thought of 'Three Represents'" (PRC Constitution 2004, Preamble).

2. The party exercises the principle of "democratic centralism" (*minzhu jizhongzhi*民主集中制) which in fact has everything to do with centralized control and nothing to do with democracy. Party organizations, from the national level to cells of three party members in the workplace, neighborhood, or village level, is rigidly hierarchical. The whole party must obey the Party Central Committee (PCC) and look to the PCC as the correct interpreter of ideology and the core leadership of political action. However, according to the principle of "democratic centralism," the whole party is ultimately subject to a paramount leader and a small group of Politburo standing members. Discussion may be allowed, but party leadership decisions are final and nondebatable. Dissent or even objective thinking is *prima facie* evidence of "bourgeois liberalism" that must be purged with "criticism and self-criticism," if one is not to be expelled from the party.

    At a national conference on party organizational work, Jiang Zemin addressed the issue of how the party can carry out the spirit of the 15th Party Congress in party construction and organizational work: first, according to the demands of the 15th Party Congress, we must bring about the new high tide of studying Marxism, Mao Zedong Thought, and Deng Xiaoping Theory; second, we must ideologically and politically keep a high degree of conformity with the PCC, resolutely carry out the major policies and decisions of the Center, consciously preserve the central authority, and unify the thought and behavior of the broad cadres and masses around the spirit of the 15th Party Congress and the decisions of the central authority; and third, we must resolutely carry out the party's principle of democratic centralism which is the fundamental organizational and leadership system.[8]

3. The party claims to shoulder a historical mission of transforming and remolding society and man, and thus has to mobilize greater political participation in the programs and campaigns of transformation. In contrast, no passion for the transformation of society and man exists in authoritarian regimes, and no official ideology in authoritarian regimes mandates an elite party, if existing, to do so. As observed in the previous chapter, the post-Mao regime has continued to use political and ideological campaigns recurrently in the last three decades to remold state and society according

to its own ideology, principles, norms, and policy needs and to educate the public about official ideology, norms, and the current political line of the regime, although the measures that have been used are more moderate than those of earlier times under Mao's regime.

To maintain the "vanguard" status, carry out the principle of "democratic centralism," and accomplish the historical mission, the party has to put itself in a constant rectification movement. The rectification movement has been the main vehicle for the post-Mao regime to re-establish ideological purity and organizational rule. The earliest rectification movement after the death of Mao was the purge of the followers of the "Gang of Four," lasting for a number of years. This was followed by the 1984–87 rectification movement, which was carefully planned to be systematic, thorough and inclusive.

The main purposes of the rectification movement in early post-Mao China were to purge the "three kinds of people" who had benefited from the Cultural Revolution (that is, those who rose to prominent position by following the Jiang Qing and Lin Biao "cliques," those who were imbued with factionalism, and those who engaged in "beating, smashing, and looting"[9]), also to normalize the organizational life of the party, strengthen party discipline and achieve conformity of the whole party to the center, improve "party style" (*dangfeng* 党风), restore the party tradition of the period before the Cultural Revolution, attack "new unhealthy tendencies," and attack any intra-party factionalism.[10] The movement was directed by a Central Commission for Guiding Party Rectification. In the earlier stages of the movement, the "liaison groups" were sent out by the Commission to supervise and coordinate rectification activities at lower levels. "Inspection groups" were often used later on to check on lower levels.[11]

Purges have been periodically conducted among party cadres and party members in "party construction" and "rectification" movements to ensure that "the party organization is pure" and to guarantee that "various leadership positions and functions are taken up by true Marxists."[12] The most extensive house cleaning after the Cultural Revolution was the purges that were carried out after the June 4 event, 1989. "Work teams" were stationed in almost all key central government organs and their subordinate mass organizations. All government functionaries, particularly party members and cadres, were required to give a detailed account of their "involvement" in the event. An unprecedented party membership "re-registration" campaign was launched in the first half of 1990. All party members automatically lost their membership unless they were allowed to re-register after satisfying the authorities of their total devotion to the "Four Cardinal Principles." The result of the purges was announced by the *People's Daily* on May 30, 1991. The total number of CPC members was 50.3 million. In 1990, 127,000 party members were either expelled, or asked to leave the CPC. In addition, 166,000 party members were subjected to internal party discipline. At the same time, more than 1.3 million new members were inducted in 1990.[13]

The emphasis has been on restoring the party's past values and the practices of the earlier stages of the communist movement and on using "traditions" to address current problems. Jiang Zemin urged the party–state cadres to uphold the ultimate ideal and firm faith in communism, strengthen the "party nature," resist various temptations, and try to be exemplary models in upholding and developing the party's fine tradition and style.[14] The emphasis on the "party traditions" is intended to improve "party style." "Party style" (*Dangfeng*) refers to a combination of all the prescribed political norms and relationships crucial to the party's operations and the maintenance of organizational coherence and obedience. The various elements of party style were first fully articulated in the early 1940s, and it is this articulation that is regarded as establishing party "traditions." If a tradition is to have any current political relevance, then it implies continuity of application. Emphasis on "party style" suggests a continued insistence on its vanguard character and on the qualitative difference between the CPC and other types of political organizations. The whole notion of "party style" demands a priority of commitment to party goals as the basis for members' political actions and relationships.[15] However, this emphasis on party "traditions" is not considered to conflict with the "shift in focus" on economic modernization. Instead, it is considered crucial for the party's survival in the economic marketization and liberalization to offset the threat posed to organizational discipline and ideological purity.

CPC party–state politics has come down in one continuous line: Mao–Deng–Jiang–Hu, and it continues its commitment to the same ideology—Marxism–Leninism–Mao Zedong Thought, the same ultimate goal and the same fundamental principles of the Leninist party–state despite some changes and modifications in post-Mao China. This chapter will introduce students to the Chinese political structure, power relationships, institutions, processes, and functions.

The party controls every sector of the state and central–local governments

In all communist Leninist states, party and state are closely intertwined and their functions are largely combined into one body, with a dominant role for the party, for which the special term "party–state" has been created. The power structure is modeled on the first communist state, the Soviet Union. The Communist Party is the center of the power, or "a state within a state." All the key policy decisions in China since 1949 have been made outside the government but are entirely monopolized by the party. The party defines its function as that of making all the crucial decisions which the government must carry out. The existence of party leading groups in units of the state organ ensures the structural dominance of the party. Members of party standing committees at various levels are each in charge of one or some governmental functions and operations. China has political institutions as the Western states

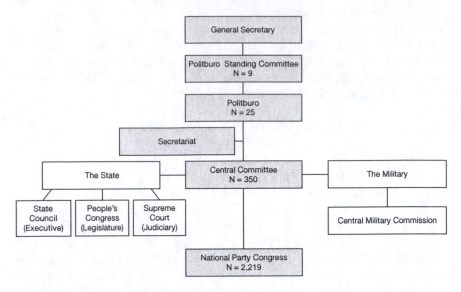

Figure 9.1 The party–state power structure.

have, for example, three branches of government, but they are organized differently. If we simply look at the three branches of government (executive, legislative, and judiciary) and their relationships, we will lose sight of the most important features of the Leninist party–state. In the politics of the People's Republic of China, we must look at the power relationships among the three big tightly interlocked *xitongs* or systems (系统), called "party–state–military" (党政军), under the direct leadership of the Party Politburo standing committee members, and many sub-*xitongs* headed by high-ranking party officials. The organizational structure of the party–state is presented in Figure 9.1.

In both horizontal and vertical power relationships, the party is the center of the power structure, and controls every level of government through an array of party organizations from top to bottom. As China is a highly centralized unitary system, a provincial or local government is subject to the "dual leadership" (双重领导) of both higher-level party organization and same-level party organization. The horizontal and vertical power relationship between the party committee and government can be illustrated as shown in Figure 9.2 in general and Figure 9.3 in more detailed illustration (an arrow means party leadership and control).

The Leninist party–state emphasizes centralism ("democratic centralism" has no meaningful relationship with "democracy") as its organizational principle, and applies it to the organization of the state institutions. China is not a federal system in its vertical power relationship, but a highly centralized unitary system, which establishes five levels of government in a hierarchy.

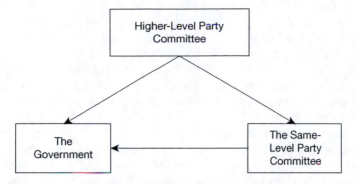

Figure 9.2 The relationship between the party and government.

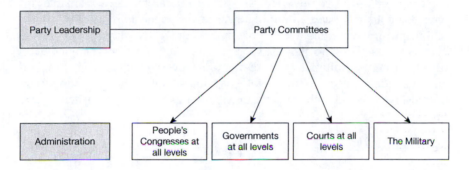

Figure 9.3 Party leadership and control.

1. Central government (中央)
2. Provinces (省), autonomous regions(自治区), and special municipalities under direct leadership of the central government (直辖市)
3. Prefectures (地区), autonomous prefectures (自治州), autonomous leagues (自治盟), and prefecture-level cities (地级市)
4. Counties (县), county-level cities (县级市)
5. Rural township (乡镇), urban district (市辖区), and banners (旗).

Rural village committees/village groups (村民委员会/村民小组) under township administration and urban neighborhood committees(居民委员会) under urban district administration, which were a basic administrative level in Mao's China, are now declared as "self-governance" grassroots organizations in post-Mao China. However, in actual reality, they are not truly free and independent of party and government control. There is a party committee established in each village and each neighborhood community, and their activities are under the leadership and supervision of the party committee at both village/neighborhood level and township level.

The State Council (国务院), which is the executive branch of central government in China, is headed by the premier, a key member of the Party Politburo. There are about 50 high-ranking members in the Council, which includes the heads of each ministry or department and agency. However, Standing Committee members of the State Council include the premier, four vice-premiers, five state councilors, and the secretary-general, who are certainly top-level party–state officials, creating a fused power relationship between party and government. The State Council directly administers various commissions, ministries, and agencies at central level and oversees government at the provincial level, which oversees prefecture-level government, which oversees county-level government, which oversees township-level government, which oversees basic-level "self-governance" grassroots organizations—a top-down hierarchical control system from the top all the way to the bottom (Figure 9.4).

Each administrative level in the power hierarchy is responsible for overseeing the work carried out by lower levels on the administrative strata. Although provincial and local governments are given more autonomy in economic policy making, they are subservient to their superiors at higher levels of administration, ultimately to the central government. At each level of administration below central-level government, there are two important political figures, and both are party members and ranking party officials. One

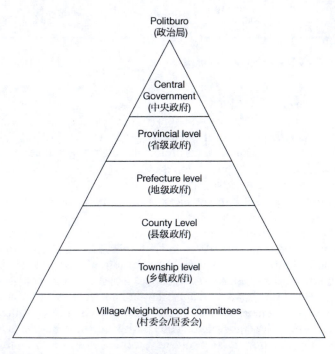

Figure 9.4 Chinese unitary system of vertical power structure.

is the Party Secretary of the party committee who is the "first-hand figure" (第一把手) and acts like the policy maker, while the other is the "second-hand figure" (第二把手) in the party committee, and serves as the head of the government to carry out the party's policy and administrative work. The Party Secretary is always ranked above the head of government. Both figures are actually appointed by the higher-level party committees, but are theoretically elected by the people or by the people's congresses.

There are 33 province-level governments, including 22 provinces, five autonomous regions, four special municipalities under direct leadership of the central government, and two special administrative regions; 333 prefecture-level regions; 2,862 county-level regions; 41,636 township-level regions; 623,669 village committees/village groups, and 80,717 neighborhood committees. Table 9.1 summarizes the levels of administration and their divisions of the area administered by the Chinese party–state as of 2005.

In summary, the party is the center of power while the function of government is to implement the party's political guidelines and policies. The party's guidelines and policies set the national goal, justify the means to achieve it, and provide bases for the government policies. It is the party's congress that sets the guidelines, not the NPC, and people's congresses that set the guidelines for the party. As a Chinese American scholar put, "If the latter are the bones and flesh of Chinese body politics, the party is undoubtedly its brain, its nerve center and its sinews. The party commands, controls and integrates all other political organizations and institutions in China. The party–state, or 'partocracy,' accurately captures China's political reality."[16] The party–state structure and the relationships of various political institutions demonstrate the following key features:

1. Party/state/military are combined and intertwined, with four parallel and highly interlocked structural arrangements: parallel positions of party leaders and state officials, parallel structuring of party organization and state institution, party ideology being the governing ideology of government, party principles being the guiding principles of government (Figure 9.5).
2. There are no checks and balances between different branches of government, with the party being the center of power and the supreme authority of politics and public life.
3. The CPC controls every sector of the state and penetrates every corner of society with a political consultation conference to incorporate the non-CPC social elite into the political system and justify its rule.
4. The party is the brain of government while government branches are its legs and arms, and carry out party policies and orders.
5. The CPC declares it works within the constitutional and legal system, but in actual reality it is the lawgiver and above the law. Laws are defined and made according to the party's ideology, norms, and political needs. There is no independent judicial system.

Table 9.1 Levels of administration of party and government

Level	Administration	Types
1.	Central-level 中央政府	Central Party Committee and its functional departments leading groups, and special agencies (中直机关) State Council with 28 commissions and ministries, and 59 agencies under the Council (国务院及直属部委)[17]
2.	Provincial-level 省级行政区	Provinces (省) (22) Claimed sovereignty over Taiwan as a province (1) Autonomous regions (自治区) (5) Municipalities (直辖市) (4) Special administrative regions (特别行政区) (2)
3.	Prefecture-level 地级行政区	Prefectures (地区) (17) Autonomous prefectures (自治州) (30) Prefecture-level cities (地级市) (283) Leagues (盟) (3)
4.	County-level 县级行政区	Counties (县) (1,464) Autonomous counties (自治县) (117) County-level cities (县级市) (374) Districts (市辖区) (852) Banners (旗) (49) Autonomous banners (自治旗) (3) Forestry areas (林区) (1) Special districts (特区) (2)
5.	Township-level 乡级行政区	Townships (乡) (14,677) Ethnic townships (民族乡) (1,092) Towns (镇) (19,522) Subdistricts (街道办事处) (6,152) District public offices (区公所) (11) Sumu (苏木) (181) Ethnic sumu (民族苏木) (1)
6.	Village-level/ neighborhood-level 村级/居委会自治组织	Neighborhood committees (社区居民委员会) (80,717) Village committees (村民委员会) (623,669) or Village groups (村民小组)

Source: http://en.wikipedia.org.wiki/administrative_divisions_of_china

The CPC and the People's Congress

The CPC is the most powerful political body in China, its decisions are determinative at virtually every level of Chinese government, and its norms and rules govern the relationship between the CPC and the NPC. The preamble to the Chinese Constitution stipulates the CPC's leading role in China. "Despite the lack of any clear constitutional or statutory authority for the CPC's omnipotence and omnipresence, the CPC has de facto control over the entire state apparatus."[18] The CPC's leading role does not require any formal legal

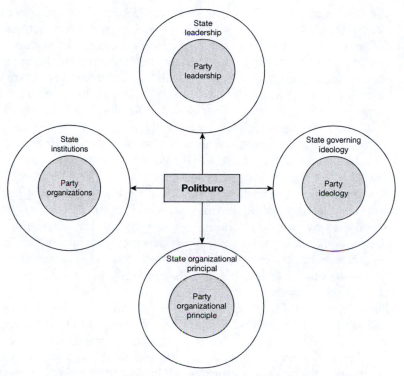

Figure 9.5 Party–state overlapping and intertwining with the party as the core.

basis because its establishment derives from the successful Communist revolution in 1949 rather than a formal legislative process. Party leadership of people's congresses is achieved and guaranteed in the following ways:

1. The CPC sets up the guidelines and policies for people's congresses to carry out according to its central tasks at each historical phase. For instance, the PCC of the CPC since 1979 has issued four major documents about legislative work to strengthen the party leadership at county and *xian* elections. To carry out the directives of the PCC, the leading party group (*Dangzu*) of the NPC laid down regulations, operating rules, and procedures for the legislative work which were specially designed to strengthen party leadership in the county and *xian* elections. All these regulations were enacted into laws immediately.
2. The CPC proposes directly to the NPC or its Standing Committee and other special legislative committee legislative bills in important state affairs, such as constitutional amendments, outlines and plans of national economic and social development, all major law-making decisions, and economic restructuring programs. Such a practice is duplicated at all levels of the party committees and people's congresses.

3.   The CPC exercises leadership of the routine work of the NPC Standing Committee and those at lower levels through specific directives or decisions. The leading party groups of people's congresses exercise the system of "asking the higher party authorities for instructions beforehand and submitting reports afterwards" in their legislative work. For example, according to the PCC Document 18 of 1986, leading party groups must submit reports on the guiding ideas and principles of all the important legislative bills in political, legal, economic, administrative, and cultural fields to the higher party authorities for approval before they are considered. Legislative bills must also be submitted to the higher party authorities for approval before they are sent to the floor for enactment.

4.   The CPC exercises leadership of the election work of people's congresses. People's congresses at all levels must set up a special leading group directly led by party committees at corresponding levels to guide the election work. Major issues, particularly personnel appointments and candidates, must be decided by party committees. Party committees evaluate all the important decisions of people's congresses to ensure correctness and authoritativeness.

5.   The CPC exercises leadership of people's congress sessions. All major leaders of the party and governmental organizations must be in charge of some work during people's congress sessions, acting in such roles as president of the congress presidium, members of the congress presidium, and heads of the congress secretariat. All the important issues of congress preparations and sessions must also be reported to the party authorities for approval.

6.   The CPC exercises the organizational leadership of people's congresses. Important personnel decisions such as people's congress deputies, leading members of congress standing committees, candidates for leading positions in state institutions, and responsible leaders of the standing committees of people's congresses are all made by party committees. In practice, all the leading positions of people's congresses are held by party secretaries, deputy secretaries, or party committee members. Leading party groups are established in all people's congresses, which are subject to the leadership of the party committees at corresponding levels. Moreover, party members in people's congresses are also subject to party discipline. The principle of "democratic centralism" of the CPC has been the organizational principle of Chinese state institutions and the people's congress, according to Article 3 of the Constitution. This Leninist party principle has been the universal principle in the political life of all communist states. The relationship between the NPC and the CPC, and the Chinese legislative structure and process are presented in Figure 9.6. This relationship is duplicated at all levels of government in China. The following will further examine the relationships of the CPC with the NPC and the lower levels of people's congresses.

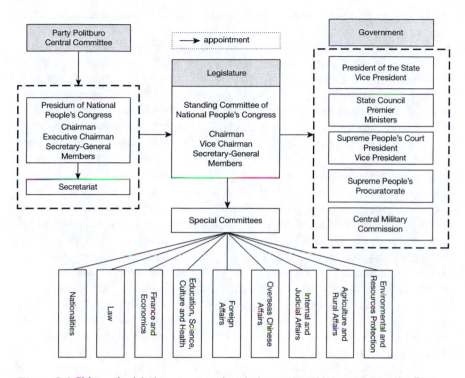

Figure 9.6 Chinese legislative structure in relation to the Chinese Communist Party.

People's congresses at each level are not truly representative assemblies or political institutions that would challenge party power and governmental decisions. First, people's congress deputies at each level are mainly politically reliable cadres, intellectuals, workers, peasants, officers, soldiers, and minority representatives who accept the contour of the CPC regime.[19] Second, about four-fifths of the legislative leaders are former cadres transferred from party or state organs.[20] Third, years of principle and practice dictate that "the party manages cadres," and the party's tightly controlled nomination procedures guarantee that even the lowest level, directly elected deputies are rarely firebrands. Fourth, about 60–80 percent of all deputies nationwide are CPC members, about four million, in a five-level system that includes the NPC, 29 provincial-level congresses, hundreds of municipal congresses, nearly 3,000 county-level congresses, and tens of thousands township congresses. Party members make up the majority of the congress deputies; they were 68.4 percent of the total 8th NPC deputies and 71.5 percent of the total 9th NPC deputies, for instance.[21] In the course of the congress, temporary party branches and party groups are always established to ensure party control over the entire course of the NPC.[22] The web of party control is pervasive and effective. All such political arrangements mentioned above are largely duplicated at lower levels.

Party leadership and the domination of people's congresses ensure that people's congresses will carry out party policy.

Party–congress relations can be best characterized as "master–servant" relations, as is evident at each level. Although formally subordinate to congresses at the same level, the heads of the government, court, procurator, and public security are actually deputy secretaries of the party committee and they outrank any people's congress leaders at that level who are in most cases members of party standing committees. In fact, people's congresses have sought greater attention and penetration by party committees. If party committee secretaries have harmonious relations with people's congress leaders, congress status will increase; if high-ranking party officials are in charge of people's congresses or more frequently attend people's congress sessions, greater attention will be drawn from party committees, and congress opinions will receive more attention. On the other hand, if a party committee regards the people's congress as a retirement home for aged cadres, the congress will be ignored. When party committees speak for people's congresses, congresses will enjoy more support and attention and be allocated more competent staff, adequate facilities, and budgets. Where joint meetings or informal discussion meetings (*zuotanhui*) are held regularly, mutual reporting and document flow will improve, congress opinions will receive more attention, congress oversight power can be respected, factories can be spurred to comply with anti-pollution statutes, fines can be levied on markets that "illegally" increase prices, unjust court decisions can be overturned, and corrupt cadres can be brought to justice.[23]

The goals of people's congresses and party committees are compatible and both strive to accomplish the yearly "central tasks" assigned by higher authorities and carry out the party basic policies. When inflation is the focus of national work, inflation is the focus of law making and oversight; when "clean government" (*Lianzheng*) becomes the top priority, people's congress priorities will change accordingly. Each province, city, or county also has its own "central tasks" (e.g., flood control, birth control, improving transportation and commodity circulation, reducing loss of farmland, encouraging foreign investment), and people's congresses at each level will devote attention accordingly. Sometimes, legislative initiative could expand the list of priorities (e.g., improving production quality, encouraging the technical transformation of enterprises), but party committees can always use people's congresses to realize the party program. The primary role of people's congresses is to transmit the "spirit" of higher levels and, by and large, they do so.[24] In short, people's congresses are the instrument for realizing party policies and carrying out the "central tasks" assigned by higher authorities.

The CPC and other state institutions

The Chinese government has three branches—a legislature, an executive, and a judiciary—but in practice there are really two branches since the Chinese judiciary functions more as a department of the executive than it does as an independent check on the other two arms of government. Similarly, the legislature only has a nominal check on the executive, though more recently it has come to see itself as a potential check on the operations of the executive and the judiciary. The branches of the government are not equal partners and there is no provision in the Chinese Constitution for checks and balances to maintain equality. As a matter of fact, CPC leaders have opposed checks and balances as a Western style that does not suit China.[25]

The State Council is the executive branch of the government that carries out party policy as the NPC does. The State Council serves as an instrument of the party dictatorship, and functions as an administrative and bureaucratic apparatus for the party. The party leaders simultaneously hold positions in governmental institutions. One leader could hold several positions. All powers are in the hands of party leaders. The party exercises "democratic centralism" by which every party member has to abide. So the party totally dominates the policy-making process within these governmental institutions. The State Council, under the Constitution, is also authorized to issue administrative regulations (*xingzheng fagui*), which make up the largest amount of legislation. Because of the significant overlap in membership of the State Council and the Politburo of the CPC, the CPC controls the content of the various regulations that the State Council passes.

As is the case with respect to the NPC and the State Council, the CPC exercises direct control over the judicial process in China.[26] The people's Courts, the judicial organs of China, are divided into five levels—the Supreme People's Court, the Higher People's Courts, the Intermediate People's Courts, the Basic People's Courts, and the Special People's Courts. Each level of court has its own "original jurisdiction," serving as a trial court within its competence. The People's Procuratorates share the identical hierarchy of the People's Courts—Supreme, Higher, Intermediate, Basic, and Special. The Procuratorates are responsible for approving arrests and for investigating and initiating prosecution against defendants. Public Security Bureaus also exist parallel to the Procuratorates at each level; these police and surveillance units are responsible for arrests and detentions.[27]

A supreme Central Committee unit in charge of the judiciary—the potent weapon of the "dictatorship of the proletariat"—is called the Commission of Political and Legal Affairs (CPLA), headed by a Politburo Standing Committee member. The CPLA members include the heads of the Ministry of State Security, the Ministry of Public Security, the Justice Ministry, the Supreme People's Court, the Supreme People's Procuratorate, and a representative from the General Political Department of the People's Liberation Army.[28] Aside from laying down yardsticks for the protection of security, law enforcement, and the measurement of penalties, the CPLA also meets to discuss major cases. For those cases that might have political significance or international repercussions, the CPLA often refers the files to the full Politburo Standing Committee meeting—and when Deng was alive, sometimes to Deng Xiaoping himself.

The politicization of justice, or the rule of man, infringing upon the judicial field, has been a political tradition of the Chinese communist party–state. In other words, the Politburo of the CPC is in effect China's "court of final appeal," which goes back to the earliest days of the CPC.[29] At the lower level, courts or judges are required to report all cases to trial committees chaired by a member of the Party Standing Committee at each level, who is at the same time the head of the Political–Legal Leading Group at each level. These committees in effect predetermine the results of the trials, thus making the actual trial a sham.[30]

The People's Liberation Army (PLA) and other armed forces constitute another critical sector of state institutions. The Chinese armed forces have always been considered as a "strong pillar of the people's democratic dictatorship," and subject to the absolute command of the CPC and the Central Military Commission (CMC).[31] Under Deng's regime, Jiang's regime or Hu's regime, the CPC has always made it clear that China "must adhere to the leading power of the CPC over the military, guaranteeing that the army must be at conformity with the PCC any time and on any occasion, and subject itself to the PCC and the Central Military Commission in its all actions."[32] Jiang Zemin made a speech at a meeting of PLA deputies to the 9th National People's Congress urging the whole army to subject itself to the command of the CPC Central Committee and the CMC: "All officers and soldiers of the army must heighten their sense of discipline, persistently subject themselves to the command of the PCC and the CMC, and always maintain a high degree of unity and stability of the troops, to excellently accomplish various tasks given by the party and the people." "Party committees at all levels in the armed forces should make persistent efforts to arm the minds of officers and soldiers with Deng Xiaoping Theory and the guidelines of the 15th CPC National Congress and carry out the party's line, principles and policies in an exemplary way," he emphasized.[33] Therefore, the post-Mao leadership has always emphasized the "revolutionization" or "politicization" of the PLA as the top priority, which does not contradict the modernization of the military and the streamlining of the size of the military.[34]

Exactly the same as in Mao's era, the PLA has extensive political, social, and economic duties to serve as "the defender and builder of the socialist system and modernization." Receiving frequent and established indoctrination in Marxism–Leninism, Mao Zedong Thought, and Deng Xiaoping Theory, as well as in policy guidelines of the current leadership, and being involved in all political campaigns, political activities, and scheduled political studies, lessons, and training classes every week, the PLA is extremely politicized though the extent is less than in Mao's era. As in Mao's era, every military unit, higher than and including the company, has an established political officer assigned as "second-in-command" in the military unit who is responsible for the political and ideological work of the troops. Since every officer and soldier must follow the party's lines and directives, all senior officers are members of the party committees established in every military unit, and the political officer or "political commissar" is usually the head of the party committee; he is actually the highest commander in the military unit. Even in some purely military situations, the political officer or "commissar" often has a decisive say in major military decisions. Only party members have a great chance to be promoted to a higher position and thus every senior officer is without exception a party member. Promotion in the armed forces continues to uphold the principle of "red and expert"—politically reliable and technically or professionally strong. All senior officers on the promotion plan must be sent to party schools at corresponding levels for advanced political and ideological training and education. The PLA leadership must commit itself to the communist ideology, the party's basic line, guiding principles, and policies, and must be loyal and subject to the "absolute" command of the PCC. The highest level officers are all appointed by the Politburo and the Central Military Commission which is usually headed by the same person, the Secretary General of the CPC.

The CPC and other "democratic parties" at the CPPCC

The post-Mao regime has reinstituted "multi-party cooperation" into its political operation, and emphasized the enhanced role of the Chinese People's Political Consultative Conference (CPPCC). The CPPCC serves as a political instrument of the post-Mao regime to recover and incorporate the eight so-called "democratic parties" that are a legacy of the "new democratic revolution" led by the CPC during its power struggle against the Nationalist Party and during the CPC regime making.

These eight political "parties" officially exist but are actually subordinate satellites of the CPC. These so-called "parties" have no independence and must accept the leadership of the CPC. Although the CPC "consults" with these parties regularly, "the reality is that they survive on the sufferance of the CPC and could be immediately crushed if they refused to do the CPC's bidding."[35] There is no interaction among the eight existing nominal political parties or so-called "democratic parties," which do not seek to control the government or vie against the CPC, for the CPC succeeded long ago in eliminating its rivals and has effectively prevented the emergence of any force that could even begin to be a nucleus for political opposition.[36]

In the 1990s the party took some major steps towards "inclusion" of the eight "democratic parties" into the polity and attempted to define and organize their activities around the leadership of the CPC. For example, the major document "On Upholding and Perfecting the System of Multi-party Cooperation and Political Consultation under the CPC Leadership" specifies that a certain proportion of the positions in the NPC and its Standing Committee as well as local-level people's congresses should be "set aside" for members of the eight "democratic parties." And when the State Council or local governments hold plenary sessions and other meetings to discuss policy, they can invite some members of these parties according to needs and circumstances.

However, the document has made it clear that "The CPC is the leading core of the socialist cause and the ruling party," and "the democratic parties accept the leadership of the CPC and work closely with it at socialist projects." "The political foundation of cooperation between the CPC and the democratic parties is insistence on the CPC leadership and the Four Cardinal Principles," the document adds.[37] As the *People's Daily* put it, the system of "multi-party cooperation" is a "creation born out of the synthesis of Marxism–Leninism and the Chinese revolution and socialist construction."[38] At a national conference on the "united front and multi-party cooperation" in 1998, Hu Jintao stressed, "facing new situations, new tasks and new tests, the CPC, as well as all democratic parties, people's organizations, and nonparty individuals within the united front, must concentrate our attention on promoting the socialist modernization, carrying out the spirit of the 15th Party Congress and the 9th National People's Congress, and implementing various major decisions." However, Hu added, "most important is the adherence to Deng Xiaoping Theory in order to ensure the correct political direction of the democratic parties."[39]

Jiang Zemin stated that the purpose of the CPC's efforts to develop the "united front" was to preserve political stability and frustrate efforts by "hostile domestic and foreign forces" to subvert the socialist system and CPC rule.[40] Deng Xiaoping had pointed to the essence of the "flower-vase politics" in early 1990: "We will never allow democratic parties to become opposition parties," and "the ban on parties should be maintained." "Why has the situation in Eastern Europe changed so rapidly?" he asked. "It happened first of all in Poland. As a result of the spread of the Solidarity Movement, a viable force of opposition took root. This quickly led to the loss of power of the Polish Communist Party. We must draw a lesson from the Polish experience. We must absolutely not allow an opposition party to take shape in China."[41]

The "flower-vase" parties are actually the CPC's satellite political organizations that follow the CPC's lead and that are completely financed by the Communist Party–state. Whenever the CPC announces a policy change, the leaders of these flower-vase parties go through the ritual of putting up their hands in support. Aside from offering support, they also provide praise for the CPC, its goals, the socialist system, the people's democratic dictatorship, Marxism–Leninism, Mao Zedong Thought, and Deng Xiaoping Theory. As Chairman of the China Democratic League Fei Xiaotong put it, multiparty cooperation suits Chinese conditions, whereas the multiparty system or two-party system in Western countries "would fundamentally not work in China."[42] All so-called "democratic parties" make it clear in their work reports addressed to their national congress that "their members must conscientiously study and carry out the spirit of the Party Congress and further seek the unity of thinking," "unite more closely around the PCC with Jiang Zemin as the core, and go all out wholeheartedly to struggle for a strong, democratic, and civilized socialist modernized country, with the guidance of Deng Xiaoping Theory."[43] What is the difference between these "democratic parties" and the CPC in goals, guiding ideologies, and central tasks? No difference.

The CPPCC status was upgraded to a certain degree in the 1990s. By 1994, 65.6 percent of the CPPCC Standing Committee members were either affiliates of the eight so-called democratic parties or other non-communist members. A special "economic sector" was added to reserve seats for 100-odd economists, state-enterprise managers, and private-sector entrepreneurs. Some of these party figures were appointed to senior positions, such as vice ministers in the State Council, and a couple of them were appointed as ministers. Various regional administrations also set aside senior positions for non-communist members. For example, about 20 such figures were slated for posts at the bureau-level or above within the Beijing municipality in 1994. Various municipal governments also formed senior think-tanks for non-communist members to provide advice on governmental affairs and to air their views on policy making.[44]

However, the CPPCC is after all window dressing for democracy and only serves as a "think-tank" or "talent bank" for the CPC.[45] Zhou Ciwu, head of the Shenzhen CPPCC, made it clear: "supervision [by the CPPCC and non-communist parties] does not mean singing rival tunes but channeling people's opinion."[46] Ye Xuanping, the Vice Chairman of the CPPCC, also pointed to the limits to the work of his consultative body. In a mid-1993 speech, in spite of his stress on the need for "letting a lot of people speak out" and ensuring that "they can say whatever they like," Ye set the basic tune: "we should do our best but not go beyond our frame of reference. We should strengthen the unity of people from various sectors." In other words, any talk and action contrary to the overall interests of unity around the CPC and political stability under CPC rule will not be allowed.[47]

It has been shown that the party is the locus of the operation of state institutions; the same will be shown later of social organizations. If any change within the system is considered necessary, it is the party leaders who decide whether such a change is tolerable or beneficial to the development of the socialist system and modernization. The decision to revamp government institutions or social organizations, or make any other reforms within the system, always comes from the party's ruling center—the Politburo or the individual paramount leader.

In short, the party continues to require the state, the military, society, and individuals to subject themselves to party leadership and policy. The party is "the core of leadership" of all state institutions and social organizations. At a national conference on the "united front and multi-party cooperation" held at the Central Party School in 1998, Hu Jintao, then President of the Party School and the Politburo standing member in charge of party organizational work and united front work, emphasized, "Deng Xiaoping Theory is the guide for all work and action of the CPC, as well as the fundamental ideological base on which the socialist patriotic united front is developed and the multi-party cooperation and political consultation system under the leadership of the Chinese Communist Party is maintained and improved."[48] During the period of the 9th NPC and CPPCC, the *People's Daily* praised the 9th NPC as a highly unified congress and called for the whole party, the whole nation and the whole people to "hold high one banner," "uphold one goal," "promote one style," "master one method," "create one environment," "adopt one strategy," and "improve one system" under the leadership of the CPC with Jiang Zemin as the core in the twenty-first century.[49]

To conclude, this chapter has examined the structure of the party–state and relationships among the party and other political institutions and organization along the five most critical empirical dimensions to demonstrate the nature, power structure, and functions of the Chinese Leninist party–state. The Leninist party–state is the pillar that sustains the CPC rule and maintains political order in contemporary China. The state-party governing principles and its ruling model are not only codified in the Chinese Constitution but also grounded in the Marxist-Leninist principles under which the state is organized and through which it is governed.

However, some reforms and changes have taken place in the past few decades since Deng Xiaoping's reform and opening policy, and these changes have complicated our understanding of the Chinese state and beg this question: Is post-Mao China still a Leninist party–state? Many scholars have used "fragmented authoritarian state,"[50] "local state corporatism,"[51] or "political decay"[52] to describe the changing nature of the Chinese state. An assessment of the nature and significance of the political change will help us to determine whether or not a fundamental change has occurred in the political character of the communist Leninist party–state regime so that we should no longer categorize China as such but as a post-communist state or something else. This will be the central task of the next chapter.

Questions for discussion

1. What is the nature and what are the hard core features of the Leninist party–state? Is the political regime of post-Mao China fundamentally different from Mao's China?

2. What are the fundamental differences between the Chinese and American political systems in terms of the relationships among various political institutions, between central and local government, political parties and government, and civilian and military authority?

3. Chinese political development has demonstrated a pattern dominated by power, ideology, and organization. What are the nature and characteristics of power, ideology, and organization in traditional China and contemporary China? What are the similiarities and differences in power, ideology, and organization in traditional and contemporary China?

Further reading

James D. Seymour, *China's Satellite Parties* (Armonk, NY: M. E. Sharpe, 1987).

Willy Wo-Lap Lam, *China after Deng Xiaoping* (New York: John Wiley & Sons, 1995).

Neil Harding, *Leninism* (Duke University Press, 1996).

Shiping Zheng, *Party vs. State in Post-1949 China: The Institutional Dilemma* (Cambridge: Cambridge University Press, 1997).

Murray Scot Tanner, *The Politics of Lawmaking in Post-Mao China: Institutions, Processes, and Democratic Prospects* (Oxford: Oxford University Press, 1999).

John Bryan Starr, *Understanding China: A Guide to China's Economy, History, and Political Structure* (New York: Hill and Wang, 2001).

10 Political development in post-Mao China

China's economic reforms and open-door policy have brought about a considerable change in many aspects of post-Mao China. However, our theoretical picture of post-Mao China and our interpretation of the nature of the post-Mao changes have been complicated and confused by contrasting situations that are coexistent in China.[1]

- Ideological campaigns are still employed while more emphasis is placed on economic development.
- The party still maintains its monopoly of power and its organizational control is still pervasive while the party–state control over people's daily lives and economic activities is relaxed.
- Party control over information and media is still tight while some civil publications are allowed within nonpolitical areas.
- Political persecutions and arrests continue while greater individual freedom is evident.
- The party still adheres to its ideological commitment while its influence on the general population is weakening. And party control over private morality is less effective than it was under Mao, while communist morality is still a whip over Chinese society and individuals.

To many people, both scholars and nonacademic analysts, post-Mao China represents a contradiction, which suggests the need to assess the changes in the last two decades and evaluate the nature of the politics regime. As Joseph Fewsmith, a leading scholar on Chinese politics, pointed out, "Any observer of contemporary China will note two seemingly contradictory facts: first, there is considerable political innovation in China, and, second, to date, none of these political reforms have gathered momentum."[2]

The Chinese political system is the area of least change in post-Mao China, compared with the economic, social, and legal areas, though the post-Mao regime has attempted some within-the-system "political reforms," including decentralization, establishment of a legal system, inclusion of the eight "democratic parties" into the political process, broadening the powers of the legislature, streamlining administration, redefining the role of party organizations and their relationships with state institutions and economic organizations, and experimenting with local grassroots elections under the party leadership, and so forth. However, to many China analysts, these reforms and changes have led to a fundamental regime change in post-Mao China— moving away from the Leninist party–state communism. Thus, they conclude that the Leninist party–state conceptualization of the current Chinese political system is no longer relevant or is outdated.

The contradiction begs the question whether post-Mao China has experienced such a "fundamental" change in the political system that the post-Mao regime has moved away from the Leninist party–state, and, in other words, whether a new political system has come into being due to these reforms and changes. The answer to the question depends on how we define the hard core of the political regime and the key indicators of a fundamental change at the regime level. For example, communist China has always repeated the cycles of streamlining–bloating and decentralizing–recentralizing both under the Mao regime and the post-Mao regime. Such institutional changes and rationalizations are clearly not the indicators of a fundamental change in the hard core of the Leninist party–state. Therefore, the answer to the question requires a coherent theory of regime identity or a clear conceptual framework by which we are able to distinguish between systemic and developmental changes and between a change of a political regime and a change within a political regime.

Let us recall Chapter 2 and Chapter 9, which have constructed a conceptual model of real-world Leninist party–state communism on a categorization to distinguish the "hard core" of the party state from other operative features, and establish the criteria for assessing the nature of political change in post-Mao China. According to the model, the above changes only suggest the post-Mao regime's attempt at institutionalization of the Leninist party–state and rationalization of the political structure and its administrative, legislative, and legal systems, rather than liquidation of the party's power, ideology, and organization, or political liberalization from the party–state power. Rationalization is a central concept used by Max Weber to refer to institutional changes involving differentiation, specialization, and standardization, and the bureaucratization of political and social organizations.[3]

In post-Mao China, political changes are institutional and administrative in nature, and political reforms are rationalized by nature. This has been more associated with the adjustment of action means and the functioning of the regime at the operative level. The post-Mao regime has retained the Leninist party–state hard core, the party's vanguard status as a total representation of the working class, new classes of the production force, and goal culture ("Three Represents"), the pervasiveness of party organizations, and party control and domination in every sector of the state structure all constitute the hard core of the Chinese Leninist party–state and account for the origin, dynamics, and essence of the communist regime. Only changes associated with the hard core components of the regime are key indicators of a fundamental type at regime level. Distinguishing between the two levels or the two different types of changes is key to our understanding and assessment of the nature of political changes in post-Mao China.

Post-Mao "political reform" and political development

The first aspect to be examined is the so-called post-Mao political reform: Has this political reform made any fundamental or systemic change to the Leninist party–state? By "political reform" the post-Mao leadership has never meant a transition from party-led party–state communism, but primarily the modernization and professionalization of the party–state institution. The so-called "political reform" is not aimed at systemic change but at so-called "self-improvement" and "moral self-restraint" of the party and government. This goal is no different from a Utopia in which government is expected to be self-disciplined, self-restrained, and self-improving without any real external checks—a system of checks and balances, constitutional democracy, and rule of law.[4] The aim of political reform, as Deng Xiaoping clearly prescribed for China, is to "raise working efficiency and overcome bureaucratism" and to make party–state cadres at various levels "better educated, professionally more competent, and younger." Its content has included "separation of the functioning of the party and the government," "decentralization of power," and "streamlining the administrative structure," but "westernization and liberalization," "separation of powers," and "Western parliamentary system" in political reforms are not allowed.[5] The CPC reiterated the "Five Nos" (*wudebugao*五个不搞):

> We have made a solemn declaration that we will not employ a system of multiple parties holding office in rotation; diversify our guiding thought; separate executive, legislative and judicial powers; use a bicameral or federal system; or carry out privatisation."[6]

This is crucial for determining the nature of the reform and its limitations. Particularly, the post-Mao leadership emphasizes that the "Four Cardinal Principles" are a fundamental prerequisite to socialist reforms and the Four Modernizations. These Four Cardinal Principles, which are the most fundamental aspects of the post-Mao regime's continuity of the Leninist party–state, determine the direction, scope, content, and limit of the post-Mao reforms. This also means that changes brought about by the reforms have not made those defining core features of the Leninist party–state insignificant.[7]

The "Four Cardinal Principles" are by no means considered by the post-Mao regime merely as rituals but as defining core elements of the system, and any attempt to weaken these principles has never been tolerated. During the 1980s the top reformist leaders attempted to open more political space or create a "more relaxed political environment," such as allowing more toleration of debate on political reforms, more press freedom, and the lifting of political taboos within the party policy line. Their limited liberal reform efforts had the unintended effect of ideological decay and increasing student and dissident activities. These reformist leaders and their political allies were removed from office by Deng Xiaoping and the party elders. Steps toward a more "relaxed" political environment were quickly reversed in the late 1980s. Instead, legitimization of the regime and individual leaders was sought through traditional political forms, such as the leadership cult and the resurrection of Maoism. We have observed a more conservative backlash in every aspect of political life.

Political reform determines the nature and degree of political change. However, there has been no evidence to prove any essential change in the political system and the power structure since reform in 1978. Post-Mao reform, either under Deng, Jiang or under Hu, has pursued a pattern of economic modernization with no attempt to fundamentally transform the Chinese communist party–state political system. Political reforms were officially regarded as a means of facilitating economic reforms, and served the purpose of strengthening and improving the Party leadership and governing capacity. Party leadership claimed that successful and further economic reform required "social stability and unity," and should be carried out only under party leadership. Thus any tendency towards political liberalization and democratization was seen as a threat to such leadership and stability. Democratic reform had little place on the political agenda.[8]

From the very beginning of Deng's reform in 1978, the Chinese party leadership never intended to have a true and thoroughgoing reform of the political system, but attempted to ease domestic conflicts and serious political tension between the Party and society through a readjustment of economic policy, or later economic liberalization and administrative rationalization, and continued to maintain the party's power in political life while relaxing control on daily life and the economic activities of citizens. Therefore, the focus of the reform policy was not on the political realm but on the economic realm, which served to facilitate economic development and attract foreign investment; the focus was on economic liberalization and not on privatization of ownership in the economic system and democratization of the political system, which would enhance and guarantee democracy and individual freedoms and rights.[9] The post-Mao communist regime has attempted to graft a "market economy" on a party–state political structure originally designed for a socialist planned economy. Such a reform strategy has led to the incompatibility between the requirement of a market economy and the political structure, between the market economy and state ownership, as China's Premier Wen Jiabao recently recognized in an interview with CNN in October 2010.[10]

Political reforms have been based on rationality and pragmatism, and are administrative in nature, such as separating functions of party and state, decentralizing decision making, streamlining administration, increasing work efficiency, and regularizing the legal system. Decentralization and rationalization of administrative power and regularization of the legal system were not implemented for the purpose of systemic and structural transformation, but for more rational economic decision making and a freer market. Therefore, it was not a systemic reform and involved no significant and fundamental transformation of the political system, power structure, and ideology. Therefore, as Tatsumi Okabe points out, "it was not a regime transition, but a within-system change (*tizhi gaige*体制改革)."[11] Even these rationalization programs in administrative, legislative, and legal systems are slow and remain weakly institutionalized, and the actual achievements are meager.[12]

A major reform step taken at the 9th National People's Congress (NPC) following the 15th Party Congress was the government restructuring program intended to streamline the size of central government to 29 departments. The reduction of size at this time is comparable to the one in the Cultural Revolution under Mao, during which the standing bodies of the State Council were reduced to 33, among which 13 bodies were actually under the control of the Party Central Military Commission and the "Central Leading Group of the Cultural Revolution," and the governmental employees were reduced by two-thirds.[13] Does this suggest that Mao's regime is less communist, or less capable than the post-Mao regime? This is another perfect example that suggests that the change in governmental size does not prove a systemic or fundamental change of the Chinese communist regime. This new plan at the 9th NPC involved greater changes. However, the purpose of the government restructuring program is to "transform functions, put relations in order, streamline administration, and improve efficiency."[14] Within four years, from 1993 to 1997, the departments and standing bodies of the State Council increased from 68 to 86, and the nonstanding bodies increased from 49 to 85; on average, 14 standing and nonstanding bodies increased per year.[15] In fact, the sixth governmental restructuring did not break the "vicious circle" of history, but just repeated it. The 11th National People's Congress in 2008 was the most recent major government restructuring and streamlining, which received wide attention in the world. However, looking only at central government, in 2011 the State council has 27 ministries, one state assets administration commission, 16 agencies under its direct supervision, 14 public institutions under its direct supervision (Xinhua News Agency, China Academy of Social Sciences, China Securities Regulatory Commission, etc.), 22 bureaus under ministerial direct supervision, totaling 80 organizations. Besides, there are 28 consultative and coordinating organs. We can simply count over 100 central government organs that rely on the state budgetary spending. Not to mention the huge duplicated and overlapped organizations at all levels.[16] In short, the Chinese communist regime has undertaken major government institutional restructuring at least seven times since the communist takeover in 1949, but it has always repeated the circle of "streamlining—bloating—streamlining again—bloating again." The purpose of the restructuring program is not to reduce the strength of the state, or to weaken the party leadership, or to promote the separation of party and government, but to cut away overstaffed administration, improve civil service, professionalize cadres or staff of governmental organizations, and simplify overlapping administrative organizations that reduce government efficiency and stand in the way of economic growth. The principle or slogan is clearly stated as "streamlining, unification, and efficiency."

In fact, instead of the separation of party and state, a major setback since the 14th Party Congress was to reinforce the "cross leadership" of the party and the state, referring to the fact that politburo members and other top leaders can concurrently take up positions in the party, government, legislature, and the Chinese People's Political Consultative Conference (CPPCC). Jiang Zemin or Hu Jintao is head of the state, the party, and the army—President of the state, General Secretary of the CPC Central Committee, and Chairman of the Central Military Commission (CMC)—in addition to many other substantial and ceremonial titles. Other Politburo members double as heads of the executive or the legislature.

All the key party leaders also occupy senior positions in the government. While the party's constitution provides that the party congress is responsible for setting political policy, that authority in fact rests with a half dozen or so top party leaders who are members of the Politburo Standing Committee of the Party Central Committee. Under Deng's regime, this small group had to refer all major decisions to Deng Xiaoping.[17] The party has two means for ensuring that its policies are implemented by government officials. The first is the power of appointment, since at each government level appointments are the responsibility of the party organization at the level just above—the central party organization appoints provincial officials, while provincial party organizations, in turn, appoint officials at the city and county level. Second, the performance of officials appointed by the party is then supervised by party organizations. At each government level and in public enterprises, a leading party group or a party committee supervises political correctness and ensures that party policies are carried out.

In fact, since the 15th Party Congress, in an effort to strengthen and improve party work in the party–state organs and bring the party grassroots organizations into full play, the Politburo of the Party Central Committee issued "Guidelines for the Party Grassroots Organizations Build-up in the Party and State Organs" and asked the party committees and the party leading groups in all provinces, all autonomous zones, all municipalities directly under the central government, all major military regions, all departments and commissions of the central party organs and the central state organs, all general departments of the Central Military Commission, all army services, and all people's organizations to carry out the guidelines without delay.[18]

The "black box" operation of the Party's National Congress suggests a big retrenchment in "intraparty democracy," of which the CPC claims to be the model for the whole nation. The election of the members of the Central Committee is separately held in hotels where various delegations or deputy groups stay during the party's congress. No information exchange is allowed between various delegations or deputy groups during this period of time. In principle, deputies are not allowed to meet visitors or go home in the course of the congress. Specially designed envelopes containing the official slate and the election form are picked up by specially appointed congress work personnel from Zhong Nan Hai (headquarters of the Party Central Committee of the CPC) and then sent to the hotels to distribute among the deputies. Deputies have no idea of the content of the envelopes until they open them up.[19] Such a "black box" operation of the election suggests no fundamental change of the communist party–state system. This party congress operation mechanism applies to all party congresses and people's congresses at all levels.

As discussed in Chapter 9, the CPC continues to be the Leninist Vanguard Party. The CPC leadership continues to require the whole party to be subject unconditionally to its leadership but also requires the state, the military, society, and individuals to be subject to the party's leadership and policy. The "Three Represents" (*sange daibiao*三个代表) codified in the Constitution gives the party's vanguard status of not only the working class but also all social classes, claiming total representation of the entire nation and total guidance of national goals, and claiming to shoulder a historical mission of socialist construction and realization of the communist ultimate goal.

The party continues to exercise the principle of "democratic centralism" (minzhu jizhongzhi民主集中制) in all sectors of the state and central–local governments. Party and state are closely intertwined and their functions are largely combined into one body, with a leadership role reserved for the party. In both horizontal and vertical power relationships, the party is the center of the power structure, and controls every level of government through an array of party organizations from top to bottom. The People's Liberation Army (PLA) and other armed forces have always been considered as a "strong pillar of the people's democratic dictatorship," and subject to the absolute command of the CPC and the Central Military Commission (CMC). The PLA has extensive political, social, and economic duties to serve as "the defender and the builder of the socialist system and modernization."

The relationship between the CPC and the People's Congress remains fundamentally unchanged. The CPC's decisions, norms, and rules govern the relationship between the CPC and the NPC. The CPC sets up the guidelines and policies for people's congresses to carry out according to its central tasks at each historical phase. The CPC proposes legislative bills for important state affairs directly to the NPC or its Standing Committee and other special legislative committees, and such a practice is duplicated at all levels of the party committees and people's congresses. The CPC exercises leadership of the routine work of the NPC Standing Committee and those at lower levels through specific directives or decisions. The CPC exercises the leadership of the election work of people's congresses. The CPC exercises the leadership of people's congress sessions. All major leaders of the party and governmental organizations must be in charge of some work during people's congress sessions. The CPC exercises the organizational leadership of people's congresses. The important personnel decisions such as people's congress deputies, leading members of congress standing committees, candidates for leading positions in state institutions, and responsible leaders of the standing committees of people's congresses are all made by party committees. In practice, all the leading positions of people's congresses are held by party secretaries, deputy secretaries, or party committee members. Therefore, the Chinese legislature, as a political institution of the Leninist party–state system, continues to serve the party's goals, acts as a rubber stamp on the party's policy change, and provides legitimation for the party rule, though it is declared as the "supreme power body" of the Chinese political structure.

The relationship between the CPC and other "Democratic Parties" at the CPPCC also remains fundamentally unchanged. The post-Mao regime has reinstituted "multi-party cooperation" into its political operation, and emphasized the enhanced role of the CPPCC. However, the CPPCC serves as a political instrument of the party–state to "incorporate" (*xina* 吸纳) the eight so-called "democratic parties," which are actually subordinate satellites of the CPC. These so-called "parties" have no independence and must accept the leadership of the CPC. The political foundation of cooperation between the CPC and the democratic parties is based on the CPC leadership and the Four Cardinal Principles. The purpose of the CPC's efforts to develop the "united front" was to help strengthen the unity of people from various sectors, maintain political stability, and support CPC rule. Therefore, the CPPCC is after all window dressing for democracy and only serves as a "think-tank" or "talent bank" for the CPC. In short, the party continues to require the state, the military, and society to be subject to the party leadership and policy. The party is "the core of leadership" of all state institutions and social organizations.

As discussed above, major core elements of and many of the political practices of the Leninist party–state still remain essentially unchanged. Although some institutional factors might be functional in determining short-term policy and personnel issues, they operate within the political and structural constraints that stem from the basic nature or essence of the Leninist party–state system.

More recent political development under Hu Jintao

The 16th Party Congress in 2002 officially marked the beginning of Hu Jintao's era. Some changes have taken place under his time of leadership in response to new challenges facing the ruling party. As a result of three decades of economic reform, economic freedom has expanded and private business has boomed. However, economic success has also created new problems due to the lack of political reform. The market-driven reform under party–state rule led to serious government corruption; social injustice; a widening of income gaps and regional disparities; collapse of the old social, health, and income safety networks; public unrest; and a worsening environment. All these problems have posed serious challenges to the ruling party, jeopardized political stability, and cast a shadow on the moral foundation of market-oriented economic reform.[20]

The World Bank has developed a Political Stability Indicator (PSI) as part of its World Governance Indicators (WGIs). The PSI measures the perceptions of the likelihood that a government in power will be destabilized or overthrown by possibly unconstitutional and/or violent means. A negative value indicates a high level of instability. In 2000, China's PSI was –0.01. By 2006, that figure has dropped to –0.37, which indicated a worsening situation in China's political stability level.[21] In 2003, there were 58,000 "mass incidents" reported by the government, and in 2005 over 74,000 incidents of public unrest were reported.[22] In 2008, there were an estimated 124,000 instances of "mass unrest" in China.[23] However, despite the increase in the number of political unrest incidents reported, China has remained relatively stable.[24] Nevertheless, these numbers should send an alarming signal to the party leaders.

The 16th CPC Party Congress, held in November 2002, and the 10th National People's Congress, held in March 2003, completed the power transfer from the "third generation" to the "fourth". Since many key leaders are protégés of Jiang Zemin, there is continuity in the party's policies. Therefore, the new leaders are not going to "rock the boat."[25] However, they seem to have reached a consensus that reform has reached a critical point where some policy adjustments are needed. There are growing interests in an alternative development model which emphasizes sustainable development, more equitable distribution of wealth, and the creation of a "harmonious society." It seems that some changes were going to happen, though not in a radical form.[26] We have observed some superficial changes in official declarations but not much in effect.

The new generation leadership under Hu Jintao has begun to search for solutions and directions. "Building a Harmonious Society" based on "Scientific Outlook of Development" has become a new catch phrase and slogan in political and academic discourse in China.[27] The new concept and goal are viewed by many as a significant departure from the efficiency-oriented developmental strategy, and a "model for the world."[28] However, the focal point of this departure is mainly economic, social, and environmental, aiming to solve the problems as mentioned above without changing the Leninist party–state rule. In practice, however, the implementation of new policies and programs has achieved very limited success in those arenas, and those problems have remained unresolved.

It is in this context the 17th Party Congress was held in October 2007. The 17th Party Congress declared to set the historical course and path of "socialist democratic building," featuring gradual, phased-in, grassroots self-governance, and intra-party democratization. The guidelines and slogans were set as follows.

• Developing the "four democracies," i.e., "democratic elections, democratic decision making, democratic management, and democratic oversight."

- Developing grassroots democracy, namely "Selfs"—"self-management, self-service, self-education, and self-oversight."
- Furthering administrative reform and building a service-orientated government, namely the "four separations," i.e. separating the functions of government from those of enterprises, state assets management authorities, public institutions and market-based intermediaries.
- Establishing a system of checks and balances, stressing that "power must be exercised in the sunshine to ensure that it is exercised correctly."
- The party should become democratic first. The party will reform the intra-party electoral system and improve the system for nominating candidates and electoral methods at the grassroots level.

These party guidelines and slogans have generated high expectations and exciting discussions for almost eight years, both within and outside China, about how political reform has been put on the party agenda. However, these reforms are set within the limit of maintaining the Leninist party–state instead of undermining it, with a goal for its "self-improvement." Hu Jintao, in a speech at the ceremony in December 2008 marking the thirtieth anniversary of China's adopting the economic policy of reform and opening up, elaborated on what kind of political reform the party has pursued, which deserves a long quote (Box 10.1).

Hu's political report actually reiterates and defines the nature, direction, and principle of political reform and claims that "socialism with Chinese characteristics" depends on "the leadership of the Party." In fact, Hu Jintao, Jiang Zemin, and Deng Xiaoping have talked about remarkably similar things about the "political reform." Therefore, the three keystones of the Leninist party–state remain fundamentally unchanged, and come down from its Leninist or Maoist origin. A comparison of the CPC under Mao's regime and under the post-Mao regime can be further illustrated in Table 10.1.

To achieve the goal of self-improvement and building social political system with Chinese characteristics, the emphasis has been on restoring the party's

---

Box 10.1 The party's definition of China's political reform

China's political reform is characterized by the self-improvement and development of the socialist political system. We must adhere to the path of political development under socialism with Chinese characteristics, integrate the leadership of the Party, the position of the people as masters of the country and the rule of law, maintain the features and advantages of the socialist political system, and proceed from national conditions . . .[29]

Hu Jintao

Table 10.1 The CPC under Mao's regime and under the post-Mao regime

	Mao's regime	Deng's regime
Power	Monopolistic and personalistic (based on the principle of "Democratic Centralism")	Monopolistic and oligarchic (based on the principle of "Democratic Centralism")
Ideology	Strong commitment, exclusive, compulsory, and coherent	Strong commitment, exclusive, compulsory, and less coherent
Goal	Twin-goals: industrialization and communism	Twin-goal: modernization and communism
Means	Mass mobilization and universal participation of all social members in the political system via constant and direct mass political campaigns for carrying out political objectives	Bureaucratic rationalization, combined with limited mass mobilization and participation in the political system via party-controlled mass organizations, political institutions, and state-licensed or controlled social organizations
Leadership	Infallible charisma (Mao)	Infallible charisma (Deng)
Membership	Elitist vanguard	Elitist vanguard
Legitimacy sources	Communist revolution and Marxist–Leninist–Maoist ideology	Communist revolution and Marxist–Leninist–Maoist–Deng–Jiang-Hu ideology

past values and practices of the earlier stages of the communist movement and on using "traditions" to address current problems. The party urged the party–state cadres to uphold the ultimate ideal and firm faith in communism, strengthen the "party nature," resist various temptations, and try to be exemplary models in upholding and developing the Party's fine tradition and style. The emphasis on the "party traditions" is intended to improve "party style." "Party style" (*Dangfeng*) refers to a combination of all the prescribed political norms and relationships crucial to the party's operations and the maintenance of organizational coherence and obedience. The various elements of party style were first fully articulated in the early 1940s, and it is this articulation that is regarded as establishing party "traditions." If a tradition is to have any current political relevance, then it implies continuity of application. Emphasis on "party style" suggests a continued insistence on its vanguard character and on the qualitative difference between the CPC and other types of political organizations. However, this emphasis on party "traditions" is not considered to conflict with the "shift in focus" on economic modernization. Instead, it is considered crucial for the party's survival in the economic marketization and liberalization to offset the threat posed to organizational discipline and ideological purity.

There has been no genuine separation of party and state since post-Mao reforms and no fundamental change in terms of the core features of the Leninist party–state. A comparison of party–state relationship under Mao's regime and under the post-Mao regime is illustrated in Table 10.2.

According to Pan Wei, a Peking University professor, China's supreme power rests on the Politburo Standing Committee of the Communist Party of China, and China's political structure is led and controlled by the Chinese Communist Party in six major ways.

1. Communist Party and its core decision-making departments, such as the Central Committee of the Communist Party of China, Politburo of the Communist Party of China, Propaganda Department of the Communist Party of China, Central Commission for Discipline Inspection of the Communist Party of China, Political and Legislative Affairs Committee of the Communist Party of China, Organization Department of the Communist Party of China Central Committee command all sectors of the state.
2. The all-powerful National People's Congress has always been under the control of the CPC.
3. All the PRC governmental departments are under the control of the CPC.
4. People's Liberation Army is under the control of the CPC.
5. CPPCC is under the control of the CPC.

Table 10.2 Party–state relationship under Mao's regime and under the post-Mao regime

	Mao's regime	*Post-Mao regime*
Government/ regime/state	The distinction between the three is blurred and fused through the CPC. The CPC constructs and molds government, regime, and state according to its own ideology, principles, norms, rules, image and requirements	Unaltered
Party–state apparatus	Party apparatus is hierarchically organized, superior to and intertwined with the state apparatus	Unaltered
State institutions	Fusion of powers of various state institutions under the CPC leadership	Unaltered
Party dictatorship	CPC dictates politics, and party organizations lead, dominate and penetrate every sector of the state	Unaltered

6.   All the semi-governmental departments, such as trade unions, women's associations, communist youth groups, are all under control of the CPC.[30]

Under Hu Jintao, the PLA has continued to be under the control of the CPC without any change. As early as 1938, Mao Zedong stated: "our principle is that the Party commands the gun, and the gun must never be allowed to command the Party."[31] Deng, Jiang, and Hu have made remarkably similar remarks: the army must be under the party's absolute command. On April 1 2009, General Li Jinai, the PLA's top political commissar who sits on the 11-member Chinese Communist Party Central Committee, reiterated that People's Liberation Army must continue taking orders exclusively from the Communist Party. In an essay published in the party's official theoretical journal, *Qiushi*, he stated:

- "Unshakingly uphold the basic principle and system of the party's absolute leadership over the army"
- "Resolutely oppose the wrong thinking of 'army-party separation, depoliticization, and army nationalization'"
- "At all times, make the party flag the army's flag and . . . in all things listen to the commands of the party, Central Military Commission and President Hu."[32]

We have examined political change in post-Mao China along the most critical empirical dimensions and demonstrated that the post-Mao regime has remained in a fundamental sense a communist party–state. The post-Mao regime has attempted to resurrect the political tradition and political theory of the mid-1950s and based the political doctrine of the post-Mao regime on the "Four Cardinal Principles" which are proclaimed as defining the core elements of the post-Mao regime and as a fundamental prerequisite to the realization of the Four Modernizations. The Four Cardinal Principles have fundamentally prescribed the direction, scope, content, and limits of the post-Mao reform. The post-Mao regime has continued to consolidate and institutionalize the totalitarian party–state apparatus that has come down from Mao's era. There has been no genuine political liberalization, but "rationalization" of the government in many ways. It continues to be the party that decides—unilaterally and unaccountably—what should be done and what steps or measures should be taken. The state institutions and social organizations are established and institutionalized as an appendage of the party, which is consistent with the Leninist party–state. State agencies are generally façades for corresponding party organizations wherein the real power lies. State institutions and social organizations act as party instruments in carrying out the wishes of the party leadership, while the party acts to ensure its predominance in all aspects of society—political, legal, economic, social, cultural, ideological, and military arenas. All state institutions, including the NPC, the CPPCC, and the PLA are instruments of the party, which the party either disregarded entirely (under

Mao's regime) or manipulates for its own ends (under the post-Mao regime). Moreover, in the post-Mao era, the security forces, synthesized with the military, are greatly strengthened and heavily politicized so that they can defend the party and its ruling order against real and imagined threat and opposition. The military and the security forces serve as sword and shield of the party. A single official party also exists in some authoritarian regimes. However, unlike the communist party–state, the party in authoritarian regimes "generally lacks the militancy, political and ideological vanguard status and may compete with the state, military and private organizations rather than penetrating and dominating them."[33]

Therefore, the post-Mao regime retains the defining characteristics of all communist regimes in the making and maintains a Leninist party that is the locus or—to use the regime's official terminology—"the core of leadership" or " the political nucleus" for all state institutions and social organizations. China has not made any significant political change from the communist party–state regime in any of those fields despite considerable economic change and some administrative and institutional changes made in the last three decades.

Questions for discussion

1. Can "self-improvement" and "moral self-restraint" provide sufficient moral bases, effective mechanisms, and sustainable legitimation for party–state rule in the long term?
2. Has the post-Mao regime moved away from the communist party–state or continued to retain the hard core of ideas, institutions, and practices of the communist party–state. In other words, has there been a change of regime or change within the regime? If so in what degree or kind?

Further reading

Kevin J. O'Brien, *Reform without Liberalization: China's National People's Congress and the Politics of Institutional Change* (Cambridge: Cambridge University Press, 1990).

Baogang Guo, *China's Quest for Political Legitimacy: The New Equity-Enhancing Politics* (Lanham, MD: Rowman & Littlefield-Lexington, 2010).

Zaijun Yuan, *The Failure of China's "Democratic" Reforms* (Lanham, MD: Rowman & Littlefield-Lexington, 2011).

Part VI

Chinese legal and legislative systems

11 The Chinese legal and legislative systems

This chapter will examine two aspects of the Chinese party–state structure: the legal system (law enforcement) and the legislative system (law making), both of which are modeled on the former Soviet Union, and continue to retain the core institutional features in the interlocking power relationship of the Leninist party–state. In theory, the legislature has the power to make laws independently while the courts have the authority to administer the law independently. However, in practice, both institutions are created by the Communist Party of China (CPC) in accordance with its political ideology, political principles, political needs, and changing policies. Both must follow the leadership, directions, and policies of the CPC. Therefore, the two systems—legislature and courts at all levels of government—operate in subordination to, not independently of, the party leadership in the confining party–state institutional context.[1] Laws, legislations, and legal regulations have been seen as the ruling instruments of the "Socialist Proletariat Dictatorship" and of the leadership of the CPC, and now are also viewed as the necessary instruments for governing and regulating the increasingly complicated and pluralistic social organizations, social relationships and business interactions of a society in transition and to accommodate the ruling party's reform policies and goals of economic and social development. To understand recent changes in Chinese legal and legislative systems, we must first study the points of departure from which they have evolved in the past three decades, and to what extent the reform and change have impacted the nature and operation of the legislature and the court.

The Chinese legal system

With the establishment of the People's Republic of China in 1949, the Chinese legal system was created on the Soviet model, in which the judiciary was not independent from the other branches of government, but an integral part of the executive branch under the Leninist party–state leadership. The legal system is undergoing gradual reform and adapting to the needs of market economic reform and the open-door policy. However, the Chinese legal system has retained the supremacy of the party leadership and thus remains fundamentally unchanged to the present day.

In contrast to the West, China's legal system is different in several important respects. For example, the CPC stresses "rule by law" (法制) or "governing the nation according to law" (依法治国), rather than "rule of law" (法治), which refers to "constitutional restraints on the exercise of power" and the law is supreme and all is equal before the law. The CPC plays a leading role in "building a socialist rule by law state" (建设社会主义法制国家). The party–state institution makes the laws and implements them; the judiciary is not independent; the presumption of innocence for the accused is not well established; mediation plays a greater role than in the West; and so forth. Moreover, there are some more significant differences between China and the West in terms of institutional setting and legal process.

People's Courts (人民法院) are one of the judicial organs of the Chinese government. China has a four-level court system. China's Supreme People's Court (最高人民法院) is the highest judicial organ, and it is responsible to the NPC and its Standing Committee under Article 128 of the Constitution. Although the NPC is the highest organ of state power, its operation is actually under the direct leadership of the CPC Politburo. Under the Supreme People's Court are three levels of People's Courts, higher, intermediate, and basic level, which correspond to the three levels of government in China: provincial, prefecture, and county,[2] and serve as their judicial arms that have jurisdiction over legal affairs. *High people courts* exist in provinces (省), autonomous regions (自治区), and special municipalities (直辖市) under the direct leadership of the central government, *Intermediate people's courts* exist (直辖市) at prefecture-level government (地区), autonomous prefectures (自治州), autonomous leagues (自治盟), and prefecture-level cities (地级市). *Basic level people's courts* exist in counties (县), county-level cities(县级市), towns (乡镇), urban districts (市辖区), and banners (旗). There are some special courts that handle legal affairs relating to the military, maritime, railroad transportation, and forestry (Figure 11.1).

China's Supreme Court has no authority to review the constitutionality of legislation and government policy, though it has the power to explain what a given law is or is not and how a given law should be interpreted according to directives of the party–state leadership, such as the Politburo (政治局) or the State Council (国务院). The People's Congress, under the CPC leadership, makes the law and at the same time retains the power of constitutional review. The CPC combines party–state–legislative bodies into one, which is called "yixing heyi" (议行合一), or the convergence of legislative and executive branches under the CPC leadership. The judiciary is in fact an integral part of the executive branch of the government at all levels, and like other political institutions, it must be subject to the CPC leadership.

People's courts at each level are composed of a president, vice-president, presiding judges, deputy presiding judges, and a number of ordinary judges. Within each court, there are several divisions, such as civil, economic, criminal, administrative and enforcement divisions, and each division has a chief and

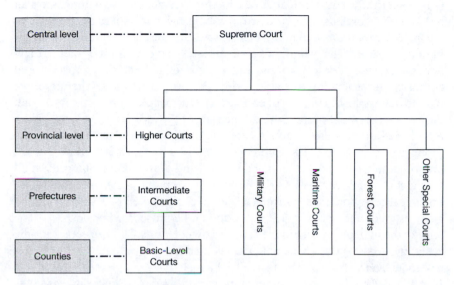

Figure 11.1 The Chinese court system.

several deputy chiefs. They are considered as government officials or civil servants at different ranks. Judicial committees are established at each court which is composed of the court presidents, division chiefs, and presiding judges, headed by the president. Judicial committees discuss and decide all major cases or law suits and judicial work of the court. It is nominally responsible to the people's congress, but is in practice subject to the leadership and supervision of the commission or leading group of political and legal affairs (政法委) of the party committee at the corresponding level. That is to say, courts at each level are subject to the dual leadership of party committees and governments at the corresponding level. The judicial process, though claimed to be independent, is in fact subject to party control, policy, and discipline, as well as to the executive power. Judges and all judicial officers are now theoretically selected and appointed by the corresponding people's congresses. In practice the appointment is overseen by the party committee and must meet the political and ideological standard to ensure that only reliable Communist Party members become judges and president of people's courts, although professional education and competence are more emphasized than before as in the selection of cadres in other governmental and public organizations. Judges are politicized, bureaucratized, and placed in the category of "state cadres," and their salary and other state welfare corresponds to their rank as state cadres in the bureaucratic administration, such as ministerial or vice-ministerial, provincial or vice-provincial, divisional or deputy-divisional, and so forth. In such a hierarchical structure, judges are subordinated to presiding judges who are subordinated to the presidents of courts. Different ranks not only mean different political status in the bureaucratic structure but also reflect the hierarchical subservience of subordinates to superiors.[3]

People's procuratorates (人民检察院) constitute the other arm of the Chinese judicial system. The people's procuratorates have a similar hierarchical structure to the people's courts, and consist of a four-level prosecutorial authority corresponding to each level of the people's courts. Therefore, we will not repeat the description of each level of the people's procuratorates. But, they serve important purposes and functions of the judiciary in China. Under Article 129 of the Constitution, the people's procuratorates are "state organs for legal supervision." The Supreme People's Procuratorate is the highest prosecutorial agency exercising and supervising prosecutorial authority at all provincial and local levels. Procuratorates examine cases scheduled for investigation by public security agencies to decide whether a suspect should be arrested or not, and whether a case should be prosecuted or not.[4]

Like the judicial process in the former Soviet Union, Chinese courts handle cases by a collegium (collegial panels) consisting of judges and people's assessors, and a judge presiding at a trial assisted by "people's assessors" (人民陪审员), who have duties similar to jurors and are drawn from citizens in the community. The people's jurors can only participate in the first trial of criminal cases. There are people's assessors in courts at all levels, and they do not rule on matters of law but can decide on a verdict together with the presiding judge to allow or deny objections. However, people's assessors are provided by people's congresses and selected by the courts, and they lack an independent role like jurors in the British or American judicial process, in which jurors make an independent assessment of facts and make an independent decision (verdict) on whether or not a criminal accusation is justifiable. If no proof of crime is found, the proceedings should end; if the defendant is found guilty, the judge will apply the law to the case and impose sentences according to the law (sentencing). However, in the Chinese judicial process, there is no clear distinction between the role and function of the judge and the jury. They all make judgment and verdict on facts and apply the law to sentencing. By law or in theory, both people's jurors and people's judges should have the same right and power in court proceedings, but in reality and in practice they do not. Since the loyalty of people's assessors is expected to be with the people and the collective interest of the state, people's assessors usually agree with or simply follow what judges say or do in the court proceedings. Besides, whether or not to form a mixed court composed of a judge and jurors is the court decision, and selection of jurors rests with the court. Hereby the court can use its judicial power at its discretion, which leads to judicial corruption, unfairness in judgments, and other serious problems. However, the most important political implication in such a party–state system is to allow the party to have an influence on the court decisions and subject the court proceedings to political pressure and interference from outside the court. Important high-profile cases or politically sensitive cases are actually decided politically by the party committee and can be easily carried out in such a party–state institutional setting. When the cases are considered important or difficult, the final decision is made by the judicial committee rather than the collegial panels that are composed of three to seven judges. This device is often used to interfere with the function and decision of collegial panels that preside over major cases. Other minor criminal cases, simple civil cases, and cases involving economic disputes can be handled by a single judge, and sometimes jurors selected by the judge participate.[5]

Public security bureaus (公安局), e.g. the police, have the responsibility of maintaining law, public safety, and social order. Specifically, according to official pronouncement, the responsibilities of the public security agencies in China include the prevention, suppression, and investigation of criminal activities; fight against terrorist activities; maintenance of social security and order; fight against behaviors jeopardizing social order; control over traffic, fire, and dangerous objects; administration of household registration, identification cards, exit-and-entry, stay and travel of foreigners in China; maintenance of border security; protection of state-assigned persons, venues, and facilities; control of gatherings, parades, and demonstrations; security inspection on public information networks; supervision and instruction of security work in state organizations, mass organizations, enterprises, and important construction sites; and instruction in crime prevention work by community security commissions. The Ministry of Public Security (MPS) is the highest authority of the public security organs and a functional body under the State Council. Public security departments (公安厅) are established in provinces, autonomous regions, and special municipalities. Bureaus, sub-bureaus, and divisions are established at different levels of local government, such as cities, sub-regions of cities, counties, towns, banners, etc., under the direct leadership of their superior public security agencies and corresponding local government and the party committee at that level.[6] The basic units are dispatched police stations (派出所) in urban streets and rural towns, which carry out the responsibilities of surveillance, investigation, registration of residential households, registration of foreigners who travel to, reside, or work in China, and other police tasks provided for them by their superior police bureaus or sub-bureaus and the local government.[7] The division of responsibilities among the public security bureaus, the people's procuratorates, and the people's courts is as follows: the public security bureaus are responsible for the investigation of crimes and the arrest of criminals, the people's procuratorates are responsible for approving arrests and prosecuting criminal cases, and the people's courts are responsible for trying the cases.[8]

Public security bureaus administer the institutions and practices of "sheltering for examination" (收审 *shoushen*)[9] and "reform-through-labor camps" (劳改农场 *laogai nongchang*),[10] both of which are legacies of Mao's China, and continue to play an important role in maintaining social order and social control. Under the system of "sheltering for examination," police can detain people as "suspects" for up to three months without the permission of courts, and detained suspects are not allowed to see a lawyer or even a family member. If the police investigation needs more time, they can always get approval from the people's congress. Such a system allows the police authority to detain anyone and do whatever they want without going through the courts. Many detained suspects, if found guilty of minor criminal offences for which criminal punishment (刑事处罚) is deemed unwarranted, will receive "administrative punishments" (行政处罚) and be sent to "reform-through-labor camps," which were created in the 1950s, and modelled on the former Soviet Union, and continue in China today.[11] Both are administered by the public security bureaus and subdivisions. It is in this area that the police can be considered as "extrajudicial power" that has little judicial oversight and external supervision. This has become increasingly controversial and attracted critical attention in both domestic and international society.[12] In 1996, "sheltering for examination" was abolished by an amendment to the Criminal Procedure Law, and since then it has been no longer used for arrest and detention by the police. However, the abolition is partial, because certain elements of the "sheltering for examination" were merged into the formal criminal process. Given the ingrained pattern of practice in China's criminal justice system, the practical impact of the amendment in protecting individual rights is limited unless it can be effectively enforced.[13]

The Chinese legislative system

Now we study how the law is made in China. Law making is a principal function of any legislature. Theoretically, according to the Constitution, the National People's Congress (NPC) appears to be the highest legislative body in China, and all governmental power rests in the NPC. The NPC also has a Standing Committee, which is actually the most powerful body of the Chinese legislature and enjoys the authority to enact or to amend laws when the NPC is not in session. The Standing Committee members are all top- or high-ranking party and state officials appointed by the Politburo, though they are theoretically elected by the NPC. In understanding Chinese politics, we must always keep in mind the difference between theory (constitution) and practice (facts). Interpretation of the Constitution is constitutionally entrusted to the Standing Committee of the NPC, although responsibility for the actual interpretation of laws is divided among the NPC Standing Committee, the Supreme People's Court and the Supreme People's Procuratorate, and the State Council, depending on whether the law in question requires "legislative," "judicial," or "administrative" interpretation, respectively. But, all interpretations must be approved by the Politburo, which is really the center of the power. The Constitution does not provide any legal mechanisms or procedures for citizens to challenge the constitutionality or legality of laws and regulations made by the NPC,[14] which is actually a party–state institution: what is made by it is the law, and the law must be obeyed by all.

The NPC is held every five years, and its plenary session is held once a year, usually in March, for about 10 days, to approve laws, legislate regulations, and to appoint important government officials. Therefore, the NPC Standing Committee, headed by the top CPC leaders, will do whatever they want without bothering to hear the opinions of the congress deputies. To ensure the CPC's policies, decisions, political appointments, and legislative bills are carried out by the NPC and other state organs, the CPC holds its National Party Congress in the year before the NPC Congress, usually in the fall, and its plenary session in the year before the NPC plenary session. This is a critical political arrangement in Chinese politics. Often, the Politburo can make a decision and implement it without bowing to the NPC, and then have it approved in the NPC or by its Standing Committee.

To ensure the CPC politburo's political appointment of all key NPC and other state leaders, the politburo controls the nomination process through the NPC Presidium. All the key state leaders, such as the NPC chairperson and vice-chairpersons, the president and the vice-president of state, premier, and chairperson of the State Military Commission, as well as cabinet members, the president of the supreme people's court and a chief procurator are supposedly elected by the NPC according to the Constitution. However, the one-candidate nomination is only in the hands of the NPC Presidium and is in fact determined by the Party politburo prior to the congressional meeting. According to the Organic Law of the NPC, the slate of the Presidium is proposed by the NPC Standing Committee prior to the opening of the NPC sessions. The slate is actually determined by the Party politburo beforehand and delivered to the NPC Standing Committee. The 150-odd-name list of the Presidium is printed before the NPC deputies step into the People's Great Hall and attend the preparatory meeting for the Congress. No deputy will propose a candidate for the Presidium. The slate of the Presidium is normally passed within a few minutes. The CPC Politburo thereby controls the nomination of all the key state leaders as well as the political agenda of the congress. The NPC deputies come only to "vote" for these officially nominated state leaders and their policy agenda.[15] In the event a candidate on the official slate fails to receive the votes of half the deputies, the Presidium will propose another candidate. If this candidate fails to receive half the votes, the Presidium will propose a third candidate. If this proposed candidate fails again, no more elections will be held for this position. The appointment of this cabinet member will be made at the second session of the NPC or by the NPC Standing Committee. In this way, the Politburo ensures all its proposed candidates are "elected."[16] The Chinese legislative structure and process is shown in Figure 9.6 (see Chapter 9).

Deputies to the NPC are supposedly elected by the citizens. However, in practice deputies are not popularly elected, but are chosen by 34 "electoral units," which are categorized into four groups: (1) people's congresses of 31 provinces, municipalities directly under the central government, and autonomous regions; (2) the "military congresses" of the PLA General Staff Department, the General Logistics Department, the General Political Department, various military regions, various military services, the Commission of the Defense and Scientific Industry, and the Defense University; (3) members of the "consultatively selected conference" of "compatriots in Taiwan"; and (4) members from Hong Kong's and Macau's "election conference" approved by the NPC Standing Committee. The distribution of the number of deputies among the "electoral units" is determined by the NPC Standing Committee accordingly, and ultimately approved by the CPC Politburo. According to the constitution and electoral law, candidates for the NPC deputies are nominated and produced by the above four categories of "electoral units." Such a political arrangement means that on the one hand, no one other than the "electoral units" has the right to nominate anyone to be a candidate for the NPC, while, on the other hand, if the politburo of the CPC is worried that someone on the official slate of a certain "electoral unit" might be voted down, it would arrange for this person to be nominated by another "electoral unit" as a candidate for the NPC. The reverse is also true: if the politburo of the CPC did not want someone to be "elected" as a NPC deputy, it could be arranged that he/she would simply not appear on the official slate of any "electoral unit." The official slate of the NPC deputies in all parts of the country is determined by the Secretariat of the Central Committee, the Central Organization Department, the Central United Front Department, Provincial Party Committees and the CPC's satellite "democratic parties." In addition to the official slate of the NPC, candidates for the NPC can also be jointly proposed by more than 10 deputies of provincial people's congresses, but in a limited number. Therefore, candidates for the 3,000-odd NPC deputy positions are largely predetermined by the party–state authorities prior to the opening session of the NPC.[17] Such an official slate system for the election of the NPC deputies is actually duplicated from the election of deputies for the CPC Congress. Such a system determines that the CPC authorities can easily manipulate the nomination process of the NPC deputies and do whatever they want.

The "black box" operation of the Party Congress is also duplicated at the NPC. The 2,000–3,000 deputies from all parts of the country are divided into 34 delegations by their "electoral units." The largest delegation is the military one with 268 deputies, while the smallest delegation is from Taiwan with 13 deputies. The Shanghai delegation has 67 deputies. Larger delegations are further divided into several "deputy groups." Deputies to the NPC are divided into more than 100 "deputy groups." It is officially arranged for all these "deputy groups" to stay at 24 hotels in Beijing, forming a "honeycomb-like structure," a phrase introduced by Yan Jiaqi. Information cannot be exchanged between "deputy groups," and can only be formally exchanged through "congress bulletins." The staff who edit the "congress bulletins" are all carefully selected from various functional departments of the party and the state. They are sent to various "deputy groups" to do "recording" and "liaison" work. They must follow the directives of the Secretariat of the Congress, which is actually the control center of the 100-odd "honeycomb-like structure." What can or cannot be put in "congress bulletins" must be approved by the Secretariat of the NPC. The "congress bulletin" serves the following three functions. (1) Since all deputies are divided into 100 groups that hold meetings or discussions separately in different locations or different rooms in the same hotel, deputies in one group can only get information about what other deputies say in other groups through this formal channel. (2) In the "bulletin," the "emotional" or "negative" elements in the speeches of deputies can be screened and eliminated or revised, and sharp criticisms can be "nullified" or "neutralized." (3) The speeches of deputies are postponed, for circulation among deputies one day after the group meetings. Such a political arrangement helps the CPC authority to control the entire course of the congress. The NPC convenes once every five years and the congress usually lasts two weeks. Seventy percent of this time is used for the meetings of "deputy groups" to discuss the issues on the agenda, while 30 percent of the time is used for the full session to pass the bills or resolutions. During the 70 percent period, deputies can only use "mouths" to speak but not "hands" to vote, while during the 30 percent period for the full session deputies can only use "ears" to listen and "hands" to vote but not "mouths" to speak. The full session is a veritable "mute congress."[18]

Deputies to all levels of people's congresses are elected every five years and they elect government leaders and approve legislation. Deputies of people's congresses at the township level in rural areas and the district level in urban areas are directly elected by citizens, but all higher level people's congresses are indirectly elected by lower level people's congresses. For example, deputies to county level or city level people's congresses are elected by township or district-level congresses, and deputies to the NPC are elected by provincial-level people's congresses. However, elections are nominal because party authorities control the nomination, appointment, and selection processes. People's congresses usually convene their sessions in the spring of the year after the party congresses hold their sessions at which major decisions have already been made on personnel appointments, legislation, and policy issues. The operational and organizational processes at the lower level people's congresses are largely duplicated from the NPC level as discussed above. The people's congresses are the political instrument for realizing party policies and carrying out the "central tasks" assigned by higher authorities.

However, the Chinese legislative and legal systems have become more complicated as legal reforms have rationalized and strengthened the legislative and legal structures and institutions, and improved the professionalism of the legislature, the judiciary, and the legal profession. The Chinese government has made a lot of laws or regulations at all levels in the past three decades, and laws have come to play an increasingly important role in China today, particularly in legal support for the party's economic reform policies and the goals of economic growth. Therefore, it is necessary to offer more detailed examination and assessment of the legal changes and their significance in the next chapter.

Questions for discussion

1. What are the fundamental differences between the Chinese and U.S./U.K.
    legal systems? To what extent has post-Mao China established judicial
    fairness and rule of law?
2. What are the fundamental differences between the Chinese and U.S./U.K.
    legislative systems? How is the law made in China—by the people, the
    People's Congress, or the Party?

Further reading

Pitman B. Potter, ed., *Domestic Law Reforms in Post-Mao China* (Armonk and
London, ME Sharpe, 1994).
Murray Scot Tanner, *The Politics of Lawmaking in Post-Mao China: Institutions,
Processes and Democratic Prospects* (Oxford: Oxford University Press, 1998).
Albert Chen, *An Introduction to the Legal System of the People's Republic of China*
(Hong Kong: LexisNexis/Butterworths, 2004).
Donald C. Clarke, ed., *China's Legal System: New Developments, New Challenges*
(Cambridge University Press, 2008).

12 Legal and legislative reforms in post-Mao China

Law making is the area of greatest achievement in the legal field in post-Mao China. The number of laws has rapidly increased since 1978. By the end of August 2009, the National People's Congress and its Standing Committee had enacted 229 laws, covering seven legal fields, i.e., the Constitution and constitutional law, civil and commercial law, administrative law, economic law, social law, criminal law, and law of procedure and extrajudicial procedure; the State Council has in effect made 682 administrative regulations; the local people's congresses and their standing committees, more than 7,000 local regulations; the local congresses of the national autonomous areas, more than 600 regulations; the legislatures of the five special economic zones, more than 200 regulations in total; in addition, the departments under the State Council and local governments vested with the power of legislation have made over 20,000 rules.[1]

The post-Mao regime has relaxed its grip on the legal professions and their practice in civil law, business law, and criminal law, though their practice is subject to party–state direction and the party–state apparatus has always intervened as needed. Ordinary people and businessmen have begun to turn to the legal profession to resolve business and civil disputes. As a result, another area of great achievement is the increased number of law offices and legal advisors in post-Mao China. By 1996, there were 90,000 legal workers or "legal advisors" in China and 7,200 law offices, among which there were more than 5,500 state-owned legal offices, 500 cooperatives, and 1,200 partnership associates. The first Lawyer Law in Chinese communist history was enacted in 1996 and regulates the different legal responsibilities of the three law offices.[2] In more recent years, lawyers and law firms have been allowed to run their business as a legal profession. By 2002, China had more than 120,000 licensed lawyers, and 11,000 law offices or law firms.[3] Foreign law firms are allowed to set up representative offices in China. By 2009, there were 117 foreign law firms in China.[4] However, their legal services are strictly restricted to certain areas by the Chinese government.[5] To implement an open-door policy and encourage the Chinese economy to participate in the global economy, "the government has developed formal legal institutions that appear to meet world standards, while using informal practices to maintain control over the administration of justice when needed."[6] However, compared with the pre-1978 period, China has made substantial progress in terms of the increased role of legal advisors in economic and civil lawsuits.

The change can also be observed in terms of the role of the people's congress when compared to the period of "Cultural Revolution." The role of people's congresses has been comparatively extended and theoretically justified in terms of representation, regime support, law making, institutional supervision or personnel oversight, and procedural rationalization, though these legislative activities must follow the principles defined by the CPC, led by the party leadership and guided by party policies.

Post-Mao legislative reform has rationalized the people's congress in many other regards. Today's congresses employ secret ballots in elections, institutionalize cadre inspection procedures, and develop job descriptions and tests for assessing competence. People's congresses also play an enhanced role in personnel oversight and legislative investigation. Congress deputies are also sent to investigate and report instances of counterfeit pharmaceuticals, impure drinking water, unhygienic markets, polluting factories, illegal gold hordes, tax-evading entrepreneurs, price gouging, and land expropriation. On some isolated occasions, local congresses have turned down party nominees to leadership posts, such as candidates for vice governors of provinces and heads of provincial or local courts and procuratorates.[7]

Post-Mao legislative reform has also brought about some organizational changes, including the strengthened NPC Standing Committee (NPCSC) and its expanded scope of action, increased specialization, procedural regularity, full-time staff, and improved internal organization. The NPCSC and its special committees have occasionally engaged in legislation drafting and revision. The Standing Committee, Law Committee, and Legislative Affairs Commission have assumed an active role in clarifying and elaborating general directives and policy changes of the CPC politburo and in making laws to ensure their implementation.[8]

Procedural rationalization aimed at improving work efficiency is another area of great achievement in post-Mao China. In the 1980s, deputies typically received draft government work reports several days before convening. Since the late 1980s they have begun to receive all draft laws, personnel name lists, and the session's agenda one month before convening in the hope that deputies would become more effective participants in discussions during the convening of sessions.[9] The Constitution (Articles 74 and 75) restores immunity for deputies granted in 1954, forbids the arrest or trial of NPC deputies without the permission of the NPCSC, and guarantees that deputies will not be called to legal account for plenary speeches or votes.[10] The Constitution (Article 73) affirms the right of deputies to address inquiries to the State Council and its ministries and commissions and requires either written or oral responses.[11] However, all inquiries have to be written and presented by full delegations or groups of 30 or more deputies—"to guarantee that the inquiries had a definite mass base."[12] Opinions, suggestions, and criticisms are submitted to the General Office of the NPCSC, which will refer them to concerned NPC committees and government departments. From June 1983 to April 1988, according to a Chinese official report, NPC committees and government departments handled 14,215 opinions, suggestions, and criticisms from deputies.[13]

Post-Mao legal and legislative reforms and changes have led many China analysts to declare that the post-Mao regime has followed the model of some East Asian authoritarian countries and moved toward a "rule of law" society. Some analysts even argue that the change in post-Mao China or "creeping democratization" is "forming subtle but important checks and balances against the ruling party's monopoly of power, strengthening the rule of law, and cultivating self-government at the grassroots level."[14]

However, a careful examination of the evidence will suggest that either "the rule of law" or "creeping democratization" is only an illusion or wishful thinking that contradicts the reality of the post-Mao legal system and misinterprets changes in the legal field in post-Mao China. Assessment of the development and achievement of a legal system should not depend on how many laws have passed but on how these laws have operated within a certain legal framework, who defines the principles, norms, and rules of the legal framework, and who makes the law. The latter, rather than the former, determine the nature of the legal system, which actually constitutes one key aspect of the Chinese communist party–state regime. If China is found to have a truly independent judicial system which is not subjugated to the party, if the party no longer stipulates its own principles, norms, and constitutional rules, and if the party authority no longer overrides laws of government, we can arrive at the conclusion that a fundamental or systemic change of the political regime has occurred in post-Mao China.[15]

The rule of law

In the assessment of legal change in terms of regime change in communist states, one critical question is: To what extent has post-Mao China moved toward "the rule of law"? Many analysts use this term without clearly defining it while asserting that post-Mao China has made the transition toward "the rule of law" or become a "rule of law" society. However, no sensible assessment can be made without defining and understanding the meaning of "the rule of law." Therefore, we must first define the term "the rule of law," which can serve as conceptual criteria for measuring the legal change in post-Mao China, in order to establish a plausible argument against such an arbitrary assertion.

"Rule of law" (法治) is usually defined as the procedural due process in which laws serve the important function of setting limits on exercising power, the political game is played according to laws, no individual or organization is above the law, and all citizens and organizations are equal before the law. However, for a country to have the rule of law, according to law professor Ralf Dahrendorf, it requires that laws are "prospective, clear, open, accessible, and noncontradictory, an independent and impartial judiciary, independent legal profession, and honest and apolitical law enforcement." He added, "independence of the 'judicial department' may indeed be regarded as the very definition of 'the rule of law': It is certainly an important part of it," and an independent bar is necessary to assure access to the courts.[16] The historical development of this concept has shown that the focus is on the limitations of state power. All definitions of rule of law agree on the importance of the law's function of setting limits on exercising power—constitutional limits on all branches of government, independent judicial review of the constitutionality of legislation, due process, including open and unbiased courts and fair hearings, and the like, and emphasize the fundamental human rights or the basic civil and political rights both at individual and collective levels that are guaranteed by the constitution—such as the principle of equality, the presumption of innocence in criminal cases, freedoms of speech, press, assembly, and association, freedoms from unreasonable searches, arrest, seizures, torture, forced confessions, and imprisonment without going through the courts, and the right to be tried before independent courts.[17]

However, by definition, there is no evidence which supports that post-Mao China is moving toward "the rule of law" or that the post-Mao government functions on the basis of "the rule of law" rather than other supreme authorities. As we will discuss later, the post-Mao leadership shares a strongly instrumental view that law is a tool to extend control over a society, maintain the existing political and economic order, and achieve its policy goals. For post-Mao communist leaders, law is seen as an instrument to subjugate all persons and all governmental institutions to the rules defined and promulgated by the "supreme lawmaker"[18]—the communist party. Law, like the police apparatus, party–state policy, mass mobilization, state planning, administrative command, and the like, is only one of the action means that are applied selectively and are always subject to change accordingly, without much concern given to the basic principles of the rule of law—for instance, that laws must be prospective, clear, open, accessible, and noncontradictory—or without any reference to an independent and impartial judiciary, independent legal profession and bar, and honest and apolitical law enforcement. This is not "the rule of law," but a kind of instrumentality of law that serves the functions of the regime other than those of "the rule of law."

Post-Mao legal changes, such as the enforcement of contracts to encourage market exchanges, the enactment of criminal, tort, and property law to protect legally earned profits, and the enactment of criminal and administrative law to curb corruption and arbitrary government intervention, reflect some aspects of legality that characterize "the rule by law" (法制) or "a system of laws," which any authoritarian regime can claim to follow. The difference between the two regimes in terms of "the rule by law" is who constitutes the "supreme lawmaker," how laws are actually made, and in what political context the law is enforced.

In post-Mao China, it is the CPC who defines and promulgates the constitutional rules and gives orders or directives to the government organs to make the laws as needed. For the Chinese communist party–state, constitutional principles and rules reflect the party's ideology, norms, values, and policy changes, and they are binding on all persons and all organs of the state, except that the supreme lawgiver—the Communist Party—has the power to change them. China's constitution is identical to Stalin's and Mao's which claimed the leading role of the Communist Party was as the vanguard of the working class and all other working people in their struggle to build socialism and realize a communist society. The party is the leading force of Chinese society, the leading nucleus of its political system, and the core of all organizations of the working people, both state and social. The party-domination clause has been emphasized and carried over into all post-Mao constitutional amendments. The primacy of one ruling party and its supreme authority are elevated to the status of a basic constitutional principle, which is certainly not the case in any authoritarian state where the supreme law maker could be the legislature, the government or a dictator.[19]

The "leading role" of the CPC is actualized in such a way that the party officials are in a position to make important decisions in all governmental and public organs as well as to confine the parameters of other social, cultural, and economic activities through the party–state apparatus. China still has no true separation between the party and the state, and the party holds all of the real power in its hands. As we will discuss in detail later, important legal decisions and laws are actually made by the party officials who fulfill all the important positions in the congress and the relevant governmental departments. It is not "congress deputies" but the "party–state institutions" that make laws. Party decisions or policy changes need not be formally justified by reference to legal rules. The party can use law to further its own ends.

Therefore, one key indicator of regime change in communist party states, with respect to changes in the legal system, is "the development of some of the key institutions for implementing the rule of law, especially an independent judiciary, an independent private bar, and the special public law jurisdictions for review of administrative action and the constitutionality of legislation. Such institutional reform is important because the rule of law is not possible without them"[20] Obviously, such institutional reform has not been attempted by the post-Mao leadership, as we will discuss later.

The nature of Chinese law and the constitution

The number of laws has rapidly increased in post-Mao China. Does the number of laws account for the nature of regime change? The answer is no. After the communist takeover in 1949, Mao's regime made great progress in law making. From 1949 to 1965, a total of 1,709 laws, administrative regulations, and other legal documents were made, among which those made by the NPC totaled 122. From 1979–93 a total of 1,888 laws, statutes, and other legal documents were made, among which the NPC passed 210 laws. Provincial congresses enacted over 2,000 local regulations.[21] From 1993–98, the NPC passed 118 laws and legal decisions, adding up to 328 laws in total.[22] Since then, more laws have been made, revised, or abandoned.

Therefore, law is not something new to post-Mao China and the number of laws does not account for the nature of regime change. The post-Mao party–state institutions have made laws in an effort to redefine and revitalize the party–state apparatus, establish a "socialist market economy," and pursue the intermediate goal of economic modernization. The key is who makes the law and defines the fundamental principles underlying it, how the law is made, and whether or not the party or the government is restrained by its own rules. Despite the fact that the post-Mao regime declares publicly that its ruling should be based on legal rules, or in their own term, "the rule by law," China is not a state where government acts or party decisions need to be authorized by law to be valid. They are valid if they can actually be carried out to meet their needs or serve a certain policy orientation according to other supreme directives (party policy or directives of individual top leaders). In this sense, Mao's regime and the post-Mao regime are similar regardless of the growth of legislation and associated institutions since 1978.[23]

A constitution is described as

> the organic and fundamental law of a nation or state, which may be written or unwritten, establishing the character and conception of its government, laying the basic principles to which its internal life is to be conformed, organizing the government, and regulating, distributing, and limiting the functions of its different departments, and prescribing the extent and manner of the exercise of sovereign powers.[24]

Communist China has had several constitutions—in 1954, 1975, 1978, 1982, and 1993. All claimed to be the fundamental law of the People's Republic of China. All defined the composition and power of political structures of the communist regime and regulated the relations of the various institutions to one another and to the citizens.[25] However, as it is observed, "the constitution seems to bear no relation to the actual government of China."[26] "The government has never been obliged to follow its precepts, and there is no mechanism for making it do so."[27] Each constitution has marked the ascendancy of a particular leading group within the party and its new policy orientation. Each has contained a clear indication of the policy directions the current leadership at that time intended to take.[28] "The constitution does not function as a set of fixed principles against which specific laws and practices are measured and overturned if found to be at odds."[29] As Donald C. Clarke observes, changes to the constitution are often intended to be the final stamp of legitimation on already existing and approved practices. Land leasing, for example, was carried out experimentally at the local level, without being approved by the NPC but with Deng's support and central government approval, while it was clearly written in the constitution that this was prohibited. People's communes were largely abolished and replaced by the contract responsibility system while they remained in writing as one of the foundations of China's socialist economy. Although the government has never in practice allowed strikes, the right to strike was put in both the 1975 and the 1978 constitutions as appropriate for a workers' state. By 1982, however, the post-Mao regime had changed its mind about how far the constitution should reflect reality: the provision was removed.[30]

Amendments suggest that the Constitution serves as the instrumental tool of a particular leading group and their policy orientation, rather than functioning as a set of fixed principles against which specific laws and practices are measured.[31] The Party is identical to the government, the regime, and the state, and it molds the government, the state, and all the key aspects of political life along lines compatible with its own political ideology, norms, image, policy orientation, and need, and it constructs laws and the constitution in accordance with this particular political ideology, norms, image, policy orientation, and need. This has nothing to do with "regime change," but is the party–state in nature regardless of changes or revisions.

Law as an institutional tool

The post-Mao leadership takes an instrumentalist view of the role of law as promoting economic development rather than trying to promote the rule of law as an end in itself. Post-Mao politics since 1978 have shifted from a Maoist leadership style that was informal, pedagogical, and highly politicized to a Dengist style that is more formal, pragmatic, and technocratic. However, the leadership's view of law has remained primarily "instrumentalist,"[32] that is, "law is considered as a needed tool for achieving economic reform and modernization and it is useful and necessary only inasmuch as it promotes that goal."[33] The primary reason that the post-Mao regime has emphasized the importance of law is simply because of the new policy orientation in which centralized state planning is no longer the sole regulator of Chinese economic activities, which have been largely based on economic contracts and increasingly in response to such market mechanisms as price, credit and interest policies, and taxes.[34] Law has therefore become a useful and necessary tool to regulate economic activity and order while extensive state intervention remains commonplace in economic activities.[35]

Market reform itself has also been carried out in such a manner as to indicate the leadership's view of law as a means of bringing about a certain economic and legal order rather than as a desirable end in itself. Examples of legal enactment designed to bring about a certain kind of economic order include the State Enterprise Law, the Equity Joint Venture Law, Bankruptcy Law, Economic Contract Law, and various regulations regarding securities markets. Moreover, under this category, there are statutes that define the structure and operation of Chinese businesses. Although they are not formal pieces of legislation, the State Council's decisions guide much of China's economy.[36]

The law and the legal system in China continue to serve a specific political agenda or the "focus shift" (*zhongxin zhuanyi*重心转移) of the CPC policy. Law reform and legislative activity have focused on economic change and the regulation of economic activities and the pace of change in law is dictated to some extent by the speed with which economic reforms can be implemented. "China's domestic economy and the legislation regulating it illustrate an attempt to use law as a control upon the economy in the broadest possible sense."[37]

Economic reforms have required extensive legislation and considerable expansion of the legal system since 1978. The content of legislation has been broadened.[38] However, a closer examination of the main aspects of legislation in past decades suggests that laws and statutes are not used to check or limit the role of the CPC but to bring about the change that the regime expects or to define the boundary of the change. According to the NPC Legislative Work Commission and the State Council Legal Bureau, (1) laws are used to regulate the subjects of the market and define their conditions and legal status, such as Corporate Law and Commercial Bank Law; (2) laws are used to adjust the relations between the subjects of the market and set rules for them to follow, such as Advertisement Law, Insurance Law, Bail Law, Accounting Law, Foreign Trade Law, and Urban Estate Law; (3) laws are used to strengthen the state's macro-administrative and economic regulation and exercise control over the economy, such as Budget Law, People's Bank Law, Auditing Law, Income Tax Law, and Value-Added Tax Law; (4) laws are used to promote the development of scientific technology, education, and agriculture, such as the Scientific Progress Law, Education Law, Teachers Law, Agriculture Law, and Land Protection Law; (5) laws are used to strengthen the state apparatus, such as Judges Law, Procurators Law, People's Police Law, State Security Law, Prison Law, and Civil Service Law; and (6) laws are used to redefine the relations between state organs, such as the organic law of state organs at the central and local levels, and election laws.[39] However, few laws have been enacted for political reforms or to limit the role of the CPC in Chinese society, the state, and the government apparatus. Legislative work in post-Mao China has mainly focused on economic, criminal, civil, and administrative law making of the legal system, particularly with economic legislation at the center of law making.[40]

The NPC Legislative Work Commission and the State Council Legal Bureau also point out some characteristics and guiding principles of post-Mao legislation: "it must serve and subject itself to the whole situation of reform, development and stability"; "it must base itself on the legislation since the Third Plenary Session of the Eleventh Party Central Committee," and "pay attention to the Chinese national character while incorporating foreign experience in order to safeguard the predominant position of the state economy and distribution according to work, and embody the essence of our socialist system while following the common law of a market economy."[41] These guiding principles regulate the legislative activities and define the boundary of the change the post-Mao regime allows.

Party authority overrides legal authority

"In any country, laws do not exist in a social or political vacuum. Their enactment, enforcement, and evolution all take place in a social context that usually determines their efficacy. In the cases of China and other socialist countries, certain institutions assume an unusual prominence, beyond the roles accorded to them in the legislative framework."[42] In post-Mao China, party authority continues to be dominant and pervasive in every aspect of the state structure and continues to override legal authority. A closer examination of some practical aspects of the legal system may provide some insight into the nature of changes in the legal field.

Party policy overrides the law

The Marxist ideology that the law is the embodiment of the will of the ruling class, the dominance of the CPC in the institutional components of the Chinese legal system, and the instrumentalist view that the law is a means to implement current party policy all influence the interaction between economic and legal reforms. In neither area can reform proceed faster than the CPC is willing to allow.[43] The purpose of legal reforms is to serve the change or the focus-shift of the party's basic line and policy: from class struggle to economic modernization, from antagonism to the West to active cooperation and promotion of foreign investment.[44]

The Chinese legal system has never assumed true independence and has always remained subservient to party policy.[45] Party policy overrides the law, and change in party policy predetermines change in the legal system. Comparing the Chinese and American legal systems, "the fundamental difference between the two legal systems is that whereas Chinese law is primarily a tool of state power, American law protects a margin of relative social autonomy."[46] The post-Mao regime has encouraged the spread of knowledge about laws, but only on its own terms: for example, the publication of statutory compilations without official authorization is illegal, news reports are subject to press discipline, and the mass media have the responsibility to carry out political and ideological education guidelines prescribed by party propaganda departments and to indoctrinate the public with the official norm of "socialist legality."

One important feature of party and government intervention in the execution of court orders and decisions is often labeled as "regional protectionism" and "departmental protectionism" or often expressed as the problem "where there is a law, it is not obeyed, and its enforcement is not strict" (*youfa buyi, zhifa buyan*有法不依，执法不严). The essence of the problem is that "policy overrides law" (*zhengcedayufa* 政策大于法) or "party overrides law" (*dandayufa* 党大于法).

Courts in the context of the socialist judicial system

The role and nature of the Chinese courts have remained unchanged from the perspective of regime change or systemic change. Judges and the courts play a limited role in the Chinese legal system because courts are "just one bureaucracy among many"[47] or a branch within a government bureaucracy. Courts at each level are subject to the leadership of party committees and governments at the corresponding level. Judges often receive party directives, documents, meetings, and even telephone calls instructing them how to decide politically sensitive cases and cases in which the party considers it necessary to intervene. The judicial process, though claimed to be independent, is in fact subject to party control, policy, and discipline, and is subservient to the executive power.

Judicial selection is relevant to the key element of the rule of law: judicial independence. In China, however, judges and all judicial officers are selected and appointed according to a political and ideological standard to ensure that only reliable communist party members become judges, although professional education and competence are more emphasized than before as in the selection of cadres in other governmental and public organizations. Judges are politicized, bureaucratized, and placed in the category of "state cadres," and their rate of pay, housing, and other state welfare corresponds to their rank as state cadres in the bureaucratic administration, such as ministerial or vice-ministerial, provincial or vice-provincial, divisional or deputy-divisional, and so forth. In such a hierarchical structure, ordinary judges are subordinate to presiding judges, who are subordinate to the presidents of courts.

Different ranks not only mean different political status in the bureaucratic structure but also reflect hierarchical obedience of subordinates to superiors. Presidents of courts and presiding judges constitute judicial committees which discuss and decide all major cases or law suits. Many discussions and decisions of judicial committees occur before a court hearing is held. Courts and procuratorial organs are also hierarchically established: lower levels are subject to higher levels.[48] Judges at lower levels must ask the higher authorities for instructions before decisions are made, and must handle the cases according the directives of higher authorities. Therefore, most of the time, appeals to higher courts do not make a great difference. Such a hierarchical structure and decision-making process of the judicial system has remained unchanged since Deng's reform, and is conducive to the control and intervention of party–state power.[49]

China does have a set of legal institutions for the preservation of social order and governmental authority, but these institutions operate on very different principles from institutions usually called "legal" (party policies, directives, and discipline) and they are subject to substantial official influence, discipline, or party policy. This is essential to understanding the Chinese legal system and the nature of its changes in post-Mao China in terms of regime change. The guiding principles of China's legal system are those of party ideology, discipline, and policy, although the post-Mao regime has attempted to justify some of its actions in the language of legality.[50]

The legal profession in the context of political embeddedness

In post-Mao China, lawyers and law firms, like other practices, are enmeshed in political structure and bureaucratic institutional networks which create dependencies, incentives, and opportunities for them to engage in activities in the direction defined by the party–state ideology, political goals, and policies.

Legal services have begun to emerge in China today, but most of them are in the economic area. To meet the growing demand for legal services, the Chinese government has now opened the legal service market to foreign law firms and allowed them to establish offices in China handling legal issues in the economic area.[51] The law of the Bar was that all members of domestic law firms were "legal workers" of the state.[52] The practice license for each lawyer and law firm is subject to annual inspection and renewal. In other words, lawyers are legal workers on an annual contract with the state. The fact is that a lawyer or law firm can lose its license or watch it expire, unless the Justice Bureau of the government agrees to extend the privilege to practice law. It serves the government well to control this critical profession. The defense of high profile cases is under surveillance and political pressure, and lawyers are expected to cooperate with the government. Lawyers acting against the government would risk losing their license to practice. In certain cases, the discretionary power is abused to such an extent that criminal charges are brought against defense lawyers who refuse to curb their submission as requested. Some recent reported cases involve the arrest of lawyers or managing partners of law firms. The politics and professional code of conduct required by the government seriously undermine the lawyers' ability and immunity to claim privilege for their clients. For example, the Code specifically says that lawyers "shall not hide evidence." This is close to a forced disclosure, or forcing a confession, breaching the privileges of the client; any confession will be used against the client. The wording leaves room for different interpretations, and the government is the interpreter. The problems are the lack of due process that guarantees the procedural fairness and equality of all, and the lack of an impartial and independent tribunal that guarantees the rights of citizens are not compromised by state power.[53]

In recent decades, China's lawyers have increased in number and quality, the number of law firms has rapidly increased, and their legal practice has achieved considerable independence as a result of market reform and economic changes as well as the change from the department management (*bumen guanli* 部门管理) to supervision (*jiandu*监督) and guidance (*zhidao*指导). However, state-funded law firms are dominant in the legal system and in legal business compared with partnership and cooperative law firms. Moreover, state law firms may be subject to more administrative direction or political pressure, and thus are less independent than cooperative and partnership law firms in handling legal cases. China's lawyers are also subject to the control and supervision of the dual management structure of the Ministry of Justice and the Bar associations under the control of the Ministry of Justice and its local counterparts, and therefore they are in many ways dependent on the government (training, license, regulation, questioning, criticism, and retaliation of the government, and business opportunities provided by the government authorization to do highly profitable business in some legal areas, etc.) and thus partially independent. Lawyers are in many ways still subject to a variety of administrative and political pressures from the government during the course of their legal practice.[54]

As one recent study based on data from the 25 city survey suggests, Chinese lawyers' dependence on state actors both inside and outside the judicial system has preserved the value of political connections inside the institutions in the context of "political embeddedness"—defined broadly as bureaucratic, instrumental, or affective ties to the state and its actors. Chinese lawyers have to cope with everyday difficulties and administrative interference in legal practice. "The challenges they routinely face include various forms of obstruction, harassment, intimidation, and even physical abuse, often at the hands of personnel in the public security administration (the police system), the procuracy (the public prosecutor's office), and courts—lumped together in common parlance as the *gongjianfa*" (公检法).[55]

The nature of legislative reform

Kevin J. O'Brien examines the three options of legislative reform in post-Mao China: liberalization, rationalization, and inclusion. Liberalization in the legislature involves "diffusing power" and "allowing political competition and organized opposition," emphasizes "responsive government" and "electoral reform," and supports "close legislator–constituent ties and active representation of individual, partial, and national interests." Rationalization involves "routinizing and legalizing political power" and "institutionalizing political power," emphasizes "fixed legal codes, formal rules, and a rational division of labor among government organs," and clarifies "jurisdictions to prevent overconcentration of power and to increase government efficiency." Inclusion refers to "measures adopted by the leaders of a one-party Leninist state that institutionally acknowledge social diversity and grant limited access and influence to nonparty forces, but do not require functioning electoral machinery or imply any right to organized opposition." It attempts to increase the system's inclusiveness, broaden the united front for achieving the modernizing goal, institutionalize the party's legitimacy, and use the legislature to integrate the political community and organize it around one-party rule.[56]

Over the past few decades, as O'Brien correctly observes, the post-Mao regime has attempted rationalization and limited inclusion, with continuing rejection of liberalization. The legislative reforms have done little to increase political competition or to institutionalize responsiveness. In the NPC, congress deputies can only discuss improving one-party rule, rather than challenging it. Longstanding ideological and structural obstacles to legislative liberalization have remained in place, while legislative functions (e.g., propaganda, education, socialization, mobilization) entrusted to the legislature under Mao's regime have continued to be embedded in the structure of the NPC and in the minds of political leaders. Despite frequent proposals to increase accountability and reform nomination procedures, talking about contested elections or open campaigns has remained an "old forbidden zone." The post-Mao regime has continued to stress the differences between China and the former communist states and the impossibility of "mechanically copying another country's reforms."[57] In what follows, we will focus on the major aspects of the post-Mao legislature and evaluate the changes and their nature in terms of representation, regime support, law making, and supervision to determine if the post-Mao legislative reform has brought about any systemic or fundamental change in the legislative dimension of the post-Mao regime.[58]

Representation has been theoretically claimed as one important function of the Chinese communist legislature. However, post-Mao legislative reforms have not brought about any significant change in terms of the representation of the legislature. The legislature continues to be unrepresentative. NPC deputies, as in the past, are not directly elected by the "constituents" whom they represent, but indirectly by the "electorate units" based on administrative districts and units, which are lower-level provincial congresses and various party, governmental, and official organizations. Local, provincial, and central party committees control the nomination lists and lead the election committees. Ethnic, gender, party, and occupation quotas are used to manipulate the composition of NPC deputies accordingly. Almost all candidates are selected and nominated by party authorities, with limited quotas of "joint recommendation" (*lianming tuijian*联名推荐) for incumbent deputies of provincial and local congresses. Nominees proposed by groups of deputies are discussed in small group meetings and few are elected. Many deputies are actually selected or arranged by higher levels of party authorities.[59]

Selecting younger and better-educated deputies suggests an effort by the post-Mao regime to enhance deputy quality. But this does not mean the Maoist style of selection has been discarded. The post-Mao regime continues to emphasize the importance of "trailblazers" in modernization and reform and the political mix of scholars, scientists, "old comrades," model workers, exemplary individuals, star athletes, heroic soldiers, poets, opera singers, inventors, sportscasters, and other "honorary deputies." This selection consideration is claimed by the CPC to be an important measure to broaden "representation."[60] However, these deputies have no "constituents" whom they represent, to whom they are responsible, but are officially selected according to some officially defined political standards and indirectly "elected" by the "electorate units" based on administrative districts and units. In other words, these deputies are "selected" not for their political skills, legal knowledge, or experience and their competition with other candidates, but for their loyalty to the regime and their obedience to the government. The only professional politicians among NPC deputies are full-time party and state functionaries who must follow the party discipline and policy line.[61] There has been little significant change in the composition of NPC deputies, but some substantial increase of NPC deputies in the categories of the CPC members and party–state cadres. The status of deputies is cross-membership; for instance, cadres who receive higher education could be categorized into deputies of intellectuals, or directors of factories could be categorized into cadres or workers, depending on the political arrangement of the distribution of deputies across categories.

Political appointment of congress deputies and "specially invited deputies" in the NPC and the CPPCC has been common practice under the post-Mao regime. The quotas for these "specially invited deputies" are decided by the CPC Politburo according to its actual political needs. The candidates for these seats will be arranged through the General Office of the NPCSC for provincial people's congresses to nominate and elect. These deputies are usually assigned to the provincial people's congresses where these special deputies used to work, or where they were born, or simply somewhere the Politburo top leaders think it appropriate. Therefore, these special deputies will not count toward the quotas of central governmental and official organizations, and the "central quota" is always guaranteed. The distribution of the quotas of deputies for 34 "electorate units" is determined on a random basis and designed to ensure party control rather than "representation" in the legislative process.[62] Although the quotas of deputies for urban and rural areas are nominally determined on the basis of population, the actual quotas for urban areas are more than four times those of rural areas and, moreover, the quotas of leading cadres for various state institutions and official organizations make up the largest portion of the quotas for urban areas.[63] The "electorate units" of the People's Liberation Army and central government produce the largest number of deputies by quota. There has been no significant change since the 9th NPC. All this suggests that the representation of the post-Mao legislature is only an illusion for the Chinese citizens, the selection process of congress deputies is totally under party control, and deputies play only a symbolic role in decision-making.

Regime support is another important function of the Chinese communist legislature. The NPC in post-Mao China plays an enhanced role in regime support based on and guided by the "Four Cardinal Principles." The NPC has been established as a state institution based on the party line and principles to supply legitimacy for party rule and support for the party policy and its implementation. Change along this dimension is insignificant. Most government reports and legislative drafts are accepted without thorough deliberation and near unanimity is often achieved.[64] Deputies' votes and speeches have rarely altered major policy or personnel decisions. Voting against a party or government proposal and candidate has remained insignificant despite the fact that more deputies have begun to cast opposed votes or abstained from voting on party and state proposals and selected candidates for state leadership positions.[65] Deputies are instructed not to understand their responsibilities narrowly in terms of maintaining ties with their "constituency," which they actually do not have, but to "take the interests of the whole into account."[66]

> NPC deputies consider important matters that involve the whole people and the whole nation; although they are elected by a certain district and certain voters, they represent the people of the whole nation and must think about the interests of the nation, not just their own district. Individual and partial interests follow the whole. Deputies must pay attention to their district but not fall prey to localism or departmentalism.[67]

This requirement is functional to party rule, which is used to justify party domination of the legislature and ensures the definitional identity of the party's will. "Electoral districts and units" exist primarily to elect deputies chosen by the party and expected to recognize the so-called "nation's highest interests," which the CPC claims to represent. Deputies are often warned not to abuse their rights and reminded that immunity from prosecution as stipulated in the constitution does not license "irresponsibility." However, these warnings are hardly necessary. Deputies are not willing to make their opposition known and attempt to avoid debating the substance of the proposed legislation.[68] Each deputy belongs to a delegation or a small group by province, business, circle, or governmental organization. In the small groups, deputies discuss items on the agenda and voice their opinions not without fear. Deputies continue to act as a group rather than as individuals and offer consent rather than opposition. The heads of delegations or groups are the party secretaries, governors, or other government leaders of the "electoral districts and units" where the individual deputies come from and they follow party leaders' instructions. They try to avoid confrontation with government departments and individual leaders. If someone dares to make his/her opposition known, he or she would be most likely to be dropped from the list of official candidates for selecting the next term's deputy. Therefore, nobody wants to be a trouble maker.

Lawmaking is claimed by the post-Mao leadership to be a third important role for the NPC to play. However, post-Mao legislative reforms have not made the NPC an effective working body in terms of law making. Legislative sessions continue to be brief, annual events, typically two weeks in duration, and deputies are not paid for their work, though subsidies for transportation, lodging, food, and entertainment are provided for deputies who attend the sessions.[69] At the legislative sessions, as Kevin J. O'Brien describes vividly, deputies file into the main auditorium of the People's Great Hall, where they sit by province or other electoral units in long rows, with special sections reserved for army representatives and government ministers. The NPCSC

President, Vice President, party and state leaders, and members of the NPC Presidium sit at the front of the stage behind a speaker's podium. Leaders speak and deputies listen. When party–state leaders address the full NPC sessions, their speeches are rarely interrupted, except by the warm applause of deputies. When the agenda is completed, if there are no small group meetings scheduled, deputies will return to their hotels to go shopping, eating, and sightseeing. The people's congress is often called "flower vase," while deputies are often called a "voting-machine."[70]

An assembly of 3,000 deputies can ratify decisions and fulfill symbolic tasks, but has no ability to initiate or revise. Strengthening the NPCSC and other NPC functioning committees becomes necessary for the NPC to be more efficient in law making. But it would not involve changing the mission of the NPC, but rather strengthening its working core. It would not challenge party control, but simply revitalize and rationalize specialized organs that are small enough to meet regularly and to conduct more meaningful discussions. A division of labor is obvious: the full NPC sessions are for discussion, information gathering, and symbolic tasks, the NPCSC and other specialized committees for law making.[71] Moreover, the Standing Committee and other specialized committees are totally under party control and staffed by party officials and members. In practice, the NPCSC has been established as "a legislature within a legislature"—China's second law-making body, which is to discuss and pass statutes that do not require NPC deliberation.[72]

A closer look at the institutional components of the legal system—who are the law makers—might provide more insight into the essence of Chinese law making in operation. As Kevin J. O'Brien observes, it is not congress deputies who make laws, but the institutions that make laws. Party policies are always first implemented, and then laws follow, elaborating and clarifying these policies. In particular, four institutions are assigned a role in translating policies or decisions of the party leadership into specific legal norms and rules.[73]

First is the Communist Party itself. Direct party involvement in law making occurs at every stage of law making—determining if an issue is ripe for legislation, drafting, reviewing, and approving a legislative proposal. The CPC may turn responsibility for drafting over to other institutions that are totally under party control. Party leading groups or committees set the lawmaking process in motion and check the results while state organs often do most of the actual work.[74]

The State Council is a second bureaucratic complex involved in law making. The State Council's Legislative Affairs Bureau has become a prime institution in legal drafting, and ministries draft laws related to the industries under their jurisdiction, such as the fisheries law, the forestry law, the accounting law, the mining resources law, and the environmental protection law. The State Council also has the power to enact "empowered legislation" (*shouquan lifa*授权立法) on issues such as retirement policy, tax reform, economic restructuring, and open-door policy beyond the realm of administrative regulations.[75] As a matter of fact, "empowered legislation" of the State Council and its subordinate ministries makes up the bulk of the Chinese legislation under both Mao's regime and the post-Mao regime.[76]

Provincial-level people's congresses make up the third set of law-making bodies. From 1983 to 1989, provincial-level congresses and their standing committees passed over 1,000 local laws on topics ranging from regional minority affairs to province-wide political, economic, cultural life, and constitutional enforcement. Provincial legislatures under Mao simply enforced laws; under Deng, they enacted them.[77]

The NPC and its committees are the fourth leg in the legislative complex. Formal NPC involvement in law making begins with "legislative planning" (*Lifa guihua* 立法规划), which is approved by the CPC Politburo. For example, the State Council Legal Research Center drew up a legislative plan, including names of regulations, proposers, issuing organizations, and drafting conditions, while the NPCSC produced a work outline that provided a list of priorities and laws to be enacted.[78] There is no separation of power but only a division of labor between the legislative and the executive. Congress deputies in plenary sessions do not alter drafts. Changes are made in small working sessions of the NPCSC Legislative Affairs Commission or the Law Committee. The NPCSC and its specialized committees are the real law-making bodies within the legislature while the NPC serves as an agent of inclusion and rationalization.[79]

Supervision is defined by the post-Mao regime as the fourth role for the NPC to play, in addition to representation, regime support, and law making as discussed above. However, the post-Mao legislative reforms have not made such a role significant in terms of regime change. The NPCSC organizes its members to carry out annual inspections of local units. Inspection tours last up to several weeks and cover a different topic each year, usually related to the implementation of laws or recent initiatives in economic or educational policy. Deputies visit schools, factories, and government offices in all 30 provinces and write reports suggesting solutions to problems with fake and inferior pharmaceuticals, toxic food, and brand-name infringement, and so forth. However, supervision and inspection tours are often "swarming like troops" (*dadui renma qianhuhouyong* 大队人马前呼后拥) and "treating inspections like pleasure trips" (*youshan wanshui* 游山玩水), and inspected units lavish deputies with banquets and gifts. Inspection and supervision, like law making, involve party–state institutions, some of which have considerably more power than the legislature. Although individual deputies may uncover problems, they do not have the authority to resolve problems and disputes outside their jurisdiction. Deputies can reflect the local situation and raise suggestions to governmental organs, but are not allowed to "meddle" in government and judicial work.[80]

According to the Chinese constitution, the NPC is empowered to modify or remove the legal decisions made by its Standing Committee (NPCSC), and the NPCSC has the power to repeal decrees or invalidate any legal decisions made by the State Council that are contrary to the Constitution or laws made by the legislature. However, up to now, no single legal decision or decree has been repealed, invalidated, or rejected by the legislature, suggesting that no such supervision power has been effectively exercised. The legislature's role in supervision thus is "primarily that of a clearinghouse that gathers information on local officials and governmental departments that are not implementing party policies"[81] and confines its scope mainly to politically nonsensitive issues and areas. It would not be inappropriate to use a Chinese proverb to describe the supervision of the people's congress as "scratching an itchy foot with the boot on."

According to Article 3 of the Constitution, "democratic centralism" is stipulated as the fundamental political system of the People's Republic of China and the organizational principle of the NPC and all other state institutions. "Democratic centralism" is one typical Leninist party principle applied universally across all former and existing communist states. The post-Mao regime has continued to apply this principle vigorously and universally in legislative practice and all other state activities. On the other hand, the post-Mao "legislative work" must also adhere to the party's "mass lines," which is another of the most typical Maoist style practices. Congress meetings give leaders the chance to hear what delegates have to say, and delegates, in turn, can have policies explained to them by the central authorities. Rather than bringing a group of representatives together to initiate laws and policies, the NPC is a group of deputies who will learn about laws and policies. While this exercise may be educational, it is not legislative in the sense we use the term in political science.[82]

In short, the post-Mao legislative reforms have not brought about any systemic or fundamental change to the people's congress and its legislative process but have continued to oppose meaningful political competition and any measures of political liberalization. Reforms mean "limited inclusion" and "procedural rationalization" to promote economic modernization and economic marketization, enhance the role of law in regulating economic activities, improve government efficiency, rationalize the civil service, and maintain the existing political order. The post-Mao legislature serves as a means to translate decisions of the party leadership into specific legal norms and codes, justify the post-Mao regime's new policy orientations and changes, and provide legitimacy for the party–state rule.

To conclude, the post-Mao regime has experienced a change from rule by policy to rule by a combination of policy and law. It has relaxed its leash to a certain degree on the legal profession and practices in civil law and business law with an increased number of law offices, legal advisors, and legal practices. Post-Mao legislative reform has rationalized the people's congress in many regards and brought about some organizational changes, including the expanded role of the people's congresses, the strengthened NPCSC and its expanded scope of action, increased specialization, more procedural regularity, full-time staff, and improved internal organization. However, all these changes or adjustments of action means are functional for maintaining the hard core of the communist party–state, and serving the purpose of policy change defined by the party line. Post-Mao legislative reform over the years has not given the Chinese people or their "representatives" remarkably more say over important matters of the state. Decision-making power has remained closely guarded, restricted to a handful. Some deputies may have spoken for the people, but not because they have an established and essential place in policy making.[83] The CPC's satellite parties, trade unions, and mass organizations were all required to accept the leadership of the CPC and the party's political, economic, and social programs. The reform aims at procedural regularity to promote modernization and to improve government efficiency. The post-Mao regime has been trying to maintain a political order in which the party–state rule is more formal, effective, and stable, "as an alternative to Mao's class-based, charismatic style of rule."[84] The major features of the legal system remain the same as before: the CPC continues to dominate the legislative initiation and law-making process; law making and law implementation must comply with the "Four Cardinal Principles" which constitute the framework and the foundation of the Constitution; although there is a functioning legal system, law administrations and bureaucracies, in practice, seldom respect it for its own value, but more often take the party policy and the directives of the party authorities as the guide for their legal actions since the legal system is not independent of party power, and courts are treated as arms of party and government authorities; law is used as a means of suppressing the discontented and dissidents and of preserving and protecting the monopolistic power of the party and the ruling class. The Chinese legal system and laws have provided "the legal prohibition against anything that might 'sabotage the socialist system,' 'disrupt the socialist economy,' 'infringe upon the interests of the state,' or incite 'acts detrimental to the security, honor, and interests of the motherland.'"[85] In this way, party–state leaders can maintain and protect their monopolistic power, justify their goals and policies, not only in the name of the class, the people, and the state, but also in the name of "law and order."

Questions for discussion

1. What is "rule of law?" What is "rule by law?"
2. What are the main functions of the National People's Congress?
3. What legal changes have taken place in post-Mao China? To what extent have such changes affected the nature of the legal system? Has post-Mao China established rule of law?

Further reading

Karen Turner-Gottschang, *et al.*, *The Limits of the Rule of Law in China* (Seattle: University of Washington Press, 2000).

Pitman B. Potter, *The Chinese Legal System: Globalization and Local Legal Culture* (New York: Routledge, 2001).

Randall P. Peerenboom, *China's Long March toward Rule of Law* (Cambridge: Cambridge University Press, 2002).

Part VII
Chinese society

13 Chinese social structure and state–society relations

According to Talcott Parsons, social stratification is defined as "the differential ranking of human individuals who compose a given social system and their treatment as superior or inferior relative to one another in certain socially important respects"[1] and "the class status of an individual is that rank in the system of stratification which can be ascribed to him [sic] by virtue of those of his [sic] kinship ties which bind him to a unit in the class structure."[2] Social classes and stratification in China have evolved from ancient times to modern times as a result of political, economic, and social changes. However, among the two most important of the continuities from ancient times to contemporary China are (1) the social class structure and stratification are not based on wealth or hereditary social standing, but on the power and the officialdom that determine one's social status in the political and social structure; (2) the state dominates and overrides society in many significant ways. In what follows, we will examine social structure and social control in traditional China, China prior to 1949, and Mao's China and then observe the general trends of continuity despite social change, and conclude that the nature of power, political tradition, ideological centralization, and organizational control over resources has determined continuity over time in social structure and stratification as well as in state–society relations in China.

Social structure and social control in traditional China

Since the ancient times of Xia (2205–1766 BCE), Shang (1766–1122 BCE), and Zhou (1122–1221 BCE), Chinese civilization, based on the "hydraulic society" dependent on large-scale water control, established a despotic, absolutist, and centralized state which gave the ruling class great power over other members of the state.[3] However, the falling apart of the central Zhou power ushered in a period of change—the Spring and Autumn Period (770–476 BCE) and Warring States Period (475–221 BCE). During this period, power became decentralized, and eventually fell apart and brought into being many warring states, each of which was ruled by a warrior king. Therefore, it was a decentralized feudal system, in which a king granted land to his nobles in exchange for their loyalty and contributing services to the kingdom, and a noble offered his peasants protection in exchange for their working on his land. Under the feudal system the people were divided into six classes, the king (天子*tianzi*), the dukes (诸侯 *zhuhou*), the great men (大夫 *daifu*), the scholars (士 *shi*), the common people (庶民 *shumin*), and the slaves (奴隶 *nuli*). The first three classes were hereditary aristocracies, while the scholars were between the noble classes and the common people, and they served various positions in the court or served the powerful as their private consuls. The commoners included peasants, artisans, and merchants. The slaves were the lowest class in society, and they "were used largely as domestic labor"[4] (see Figure 13.1).

However, this feudal system only lasted for several hundred years and was ended in 221 BCE by the unification of all warring states under Emperor Qin, who re-established a despotic centralized dynasty, the Qin dynasty, based on a highly centralized bureaucratic state, which endured to modern times, although there were several hundred years of civil wars, divisions, and unstable periods of central imperial rule between the Han Dynasty and the Tang Dynasty. After the Tang dynasty (618 AD), the central government implemented the imperial examination system to rebuild the highly centralized bureaucratic state based on the domination of Confucianism as the governing philosophy, which had a long-term impact on social class formation and stratification, enduring to the end of last imperial Qing dynasty, regardless of dynastic changes.

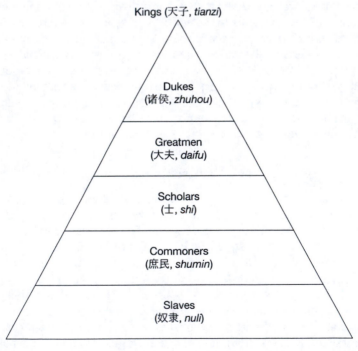

Figure 13.1 Traditional Chinese social structure (pre-Qin China).

Traditional Chinese society from the Tang to Qing dynasties was divided and ranked by four social classes or categories: scholar-gentry (士), peasants (农), artisans (工), and merchants (商).[5] The top level class consisted of gentry, Confucian scholars, and officials who had land, knowledge and power, but without hereditary aristocratic titles and their positions and status were not hereditary. That is to say, except for the emperor and his family, nothing was hereditary.[6] The second class consisted of the peasants, who were the economic base of the country. The third class consisted of the artisans who were skilled and economically self-sufficient. The fourth class consisted of the merchants who engaged in business and sales of goods.[7] The social structure of the four classes was despotic and hierarchical, with the emperor at the top of the pyramid of power; all things were done in his name and under his authority. No significant local forces, independent social forces, churches, or nobility, as in feudalism in the Western context, could challenge the monarchy, and the emperor ruled absolutely based on a highly centralized bureaucratic state. In the West, "a hereditary nobility often limits the power of the central ruler, since nobility carries a prestige and authority of its own as in Western Europe where kings fought for centuries to curb the power of the nobles" as well as the authority of the church.[8] China also lacked another feature of the early modern West, an independent urban middle class or bourgeoisie.[9] Therefore, a Chinese monarch is absolute compared to a Western monarch.

The bureaucratic elite (the Mandarins) at central, provincial, and county levels were recruited by virtue of imperial degrees obtained through national civil service examinations on state ideology, Confucianism, and literary classics, given at the county, province, and central levels. To be eligible for the higher levels a candidate had first to pass the lower exams, with the attrition rate increasing at each level: 10 percent would pass the county level exam, but only 2–3 percent would pass the provincial and central levels.[10] Therefore, social control was based on ideological centralization, Confucian indoctrination, and scholar–gentry officialdom.

Scholar–gentry officialdom was the ruling elite that ruled society on behalf of and for the emperor based on a highly centralized, hierarchical bureaucratic state. Below the ruling elite were powerless peasants, artisans, and merchants. The basic class distinction was between the powerful and the powerless. Social structure and stratification were not based on wealth or hereditary social standing, but on the power and the officialdom that determined one's social status in the political and social structure (Figure 13.2).

Pre-1949 social structure and state–society relations

During the late Qing period, old merchants and newly emerged capitalists began to grow into national capitalists. They organized chambers of commerce and industrial associations, promoting ideas of constitutionalism and local self-government assemblies.[11] However, long before the late Qing, Chinese people had organized themselves into clan or family groups that supported the temples

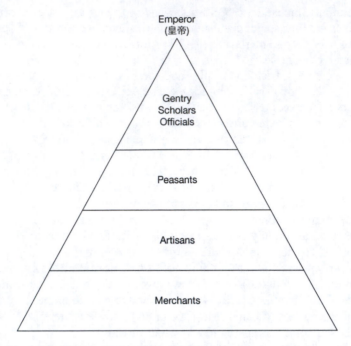

Figure 13.2 Traditional Chinese social structure (from Tang to Qing).

and schools, and other charities, and also into merchants' associations that provided mutual support to merchants who traveled to and from distant cities.[12] Scholarly associations and private professional institutions in sciences, medicine, education, and other public services also appeared in China, particularly in some major cities and coastal areas after the turn of the twentieth century.[13]

However, after the KMT's seizure of national government in 1927, due to the shortage of capital, wartime turbulence after the Japanese invasion, and the civil war, industrialization was not a success, and this most dynamic element of capitalism never gained ground. This sector mainly concentrated on light industry especially textiles, not on heavy industry such as steel production and machine building.[14] By 1933, modern factories only produced 2 percent of GDP with only a million workers, which constituted only 0.4 percent of China's labor force. Modern industry began in enclaves in the Treaty Ports during the twentieth century, with mainly textiles and light industry concentrated in some cities, such as Shanghai, Tianjin, and Qingdao. The Japanese government and its quasi-official affiliates, however, invested in heavy industry and railroads in the northeast, which was then called Manchuria, to aggressively exploit the rich deposits of coal and iron ore in the region for the Japanese domestic industrialization while preparing these heavy industries for its strategic objectives as shown in the later full-scale military aggression in China and the wars in southeast Asia against other major powers in the region. However, these Japanese heavy industries tightly controlled by Japanese nationals had few linkages and spillover effects to other regions of China.[15]

After the collapse of the last imperial dynasty, Qing dynasty, in 1911, an industrial working class emerged in some major cities, such as Beijing, Shanghai, and Hong Kong, but remained a minority among the Chinese population because China remained predominantly an agrarian society. Between 1920 and 1949, the industrial working class had only increased by less than three million, mainly women and children working in cotton mills. However, the upper class changed dramatically—a new group of elite emerged to lead the country: military and political leaders, new intelligentsia, national capitalists, landlords, and state technocrats.[16] The social structure and stratification continued to be based on the power and wealth that determined one's social status in the political and social structure (Figure 13.3).

Despite the authoritarian rule of the KMT, a civil society clearly existed in China. Civic organizations or NGOs in the social, economic, and cultural spheres were self-generating, self-supporting, and independent of the state, promoting autonomous associational life and activities, except for some organizations under the leadership of the KMT. Labor movements, student movements, peasant movements, etc., which were independent of the KMT government, became the driving force and training ground of the communist

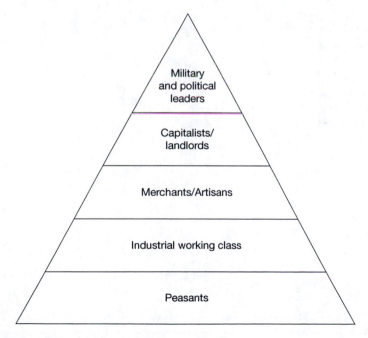

Figure 13.3 Chinese social structure pre-1949.

revolution despite the KMT suppression. Traditional social organizations, such as kinships, clans, and religions, remained the basis for traditional social relations and allocation of resources, except for rural areas where the Communist Party of China (CPC) created "guerrilla war bases" for fighting against the KMT.

Social structure and social control in Mao's China

In traditional China, social relations and the allocation of resources were primarily founded on the basis of blood kinship networks, familial lineages, neighborhood relationships, and interpersonal relationships that were formed on the basis of a shared location where people had grown up, such as a place of birth, or the same town or neighbors. It was on such a basis that individuals developed their dependence on and loyalty to such social relationships. However, after 1949, as a result of socialist transformation as well as political, economic, and ideological campaigns, resources, employment, location of living, and opportunities for mobility and career advancement were all monopolized and coercively redistributed by the state, and traditional social organizations were replaced by mass organizations led by the party, which actually destroyed the bases of those traditional relationships and created new political, social, and economic bases for social relationships and social status. People were divided into three social classes, a small tiny ruling class of cadre,

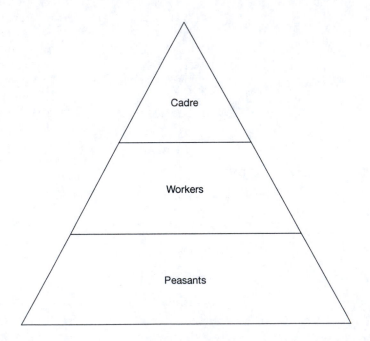

Figure 13.4 Chinese social structure from the late 1960s to the late 1970s.

a small urban working class of workers, and a large rural class of peasants, because peasants constituted the large majority of the population[17] (Figure 13.4).

Such patterns of social structure and stratification were based on social members' positions and relations in the political and administrative systems and reinforced by the following identity systems: urban–rural residential registration system, work unit identity system, and cadres-masses identity system.

1. *Urban–rural residential registration system.* This system divided people into two residential categories: urban and rural, and any change or switch between urban and rural residential areas was strictly controlled and approved by the party–state agencies. People had no choice of where they wanted to work and live. In fact, such a residential system created a *de facto* divided and dual social structure. Living and working in urban areas became a symbol of identity and privilege.

2. *Work unit identity system.* Almost all urban residents belong to work units. Work units were at the grassroots of governmental administration and party organizations in the power structure. They could be schools, factories, business organizations, public organizations, or any work place where people were employed. Work units were carriers of state planning, ideological and political campaigns, administration orders and policies, as well as networks of social relations and cells of political socialization and mass mobilization. Small group political study and mutual criticism were the most frequent, longstanding forms of brainwashing in the work units. Individuals were required to place their commitments to the party and its cause above personal affections and obligations, and they were required to report their innermost feelings and criticize errant tendencies in others in group meetings. Interpersonal relations were fundamentally affected. All units were ranked according to levels of administrative jurisdiction, called "administrative ranks" (行政级别), which were entitled to different powers, responsibilities, privileges, and benefits in the hierarchically organized party–state structure. Each person had to be associated with a work unit in order to have a work unit identity card (工作证), be employed, supervised, and disciplined if wrongdoings were found, and guaranteed the minimum state welfare in exchange for obedience to the state authority. Therefore, social members were unitized, i.e., all individuals were organized into work units, and social resources were unitized, planned, and distributed by work units. Individuals were entitled to the right of having a certain portion of the social resource only if they were unitized, such as salary, welfare, pension, medicare, housing, school, etc.

3. *Cadres–masses identity system.* Cadres were those on the official nomenclature list and payroll system, and enjoyed certain privileges in salary, housing, welfare, and services that the masses did not. As allocation of resources by ownership was replaced by central planning, obtaining the

status and the identity of cadres was honorable and admirable, and permitted career advancement and moving upward in the hierarchically centralized political structure of the party–state apparatus. Cadres were classified in a hierarchical order into ranks (级别) which were associated with their positions, responsibilities, salaries, and privileges. A cadre's rank was associated with salary levels, welfare, and privileges, and such cadre identity was permanent, even after retirement. Cadres were the elite of the party–state.[18]

Such a social structure was created as a result of the major social, political, and economic transformation in the People's Republic of China. The first major transformation of society took place during the 1950s in a series of major campaigns carried out by the CPC.

In rural areas, an initial land reform after the communist takeover in 1949 redistributed land to those who did not own land. This was quickly followed by a series of agricultural reforms that increased the level of collectivization of land and the scale of organization, from mutual aid teams (groups of joint-operating farmers from individual farming households), to agricultural cooperatives, and finally to large People's Communes. By the fall 1958, some 23,500 communes were incorporated from some 750,000 agricultural cooperatives, each averaging 5,000 households, or 22,000 people. By the early 1960s, an estimated 74,000 communes had been established.[19] The communes are the administrative and economic units of the party–state apparatus in rural China.

In urban areas, virtually all private enterprises were nationalized by the mid-1970s into SOEs or cooperatives that were run by central and local governments. Socialist transformation campaigns had periodically launched and basically wiped out any independent political, social, economic, and cultural organizations, with all aspects of Chinese society being controlled by the party–state apparatus and its mass organizations in workplace or work unit (*Danwei*). Individuals were absorbed into a collective (a unit), with no free mobility, including job change, residential relocation, and traveling, relying on the state for everything through the work units where they are employed. Individuals were required to subject their self-interest to the state interest. All units had their superior administrations which were hierarchically structured and controlled from the top down. All units carried out their superiors' plans, policies, and orders. Work units had political, economic, and social functions, and dominated all these spheres of Chinese society, such as indoctrination, political campaigns, education, public health, welfare, housing, individual dispute and conflict resolutions, and maintaining social order, etc. Individuals could only play a role through the units where they were employed, and their roles were defined and controlled by the units. Party organizations were established in all work units, and penetrated every corner of Chinese society. Citizens were compelled to participate in different organizations within their work units, such as the Youth League, Women's Association, Trade Union, and the CPC. Andrew G. Walder's elaboration on the work unit is so precise and insightful that a substantial quote is necessary to our understanding of the organizational features of the communist party–state and its political implications for the system maintenance and social control:

> In a communist regime, the state has a double impact. Not only does it have the organized capacity to shape political relationships and activity more thoroughly than other types of authoritarian regimes; in China and the Soviet Union, the contemporary working class is itself a creation of the industrial drive directed by the party–state. They have in reality created their modern working classes and mobilized them into the political organizations that are grassroots extensions of the party–state itself.[20]

The household registration system (*hukou*) and the work unit (*Danwei*) were two of the most important means of social control and were integrated into a system of administrative management of Chinese society. In the household registration system (*hukou*), every household was officially registered with the local police station; every registered household was issued a residence booklet; reported any changes in the household to local authority; personal records were kept in the local police authority; residents had to go to the local police authority to process the change if they were going to switch jobs from one area to another authorized by the work unit, and reported to the police station when they arrived at the new location.

Society was politically and ideologically constructed to achieve the Party's goals of social transformation, and was divided into two major categories, "black" and "red," based on class and class birth categorization, which received different treatments. The good or "red" category included workers, peasants, soldiers, intellectuals, and cadres while the bad or "black" category included landowners, rich peasants, bourgeoisie, counter-revolutionaries, rightists, and criminals. Those in the "black" categories were victimized and treated as the "class enemy." This class categorization was based on the Marxist class division between the proletariat and the bourgeois and social members' political attitudes and ideological orientation towards the Chinese revolution and the CPC. The categorizations were used as criteria for party–state social control, allocation of resources, employment, career development, advancement, and almost every area of social life, and applied in every political and ideological campaign in which those who were labeled as "black" were attacked by mass movements mobilized by the party led by Mao Zedong to achieve the political goals of "class struggle" and "constant revolution under the proletariat dictatorship."

Traditional Chinese society's associations such as kinships, clans, and religions were replaced by government bureaus or party–state led "mass organizations," such as trade unions, peasantry associations, women's associations, youth leagues, and many others. Virtually everyone belonged to a work unit, such as a factory, school, government office, shop, or village production team. The consequence of such social transformation was that most aspects of social differentiation, stratification, mobility, and tension were all played out within the party–state institutional framework and controlled by party–state organizations. Party–state power controlled, dominated and penetrated every corner of Chinese society through a powerful network of political and administrative power, such as party organizations, work units, mass organizations, street and neighborhood committees, and the residential *hukou* registration system. The state–society relationship can be characterized as totalistic domination, command, mobilization and indoctrination by the party–state, and no social organizations or social members are independent of the state.

Changes in social structure in post-Mao China

In post-Mao China, the simple class division or "black–red" labeling has been officially abolished. The social structure of cadres, workers, and peasants based on identity, work unit, and the administrative system has been increasingly diversified because Chinese society has become more diversified and pluralistic due to changes brought about by market-oriented economic reforms, diversified ownership structure, and social stratifications.[21] The household registration system (*hukou*) and the work unit (*Danwei*) have been watered down as peasants began to look for jobs in urban areas, and state and collective workers began to work in the private sector. We have witnessed the emergence of some new "classes," such as the "new rich" in SOEs and other economic sectors, middle class (managers and professionals), capitalists (private business owners), and other social classes.[22] Social mobility has been increased among these social classes, but mobility is still constrained by party–state policy and political-economic confined context.

In 2002, a research team of China scholars led by a prominent sociologist, Lu Xueyi, published important work based on their nationwide empirical research, titled *Research Report on Contemporary China's Social Stratums*, which divides Chinese society into 10 social strata and five social classes based on the criteria of organizational resources, economic resources, and cultural resources controlled by different social groups. Organizational resources refer to the control over administrative and political resources, particularly party–state organizational systems that control political, social, and economic resources. Economic resources refer to the ownership, control, and management of the means of production. Cultural resources refer to the ownership, control and management of cultural and technological resources. In China today, these three resources determine the social and economic status of individuals, their occupations, and positions in social classes. The 10 social strata include the party–state officials, managers, private owners, engineers, staffers, small business owners, self-employed individuals and service employees, industrial workers, rural peasants, and unemployed social members. The five social classes include (1) high class (high ranking government

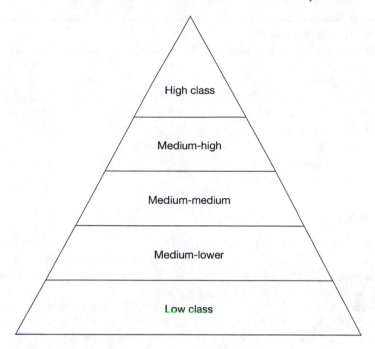

Figure 13.5 Chinese social structure in post-Mao China.

Source: Lu Xueyi, ed., *Research Report on Contemporary China's Social Stratums* (Beijing: Social Science Literature Press, 2002), p. 4.

officials, senior managers of large-scale enterprises, senior technical professionals, and big private owners); (2) medium-high class (medium-lower ranking officials, medium-level managers of large scale enterprises, managers and technical professionals of medium-small enterprises, and medium scale business owners); (3) medium-medium class (junior level technical professionals, small business owners, staffers); (4) medium-lower class (self-employed individuals, retail and service employees, workers, and peasants); and (5) low class (unemployed or semi-unemployed workers, rural and urban populations who live below the poverty line) (Figure 13.5).

The ranking of social members in social status and position is determined by the quantities and capabilities of their control over the three resources, and the important values of resources under their control. Of the three resources, organizational resources are the most important and decisive, because the party–state controls the most important and largest resources in the whole society. Control over economic and cultural resources has become increasingly important in market reforms and socioeconomic development, but it is dependent on party–state organizations and agents in many important ways, including survival and development. Moreover, party–state political and ideological systems have increased their control over those with increasing economic and cultural resources and have curbed their increasing influence over the society and politics.[23]

This begs the questions: Does the basic pattern of social control in China that was established during the period of Mao Zedong still remain fundamentally unchanged despite considerable changes in many aspects of the social and private lives of individuals in post-Mao China? Does the basic social structure and identity system of cadre, workers, and peasants remain essentially unchanged despite the changes in social stratification in post-Mao China? Is there any fundamental change in the state–society relationship? Therefore, it will be the central task of the next chapter to examine the social changes and social control in post-Mao China.

Questions for discussion

1. How has the nature of power, political tradition, ideological centralization, and organizational control over resources determined the continuity over time in social structure and stratification as well as state–society relations from ancient times to contemporary China?
2. Which forces, tradition or modernization, would be more powerful in determining the future trends of social structure and state and society relations? What might be the necessary conditions for a fundamental change in China's social structure and state–society relations?

Further reading

A. Doak Barnett, *Cadres, Bureaucracy, and Political Power in Communist China* (New York: Columbia University Press, 1967).

James L. Watson, ed., Class and Social Stratification in Post-Revolution China (Cambridge University Press, 1984).

Andrew G. Walder, "Social Change in Post-Revolution China," *Annual Review of Sociology*, vol. 15, 1989, pp. 405–24.

Hong Yung Lee, *From Revolutionary Cadres to Party Technocrat in Socialist China* (Berkeley: University of California Press, 1991).

Tiejun Cheng and Mark Selden, "The Origins and Social Consequences of China's Hukou System," *The China Quarterly*, no. 139, 1994, pp. 644–68.

Wing Chan Kam and Li Zhang, "The Hukou System and Rural-Urban Migration in China: Processes and Changes," *The China Quarterly*, no. 160, 1999, pp. 831–40.

Fei-Ling Wang, "Reformed Migration Control and New Targeted People: China's Hukou System in the 2000s," *The China Quarterly*, no. 177, 2004, pp. 115–32.

Yi Li, *The Structure and Evolution of Chinese Social Stratification* (The University Press of America, 2005).

14 Social changes and state–society relations in post-Mao China

Post-Mao reforms have brought about some considerable changes in Chinese society, particularly in terms of state–society relations. Chinese society itself has become more pluralistic and complex, with a greater variety of groups and interests, as a result of the market reform and economic modernization.

First, action means of state control over society have been diversified. Instead of relying solely upon the traditional administrative command, central planning, and ideological control, the post-Mao party–state has skillfully taken advantage of economic, legal, and other means of social control.

Second, decentralization has greatly affected not only the relations between the center and the provincial/local governments but also the changing state–society relations and the freedom of individuals in economic activities, daily life, and lifestyles. The government at all levels has faced rising public unrest and protests over land seizures, environment concerns, and corruption, ethnic conflict, labor–capital conflict, migration settlement and migrant protest, environmental disputes, homeowner's rights movements, resistance to family planning and other governmental policies, and internet challenges to the government.[1]

Third, the ownership structure has shifted from state and collective ownership to the coexistence of multiple forms of ownership, which has resulted in great change in social stratification and interest differentiation. Chinese society has become more complex in terms of industrial structure, employment structure, urban–rural structure, and social stratum structure. Existing groups have become internally more complex as a consequence of diversification in economic sectors, forms of ownership, and levels of income. Post-Mao China has witnessed the emergence of a new rich class in Chinese society, who are successful private business people or state or collective firm top-level managers, and a widening income gap between the new rich class and the general population.

Fourth, decollectivization of agriculture by dismantling the commune system and economic modernization has liberated peasants from collective farming and allowed them to pursue economic activities in their own ways. The change has also provided an enormous opportunity for 200 million peasants to go to urban areas to find jobs and become industrial workers, and this rural to urban migration is paralleled by more social mobility in the population and labor force in urban areas. As a result, the traditional management system of urban residents based on the permanent residential household system (*hukou*单位) and work units (*danwei*户口) is being watered down, because control over the floating population is difficult, though such a control system is still effective and continues to serve important functions in social, economic, and political life. The so-called "floating population" refers to those migrants who move to places where they do not have permanent household registration status and thus do not receive the various benefits and advantages of those who have household registration status.

Fifth, post-Mao China has witnessed the proliferation of semi-official and popular (*minjian*) social organizations (not without rigid limitations by the state), such as the Individual Laborers and Private Enterprises Association, the Stamp Collecting Club, the *Qigong* Research Association, and the Old People's Exercise Association, while the party–state still contains their development and excludes their influence on politics. In 2011, it was officially reported that there were 440,000 social organizations in China, among which 195,000 were NGOs.[2] The figure does not include those unregistered social organizations.

These changes are clearly evident. However, despite these changes, the party–state has not retreated from society, instead it has employed different methods to maintain control over development, and incorporated them into the party–state controlled interdependence of economic, social, cultural, administrative, and political institutions. Society is not free from the arbitrary interventions of party–state institutions and local officialdom, and their sphere of activity has been carefully defined and regulated by the party–state.

Actually, the post-Mao decentralized, market reform has given state bureaucracies and local officialdom substantial control over new resources such as market information, business licenses, fees, and tax collection, creating new commercialized societal dependencies on state bureaucracies and local officialdom. Their power is redefined but not necessarily diminished. In village politics where village committees now function as the board of directors of a village economy, party committees continue to exist and the party secretary acts like the boss.[3]

Furthermore, a "pluralistic society" and a "civil society" are two totally different concepts that cannot be treated interchangeably in political analysis. A more pluralistic society does not necessarily mean that the Chinese communist regime has developed into a pluralistic polity if diverse economic interests, social groups, and specialists are all incorporated into the party–state political context. State–society relations are defined, controlled, and dominated by the party–state. The role of these groups and interests is still so limited that in no way could they challenge and check the party–state institutions or become truly independent of the party–state establishment, though informal politics through personal networks and bargaining between the state and these groups may play a certain role in the conduct of public affairs. Such contradictions require reassessment of post-Mao changes, and assessment of these changes should enrich our understanding of post-Mao change.

The assessment must be based upon the general conceptual framework of state–society relations. One key indicator involves the party's substantial retreat not only from the state apparatus but also from society. As Zbigniew Brzezinski put it, the emergence of an autonomous civil society is the point of departure for the eventual self-emancipation of society from communist control, and the autonomous political dialogue thereby surfacing might contribute to the transformation of dissent into actual political opposition capable of challenging and negotiating with the ruling party and, eventually, it might contribute to democratic transition.[4] However, post-Mao development has not suggested that the party has made a substantial retreat either from the state or from society, though the party–state has relaxed its control over the daily life and economic activities of its citizens.

Chinese society in the context of political embeddedness

Civil society is a concept that has been commonly used in the study of social change and state–society relations in post-Mao China. Civil society is defined as the public realm of organized social life that is voluntary, self-generating, self-supporting, and autonomous or independent of the state.[5] Civil society is usually used in two senses. In the first sense, civil society stands in opposition to the state as a forum for setting limits to state power and checking excesses. There is no evidence that supports the existence of a civil society in this sense. In the second sense, civil society refers to those social organizations or associations that are assumed to arise voluntarily outside the state and to operate autonomously from the state.

It seems that there are emerging many new social organizations in post-Mao China with the introduction of market reforms.[6] Some of the new social organizations seem to display certain features associated with a civil society: initiated from the bottom with a voluntary membership, independent of the state, and occupying space outside the state. Associational life has flourished in post-Mao China as people seek out interests that differ from those of the state, and even attempt to influence party–state policy making in many areas, which has led to increasingly open discontent and friction between the party–state and society.[7]

But the key question is: to what extent do we find that "civil society" exists in post-Mao China? In other words, to what extent are these social organizations independent from the state, and voluntary or spontaneous? Assessment requires a clearer categorization and a closer examination of these organized social groups or social organizations based on the defining features of civil society.

Since there is no evidence that supports the existence of a civil society in the first sense, this study will focus on the post-Mao social change in the second sense. In the second sense of civil society, four broad categories of social organizations have been identified in Table 14.1 in terms of their autonomy, voluntariness, and spontaneity.[8]

A social organization is autonomous if it is able to set its own goals, determine its own structure, and rely upon its own financial resources. A social organization is voluntary if its members choose to participate in the organizational activity of their free will rather than being asked by the government to do so. A social organization is spontaneous if its members founded the organization of their own accord.[9] The four broad categories along this continuum are the official mass organizations, such as Youth League, Trade Union, Women's Association; the new semi-official social organizations such as the Private Entrepreneurs' Association; the new, popular social organizations such as stamp clubs or Qigong societies; and illegal organizations such as secret societies or underground political organizations.

The official mass organizations, with more than a hundred national organizations and tens of thousands of local subordinate branches, such as the Communist Youth League, China Young Pioneers, the Trade Union, the Women's Association, China Film Critics Society, the Writers' Association, the Artists' Association, Chinese Legal Consultant Center, Chinese Buddhist Association, Three-Self Patriotic Movement Committee of the Protestant Churches of China, Red Cross Society of China, and so many more, stand near the pole of no autonomy, no voluntariness, and no spontaneity. They are vertically integrated into the top-down party–state institutions at all levels and have functioned as "transmission belts" between the party–state and society. Their staff are officially appointed and paid by the state, and they basically serve as implementers of party–state policy. Their roles, functions, responsibilities, governing ideologies, and norms have remained fundamentally unchanged compared to those in the pre-reform era. These organizations and institutions also administer important functions of political and social administration on behalf of the party–state, for example, as responsible administrative units and agencies (*xingzheng zhuguan danwei* 行政主管单位) for those registered social or popular organizations, in addition to fulfilling their own responsibilities, thus becoming an extension of the state apparatus. Their role and influence has not been weakened over the past 30 years but remains effective, pervasive, and predominant in almost all important fields of society—political, ideological, social, cultural, and economic.

Table 14.1 Four broad categories of social organizations in post-Mao China

Four categories of social organizations	Autonomous	Voluntary	Spontaneous
Official mass organizations	No	No	No
New semi-official social organizations	Yes, limited	No	No
New popular social organizations	Yes, limited	Yes	Yes
Illegal organizations	Yes	Yes	Yes

The new semi-official social or business organizations such as the Individual Industrial and Commercial Laborers Association, the Private Entrepreneurs' Association, the Self-Employed Workers' Association, and the Lawyers' Association enjoy greater autonomy than the old, official mass organizations, but less than popular or illegal organizations. These semi-official organizations are not self-generating either. Private entrepreneurs and self-employed businessmen automatically become members of their respective organizations upon registering their business, though there may be some enterprises and individuals who fail to obey the state's call to join the organizations. They are mainly concerned with economic, technical, and professional issues and enjoy some degree of autonomy partly because it is in the interests of the state for them to do so. The economic reforms since 1979 have led to the emergence of many new economic sectors and activities. In this context, these new institutional forms provide their members additional official channels for communication and ideological education, a mechanism for linking individual economic actors with various state agencies, and maintain the official influence and control of the party–state in these new sectors of the economy and society. These organizations are allowed to benefit their own members by promoting their interests through the state agencies or local officialdom. At the same time, however, this also enables the state and local government to manage the sectoral policy and control these new sectors more effectively. This is called "integration of social organizations" (整合社会) into party–state institutions.

These new business organizations are semi-official because the state is involved in their goal-setting, organizational structure, management, and funding. Leaders and staff are drawn from related governmental departments or bureaus, though some leaders may be chosen from private enterprises or other economic organizations. They are not organized voluntarily and spontaneously, or "self-generating," but established compulsorily according to the need of party–state control and party policy in post-Mao reforms to "bridge the gap between the state and society." Although they claim to represent the interests of the individual entrepreneur or sectoral interests, they are established and directed by the State Administration of Industry and Commerce, which is the state office in charge of licensing and policing both private and public enterprises. Thus, these new business organizations have become part of the Leninist or Maoist "transmission belt" organizations designed to gain control of independent activity, rather than presenting themselves as a challenge to the government's current policy and basic ideological principles. Some individual entrepreneurs may attempt to take advantage of these organizations to pursue their interests but many others view these organizations simply as another organ of the state trying to intervene in their affairs and keep their activities under control. Therefore, the development of new social or business organizations reveals "the strength and the power of the state socialist system" to structure the self-organizations of individual and private entrepreneurs and "the Leninist strategy used by the party–state to co-opt and control societal forces."[10]

The new popular social organizations such as stamp clubs, chess clubs, poetry societies, or *Qigong* societies stand more toward the pole of greater autonomy, voluntariness and spontaneity. They rely upon their own fund-raising efforts, set their own goals, and manage their organizations with volunteers. They were created voluntarily to bring together people who share similar cultural interests. They are not totally autonomous, however, because they are required to register with the state and they are subject to annual review by the governmental agency. As long as they operate within the scope of their registered activities and confines of state policy, and do not challenge the government, they have considerable autonomy in their activities. Moreover, although the popular organizations have in general been founded by their members, their creation has been conditional upon party–state tolerance for such organizations and their activities have been restricted to nonpolitical issues.

Illegal social organizations are the most autonomous, voluntary, and spontaneous of all the four categories, precisely because they are not legally permitted. Examples include some secret societies, ethnic associations, and underground political groups. They set their own goals, raise their own funds, and manage themselves. However, party–state control of social life has been tightened to an unprecedented extent, and there are no records of such unregistered organizations.[11]

Among the four broad categories, the last two social organizations are actually marginalized in political life, and, as a matter of fact, they have few channels to exercise their collective influence on the politics and checks on the government. The second and third categories are allowed to develop in nonpolitical areas and are organized in ways that enhance the power of government agencies that have jurisdiction over them. In more recent years, these organizations have been allowed to participate in the conduct of public affairs, for example, public service delivery, consultative meetings, local issues that affect the community. The last category is actually excluded from participation in political life, and also has the lowest degree of institution-alization, because all organized activities not licensed by the party–state are not legally permitted. Post-Mao reforms have brought about more diversity of social organizations and a flourishing of associational life in China. But nothing suggests a fundamental change in state–society relations. Party–state dominance has remained in the social organizations of political and social significance; party–state control and penetration in society and the economy have remained in effect, and are even more tight than the 1980s. Civil society in both senses has remained largely disorganized and underdeveloped in post-Mao China. To establish a plausible argument for this, a closer examination is needed.

The presence or absence of a strong and organized civil society makes a significant difference in the transition from the party–state system. Civil society, in the context of communist countries, refers primarily to the public realm between the state and the private sphere. Under the communist regime, this "intermediate" public sphere is party-led, government-controlled, or state-certified, since the party–state controls this sphere to a great extent. Typical for a civil society is its independence from the state, and the building of such a civil society with independent social institutions and organizations is an integral part of democratic transition. Such a civil society is a "proving ground" for democracy, for it is in this realm that the social forces act as checks on the ruling elite and can be well organized and prepared to provide a real challenge to the ruling elite while citizens can develop a democratic attitude and mentality.[12] Therefore, whether or not the party–state allows civil society to develop or to what extent it is permitted to develop will also determine the nature of the transition.

This is an overriding constraint during the transition that comes from the nature of state–society relations: will the party–state apparatus permit the development of civil society to undermine their monopoly on power and transfer substantial public assets to private persons?[13] Under communist party–state leadership, economic reform or economic liberalization itself will not necessarily create a civil society but only provide certain opportunities for the emergence of social or economic institutions which may have little function or checks on the government. Their further development has been constrained by party–state permission. Any attempt to register an independent political group or party was not allowed, and their activists would be charged with attempting to "sow social unrest" or "disturbing social stability and unity;" the members of any "underground" political groups would experience persecution and imprisonment. However, nonpolitical professional groups, clubs, or associations must register with party–state institutions or official mass organizations, and are regulated and overseen by government restrictions and prohibited from engaging in political activity.

After the Communist takeover of power in China, the previously existing structures of civil society were destroyed and replaced by official "mass organizations" controlled by the party–state apparatus. The party–state excluded any social forces that could challenge the party–state and subjugated individuals to party–state domination.[14] The Post-Mao economic liberalization did not bring about any substantial change in this regard. Truly independent civil society organizations are not permitted. However, the people's demands to participate in conducting public affairs have now been selectively recognized as the CPC's governance practice, accommodated and incorporated by party–state organizations, or official "mass organizations" that have in fact been institutionalized into bureaucratic organs. Therefore, a change in state–society relations has taken place in the context of "political embeddedness"—social organizations are enmeshed in the party–state political structure and bureaucratic institutional networks, which create dependencies, incentives, and opportunities for social organizations to engage in activities in the direction defined by party–state ideology, political goals, and policies.

Statization of society through state license system

Over the past three decades, the party has institutionalized its control over almost every sector of the state that was undermined by the Cultural Revolution, including state bureaucracy, the legislature, the judiciary, the military, the media, education, culture, and society. Recent developments in China have not suggested that the party has made a substantial retreat either from the state or from society. One of the essential features of the Leninist party–state is the statization (国家化) of society, by which party–state power penetrates almost every important aspect of society, to empower the party–state, not society, in state–society relations. In recent years, the party–state has required state agencies to incorporate civil society organizations in selected areas of public affairs, such as welfare and public service delivery, to achieve the party's policy goals. In Leninist party–state countries, since the communist party is identical to the state, government, and the regime, party organizations and their control via the state apparatus are thus pervasive in society. Such statization of society involves two political aspects: statization of social organizations and penetration of state power into society.

In the process of statization of society, since the party is completely intertwined with the state, all sectors of the state have turned into administrative agents of the ruling party as well as being institutionalized into a hierarchically controlled "administrative state" that administers a unified administrative control over the major means of production and exchange, the key industries of the national economy, and major economic, social, and cultural organizations and activities, including major SOEs, state-owned banks, schools, social organizations, and cultural, scientific, and academic institutions. These organizations and institutions also administer important political and social functions on behalf of the state in addition to fulfilling their own responsibilities, thus becoming an extension of the state apparatus. Although they are different from state institutions, they have almost become another version of the state apparatus, because these organizations share many similarities with state institutions: they are all managed under responsible administrative agencies (归口管理*guikou guanli*); they are not organized voluntarily and spontaneously; leaders are not elected by their members voluntarily, and staff are paid by the state fiscal expenditure; they are hierarchically organized and act like state institutions; and so forth.

On the other hand, the statization of society has brought about substantial penetration of party–state power in society, and the administrative state has extended into an "administrative society" in which individual citizens, through the "transmission belts" of official or state-sanctioned social organizations and institutions, are influenced by and subject to state power relations and control of the administrative state. State power has become the major means of transforming society and citizens in line with the party's ideology and goal. "Democratic centralism" is the organizational principle not only of the ruling party but also state institutions and social organizations, thus guaranteeing the effective control of superiors over subordinates within party–state institutions and effective control of the party–state over these organizations and society as a whole.

Has "de-statization" occurred in post-Mao China since reform and opening? China has indeed witnessed the growth of civic organizations growing out of participation defined, guided, regulated, and controlled by the party–state.[15] However, the dual structure of the "administrative state" and "administrative society" has remained fundamentally unchanged, and state power has continued to perform comprehensive functions of administrative, political, and ideological leadership—the economic function of organizing major economic activities through large and medium-sized SOEs, the social function of administering major means of distribution and exchange of public goods, the ideological function of cultural education, and the political/legal function of maintaining socialist political and legal systems. Government penetration and control of mass communication, social and cultural organizations, and major economic activities are still significantly strong in post-Mao China.

Although the state is beginning to permit some new semi-official or popular social organizations to register and develop, the state still contains their development and restricts their influence on Chinese politics and government. All associations must register with the state authorities and restrict their activities to those areas for which the group has been registered and approved by party–state authorities. For example, the State Administration for Industry and Commerce (SAIC) can refuse to register or expel any association on any legal or policy grounds, including affiliation with an overseas organization that is considered anti-China or anti-Chinese government. In 1998, three new administrative regulations were made to ensure austere and total party–state control over the new semi-official and popular social organizations and provide a legal basis for such control. Violators of these regulations would be banned and punished.[16]

Among the officially registered national social organizations and regional social organizations, the official "mass organizations" such as trade unions, youth leagues, and women's associations are predominant in political, cultural, ideological, economic and social life of Chinese citizens. Almost all or most social organizations are "people-run" (民办 *minban*) in name, but "officially run" (官办 *guanban*) and administrative in nature. China's "Rules of Registration and Regulations of Mass Organizations" (RRRSO),[17] which were implemented in 1998 and have not been amended for over a decade, are the world's most stringent and toughest regulations for restricting freedom of association, and in practice they prohibit "freedom of association," which only on paper is stipulated in the Chinese constitution. China's regulation of "mass organizations" is a perfect example of the "rule by law" (法制) with Chinese characteristics, providing legal prohibition against the political and civil rights and liberties of its citizens rather than protection of them (法治).

1. *License system.* According to Article 2 of the RRRSO, "all mass organizations in the People's Republic of China must apply for registration

following the rules. No activity is allowed without the approval of the application." Under this rule, freedom of association is a "freedom" with the approval of the government. It is the government that determines who has access to the "freedom" and what type of association and activity is allowed under the communist party–state rule. More crucially, under Article 2, the registration authorities only accept applications for creating societies, associations, foundations, academic groups, and the like, but do not accept applications to create political parties. In other words, in practice, citizens' rights of association, which are theoretically stipulated in the Constitution, include only those social organizations defined and allowed by the government and exclude the right of creating new political parties. Any attempt to register a political party would have no legal basis, and any activity in the effort to form a political party without legal approval is illegal and will be charged as "a criminal offense" according to the new Criminal Law, and the activists will be arrested and sentenced as "criminal gangs."[18]

2. *Monopoly system.* According to Article 16 of the RRRSO, "no two similar or identical mass organizations are allowed to establish in the same administrative areas." Under this rule, any "political" mass organizations other than those officially run are not allowed. For example, according to the Law of Union, the All Federation of China Trade Union (AFCTU) is the highest leading organ of all trade unions in China. The creation of any trade union must report to the AFCTU and its leading subordinate industrial and regional trade union organs in the same administrative areas. Thus, no trade union other than official ones will be approved and no such activity other than official ones will be allowed in China.

3. *"Hang-on" system* (挂靠 *guakao*). According to Articles 6, 8, and 9 of the RRRSO, all applicants for the registration of mass organizations must first of all obtain the review and approval of concerned business or professional superiors or responsible departments or institutions (有关业务主管单位 *youguan yewu zhuguang danwei*) before they may proceed to apply for registration. Moreover, the concerned superiors or responsible departments have the power to conduct daily supervision and management over the approved mass organizations. In this way, almost every social organization in China has to find a "hang-on" (挂靠 *guakao*) superior within the scope of its own industrial, professional, or business activity and becomes the "hang-on unit" (挂靠单位 *guakao dangwei*) of this "responsible unit" (主管单位 *zhuguan dangwei*) before the application for registration can be considered by the authorities concerned. Thus, all social organizations approved by the authorities are under the supervision and control of governmental institutions and become their satellite "mass organizations."

4. *Annual examination system.* According to Article 24 of the RRRSO, "registration administrative organs conduct annual examination over the mass organizations which must submit annual examination reports and related materials to the concerned organs in the first quarter of every year."

This gives the authorities powers and opportunities to censor and censure these organizations and their associational activities. Once something not in line with the party line and policy is found, it must be corrected immediately.

It is clear that the de-statization of society has not occurred in post-Mao China. Chinese society is a long way from being "civil." The "administrative state" and "administrative society" of the Chinese party–state system have remained fundamentally unchanged, and the state power has continued to perform all-embracing functions of administration of all social organizations. China's mass organizations are in essence formed in the associational administration system with the administrative authorities as the core. Under this system, all social organizations become party-led, state-licensed, or government-controlled without the real meaning of self-government, independence, or autonomy. Furthermore, this is one example of how laws have been employed by the post-Mao leadership to fit its own purpose—laws are actually used to protect and strengthen the party–state control rather than the political and civil rights of its citizens.

Social control has been beefed up

An inescapable concomitant of more mature industrialization is increased functional differentiation and societal complexity. At this point the government is forced to relax some of its clearly dysfunctional controls, such as the use of mass mobilization and mass terror, the tight control over people's daily life and mobility, and all-embracing state planning, which appear to be no longer desirable and necessary in experimenting market reforms.[19] However, the Chinese government has selectively relaxed control in some areas but tightened control in others. Although the post-Mao regime has relaxed control on people's daily life and economic activities, it has never relaxed control over the key sectors of the economy, the government, the ideology, cultural and artistic activities, civil society, and any potential dissent threat to the regime. In recent years, the Chinese government has made an all-out effort to boost the muscle of the "dictatorship of the proletariat"—the state police apparatus.

The security forces, both regular police forces and armed police forces, have been greatly strengthened, armed with sophisticated electronic surveillance equipment and specialized security equipment, heavily politicized, and put directly under the control of the Party Central Military Commission so that they can serve as a powerful party instrument intended to remove all political opposition, if formed, and to guard against any potential threat and dissent through both the political and the police apparatus. To accomplish the special policing task of defending party–state—surveillance of state agencies and society—an internal secret political police organization, called the "political defense branch," organizationally distinct from the foreign intelligence offices of the state security agency, has been established at every level of the police force, with all policing powers of search, arrest, and seizure either formally or informally, to penetrate and investigate any undesirable activities and even party–state officials both inside and outside the system. Based on limited data, with less than 1 percent of the security forces, this special branch accounts for roughly 10 percent of the country's total security expenditure.[20]

Identifying enemies and potential enemies of "the Dictatorship of Proletariat" and the socialist system is the main task of this special branch, and this very responsibility means that service personnel are involved in the penetration of every corner of society and all government, social, and religious organizations as well as in the collection of information about suspicious speech and activities of individuals and groups. A nationwide monitoring network has been established at every level of the police force. Agents in plain clothes (便衣警察 *bianyi jingcha*), for example, infiltrate church services and report on what is preached and the degree of support for the regime, or attend student meetings voluntarily organized on campus and report on attendance, topics discussed, and any dissenting opinions voiced. "Agitators" and any supporters of "anti-revolutionary agitation" will be identified and promptly arrested. The political police branch acts not only as the eyes and ears of the government but also as a special force to crack down on dissenters and their organizations.

The role of the People's Armed Police (PAP) as a tool for the dictatorship has been enhanced since late 1980s. The PAP is under the direct control of the Central Military Commission of the CPC. The power of the PAP has been specially strengthened, and tens of thousands of PLA officers and soldiers are converted into PAP officers and soldiers. The apparatus of the PAP and the regular police has been boosted nationwide. At the same time, anti-riot, anti-terrorist, and other crack units were formed in major cities. They often hold exercises in downtown areas to instill fear in the heart of potential "troublemakers."[21]

The size and the power of the State Security agencies have expanded. China's police-state apparatus has grown to the extent that police, secret police, and other security officers make up 24 per cent of the personnel establishment of China's provinces and center-directly-administered cities. The percentage in some major cities is even higher. These figures refer only to personnel with cadre or officer ranking employed by the provincial and municipal governments. They do not include the PAP or lower-level employees such as policemen or agents working at the national headquarters of the Ministry of Public Security and State Security.[22]

The inter-departmental leading group—the Central Commission for the Comprehensive Management of Social Order—was established in 1992 to coordinate the anti-crime and anti-subversion efforts of units including State Security, Public Security, fire prevention, drugs, customs, and border patrol. While the strength of the PAP increased, new units including police patrols in large urban areas and *anti-tufa* squads ("political emergency incidents") were created in all major cities.[23] "Maintaining stability" (维稳 *wei wen*) has become the top priority, with the Chinese government spending more money on maintaining stability than on national defense. In 2011, the government budget for police, state security, armed civil militia, courts, and jails was set at 624.4 billion yuan (US\$ 95.0 billion) while military spending was set at 601.1 billion yuan (US\$ 91.5 billion).[24]

The state police apparatus also includes other tools of the "dictatorship of the proletariat" such as the judiciary and the courts. In the Chinese press, as well as internal talks, the top Chinese leaders made no secret of the fact that the courts, procuratorates, and the prison system were primarily the CPC's weapons to ensure the "dictatorship of the proletariat." Ren Jianxin, former President of the Supreme People's Court, and also a member of the Politburo, made very explicit the "political" nature of the practice of law in China: "judicial cadres" must abide by the instructions and policies of the party as much as legal codes. The chief judge pointed out that, in addition to the law books, judges had to study "Marxist–Leninist theories on the state and law, as well as Chairman Mao's writings on class struggle." He stressed that "courts at all levels must self-consciously follow party leadership." "All the trials conducted in our country's courts at various levels should be beneficial to ensuring social stability," Ren added. He reminded judicial cadres that their task was to safeguard the party leadership and the "people's democratic dictatorship" and it was wrong to forget that "within certain parameters, class struggle will exist for a long time."[25] Ren's talk was echoed by Liu Fuzhi, then head of the Supreme People's Procuratorate and a former minister of public security. Liu pointed out that procuratorates, which are in charge of investigation and prosecution of crimes, must "take the initiative to fight for party leadership of judicial work." "In important circumstances and difficult cases, we must report to the party and government leadership," he said.[26] Cai Cheng, then head of Justice Ministry, stressed that "as a class tool, the law cannot be divorced from politics. Since our law is socialist law, it will without question serve the politics of the proletariat class, socialist construction, reform, and the open-door policy, as well as the consolidation of the dictatorship of the proletariat."[27] Therefore, courts have served as the regime's instrument to stigmatize and lock away its vocal opponents.

Social stratification, rural–urban mobility, *hukou*, identity, *danwei* systems

Post-Mao reform has brought changes in social stratification and social classes. China's social class has become more diversified since reform and opening up. The simple class divisions and social stratifications (cadres/workers/ peasants or "black" and "red") have been changed into 10 social stratum and five social classes depending on organizational resources, economic resources, and cultural resources controlled by different social groups. Social and economic differences between social classes have greatly increased, particularly between the social classes that control resources and those who do not. Such differences are largely influenced and determined by the political and institutional arrangements of the party–state, such as ownership structure, industrial differences, *hukou* system, and powerful state control over organizational, economic, and cultural resources. The party–state controls the most important and largest resources in the whole society. Control over economic and cultural resources has become increasingly important in market reforms and socio-economic development, but it is dependent on the party–state organizations and agents in many important ways. Moreover, the party–state political and ideological systems have increased their control over those with increasing economic and cultural resources and curbed their increasing influence over society and politics.[28]

Post-Mao market reform has brought many job opportunities for peasants who have moved from rural to urban areas to find jobs, which has increased rural–urban mobility. Relaxation of migration and employment control has also facilitated the increase of rural–urban mobility. However, the distribution of political, social, and economic power among social classes has not changed, and these migrant workers are still considered as lower social classes without being provided with basic social welfare coverage and insufficient social service support.

In recent years, China has begun some reform experiments of the *hukou* resident registration system in some major cities, such as Shanghai, Chongqing, Chengdu, and Shenzhen, as the government has recognized the floating population (流动人口) has watered down the system, accompanied by many problems that need to be tackled effectively. The reform is an attempt to strengthen the control and administration of the floating population, which gives the police authorities (bureaus of public safety) at local and basic levels the responsibility to register the floating population and issue residential cards for better administration and control. This has caused some confusion about the effect and result of the *hukou* reform, and even makes some people think the government is abolishing the *hukou* system.[29]

In Kam Wing Chan and Will Buckingham's recent study of the Chinese *hukou* system, they found that various reform measures of the *hukou* system have not resulted in

> the abolition of the *hukou*, but devolution of responsibility for *hukou* policies to local governments, which in many cases actually makes permanent migration of peasants to cities harder than before. At the broader level, the *hukou* system, as a major divide between the rural and urban population, remains potent and intact."[30]

Wang Feiling, another expert on the *hukou* system, recently pointed out that the rigid rural–urban division remains and continues to exclude and discriminate against rural residents in China. "The *Hukou* system gives the government the power to register, manage, and control everyone," and "the *Hukou* system remains to be one of the last Mao-era institutions that have their basic structures and leading functions largely intact so far."[31]

Cadres were the elite of the party–state. Cadre's ranks were associated with salary levels, welfare, and privileges, and cadre identity was permanent, even after retirement. Such a cadre system has remained unchanged despite the fact that the government has adopted civil servant examinations to recruit college graduates for positions in the party and state institutions and the public sector. The cadre identity and the mass identity continue to be a major division between social classes. Cadres are managed by personnel departments/bureaus (人事局) while workers are managed by labor departments/bureaus (劳动局), and social mobility between the two is restricted by the identity barriers. Cadres also enjoy many privileges that the masses do not. For example, entry into many positions requires cadre identity, and many benefits, such as housing allowance, medical benefit and service quality, vacation with pay, and full pay at retirement are reserved only for cadres. One's identity continues to determine one's social status.[32]

The *danwei* (单位) system is a unique controlling system in urban areas for the party–state to utilize and control society. In its heyday, the unit was a key element in the CPC's system of social control, and virtually every Chinese citizen was affiliated with a unit. It was the responsibility of the unit to keep tabs on the lives of its individual employees and files (档案 *dang an*) on unit members containing biographical data, employment history, criminal records, and information on political attitudes.[33] According to Andrew G. Walder, the economic and political control of a work unit over its employees makes employees not only economically but also socially and politically dependent on their work units, which allows the regime to gain full control over employees' lives.[34]

However, with the gradual emergence of a labor market in the past decades, more and more Chinese find themselves cut loose from both the support and the watchful eyes of their units. Today the 200 million population floating from rural to urban areas are not affiliated with the *danwei* system, nor are millions of employees who work in the private sector. This is a major reason for many observers to feel that the post-Mao regime is less intrusive in people's daily lives than it once was. Many analysts observe that this *danwei* system has been watered down, which has punched a hole in the whole party–state communist system. However, the fundamental issue is whether or not party control and domination have been weakened or diminished in the work unit and other economic sectors in post-Mao China.

The defining feature of a Leninist party–state system is an array of the party organizational structures that supplement government institutions from top to bottom that a regular authoritarian regime does not have. In post-Mao China, the undeniable fact is that the CPC continues to be organized in every workplace, down to the very basic units, and the party–state cadres and loyal activists continue to dominate all the leading positions from top to bottom. The CPC has not attempted to retreat from the work unit but sought to reorganize it in such a way that party control remains firm and pervasive in every workplace, and private interest groups cannot find organized expression.

Communist party cells continue to be well organized and active in the workshop. Rank-and-file members on the shop floor are organized into a party branch (支部 *zhibu*), usually divided into party groups or cells (小组 *xiaozu*). The heads of these cells are members of the workplace party branch committees. The heads of these branch committees, the party branch secretaries, are members of the workplace party committees. The secretary of the party committee is the top political official in the workplace. This interlocking network of committees and cells forms a hierarchy of communication, command, and discipline.

Fewer people would recognize the fact that the work unit continues to be the place where the Communist Party educates, resocializes, monitors, and transforms the thinking of the masses in accord with the party's definition of "correct thought" in China today. In its heyday in the 1950s and 1960s, this practice became known as "brainwashing" in which every citizen, particularly enemies of the regime, had to go through an intensive, coercive process of ideological conversion. In the post-Mao era, however, "brainwashing" in the form of small group political study has not been abandoned and is still often used as needed, while its extent and frequency have been considerably reduced. The party still keeps abreast of the thinking of people in the units and indoctrinates them with the party's basic line, ideology, values, and new policy orientation. As central party documents put it, "Party organizations at every level must keep abreast of the thinking of the masses in the enterprise, and concretely solve thought problems among the masses. The advanced workers and staff must be distinguished from the backward, in regard to both the level of their political consciousness and how well they complete their production tasks and work responsibilities." Every party member is part of an organization and must obey the organization. "Every party member should propagate the Party's view, thoroughly carry out the Party's directives, obey Party decisions, complete their responsibilities in an outstanding manner, and use their own model behavior to influence and spur on the masses."[35] There has been no fundamental change in this practice.

To accomplish the party's policy goals of economic modernization and institutional rationalization, the party organization has begun to alter its role in the factory and other economic organizations. Party committees would not interfere in the day-to-day operations of the factory, but they have a new role to play in enterprises. They support the directors of firms in exercising their authority in production and operation, guarantee and supervise the implementation of the principles and policies of the party–state, strengthen the party's ideological and organizational work among administrators and workers, and strengthen their leadership over trade unions, youth leagues, and other mass organizations.

However, the form of party organization is virtually unchanged: it continues to staff its array of offices internally; it continues to cultivate loyal activists for positions of leadership in the shop hierarchy, youth league, union, and propaganda department; it continues to organize study meetings as the party may order, and production campaigns as the factory directors may need; and it continues to play the role of the political core and supervise the implementation of the principles and policies of the party–state. CPC cells and other party satellite organizations were strengthened among local-administration units as well as in factories, farms, and colleges in the wake of the "misguided" attempts at "separating the party and government" in the late 1980s. Party cells were also established even in joint-venture enterprises. Hu Jintao emphasized,

> to play the leading core role of party cells in enterprises, we must concentrate on two fundamentals: one is that party organizations must participate in major decision-making in enterprises and ensure the full implementation of the party's line, guiding principles and policies in enterprises; the other is to uphold the principle that the party must be responsible for the cadres in enterprises and ensure the implementation of the party's line, guiding principles, and policies of cadres.[36]

The 4th Plenary Session of the 15th Central Committee held in September 1999 continues to emphasize "the leading core role of party cells in enterprises, which must never be shaken" and "guide cadres and workers to uphold correct outlook on world, life and social values."[37]

Moreover, most of the SOE directors and managers are actually CPC members, state functionaries, government administrators, or at least persons who can be trusted by the party and the government. In some other work units, such as schools, the army, and governmental organs, the party organization continues to play an active, significant role. Despite all the changes in the factory, the most fundamental role played by the party—and the one that serves to distinguish the communist party–state from authoritarian corporatist states—has remained unchanged: the party organization still acts systematically to prevent organized group activity among workers independent of the party–state, except those activities allowed and promoted by the party itself. The organized capacity of the party–state to place workers in a politically and economically dependent position has not changed either, though the past years have witnessed a growing depoliticization and de-ideologization of the management of enterprises.[38]

The role of party organizations in the nonstate sector is greatly emphasized in the context of its greater development. The regime has repeatedly stressed the role of party organizations as a "fighting stronghold" in nonstate enterprises, with particular attention to party building in the nonpublic sector, such as private enterprises, joint ventures, and even foreign enterprises. Party cells in the economic organizations of this sector are considered as an organizational guarantee to ensure the "healthy" development of the economy of nonpublic ownership. It is now required that party branches also be established in nonpublic enterprises, including foreign-funded enterprises where more than three party members work as employees. These party cells should be reviewed, organized, and led by the party leading groups in the department of industrial and business administration under their jurisdiction. An official document issued in mid-1991 stated that 20 percent of the nation's 26,400-odd foreign-funded enterprises had party cells or other kinds of party organizations. In Guangdong, 41 percent of the foreign-funded enterprises had party cells. The document pointed out that a key task of the party cells was to prevent the "infiltration" of capitalist ideology and lifestyle and to boost the Marxist consciousness of the workers.[39] This has been a major task for "party building" since then.

At the same time, establishment of official trade unions in all nonpublic enterprises has become the central task of the All-China Federation of Trade Unions since 1996. The major measures undertaken since then include three simultaneous actions: incorporating the provision of trade unions into enterprise regulations at the time of signing contracts; preparing for the setting up of trade unions at the time of preparing for the setting up of enterprises; and establishing trade unions at the time of establishing enterprises. By 1998, 53,634 trade unions had been established in foreign enterprises and more than 23,000 trade unions in private enterprises.[40] In 2008, a new labor law was passed to force all business corporations, including foreign-owned companies, to create an All-China Federation of Trade Unions (ACFTU)-chaptered trade union within them. The ACFTU is the sole national trade union in China, and part of the party–state institution. Since then, ACFTU has been emboldened to push for the unionization of all foreign companies across the country. Those that do not comply with the requirements would be punished with fines. By 2009, according to official reports, unions had been set up in 83 percent of foreign multinational corporations.[41] All this suggests that party control and domination of society has not been significantly weakened but is still effective and pervasive, though such control might be weakened during certain periods of time in certain places or areas.

Village elections and party control in rural areas

Village elections had been officially implemented by the CPC for over two decades when "The Organic Law of Villagers' Committees in the People's Republic of China" was enacted by the NPC in 1987. Many empirical studies on village elections have suggested some significant changes in rural areas while others have pointed out that the village elections have not significantly improved village governance.[42] This is another important area we need to look at in terms of the post-Mao social changes.

After the people's communes were abolished, the traditional leftist approach based on mass mobilization and political campaigns was considered no longer workable in the changing countryside and even dysfunctional in rural economic reforms and growth. Rural residents have become less interested and less involved in politics and party ideology. The post-Mao regime intended to encourage villagers to be involved in political, economic, and cultural activities defined by the regime policy through the "rural grassroots organizational build-up of the state"—villagers' committees and "rural grassroots democratic elections."[43]

According to Article 111 of the Constitution, "residential neighborhood committees in urban areas and villagers' committees in rural areas should be respectively established as the grassroots mass self-government organizations."[44] However, neither urban residential committees nor rural villagers' committees are truly "self-government organizations." Both serve the purpose of the party–state to administer and control the general population in urban and rural areas. Villagers' committees are established, under the leadership of the CPC, to help consolidate "the dictatorship of people's democracy," maintain stability and order in rural areas, and carry out the party–state current policy in agricultural economy and social public affairs in rural areas.[45] According to the directive of the Ministry of Civil Affairs, "the guiding idea of the construction of the villagers' committees is to pursue the goal of building a new socialist countryside, with economic construction as the central work; ensure the implementation of the party's basic line and the state's law and policy; and exercise self-government, self-education, and self-service under the leadership of the party and within the scope of the state law and policy."[46]

The mid-1980s saw the emergence of villagers' committees in rural areas in response to the need for streamlining rural administration, compelling mass participation, and strengthening local government in villages after the dismantling of the old production brigades. After the passing of The Organic Law of Villagers' Committees in the People's Republic of China in 1987, pilot projects were launched in selected villages in 1,093 counties in 14 provinces, and villagers' committees mushroomed. By 1990 the party leadership decided to establish "demonstration villages" that would introduce the new system and provide "models" for others to emulate. By mid-1992, it was reported that 18 provincial people's congresses had enacted implementing regulations and 80 percent of China's villages had completed two rounds of elections. By late 1995, 24 provincial and centrally administered municipal people's congresses had passed local legal regulations and 90 percent of villages had elections. However, villagers' committees are often dominated by township appointments and party members, although some unpopular cadres are removed from office.[47]

The Organic Law of Villagers' Committees gives villagers' committees responsibility to "manage the public affairs and public welfare services of the village, mediate disputes among the villagers, and help to maintain public order"; "to support and organize the villagers in cooperative economic undertakings"; "to administer affairs concerning the land and other property owned collectively by the villagers"; and to draw up "rules and regulations for a village" covering all aspects of village life.[48] Villagers' committees are theoretically classified as "nongovernmental institutions." On the one hand, they are defined as "the primary mass organization of self-government, in which villagers educate themselves and manage their own affairs." On the other

hand, however, they are supposed to assist township government and implement party–state policies in villagers' economic, cultural, and political life.[49]

In practice, villagers' committees have never been considered as outside the
state system. The Ministry of Civil Affairs is responsible for "the standardized
construction of township and street basic governments as well as the
construction of villagers' committees and neighborhood mass organizations
of self-government."[50] The township government should "give guidance,
support and help to the villagers' committees," while "the villagers' committees
must stand for the leadership of the Party."[51] There is elasticity in interpreting
the distinction between "leadership" and "guidance." Those asserting the
power of township and party control emphasize leadership while those making
the case for village autonomy argue for guidance of township and party
organizations.[52] In reality, within the general political framework of the
communist party–state, villagers' committees act in the context of political
embeddedness, and actually do not enjoy real autonomy in policy making from
either township governments or party branches, which will be demonstrated
later.

The post-Mao regime has been exploring the relationship between the
party leadership and the villagers' committees, how to transform the will of
the village party branches into the action of the masses, and how to bring the
role of villagers' committees into full play according to the principle of
the grassroots organizational construction with party branches as the core
of the leadership.[53] So far the party–state has not seen the necessity of all-
embracing control in village life, but hopes to increase the autonomy of
villagers' committees in "pursuing wealth" in their villages and maintaining
social order. However, the post-Mao regime has never intended to weaken the
leading power of the village party branches while granting the villagers'
committees more autonomy in economic activities.

The party organizations at all levels are the organizers and leaders of the
construction of villagers' committees.[54] Township party committees and
governments are directly responsible for the leadership of the village-level
organization construction. Nothing is more obvious than the following
directives issued by the CPC Central Committee in regard to the relation
between party–state and villagers' committees. To ensure the implementation
of the party's line in villagers' committees, the CPC central committee issued
directives:

> village party branches must strengthen the leadership of villagers'
> committees and support their work in accordance with the law, while
> villagers' committees must voluntarily subject themselves to the leadership
> of the party branches and actively do a good job within the limits of their
> functions and responsibilities. Township governments should respect
> the legal status of villagers' committees and support their work, while
> villagers' committees should look for the guidance, support, and help
> of township governments, implement the functions of villagers' self-

management, and actively accomplish the tasks assigned to them by township governments.[55]

In practice, electoral leading groups in villages are established, usually with the party secretary as the head, to direct the election of villagers' committees. Local party committees also regulate, in the official documents on villagers' committees, that "villagers' committees must obey the leadership and the nucleus status of the village party branch."[56] Villagers' committees usually determine the agenda, contents of discussion, and time and place for the meetings of the villagers' council according to the proposals of village party branches. While the percentage of nonparty members on villagers' committees has increased, the key decisions continue to be made by the village party branches. Central and local party and government organizations have also established unified regulations and criteria for such things as election slogans, villagers' committees' notices, work regulations, organizational structure, tenure goals, election registration, nomination forms, speech guidelines, criteria of candidates, candidate nomination, and determination, "village regulations and villagers' agreements" (*cungui minyue* 村规民约), election propaganda guidelines, election regulations, stages and procedures, criteria for "demonstration villages" and checks before acceptance.[57]

All this has suggested that villagers' committees and villagers' self-management are placed under the control of local party and government organizations and easily manipulated by local party–state officials. Those elected officials exercise their authority only on the sufferance of and within constraints set by party–state authorities. Many recent field studies in China have provided evidence supporting the view that villagers' committees do not in reality enjoy much autonomy from the local township government and the local party branches as well as the view that "grassroots participation" in China differs in fundamental respects from that found in more open societies. As M. Kent Jennings correctly observes,

> the existence of powerful governmental and party organs, the thorough penetration of society by the state, the scarcity of independent advocacy groups and other mechanisms for interest articulation, a shackled mass media, and the long absence of free and competitive elections have supplied a different meaning to the construct of participation.[58]

Potter and Potteron, on the basis of their fieldwork in Zengbu village in Guangdong near Hong Kong, note that although villagers' committees "have some autonomy in managing their village's affairs, they are still under the authority of the Zengbu *xiang* (township) Party Committee and the *xiang* government, which ensure that they follow general party policy." Candidates for the villagers' committees "had to be chosen from a slate approved by the party." They conclude that "all general policies of import to the countryside are made by members of higher party levels, or the center, and then transmitted to the local levels of the society, to be implemented by the rural cadre."[59] According to another report, the election of villagers' committees is largely manipulated by the township and village government (TVG) and party organizations. "In the selection of village cadres, the nomination right and the final appointment right are actually in the hand of township or village party branches," although the process involves four types of nomination: nominated by the party branch, by villagers' groups, jointly by villagers, and self-nominated.[60]

Kelliher D. Kelliher observes that China's recent change "leaves much of the former relationship between state and countryside intact. Villagers' committees enforce state policies on family planning, health, and education." Villagers' committees still wrestle "with state directives and targets, mediate disputes, maintain public order, and provide welfare services while economic reform has meant that these committees have come to involve themselves in a range of new economic tasks." Township leaders always "seek to restrict the village autonomy because they fear that they will 'lose their legs' if they cannot rely on villagers' committees to carry out party–state policies in the same way that production brigades followed commune instructions in the past under Mao's regime."[61]

Yang Zhong's more recent field study has also shown that local governments and party organizations perform enormously important tasks for the central government in political, economic, social, and many other areas. Political control by local governments is strengthened rather than weakened, and party organizations at various levels are still the power center.[62] The local TVGs control village grassroots organizations in many ways, including personnel appointment, financial supervision, administrative intervention, penalty and reward, political, ideological and policy guidance, and so forth.[63]

Chinese scholars in mainland China have also conducted their own field studies which have confirmed that the top-down party control system has remained effective and pervasive in rural grassroots organizations in the post-Mao economic transformation after the discontinuity of the People's Commune system, and has continued to play a role as the core of leadership of rural economic, political, and cultural development. In many areas, a leadership system of "party–village–enterprises integration" (party branches, villagers' committees, and village-run enterprises) has emerged as a dominant form of governance structure in rural grassroots society, in which the party branches occupy a dominant position in almost all aspects of village political and economic life, such as household contract responsibility system, industrial development, village elections, villagers' committees, village-run businesses and enterprises. For example, in the village-run shareholding cooperatives, party secretaries usually serve as the chairmen of the board of shareholding cooperatives, deputy secretaries as general managers, and members of party organizations and villagers' committees as the board members. Thus, party secretaries actually make decisions, while villagers' committees implement party decisions.[64]

Variations might exist from village to village, from coastal areas to interior areas, and from economically more advanced provinces to poor and more remote rural villages; but variations do not prove a fundamental change in the party–state control over the village life. If those local power structures come to work against central intent, the party–state apparatus can easily reassert their power over village affairs.[65] This no-fundamental-change picture of village politics is reinforced if we examine how the post-Mao regime has strengthened party control of rural grassroots organizations and the building of village party cells after the establishment of villagers' committees in village politics. Strengthening the village-level organizational building of the party branches as the leading core has been considered as the party's urgent task in China's rural political development under Jiang Zemin and Hu Jintao. Several measures have been taken to overhaul and consolidate the village party cells.

First, to strengthen the party's leadership and control of rural grassroots organizations, provincial and local party–state organizations have incorporated "the construction of villagers' committees" into the general framework of "unified planning, unified procedure, and unified check before acceptance." Coordinating and leading groups of the construction of rural grassroots organizations and villagers' self-management work are established at the provincial level, with a key responsible party secretary as the head, jointly constituted by leaders of various departments such as party organization, agriculture and industry, propaganda, civil affairs, and official mass organizations. Similar leading groups are also established at the municipality and county level, headed by the leaders of the party, government, and people's congress.[66]

Second, party committees at all levels have undertaken measures to strengthen the leadership of the rectification of the village party cells. Party committees at all levels have made a three-year and an annual plan for the party rectification and also established the responsibility system of party rectification. Every key leader of party committees at all levels is responsible for some "networking villages" for the rectification of party cells.

Third, governmental cadres at all levels are sent in a planned way to be "stationed" in those villages to help and guide their party rectification or hold key leading positions in the rectified village party branches. Millions of cadres have been sent to help those rectified villages, and the villages where help was most needed, and to hold leading positions of the party branches.

Fourth, in the rectification of village party branches, great attention has been given to the effort to construct "a complete organizational system with the party branch as the leading core," including party branches, villagers' committees, village collective economic organizations, communist youth leagues, village militia, and women's associations. All these organizations are united, in the "principle of democratic centralism," around the grassroots organizational system with the party branch as the leading core.

Fifth, every year, rural party cadres are sent in turn for training at party schools at different levels. Province, district, county, and township party authorities are responsible for the training work. In 1997 only, 20,146,000 rural party members and cadres were trained, of which township cadres were 1,055,000, village party secretaries and villagers committee directors were 1,156,000, and rural party members were 17,934,000.[67] Such training is set as the party's long-term program and it has continued since then.

Apparently, political control of villagers' political and social life by local government and party organizations has not been weakened, but instead it has been strengthened. Party control and domination are pervasive and effective in village politics. Villagers' committees and villagers' self-management are confined by the principle of the grassroots organizational construction with the party organizations as the core of the leadership and totally under the control of local party and governmental organizations. Village elections have come into being in China since 1987, but the government has yet to allow direct elections at its basic administrative levels, such as township- and county-level, because it worries that elections will weaken its power base in the rural areas. Self-government at township level was even practiced 100 years ago under the Qing Dynasty in 1908,[68] but it has yet to come into being in present-day China.

Questions for discussion

1. What is "civil society?" What social changes have taken place in post-Mao China? To what extent have such changes created a "civil society" in post-Mao China and to what extent have such changes affected the nature of the political regime?
2. Why and how has the party–state integrated social organizations into the interlocking structure of power, ideology, and organizational control while allowing them some legal and public space for their growth?
3. What are the main characteristics of the changing pattern of social structure and state–society relations in contemporary China compared to traditional China and Mao's China?

Further reading

Deborah S. Davis and Ezra F. Vogel, eds., *Chinese Society on the Eve of Tiananmen: The Impact of Reform* (Cambridge, MA: Harvard University Press for the Council on East Asian Studies, 1990).

Elizabeth J. Perry and Mark Selden, eds., *Chinese Society: Change, Conflict and Resistance*, 3rd edition (New York: Routledge, 2010).

Part VIII
The Chinese economy

15 State socialism and the Chinese communist economy

Following the 10-year turmoil of the Cultural Revolution (1966–76), the CPC has made a "focus shift" from "class struggle" to the economic development characterized by the "four modernizations" of industry, agriculture, national defense, and science and technology, and adopted market-oriented economic reform and an open-door policy. However, how can we understand the legacies of state socialism and the Chinese communist economy established after the communist takeover in 1949 in Mao's China and how these legacies continue to influence the reforming Chinese economy? How can we understand the current Chinese economy and evaluate the considerable changes in post-Mao China? We need to define state socialism and examine key characteristics of its application in the Chinese economy, so as to establish a reference point from which the Chinese economy is transitioning, and evaluate economic changes in post-Mao China.

The starting point for any study of the economic transition in communist states is the centrally planned economy modeled on the Soviet economy. This chapter will define state socialism as the tradition of the Soviet centrally planned economy, and employ this concept as a theoretical framework by which to examine the pre-reform Chinese socialist model that constitutes the point of departure from state socialism or a centrally planned command economy, in order to define the beginning and the end of transition from state socialism and conduct a sensible assessment of economic change in the next chapter.

Two ideal-type political economies

Any society has to face some basic questions and know how to answer those questions. In distinguishing a centrally planned command economy from a free market economy, five fundamental questions can be formulated. The answers to these questions establish the nature and characteristics of the two economic systems[1] (see Table 15.1 for explanations).

1. Who controls the means of production and the factors of production?
2. Who determines what goods are produced?

Table 15.1 Two ideal-type political economies[2]

Key points	Market economy	Command economy
1. Control of factors of production	Every economic actor controls own factors	State owns and controls all factors of production
2. Production decisions	Sum of all private actors' decisions ("invisible hand" of market); demand oriented	State decisions defined in detailed plan; supply oriented
3. Value established	Exchange value in the market	State sets values attached to all goods
4. Distribution decisions	Choices by private actors	State determines who will receive what products at what levels
5. Role of the state	Generally passive; enforces rules, provides minimal protection to actors	State dominates, owns, plans, controls, and regulates all economic activities

Note: The means of production include energy resources, land, raw materials, tools, machines, and factories. The means of exchange include transportation and communications facilities, wholesale and retail outlets, banking and credit institutions, etc.[3]

3.   Who establishes the value attached to different resources and goods?
4.   Who decides how resources and goods will be distributed?
5.   What is the role of the state?

In the history of economics, Adam Smith and Karl Marx presented two ideal types: the "free market economy" of capitalism and the "planned command economy" of communism. In a free market economy, it is private citizens or private firms who own the private property or the means of production, and therefore control their own factors of production, determine what should be produced, and have the right to the residual income from their asset. It is the "invisible hand" of market forces that establishes the exchange value while the state plays a passive role allowing private actors to operate freely in the market and prevent private actors from doing violence to each other or violating the rights of others. In a planned command economy, it is the state that owns the means of production, controls the production, distribution, and exchange, and determines what to produce and who will receive what products at what levels according to the state plan. It is the state that sets the official values for all exchanges of goods and services.[4] The centrally planned command economy as an economic system is also theoretically conceptualized as "state socialism" in contrast to market capitalism.[5]

State socialism as an economic system

State socialism refers to the economic system in communist states, such as the Soviet Union, formerly communist states in Eastern Europe, China, Vietnam,

North Korea, and Cuba. In contrast to various forms of socialism in Western countries, which advocate direct workplace democracy in daily operation, or democratic self-management of factories by workers, or cooperative ownership of the means of production by citizens, state socialism in communist states is based on (1) state ownership of the means of production, (2) state-directed central planning, (3) bureaucratic management of workplace and economic activities, and (4) the domination of the communist party and its ideology in the direction, planning, and operation of the economy.

In practice, the government in state socialism owns the means of production and resources, and plans, controls, and manages the economy through state-directed central economic planning and state-appointed party–state officials in the management of the workplace. The government controls almost all aspects of economic life, including capital, labor, industries, farms, schools, transportation, financial institutions, trade, and allocation of resources. Thus, a highly centralized bureaucratic state was created by the communist party to plan, control, and manage all economic activities in communist states. The communist party in a communist state declares itself to have total representation of the people and total guidance of national goals. The party itself is also organized bureaucratically and intertwined with the state bureaucracies, but it leads, dominates, and penetrates them through a parallel network of party organizations established in the state bureaucratic institutions. The party is the brain or the central nervous system of the state body, which executes the party's directives and policies in directing and organizing socialist economic activities and accomplishing the party's short-term, intermediate, and long-term goals and tasks through the central planning system and commands.[6]

The Soviet Union was the first communist state in history to create state socialism as an economic system, which is often referred to as interchangeable with a centrally planned command economy. It became the model for duplication in the nationwide, massive, radical socialist transformation under Mao leadership from 1953 forward (see Chapter 6 for details). Therefore, we will use state socialism as a theoretical framework for an explanation of the type of socialist economy established in Mao's China.[7]

Chinese economy prior to market reform in 1978

The Chinese socialist economy encompassed all key elements of state socialism before the market reform and opening up of 1978, which was characterized by the attempt by the CPC to establish a new socialist planned economy based on complete public ownership including collective and state sectors, wiping out virtually all private enterprises and other forms of private ownership. The result of this transformation was the establishment of a Soviet-type "centrally planned command economy" in China, although the Chinese economy may differ from the Soviet economy to a certain degree and in some ways. The characteristics of Mao's model of the socialist economy from 1949–78 can be summarized as follows: (1) Soviet-type state socialism based on a highly centralized bureaucratic state, (2) heavy industry priority industrialization strategy, (3) a collectivized agricultural sector, and (4) mobilization and campaigns as incentives and means to accomplish goals. As a model it is an abstract construct that incorporates certain most important elements and features from reality, and thus it does not have to incorporate all elements in reality, but serves as a blueprint to explain Chinese state socialism and the operation of the centrally planned economy.[8] For example, "self-reliance" was adopted by Mao as a state policy and an ideological slogan when China was isolated from the outside world, particularly after the Sino-Soviet split. This may be considered an element or feature of the Chinese economy in the Mao era. However, after U.S. President Nixon's visit to China in the early 1970s, with China being internationally recognized by the international community, China has adopted an "open-door" policy and even joined the World Trade Organization. Therefore, "self-reliance" may not necessarily be considered as a key feature of socialist economy. In what follows, we will examine each of the four key characteristics to understand state socialism in Chinese practice.

Soviet-style state socialism based on a highly centralized bureaucratic state

Soviet-style state socialism is a centrally planned economy or centrally planned command economy. In Mao's China, the state owned and controlled the major means of production and exchange and therefore virtually all factors of production. That is to say, the government owned all large and medium-scale factories, transportation, communication, banks, and all strategic sectors and resources, and some medium-sized and small enterprises were owned and administered by local governments. The smallest enterprises were owned by local communities in urban areas (street and neighborhood committees) and by communes and brigades in rural areas. By 1981, there were 84,200 state-owned enterprises, 296,800 collectively owned, and 185,500 commune-run, accounting for 78.30 percent, 14.80 percent, and 6.24 percent of gross industrial output value, respectively, leaving 0.66–1 percent accounted for by "others."[9] There was virtually no private ownership of enterprises in China, except for some individual shoe repairs or street vendors or private plots behind the houses of peasants during the time when the economy was in difficulty and party policy allowed such activities. Therefore, virtually no significant private ownership existed by the late period of Mao's China, and all means of production were state owned or collectively owned. The party–state initiated and implemented reforms or adjustments if necessary but established the limits of reform and adjustment, such as the degree of centralization and decentralization, size of private plots peasants could operate, and other policy changes.

The state institutions that were in charge of central planning and coordinating among ministries under the State Council were the State Planning Commission, which had overall responsibility for economic planning, and the Economic Commission, which reviewed the fulfillment of the annual plans of ministries, provincial and local governments, communes, and other state-owned economic units. Overall, central government prepared and executed its economic plans through different administrative units from top to bottom.[10]

The government centrally planned the production and distribution of major industrial and consumer goods, and set values/prices attached to goods, supplies, and services. The government determined who would receive what products at what levels, and directly allocated and distributed resources and factors of production among producers and those in need of them according to state planning. The state dominated, owned, planned, controlled, and regulated all major economic activities. The party–state central planners set the goals, plans, policy agenda of the national economy, prices, wages, and output quotas or production targets, and allocated supplies, financial investment, products and resources to enterprises and communes according to national plans. Central planners used "material balance planning" to calculate and balance supply and demand among producers (deficits of some units were balanced by surpluses from other units), and they assigned "quantities" and ignored "prices." "There were output plans for industrial producers and supply plans that transferred resources among producers."[11] However, there were no "hard budget constraints" on the enterprises, and their behavior was politically motivated, monitored, and supervised by the government. Enterprises sought to fulfill plan targets and output quotas, and they were not concerned about economic efficiency and productivity. Loss-making enterprises asked the government for budgetary grants, supplies, and assistance, while the government would try to meet the needs through the bureaucratic redistribution of profits. This created the so-called "soft budget constraint" in state socialism as described by Janos Kornai.[12]

The state appointed party–state leaders and officials as managers and heads of enterprises and communes. Personnel appointments of some large and strategic enterprises were directly appointed by central government with the assignment of equivalent political ranks on the party–state *nomenklatura* system that was a duplicate of the Soviet model. Personnel appointments of medium-sized and small enterprises and communes may be assigned by provincial and local governments under their jurisdiction and supervision. The plan targets are not recommendations but commands from the central authority and higher-level authorities, and all enterprise leaders are obliged to fulfill the planning targets.

All foreign trade and business was monopolized and administered by the Ministry of Foreign Trade or its equivalent through specialized state trading corporations. Protected from the threat of both domestic and international competition, industrial enterprises and industrial ministries had little incentive to reduce their costs, raise productivity, or improve the quality of their products.[13]

In short, power was centralized in the hands of communist party organs, the central planning agencies, and industrial ministries. Decision making was highly centralized. Central planners drafted and proposed long-term national development goals, five-year plans, and annual growth goals, approved by the CPC Politburo and then tailored by various industrial departments/ministries into departmental plans that were given to local governments, industrial enterprises, and agricultural communes as orders or commands for their implementation. Central planners allocated resources to prioritized industrial sectors, particularly heavy industry. Taxes and profits were accumulated by central government and reallocated as budgetary grants to local government and as investment grants to industrial enterprises throughout the country. Industrial ministries oversaw all economic activity and had national industrial monopolies. Local government and enterprises had no autonomy in decision making unless some decisions were decentralized during the time of economic difficulty and policy readjustment (e.g., the "readjustment" from 1961 to 1963).

Heavy industry priority industrialization strategy

"Giving priority to the development of heavy industry"(优先发展重工业) was the development strategy adopted for almost 30 years by the CPC leadership under Mao. There were many reasons for the CPC leaders to adopt this rapid and prioritized development strategy, such as the historical trauma of humiliation and the revolutionary enthusiasms of political elites and masses, intermediate goal of communism, international isolation by the U.S.-led embargo, "leaning toward one side" (the Soviet Union) foreign policy, and the practical needs of building industrial bases for industrialization.

This strategy gave policy priority, investment, and resources to heavy industry, at the cost of consumption, light industry, and other economic sectors. Such a strategy cannot be realized by the allocation of resources in a free market economy. As China lacked investable capital, foreign currency, and necessary technological skills during that period of time, the Chinese leaders deliberately suppressed the prices or exchange values of resources and other factors of production, and allocated most investment and resources through central planning to heavy industry, and poured massive resources into it, which created rapid industrial growth, but it also resulted in a shortage economy, resulting in the country's supply and consumption being rationed. Once this strategy was adopted, the logic of the central planners' organization and economic policy would not allow private ownership and a market economy to exist, because the latter would operate by a different economic logic.

The Chinese government also designated a region as the main base of heavy industry, and launched major construction campaigns to build heavy industries in the northeast of China during the 1950s when China received Soviet aid, and then massive construction programs focused on inland regions (such as Sichuan and Guizhou), called the "Construction of the Third Front" (三线建设), beginning in the mid-1960s when Sino-Russian relations deteriorated and Chinese involvement in the Vietnam War increased. By building industrial bases in these remote areas and regions, the Chinese leaders hoped that China's industrial bases would not be vulnerable to Soviet and American military attack.[14] Both economic construction campaigns created new factories and modern industries that China had never had previously, and laid the foundation for China's industrialization. The construction of heavy industries received high priority in investment, manpower, and resources through central planning and commands. However, Chinese people, from young to adult, were indoctrinated by the government to "tighten their belt" (勒紧裤腰带) to support the socialist economic construction. People's consumption was suppressed, and service and light industries were neglected.[15] College graduates and engineers were mobilized and sent to those regions to participate in the construction programs.

Agricultural collectivization

As discussed in Chapter 6, as an integral part of the post-revolutionary socialist transformation movement, agricultural collectivization started in the early 1950s and was pushed through gradually and voluntarily till 1957, establishing various collective forms such as "mutual aid teams" (互助组), "elementary agricultural cooperatives" (初级合作社), and "higher cooperatives" (高级合作社). Beginning in 1958, Mao launched a nationwide campaign of the "Great Leap Forward" (大跃进), which included the nationwide "people's communization movement" (人民公社化运动) that transformed all cooperatives into people's communes (人民公社) throughout China's rural areas. Within several months in 1958, 98.2 percent of the total number of peasant households were converted into 26,425 communes, and by 1981, 54,371 communes had been established.[16] In the meantime, some large state farms were also created in some regions directly under central government control, such as Xinjiang Production and Construction Corps (新疆生产建设兵团)—a unique semi-military organization that created farms, ranches, settlements, towns, and even small to medium-sized cities across Xinjiang, settling disbanded military units and cultivating frontier lands for food and cotton production. By the early 1960s, virtually all land was state and collectively owned, and private ownership was completely abolished.

The rural collective organization consisted of three hierarchical levels: communes, brigades, and production teams, which is the basic level or economic unit. Communes were both political-administrative units and economic units of production that carried out central directives.[17] Each unit received input allocations and subsidies for targeted output quotas according to annual and seasonal plans tailored and set by the central planners, and in return each was obliged to deliver to the state a specified quantity of produce or state procurement quotas (compulsory purchase at the state price) set by central planning. All means of production, including the land, machinery, draft animals, and industrial facilities were collectively owned. Annual and seasonal plans were ultimately assigned to the lowest level of economic unit, the production team, which would carry out production targets and assign tasks to individual team members who worked in groups on land. The incomes of all team members, largely in material quantities, were distributed proportionally based upon their work points assigned for tasks that were accumulated annually. However, the total net income of the team members (grain, other material, and cash) was calculated and retained for distribution among members only after subtracting state procurement quotas and the collective retaining portion for the public fund. This is called the "annual earning distribution" (*nianzhong fenhong* 年终分红)) after the harvest. According to household surveys in 1978, average distributed collective income amounted to 88.5 RMB per person (a little over US$50 at the prevailing exchange rate). However, most of this was received in the form of distributed grain, and less than a third of the total was in cash. Besides collective distributed income, each household also earned some cash by selling produce from their small private plots and animals raised in their houses or backyards (pigs, chickens, and eggs).[18]

Mobilization and campaigns as incentives and means to accomplish goals

The party–state organizations systematically employed mass mobilization and economic campaigns as means to achieve economic growth, because economic growth and industrialization were considered to be one of the main goals after the successful communist revolution—as the "transfer goal" or "intermediate goal" that the CPC pursues to achieve the "ultimate goal" of communism. The mass campaigns were of vital importance to the CPC leadership in carrying out various economic, social, ideological, and political programs, policies, and decisions. In the meantime, the campaigns also destroyed the old political, economic, and social structures, organizations, and institutions, and created new ones!

In pursuit of the various CPC goals, mass mobilization and campaigns were repeatedly employed as the main means and incentives for motivating the Chinese people to follow the party line and mobilization. There have been at least 50 major political, ideological, and economic movements and campaigns since the CPC's takeover in 1949—just to mention a few examples: the "Campaign on Eradication of Illiteracy" (扫除文盲运动), the "Land Reform Movement" (土改运动), the "Suppression of Counterrevolutionaries" (镇压反革命运动), the "Campaign to Resist U.S. Aggression and Aid Korea" (抗美援朝运动), the "Three Anti and Five Anti Movement" (三反五反运动), the "Socialist Transformation Movement" (社会主义改造运动), the "Party Rectification Movement" (整风运动), the "Agricultural Collectivization Movement" (农业集体化运动), "Let One Hundred Flowers Blossom and One Hundred Schools Contend" (百花齐放，百家争鸣), the "Anti-Rightist Movement" (反右运动), the "Great Leap Forward" (大跃进), "the Nationwide Iron and Steel Production Campaign" (全民大炼钢铁运动), the "People's Communization Movement" (人民公社化运动), "socialist education movement" (社会主义教育运动), "four cleanups" (四清运动), the "Learning from Lei Feng Movement" (学雷锋运动), the "Learning from Daqing in Industry, Learning from Dazai in Agriculture, and Learning from the People's Liberation Army in the whole country" (工业学大庆、农业学大寨, 全国学人民解放军), the "Great Proletariat Cultural Revolution" (无产阶级文化大革命), the "Down to the Countryside Movement" (上山下乡运动), the "Campaign to Criticize Lin, Criticize Confucius" (批林批孔运动), the "Repulse Right-Deviationist-Verdict-Reversal Movement" (反击右倾翻案风运动), the "Four Modernizations" (四个现代化), the "Anti-bourgeois Liberalization" (反对资产阶级自由化), the "Anti-Spiritual Pollution" (反对精神污染), "Socialist Spiritual Civilization Construction Movement" (社会主义精神文明建设), the campaign for "Eight Honors and Eight Shames" (八荣八耻), and the "anti-three-vulgarities movement" (反三俗运动), and so on.[19] Such nationwide mobilization and campaigns have been repeatedly employed by the party–state under different generations of political leadership even until today (e.g., the campaign for "Eight Honors and Eight Shames," and the "anti-three-vulgarities movement" under the leadership of Hu Jintao). These nationwide campaigns and movements have been used by the party–state as the means to push through socialist transformation and economic construction programs, accomplish the party's social and economic policy goals, achieve the political leaders' political purposes, conduct brainwashing and thought control, purge dissidents from their ranks, or punish ideological and political deviants. These campaigns and movements shaped and conditioned the political and cultural context in which Chinese socialist economy was created and developed under the CPC leadership. The CPC might top the historical record in the number of campaigns in human history.

During Mao's era, there were at least five successive waves of economic "leap forward" campaigns that corresponded to a period of rapid investment growth and economic construction programs—1949–53 (post-revolutionary campaigns and land reform), 1953–56 (first five-year plan and socialist transformation), 1958–59 ("great leap forward"), 1964–66 ("Third Front" construction), and 1970–71 (*zhua geming, cushengchan* 抓革命促生产 during the Cultural Revolution). Each "leap" was a phase of more rapid and radical social and institutional transformation.[20]

Mass mobilization and campaigns need propaganda and organization. The CPC had learned and mastered a great deal of experience in mobilizing and organizing the Chinese people for the communist revolution, and such experience was then vigorously and systematically employed to accomplish the goals. Endless production campaigns or a series of economic campaigns—led by party cells in workshops and in production teams, but pioneered by activists (积极分子) and activists groups mobilized and organized by the youth leagues, women's associations, trade unions and all other "official" mass organizations—were launched nationwide, often periodically repeated, and down to the grassroots to arouse people's revolutionary enthusiasm for participation and direct their energies to the planned production targets, quotas, and various policy goals, while in the meantime such campaigns were always accompanied by the party's ideological indoctrination and brainwashing aimed at transforming human nature and political thinking to create a "socialist new man" (社会主义新人) and "correct erroneous thoughts among cadres and masses" (克服干部群众存在的错误思想). Work teams (工作组) were always sent from a higher level of the party–state authorities to work units (schools, factories, shops, government institutions, army units, etc.) in urban areas as well as communes, brigades, and production teams in rural areas to direct, supervise, and energize the mass campaigns, which were always accompanied by nationwide propaganda campaigns—led and organized by the party propaganda departments at all levels—through the party–state newspapers, radios, and other media organizations as well as other educational methods, such as study sessions, mass meetings, wall newspapers (*dazibao*大字报) listening to leaders' speeches, selecting heroes and models of campaigns, and their reports of meetings to recommend them as examples for emulation.

In short, campaigns involved the whole of society, every individual, and covered all fields of social, economic, cultural, and political life. All mobilization actions in economic, technological, social, etc., fields were also politically determined, with important political goals and values. All campaigns were also ideologically directed towards the transformation of people and society into new forms, with ideological indoctrination and propaganda as the main means.[21]

Transition from state socialism in post-Mao China

The death of Mao and the demise of the "Gang of Four" ended the Cultural Revolution. Deng was reinstated, as were many reform-minded leaders who had been previously purged during the Great Leap Forward and the Cultural Revolution. Left-wing ideologues who came to power during the Cultural Revolution were dismissed. New policy was established at the Third Central Committee Plenum of the 11th National Party Congress in 1978—the party's "focus shift" from the "class struggle" to the "Four Modernizations." However, Barry Naughton has pointed out, despite the fact that China has gradually dismantled the centrally planned command economy, its legacy to the contemporary Chinese economy is large and complicated, and no area of the post-Mao Chinese economy completely escapes the after-effects of the command economy.[22]

The 1980s and 1990s were characterized by economic reform as prescribed by the Four Modernizations doctrine. Economic liberalization began first in agriculture with the People's Communes replaced with the "household responsibility system" and farmers' markets created to facilitate commercial exchange among farmers and between urban and rural areas. The CPC also adopted a cautious open-door policy to promote foreign trade and attract foreign investment by creating a special economic zone in the southern city, Shenzhen, Guangdong Province, which was followed by four special economic zones (SEZs) along the southeast coast, Shanghai, and some other coastal cities in later years. The transition is partial, gradualist, experimental, and phased in, with the party–state in control of the entire process. Plan and market are both considered as the methods of economic development and modernization regardless of capitalism or socialism. However, throughout the 1980s, the mainstream of economic thought in the CPC was to maintain the central planning system within which the market would play a supplemental role in the allocation of resources. The move away from this more traditional socialist doctrine was a more pragmatic policy of transition toward a market-based economy—"Socialist Market Economy"—a skillful compromise between reformers and conservatives in the 1990s. By the mid-1990s, the CPC finally confirmed that its long-term objective of economic transition was the establishment of "a socialist market economy with Chinese characteristics" while fully utilizing the world's free markets, capital, advanced science, and technology to advance the Four Modernizations.[23]

With leadership devolving from Deng to Jiang to Hu, China remained steadfast in its economic transition from a centrally planned economy to a market-oriented economy. Many elements of a market economy have come into being in the past two decades, and transformed the Chinese economy into a diverse structure of ownership with state, collective, personal, private, foreign, and joint-venture enterprises and businesses coexisting in the economy—a mixed economy combining capitalist dynamics and socialist principles. Economic liberalization and marketization have made significant progress and maintained a high economic growth rate for more than two decades. However, the political system with the communist party–state at the core has remained unchanged, and defined the political context and the parameters within which the economy can operate and move around. The CPC leadership, Hu and Wen, seems intent upon expanding China's economic liberalization even further along the same path to becoming a more advanced socialist market economy in the twenty-first century.

Questions for discussion

1. What is state socialism? What might be the major problems of state socialism as an economic system in contrast to market capitalism?
2. What are the key characteristics of Chinese socialist economy under Mao? To what degree would a "socialist market economy" in post-Mao China differ from state socialism in the Mao era? How can we capture and describe continuity and change from Mao's state socialism to post-Mao market socialism?

Further reading

Janos Kornai, *The Socialist System: The Political Economy of Communism* (Princeton, Princeton University Press, 1992).

Maurice J. Meisner, *Mao's China and after: A History of the People's Republic* (New York: The Free Press, 1999).

David Lane, ed., *The Legacy of State Socialism and the Future of Transformation* ((Lanham, MD: Rowman & Littlefield Publishers, 2002).

16 Market socialism and economic transition in post-Mao China

China has been the world's fastest growing economy for over three decades. The rapid growth has been accompanied by a significant reduction in poverty, an improvement in most measures of wellbeing, and an increase in the share of world trade and production. The rapid growth has been largely the result of embracing market competition, opening to foreign trade and foreign direct investment, the high level of savings and investment, and local entrepreneurship. However, despite the impressive economic performance for over three decades, China remains in the ranks of the world's low-income economies.[1] China faces serious challenges in many social, economic, environment, and energy arenas as well as major institutional and political obstacles to sustainable economic development and political development in the long term. Therefore, political science students often ask such questions: Is China still a socialist economy or a capitalist market economy? What are the most significant changes in the Chinese economic system compared with Mao's China? What are the institutional and political obstacles to China's sustainable economic growth and political development in the long term? In what follows, we will examine what has changed and what has not, and evaluate the nature and magnitude of change over the past three decades in post-Mao China.

The most significant change in post-Mao China has occurred in the economic field. The Chinese economy has become market and outward oriented compared with the economic policy in Mao's era. Moreover, significant changes have occurred in the industrial structure, ownership structure, decision-making power, and administrative organization. The ownership structure has become mixed. While public ownership is still dominant, state ownership has shrunk. Local governments and basic economic units have been granted greater autonomy in economic decision making. Emphasis has been on the importance of market forces and guidance plans in directing economic activities and on the importance of laws and economic mechanisms in regulating economic activities while administrative means have continued to be employed to a great degree if they are considered necessary.[2]

Since reform and opening up, agricultural production has been decollectivized with a return to individual family farming, aiming to improve rural productivity and increase agricultural output; state-owned enterprise (SOE) management has been given greater autonomy in production, pricing, and distribution of nonplanned output by the "separation of ownership and management," designed to stimulate enthusiasm for production and increase economic efficiency; the planning system has shifted from "mandatory planning" (state direct administrative control over targets, quotas, and so on) to "guidance planning" (state indirect economic control, such as taxation, interest rates, price, etc.), aiming at rationalizing state economic performance and policy making; circulation of commodities through the marketplace and close economic ties with the world economy have been promoted.[3] The unitary structure of ownership has changed into a "mixed economy" with various ownership forms and sectors, under which a dominant public sector (state ownership and collective ownership) is coexistent with individual, private, foreign-funded, and joint-venture economic sectors.

Shareholding reform since 1992 has been employed by the government to further restructure China's economic organizations and ultimately establish a "modern enterprise system" through the "corporatization" of SOEs into shareholding companies based on a new Company Law. Considerable progress has been made since then in extending and formalizing the shareholding system throughout the other economic sectors. Greater diversification has taken place in the ownership structure of the economy, while the government has emphasized the maintenance of public ownership as the cornerstone of the economy in the new phase of economic reform.[4] In short, all efforts have been made to bring about a market-oriented and outward-oriented economy, and marketization has achieved considerable progress in the direction of economic liberalization and the establishment of a "socialist market economy."

The post-Mao economic reforms have led many China analysts to declare that post-Mao China has been moving toward capitalism. Nicholas Kristof, Beijing bureau chief of the *New York Times*, wrote that "China is no longer a communist country in any meaningful sense," because no communist country "has ever so fully embraced stock markets. In the 1990s the business of the party is business."[5] Some others have observed that "the rapid rise of the capitalist and entrepreneurial class, accompanied by large-scale privatization and foreign investment in urban China, is undoubtedly one of the nation's most important politicoeconomic developments today,"[6] and that "the dynamism of the market economy, including the rapid development of the stock market, private enterprises, and foreign investment, has been one of the most notable features of China in the 1990s."[7] The massive shrinkage of the output share of SOEs in Chinese industry is often used as evidence supporting the above argument.[8]

"China moving toward capitalism" has mainly referred to the three empirical aspects of the economic change in post-Mao China: the existence of capitalist elements, the enlarged share of the nonstate sector, and the enhanced role of the market in the economy. However, this argument fails to capture the central realities of post-Mao China. While the public sector is still dominant in the post-Mao Chinese economy, the essential features of state socialism (soft budget constraint, government intervention, and the employment relationship) have remained intact.[9] As Janos Kornai pointed out, "the nature of political power, the prevailing ideology, and the property relations determine jointly the part (or at least the main feature of the role) that various coordination mechanisms can play in society."[10] In what follows, we will demonstrate that China has actually transitioned from centrally planned state socialism to market socialism. This chapter will begin with a conceptual framework of "market socialism," and then examine the post-Mao economy along three key empirical dimensions—the "socialist primary stage" with the coexistence of socialist and capitalist elements, the ownership structure of Chinese market socialism, and the roles of state and market in the "socialist market economy".

Conceptualizing market socialism

Market socialism is a type of economic system that combines the basic socialist principle of public ownership with the basic principle of the market economy, with public ownership predominant in those areas deemed critical to the implementation of socialist principles and social policy.[11] It is described as "a species of economic system which is, in a number of ways, a cross between capitalism and socialism"[12] Central to market socialism is the belief that the market is not a mechanism exclusive to capitalism, but is also compatible with public ownership and socialist principles.

The general literature on market socialism suggests a number of proposals for a hybrid form of political economy, one that operates within and adheres to socialist principles while allowing market forces a substantial role. Despite variations in measurement schemes, these studies agree upon a basic definition of market socialism as a type of economic system that combines the socialist principle of public ownership with the principle of the market economy, with predominant public ownership in those areas deemed critical to the implementation of socialist principles and social policy. It resides in the middle of the spectrum, bounded by a pure market economy at one end and a pure command economy at the other. Market socialism is a prime example of a mixed economy with allocation decisions undertaken by both governments and markets. Therefore, market socialism incorporates some methods kindred to capitalism.

While Adam Smith and Karl Marx presented two *ideal* economic types: the "free market economy" of capitalism and the "planned command economy" of communism, in between exist mixed systems, since states and markets play varying roles in different countries. Even within the same type of political economic system, such as capitalism, variations exist such as those between the United States, Great Britain, Japan, and Germany. They do not all exhibit the key characteristics of market capitalism to the same degree due to differing traditions and political contexts; however, sufficiently similar characteristics allow them to be placed in a common classification. Likewise, the same situation may occur in other economic systems. All actual political economies are "mixed," but this does not mean that all political economies are basically the same—the mix of elements varies a great deal from country to country. The interaction between states and markets exists in every country, but the manner in which they interact and the extent to which the state or the market plays a role in society varies a great deal from country to country. Politics and values or regime types and belief systems in given societies play a powerful role in establishing what kinds of interventions the state will undertake and what values and interests the state will serve.

"State capitalism" and "market socialism" are the two most important hybrid prototypes between the two extremes: the market economy and the command economy. Although the models may not be a perfect reflection of the real world, these four categories or prototypes are useful for simplifying and generalizing the diversity of modern economic systems. Figure 16.1 illustrates the differences and similarities between the four ideal prototypes.

The model locates ownership and control at points between the two extremes. Ownership and control are the two most important indicators that distinguish one type of political economy from another and constitute a feasible analytical framework against which to examine and evaluate the transition from communism. In this spectrum, the horizontal axis indicates the ownership dimension between the state and private sectors. The vertical axis measures the relative role of the state and the market in the economy. It provides a general picture of mixed political economies between two ideal types as a result of varying combinations of ownership and control between state and market. However, the model is not meant to suggest that all change is linear. For example, a command economy may not necessarily make a

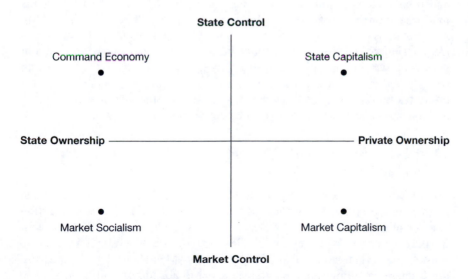

Figure 16.1 Four types of political economy.

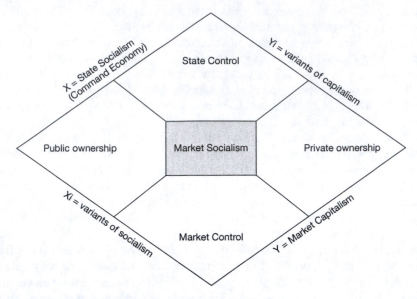

Figure 16.2 Multidimensionality of market socialism.

transition toward a market economy in the linear form, but could end in a mixed political economy, such as market socialism or state capitalism without moving further toward the market economy of capitalism.

Figure 16. 2 highlights the multidimensionality of market socialism. Public ownership with state control represents the planned command economy (USSR and Mao's China), while public ownership without state control represents market socialism (Yugoslavia, Hungary, post-Mao China, and Vietnam). Alternatively, private ownership with state control represents state capitalism (Japan, Germany, Taiwan, and South Korea), while private ownership without state control represents a *laissez-faire* market economy (UK in the nineteenth century and U.S. prior to the New Deal). Conceptually, market socialism embraces public and private ownership as well as state and market control, and a market socialist state allows substantial freedom of markets.

The "socialist primary phase" with the coexistence of socialist and capitalist elements

The post-Mao regime has supplied a theoretical justification for its economic restructuring program by introducing two keystones for Chinese modernization and socialist construction: "the Socialist Primary Phase" and "the Socialist Market Economy." The essential elements of the theoretical keystones, however, do not suggest any attempt by the post-Mao leadership to transform the Chinese economy into a capitalist one or to abandon its ultimate goal of communism.

The ultimate goal of the Communist Party is to eliminate private ownership and to accomplish communism. Complete public ownership, in whatever form, of the economy is clearly the goal of the Chinese communist revolution. In the context of the communist ruling, the fact that private enterprises are allowed to exist and develop contradicts the communist doctrine. However, this practice is not something new under the post-Mao regime, but recurrent in the history of communist states either in the former Soviet Union, formerly communist states, and in China. Such a practice of allowing and encouraging the development of private business was exercised during the period of Lenin's New Economic Policy (NEP) in the early 1920s, when the Soviet Union encountered economic difficulties and political crisis. Almost all the forms of practice during the period of Lenin's NEP, such as leasing, contract, sell-off of some SOEs, private business, foreign direct investment, and foreign-owned enterprises, have been employed in post-Mao China. Such practices, however, were also exercised during the readjustment and retrenchment from 1961 to 1963 during the Mao era, and then repeated during Deng's economic reforms in 1978–89. Both regimes tolerated the role of private business in the socialist economy.[13] In more recent years, since the 1990s, the post-Mao regime has shifted its policy from "tolerance" to "encouragement" to achieve the immediate goal of "a socialist market economy." However, either "tolerance" or "encouragement" is only a measure for overcoming economic difficulties and accomplishing intermediate goals, rather than a substitute for a long-term goal of the Chinese Communist Party. To the communist state, the existence and development of private enterprises is a useful and controllable practice at the "socialist primary stage." In this regard, the post-Mao economic policy and transformation can be compared to the example of Lenin's NEP, which Lenin considered as a "tactical retreat" on the road toward communism. The coexistence of public and private ownership was considered a concession. As Lenin pointed out, "we have learned an art that is indispensable to our revolution—pliability, the ability to alter our tactics quickly and abruptly . . . choosing a new road to our goal if the former road has proved to be inexpedient or impossible for the time being."[14]

The post-Mao regime recognizes that Mao committed a serious mistake in handling the socialist economy; that is, Mao became impetuous in bringing about the transformation of rural cooperatives into "People's Communes" and of urban collectives into "the whole people ownership" (全民所有制) and pursuing "larger in size and a higher degree of public ownership" (*yidaergong* 一大二公). The post-Mao leadership recognized that such a high degree of public ownership was not fit for the "socialist primary phase" and could not promote initiative and creativity of laborers and producers, and thus failed to promote the development of productivity.[15] The post-Mao leadership also recognized that China's economic modernization and the development of a requisite infrastructure and scientific technology can only come about with outside help through an "open-door policy." Therefore, a transition period is needed in which state and nonstate ownership, public and nonpublic sectors, can exist side by side, with the former in a dominant position. This transition period for Chinese socialist economic construction is theoretically formulated as the "Socialist Primary Phase," during which the CPC retreats from Mao's strategy of pursuing "larger in size and a higher degree of public ownership." Such a retreat is essentially the equivalent of Lenin's NEP; the existence of capitalist elements and the role of the market mechanism in the economy does not suggest a fundamental change in the economic system or abandoning the ultimate goal of communism.

Deng's reform was advanced in the late 1970s when Mao's leftist policies such as the "Three Red Banners" and the "Cultural Revolution" proved to be ineffective, just as Lenin's NEP was advanced in the Soviet Union when "military communism" proved to be a failure there. In other words, both Lenin's NEP and Deng's economic reforms were designed to avert an economic crisis and aimed at arming the socialist economy with advanced foreign capital and technology in their respective countries.[16] The post-Mao economy and the Soviet economy during Lenin's NEP not only share some similar forms of practice but also show a notable similarity in the mixed ownership structure. Obviously, capitalist elements exist in the economic sector in post-Mao China today as they existed in the Soviet economy during the NEP period.[17]

After the 15th Party Congress, the CPC has acknowledged the positive contribution by individual and private economic sectors to China's economic modernization, and encouraged the development of privately owned enterprises, but under party–state control and within the legal and policy framework defined by the regime. The 4th Plenary Session of the 15th Central Committee held in September 1999 continues to emphasize the political direction of restructuring SOEs and adheres to the basic socialist economic system with public ownership in the predominant position while at the same time allowing the development of multiple economic sectors, including private, foreign-owned, and joint venture firms. Privatization is once again denounced as contradicting the whole purpose of reforms and running counter to the party line and policy of the 15th Party Congress.[18] Therefore, the post-Mao economic transformation toward capitalism is a misinterpretation of the central reality of post-Mao economic reforms.

The ownership structure of Chinese market socialism

The ownership system is fundamental to China's economic transition. It is in this most important domain of China's economic reform that the dispute over the nature of China's economic reform—capitalism or socialism—has centered in post-Mao political and ideological discourse. "Ownership" has been defined as the core of the relations of production, determining the nature of an economic system. Ordinary usage suggests that socialism and capitalism represent two contrasting economic systems. "An essential, though not exhaustive, trait of capitalism is private ownership of the means of production and exchange."[19] Therefore, there has been a clear distinction between socialism and capitalism: socialism is an economic system in which the means of production and exchange is publicly owned and major economic activities are performed by governmental, societal, or public agencies, while capitalism is an economic system in which the means of production and exchange is privately owned and major economic activities are performed by private organizations.[20] However, as the history of modern socialist movements and communist practice has suggested, socialism does not have public ownership of all the means of production and exchange, but can coexist with private ownership in some economic sectors, for instance, agriculture, handicrafts, retail trade, and small and medium-sized industries. Socialist countries not only differ on the method of socializing the economy but also vary greatly in the degree to which their economies are socialized.[21] There are significant differences in the operation and experience of these countries because of the widely different political cultures of these countries. Even then, however, the single most essential trait of ownership is sufficient to allow these countries to be placed in a common classification.

The post-Mao regime has encouraged the development of the nonstate sector and emphasized the important role of this sector in economic growth. Over recent decades, nonstate-owned enterprises have been growing rapidly and they have accounted for a larger share of the gross value of industrial output (GVIO) than have SOEs. However, the definition of the nonstate sector in the Chinese context needs to be clarified more specifically and clearly in order to assess the change in this sector and its significance in the economy.

Categorization of the Chinese economic sectors

According to the State Statistics Bureau and the State Administration Bureau of Industry and Commerce, the post-Mao Chinese economy has become a mixture of eight sectors: state-owned, collective-owned, private-owned, individual-owned, cooperative or joint-venture, shareholding, foreign-owned, and others (Hong Kong, Macao, Taiwan, and other overseas Chinese investments).[22] There are five layers of government in China: central, provincial, municipal, district or county, and township. Enterprises that are under the direct authority of the central government or of provincial governments are considered state-owned or SOEs and all others are considered the nonstate sector. But, the nonstate sector includes collective enterprises, individual and private business, foreign-funded enterprises, and joint-ownership enterprises.

What needs to be clarified is the nature of the collective-owned enterprises which make up the largest portion of the nonstate sector. In legal terms, title to the assets of a SOE is vested in "the whole people"—all the citizens of the country (can be national, provincial, or municipal). Title to a collective's assets is vested in its members who make up a *danwei*, a workplace or residential unit.[23] Collectives are public in nature and can be urban or rural, depending on their affiliation. Urban collectives include urban "large collectives" (*dajiti*), "small collectives" (*xiaojiti*), and urban cooperatives. Enterprises affiliated with a district government under a municipality or a county are regarded as urban "large collectives." Enterprises affiliated with a neighborhood (grassroots governmental organizations in urban areas) are labeled "small collectives." Urban cooperatives are included in the category of urban collectives. Rural collectives include township and village enterprises (TVEs) and rural cooperatives. What distinguishes collectives from SOEs is that they are not managed by, nor do they report to, the industrial ministries/bureaus or any representatives thereof. They operate largely on their own in a more market-based environment. From the point view of ownership, collectives are regarded as publicly owned because in principle their ownership is shared by the community. The remaining categories of the nonstate sector include individual businesses owned by a household or an individual that employs several people; private enterprises owned by a household or an individual that employs more workers; foreign enterprises; and joint ventures.[24] However, SOEs and collectives together, as the public sector, continue to constitute more than 60 percent of the economy in almost every key respect, such as industrial assets, labor force, and industrial output.[25]

TVEs are the fastest-growing category of industry, and rural industrialization is an extension of the country's urban industrial program. TVEs are categorized into the nonstate sector, but they are not the private sector. "Chinese TVEs are by no means reducible to the canonical capitalist firm," which is characterized by market-controlled, individualistic property rights—"they are collectives, not private."[26] Many new TVEs have emerged as a result of urban industrial expansion. Factories in large cities increasingly sub-contract activities to neighboring rural areas as a way around restrictions on their ability to hire more labor or to acquire more land for expansion.[27] However, TVEs can be traced back to the late 1950s as commune- and brigade-run enterprises under Mao's "walking on two legs" policy, which anticipated the coexistence of labor-intensive small rural industrial enterprises with medium-sized and large urban industrial enterprises. These rural industrial enterprises were created to mobilize surplus labor and other local resources in the countryside to enhance local self-reliance and help rural industrialization. With the replacement of the commune system with the township–village system in the late 1980s, these enterprises were renamed TVEs. Therefore, TVEs are not something new under the post-Mao regime in terms of their origin, purpose of creation, and local controlling system.[28] Some efforts have attempted to address the nature of TVEs.[29] Some studies examine the ownership structure of the TVEs along two dimensions: the control right and the benefit right, and they conclude that the TVE is controlled by the Township–Village Government (TVG), not by its nominal owners, the local citizens, and the benefits produced by the TVE are shared between the TVG and the citizens. Workers as property "owners" are actually nominal and receive a very limited amount of benefit from the property. The TVE in its very nature is "public" rather than "private." The ownership structure of the TVE is designed for two main purposes: one is that the existing political system must be maintained and the other is that local agents must be provided with economic incentives.[30] Therefore, the ownership structure of TVEs is not the result of free contracting among private agents as in a free market economy, but a product of an environment in which the party–state power plays a dominant role in economic life.[31]

A field study has also shown that local governments and party organizations perform enormously important tasks for the central government in political, economic, social, and many other areas. Political control by local governments is strengthened rather than weakened, and party organizations at various levels are still the power center.[32] As many scholars of Chinese economic reforms point out, the collective sector, including the TVE, is best regarded as the local government sector of the Chinese economy.[33] An article published in the *People's Daily* admitted that policies of TVEs are "often decided by one person, randomly modified or changed by one person, and many TVEs are victimized by such changeable policies and random fees and allotments."[34] At the TVE Work Conference of Jiangsu Province in May 1998, Xu Guoqiang, Party Secretary of Changshu City, also complained that

> local governments have always seen the TVEs as their own appendage. Whenever there were instructions from above to develop the TVEs, our local governments would take immediate actions to become the subject of the development, taking on what ought to be done by the TVEs, consequently resulting in too much interference with the business of the TVEs, which can hardly become independent subjects of the market competition. The resolution of this problem requires our local governments to divest themselves of their power, separate government from business, and change government functions.[35]

Therefore, from the viewpoint of scholars, national newspapers, or local officials, TVEs in most areas of this country are best defined as "the local government sector of the Chinese economy" or "the collective sector" which is a constituent part of public ownership.

In short, "collective" enterprises, including urban collectives and rural TVEs, are "nonstate" in name, but "public" in nature, and they are in reality not essentially different from the state enterprises in terms of their administrative jurisdiction and party bureaucratic control. If the private sector made up the major part of the GNP or GVIO, that would suggest an essential change in the economic system. However, the reality is different, and the statistical figure suggests that public sectors including state- and collective-owned enterprises still account for more than 60 percent of the total industrial output value, the total industrial assets and the total labor forces. According to Deng and post-Deng leaders, the public ownership includes not only the state enterprises but also the rising collectives and the TVEs, and stockholding companies are considered as publicly owned if the state has the majority of shares or controlling shares.[36]

Land is still publicly owned

The ownership of land is another critical aspect of change in the ownership system since the reform. The formal ownership of land has changed little and remains almost exclusively under some form of public ownership, although a great change has occurred in land management systems. From 1949 through 1977, agricultural collectivization not only transformed the entire ownership of land into the hands of the state, though it was said to be "collectively owned," but also transformed the management of land into a three-level system in which village households were organized into "production teams," which in turn were organized into "brigades" and ultimately into "communes." Private plots were tolerated on a limited scale. Under this system, land was collectively owned, and the basic production unit was the team, consisting of 20–30 households.[37]

Since 1978, the reform in rural areas has changed the management system of land into a "household contract responsibility system," because arable land was distributed among village households based on family size and the availability of labor. Production decisions became the responsibility of the household governed by contracts with the relevant rural collective economic organization. However, although the old system of communes, brigades, and production teams was abolished, these entities were reconstituted as townships or villages, the government of which was charged with the responsibility for land management and the negotiation of contracts with the households. Moreover, land remains under public ownership.[38]

Agricultural decollectivization is not an equivalent of "privatization," as described by some China analysts, but only the transformation of the rural economy into "a new type of collective economy, characterized by combining public ownership of the land with totally individualized operations of production."[39] To the post-Mao leadership, such an arrangement is defined as the "separation of land ownership rights and land use rights" by contracting land use rights to individual households, and thus it retains public ownership of the land as the main means of production while providing working incentives and productive freedom for peasants.[40] Land ownership rights are forbidden from sale while the transfer of contractual rights could be achieved through negotiations among involved parties and must be ratified by villagers' committees or higher authorities. When land is owned by the state (one owner), it is not a commodity; what is on the market for exchange is not land ownership rights but land use rights.[41] This is absolutely not tantamount to a transfer of private property rights in capitalist economies or a policy of privatization of public ownership in post-Soviet or post-communist economies.

Contracting land rights to individual households has led to the problem of land associated with small, fragmented land holdings. To solve this, another important reform has been introduced: the emergence of shareholding cooperative systems in various parts of the country, by which land or property under the direct control of the collective ownership is valued and divided into equal shares. Some shares are reserved for collective ownership and the rest are distributed among the village households. These shares for individual households cannot be traded but earn dividends. In this way, villagers in cooperative systems no longer cultivate small pieces of land but give their contracted land to the cooperative in return for shares upon which they earn dividends. The cooperative may cultivate the land or use it as a factory site, but must get the approval from higher government authorities and hire labor from the households involved in the cooperative arrangement.[42]

However, such a practice has had little change in the ownership of land. The collective retains a dominant share in the cooperative and controls the decision-making power in the use of land, while the villagers actually do not own those shares distributed among them nor can they trade those shares. Neither do individual households have the decision-making power in how to use the land since they have given their contracted land to the cooperative in return for shares upon which they earn dividends. Moreover, the use of land or trade in the usage of land is tightly controlled by the township, county, or provincial governments, depending on the government guidelines for the use of land and the administrative jurisdiction of the land. There are very strict administrative procedures for approving the use of arable land for purposes other than agricultural production.

In 1999, the General Office of the State Council issued a "Circular of Strengthening Administration of the Transfer of the Use Right of Land and Strictly Forbidding Speculation on Land" which regulated that the collective was not permitted to sell, transfer, lease or use rights of land in rural areas for purposes other than agricultural production; individual peasants were prohibited from selling their houses to individuals in urban areas; the use and development of land must be strictly restricted by the state general and annual plan; no individual or organization was allowed to sign contracts relating to the use of land with rural collective economic organizations without the approval of the higher authorities responsible for land; and so forth.[43] Obviously, land, as the most important factor of production, has been publicly owned, controlled by the state, and not considered as a commodity for free exchange in the marketplace. So-called "privatization" of land is a misuse of the concept in interpreting changes in post-Mao rural reforms.

State-owned enterprises are still dominant

SOEs continues to control the "commanding heights" of the Chinese national economy—basic industries, infrastructure industries, banking, insurance, pillar industries, key strategic industries, and high-tech industries. This term was used by Lenin and then used by Janos Kornai to refer to the state dominant positions in those areas "that allow the other, nonstate sectors of the economy to be dominated."[44] The sales and profits of the 300 major SOEs are responsible for more than 50 percent of the total SOEs sales and profits, although these major enterprises are only 1 percent of the total SOEs.[45] "SOEs are still responsible for a substantial share of China's GDP, but the government's control of the economy goes far beyond those enterprises it directly owns. State-issued economic plans set policy on all ventures, including private and foreign-owned ones."[46] The state sector not only has increased in total asset value but also continues to control and monopolize the "commanding heights" or "economic lifelines" of the national economy, such as electric power, petroleum, natural gas, petroleum processing, metallurgy, transportation, assembly machinery manufacturing, chemicals, telecommunication, railway, aviation, and finance.[47]

The large and medium-scale enterprises (LMEs) in the Chinese SOEs are at the heart of China's traditional Soviet-type economy, and the reforms of LMEs should represent the core of China's overall economic systemic transformation.[48] The same logic would be that the abandonment of the "Four Cardinal Principles" should represent the core of China's overall systemic transformation. Even after the wave of corporatization of SOEs into joint-stock companies, the majority of these corporatized firms have the state as the dominant owner and, more crucially, the essential features of their governance structure (soft budget constraint, government intervention, and the employment relationship) have remained intact.[49]

The reform of SOEs is to promote rather than to discourage their development. SOEs are experimenting with the reform of the joint share system, the joint stock cooperative system, leasing, and people's management of public-owned enterprises, and they are implementing the party policy of "seizing on the big and letting the small go" (*zhuada fangxiao*).[50] The state provides beneficial policies to these key enterprises and enterprise groups in such ways as the self-managing right of import and export, bank loans, technological renovation, and restructuring of enterprises.[51] The 300 largest SOEs chosen by the central government and the 2,500 large and medium-sized SOEs chosen by the provincial governments are to experiment with the reform of the joint share system and corporatize themselves into large enterprise groups or mother–son corporations.

Small SOEs are those nonkey industries of the national economy with poor technological equipment and low productivity. Losers or deficit enterprises of small SOEs have become a heavy burden on the government budget.[52] Therefore, the new policy of "seizing on the big and letting the small go" (*zhuada fangxiao* 抓大放小) is to resolve this situation. Small SOEs are to be invigorated and transformed into new firms by way of reorganization, association, merger, leasing, contract, shareholding cooperatives, and sell-off. These practices are considered as "exploring various new forms for realizing public ownership" and will not change the nature of public ownership.[53] Most of these enterprises have been reorganized or incorporated into public-owned large corporations. Selling some of the small SOEs to private owners will not affect the nature of the entire economic system, because the role of these SOE losers is small in China's economy. Post-Deng leaders have emphasized that the policy of "seizing on the big and letting the small go" is to restructure and develop SOEs, not to do it in the opposite direction. "Letting the small go" is to "invigorate them" (*fanghuo* 放活), not to give them away or abandon them.

There are many ways to "let the small go," such as reorganization, association, merger, delegation of administrative power, leasing, contract, shareholding cooperatives, and sell-off. Sell-off is only one of many forms of "letting go" and the policy is not to sell all the small state enterprises or simply give them away. Many small SOEs can be invigorated and transformed into new corporatized firms without changing the nature of their public ownership.[54]

Shareholding reform

Shareholding reform since the 1990s is characterized by diversification of the ownership structure and the forms of public ownership. In 1992, provisional regulations were issued for two types of shareholding experiments, namely, the limited liability companies and the limited joint-stock companies. In the former type of company, the capital of the company is not necessarily divided into equal shares which are closely held among a small group of investors, and transfer of ownership rights is more restricted, while in the latter type of company, the equity of a company is divided into equal shares which can be held by many owners and ownership can be transferred. The aim of this reform is to establish a "modern enterprise system," which is to be achieved through the "corporatization" of SOEs, that is, the conversion of SOEs into shareholding companies based on public assets through the implementation of a new Company Law. The majority of the enterprises are to be converted to limited liability companies rather than joint-stock companies. Through this the government authorities hope to achieve a separation of the ownership functions of the state from the management functions of the enterprises within the framework of greater autonomy and accountability. A pilot project for this purpose was launched shortly after the 3rd Plenum of the 14th Central Committee in November 1993, with 10,000 medium-sized and large SOEs involved. Considerable progress has been made since then in extending and formalizing the shareholding system. At the same time, greater diversification has also taken place in the ownership structure of the economy over the years, while the new phase of enterprise reform has emphasized the maintenance of public ownership as the cornerstone of the economy.[55]

Shareholding reform, as clearly demonstrated in leaders' policy speeches and party–state documents, must adhere to the basic principle of "the predominant position of public ownership with diversified forms of ownership" and ensure majority shareholding of the state or collective corporations in "state-collective–private mergers," prohibiting private citizens from controlling the majority share.[56] The party–state policy statements and related legal documents regarding shareholding reform have actually specified which industries or enterprises are allowed to practice the shareholding system and which are not. They have also regulated, in those enterprises where the shareholding system is allowed, what should be allowed for private shares and what should not be allowed, and what percentage must be held for the public ownership. All these regulations are implemented to ensure the nature of the socialist public economy as a whole.[57] To equate shareholding reform with privatization is a misunderstanding of the post-Mao economic policy and practice.

The present various shareholding cooperatives and joint stock companies do not affect the nature of Chinese national economy, regardless of all kinds of mergers of state–collective, state–foreign, collective–foreign, collective–private, or joint–venture cooperatives. In China's constitution, shareholding cooperatives are viewed as a new form of collective economy, incorporating some forms of shareholding companies with the combination of labor cooperation and capital cooperation. These firms combine "the distribution according to work" and "the dividend distribution according to share." Shareholding cooperatives are considered an effective form in the restructuring of small SOEs and collective enterprises.[58] However, the government has also recognized that the shareholding reforms have so far failed to resolve old problems such as redundant employees, bad debts, all kinds of burdens and charges on enterprises. Furthermore, "the shareholding co-operative system does not clearly define the responsibilities and rights of shareholders. Egalitarianism has existed in many enterprises where workers hold an equal number of shares, thus hampering flexible management of these enterprises."[59]

It is true that the post-Mao regime has attempted to promote "diversity of ownership" and "diversity of forms for realizing public ownership." However, diversification of ownership is experimented with on the basis of the predominant position of public ownership. The diversification of forms for realizing public ownership is not equal to the privatization of the state economy but rather involves the transformation of operational forms of public-owned enterprises, which has not weakened the dominant position of public ownership or reduced the scope of its influence in socioeconomic life. For example, according to some Chinese economists, in implementing the joint share system and joint stock cooperative system, the state or collectives can control 100 percent of enterprise capital by controlling 51 percent of the total shares, thus expanding the scope of the state capital's influence on the economy.[60] Both the joint share system and the joint stock cooperative system are not considered as the "patent" of capitalism but "as the necessary result of the socialization of production in an advanced commodity economy."[61] In other words, the shareholding system is an economic organization or an operational form of socialist market economy, which can be used to aggregate floating capital, facilitate economic corporation, and improve the allocation of resources.[62] This holds the key to the understanding of the shareholding reform which the post-Mao leadership employs as the means to revitalize and modernize Chinese economy. As the *People's Daily* states, the shareholding system should not be equated with privatization of the state assets but considered as "new specific forms for realizing public ownership as a result of the self-reform and self-perfection of socialist public ownership."[63]

The transformation of SOEs into shareholding companies is essentially to delegate the power of state asset management to core enterprises of the concerns, rather than to "privatize" the state assets into "private enterprises." The vast majority of these corporatized companies are member enterprises normally retaining the same ministerial or local-governmental affiliations, the same channels of tax-and-profit remittance, and the same ownership systems— so-called "three unchanges." Even the wave of agglomerations, mergers and takeovers took place mainly within these boundaries. Core state industrial enterprises are the country's financially most powerful and technologically most advanced. They are granted the autonomous power to adopt various forms of firm organization. Core state enterprises are however required to centralize decision making, which covers major aspects of the activity of the industrial concerns: formulation of mid-term and annual development plans, concluding contracts with the state, dealing with the bank in borrowing for capital construction and technical renovation investment, imports and exports, the accumulation and transaction of state assets, and the appointment of the leaders of main member enterprises. Therefore, "the delegation of power" to the most advanced sector of Chinese industry is to enhance the mobility of productive factors and assets across localities or ministerial affiliations, promote growth and productivity through dynamic economics of scale, and to strengthen the international competitiveness of Chinese industry, rather than to implement a policy of privatization of Chinese industry. The essence of the reform is best captured by the term "rationalization."

Private enterprise

The private sector has been the fastest growing part of the Chinese economy in recent years. About two million rural residents are employed in privately owned enterprises. Another eight million are self-employed, primarily in handicrafts and other sideline activities.[64] Many individual and private enter- prises tend to merge with the local government economy (the collective enterprises) not only because they require political insurance but also because local government can offer access to land, labor, material, and even capital. Therefore, the mix of the individual, private, and collective sectors is a particular developmental feature of some areas, particularly of the Wenzhou economy in the Zhejiang province. Such practices actually reflect the state socialism context. As Kristen Parris put it, these private entrepreneurs operate their business and pursue their interests "within the context of state socialism." The relationship between state and society is being redefined but this process is shaped by existing power structures and ideologies. Such practices illustrate how existing state institutions and ideologies can condition local and individual economic activities, even in areas that are remote from the center.[65]

However, the Wenzhou model does not represent the overall economic practice of the post-Mao regime. In some regions of China, private entre- preneurs have become even more intimately connected to, and dependent on, the state through formal contracting arrangements which allow them to avoid market risks under the communist totalitarian regime by securing supplies and buyers for their products from the public sector.[66] Therefore, such practices are no more than another version of the "state capitalism," a Leninist strategy practiced in Soviet Russia during the period of Lenin's NEP in the 1920s. It is a practice that is allowed, designed, and controlled by the socialist state and operates as an economic element within the context of a socialist public economy.

Provincial variations in the structure of ownership are apparent in national statistics. Heilongjiang's economy remained dominated by its state sector, despite many years of economic reform. Jiangsu had a very large collective sector but an insignificant private sector and a small foreign-funded sector. Guangdong's economy was dominated by its foreign-funded and collective sectors. Guangxi had the largest private sector (as a proportion of provincial GVIO) even though industrial production remained dominated by the state sector. Table 16.1 provides data on GVIO by ownership sector for selected provinces. These provinces are selected because they broadly represent different geo-economic regions in China.

The figures in Table 16.1 are a reflection of the economic transition pattern in China, and such a trend has continued since the 1990s. The figures also suggest that the public sector (including SOEs and collectives) maintains a dominant position in all geo-economic regions in China. Also noteworthy is the fact that private and individual entrepreneurs continue to face discrimination in obtaining bank loans, raw material, licenses, legal status, and so forth, and struggle for a place within the framework of state-dominated market socialism. In shareholding reform, as CPPCC member Chen Hong complained, "the nonstate economy is not treated in the same way as state-owned enterprises in acquiring property rights and merging with other enterprises."[67]

In more recent years, particularly since the 2008 financial crisis, there has been a trend—using the catch-phrase among the Chinese—"the advance of the

Table 16.1 Provincial GVIO by ownership, 1994

Province	State sector(%)	Collective sector (%)	Private sector(%)	Foreign-funded sector* (%)
All provinces	34.1	40.9	11.5	13.6
Heilongjiang	69.3	17.4	6.2	7.2
Jiangsu	20.0	63.0	5.0	12.0
Zhejiang	16.1	56.4	17.7	9.9
Guangdong	21.7	33.4	7.3	37.7
Hainan	49.7	13.3	10.3	26.1
Guangxi	42.9	26.4	22.1	8.5
Shanxi	43.7	36.5	17.3	2.5

GVIO, gross value of industrial output.
*Including joint-venture enterprises.
Source: Derived from table 12-6: Zhongguo tongji nianjian 1995 [China Statistical Yearbook 1995] (Beijing: Zhongguo tongji chubanshe, 1995), p. 379.

state enterprises and the retreat of private enterprises" (国进民退 *guojin mintui*). The private sector has suffered financial straits, and a lot of private enterprises were forced to shut down while SOEs have received large amounts of state bank loans to advance their monopolies and market shares. "Most of the government's four trillion yuan, or US$586 billion, stimulus package, already designated for rebuilding infrastructure such as railroads, highways, airports, and construction, were contracted to centrally controlled SOEs. In addition, these enterprises also enjoyed privileges by borrowing from state banks. In 2009, around 80 percent of bank loans, nine trillion yuan, or US$1.4 trillion, went to SOEs."[68] Directed by the central government, large SOEs have been encouraged to merge with medium-sized and small private enterprises in almost every industry to transform them into part of state-owned conglomerates. SOEs have also advanced into many areas that used to be dominated by the private sector, such as the real estate market, and the share of SOEs has increased to 60 percent. "Currently, the SOEs enjoy a monopoly over almost all of China's resource industries: petroleum, telecommunications, electricity, tobacco, coal, civil aviation, finance, insurance, etc. As a consequence, private enterprises had to exit from these industries."[69] It is reported that 120 of the largest central SOEs increased their profit 42.8 percent compared with that of the first two quarters of 2010 while the profit of most of private enterprises dropped dramatically and many were bankrupted. In China today, whoever gains most depends on lower interest loans, cheaper land and resources, and government financial subsidies, which are all controlled by the government.[70] Therefore, it is premature to conclude that post-Mao China has been moving toward capitalism.

State and market roles in the "socialist market economy"

A free market economy is an economic system in which the market is the invisible hand that ensures resources are allocated to their most productive uses in line with the principle of consumer choice and utility maximization.[71] The basic indicator of a free market economy is "the achievement of the conditions of a competitive environment in which market prices reflect relative scarcities, and enterprises and individuals make decisions mainly in response to *undistorted* market signals."[72] The very foundation of a free market economy is private ownership. According to Kornai, the SOEs in socialist countries are characterized by the "soft-budget constraint"—"the residual income that emerges as the difference between receipts and expenses does not pass into the pockets of natural persons, and the losses are not covered by the same natural party."[73] This embraces the central thesis of the property rights approach—it is only the natural–personal owners who control and direct production and distribution of residual income and it is only based on this condition that modern capitalist economies have developed. Private property rights are the very foundation of the free market economy.[74] To what degree has a market economy been established in post-Mao China? To what degree has the Chinese economy been transformed in terms of private property rights?

The above discussion has suggested that the public sector still dominates in the Chinese economy while private and other sectors have also emerged, creating a mixed ownership structure that combines socialist principles and market principles.

Legacies of a centrally planned economy

The "socialist market economy" is another keystone of this transition period of the Chinese socialist economy which is to restructure the Chinese economy at the "socialist primary phase" with the enhanced role of the "market mechanism." But the economy to be restructured must be "socialist" rather than "capitalist." The post-Mao leadership has emphasized that markets are value-neutral mechanisms of which both socialism and capitalism can make use. The concept contains two components: "socialism" and "market." The relationship between the two components is interpreted as the interplay between "highly efficient resource allocation and productivity of labor" and "social justice and common prosperity." Former Premier Zhu Rongji explained that "resource allocation under a market economy is more efficient than that of a planned economy," but "maintaining a just society and working towards common prosperity of its people is a socialist ideal. Public ownership of property can better maintain social justice and increase common prosperity than systems which encourage private ownership." Therefore, Zhu claimed that "China can establish a market economy while public ownership continues to predominate."[75] Li Peng, another former premier, argued that planned and market economies each had their own strengths and weaknesses and that China needs to draw upon the strengths of both in order to build an integrated mixed economy.[76] Jiang Zeming, former party general secretary, also claimed that China should be able to establish a market economy under a socialist system which "can and should operate better than one under the capitalist system."[77]

Therefore, such an economy should be theoretically conceptualized as "market socialism"—with an enhanced role of the market and competition but not necessarily a replacement of public ownership with "private ownership" as in a capitalist system. The party's objective is to retain the predominance of public ownership supplemented by nonstate and private ownership while achieving an effective separation between the ownership and management of enterprises.[78] As Jiang Zemin pointed out,

> We must continue to adhere to the policy with public ownership as the principal part of our economy while at the same time allowing the development of multiple economic sectors. However, the dominant position of public ownership must not be weakened or abandoned.[79]

The post-Mao economic reform has made considerable progress since the 1990s in terms of economic "marketization" (市场化). However, the central planning system remains and continues to play a significant role in the Chinese economy. China has begun to implement the 12th Five-Year Plan, which is one of some important legacies of the Chinese central planned economy in the Mao era. Although the five-year plan is now less powerful and pervasive than in the past, its implications are still significant because the plan sets the direction and pace of economic development for the five-year period, provides a roadmap which outlines major structural changes, and defines the environment in which the economy operates. China's chief reform architect, Deng Xiaoping, made it very clear that

> we have not changed and will never change the policy of integrating the planned economy with the market adjustment. We can adjust the degree accordingly in our practice, sometimes with more market functioning, and more planning performances in other cases.[80]

In practice, the post-Mao leadership has never attempted to dismantle but to rationalize and improve the state planning apparatus.

The five-year plan does not include specific details on the operation of all aspects of the economy; much of that was left to the sectoral economic plans tailored by government ministries in the traditional planned economy. Currently, many of the specific details are left to policies tailored by government ministries and the local governments. The original sectoral plans are not being abandoned outright but rather replaced with specific, informal government policies and new industrial plans. Whether it is called an industrial policy or merely a policy on foreign investment, civilian aircraft, import and export, private enterprises, or special economic zones (SEZs), it has the same policy effect.[81] Broadly speaking, five-year plans provide a broad outline for government economic policy and indicate the direction of policy changes in the coming five years. "Five-year economic plans are the hallmark of the communist economic system. The continuing existence of a government planning structure does indicate an unwillingness to rely upon the market to make resource allocation and other economic decisions."[82] Most importantly, the stated goal of post-Mao reforms in any party–state policy statement and document is not to move the economy to a capitalist system but to improve and strengthen the socialist system.

The concept of planning has also been renewed. Under the new ideological doctrine, the market mechanism is merely an instrument of economic development and not a defining characteristic of a social system; the socialist character of the economy is preserved by the predominant ownership of the means of production by the public sector (including the state and the collectives). The market system is therefore considered fully compatible with either capitalist or socialist systems. Therefore, the objective model of the post-Mao economic reform is to transform the economy from a predominantly central planning system to one in which market mechanisms play an important role.[83] The main task of planning will be to set rational strategic targets for national economic and social development, to forecast economic development, to control total supply and total demand, to readjust the geographical distribution of industries, and to master the financial and material resources necessary for the construction of important projects.[84] As Zheng Peiyan, former Commissioner of the State Development and Planning Commission (SDPC), put it, "the government restructuring does not mean any weakening of the functions of the SDPC but brings the new functions of the SDPC in line with the requirements of the socialist market economic system and enables us to make a flexible use of economic and legal means as well as the necessary administrative means."[85]

In a free market economy, business firms have freedom of entry to and exit from the market, either investment in a certain industry or business or withdrawal from it, depending on the market competition, demand and supply, and they equally have the opportunities of investment and withdrawal from the market. But, in the post-Mao "socialist market economy," the government plans, defines and decides the parameters of who can run certain businesses and who cannot. The "commanding heights" of the Chinese economy are reserved for SOEs, and state policies and license systems are employed to block the private and foreign companies from running business in those industries (if allowed to joint venture with SOEs, the state sets the terms and policies), while leaders of SOEs actually do not have the freedom to withdraw from those areas, because it is the government authorities that decide whether to liquidate, break up, or merge those businesses. Only in the economic sectors of "non-commanding heights" can business firms have freedom of entry and exit, but often the SOEs have the upper hand or more opportunities than private firms.

In short, even though admitting the considerable economic changes, China still manifests a dominance of the public sector in the economy, the presence of administrative controls in economic daily life, the government allocation of resources and materials, the limitation of market mechanisms, and the maintenance of socialist economic principles and norms. It is true that economic activities are more responsive to the market today, but they are still deeply involved in and restrained by the "political embeddedness" or the controlled interlocking interdependence of economic, social, cultural, administrative, and political institutions.

Government intervention in the economy

Compared with the situation in the Mao era and in the early reform era in 1980s, the level of government intervention in economic activities has been significantly reduced. But government intervention in all forms has not been removed. The state is not withdrawing from its role in the economy but redefining it. Most of China's enterprises and economic activities actually remain within the scope of government administrative or nonadministrative intervention and adjustment since the dominant position of the public sector has remained unchanged. As far as the state ownership system and administrative control are concerned, post-Mao recent theory and practice have evolved without causing any fundamental change or structural transformation. A free market economy, with the system of free private enterprises as its base and market forces as its constant regulator, has not been established. What has emerged is a new form of market socialism in China.

In the post-Mao economic reform, some important measures were introduced to draw a clear distinction between state administrative organs and individual state-run enterprises, include the distinction between profits and taxes, the right of enterprises to distribute wages and bonuses to their employees, and the right of enterprises to set factory prices for certain commodities whose prices were previously fixed by the administration.[86] However, while these measures allowed industrial enterprises greater independence from state administration, interference in the affairs of industrial enterprises has remained commonplace. For instance, the higher administrative levels can renege on any contract or agreement stipulating the share of the profits an enterprise can retain, or the percentage of commodities produced by that enterprise which the enterprise itself can market. The final arbiter on disputes between enterprises is in most cases the industrial bureaus of the state administration or other higher administrative organs.[87]

State intervention, which remains commonplace in post-Mao China, has inhibited market efficiency and competition. Administrative authorities continue to intervene in business affairs in post-Mao China. Bureaucratic inspections and tedious appraisals and examinations still divert much of the enterprise leaders' attention from their management work. Random policy changes, fees, fines, and taxes imposed upon state enterprises and other economic organizations under various pretexts also increase production costs and discourage their production initiative. At present, most public enterprise leaders, those in state-owned, collective-owned, and state- or collective-predominant cooperatives and shareholding companies, are appointed by their superiors rather than being elected or chosen through modern employment mechanisms. Their promotion or demotion depends not on their performance but on their superiors' likes and dislikes. Because of these old practices, most public enterprise leaders, particularly SOE directors, focus more on building good relations with their superiors than on improving the enterprise's efficiency and productivity. All such administrative interventions have greatly inhibited fair, free, and efficient competition in the marketplace.[88]

According to Chen Xiaolong, who has conducted an in-depth examination of the current situation and the tendencies of China's economy, the planning administration is weakening while administrative intervention from the government, and monopolistic state economic institutions has not been reduced but rather strengthened and became more "random" or "casual" along with the decentralization of administrative power to local governments. The post-Mao economy is not one dominated by the market but a "dual track" system with partly market exchange and partly "randomized" administrative intervention. In socialist states, after the abdication of command planning, a "commercial market" could develop rapidly. The commercial sector is free in the sense of exchange, but this free exchange in commerce does not mean a free market in resource allocation. In other words, marketizing commercial exchange does not necessarily bring about the marketization of resource allocation. A nonmarket allocation of resources can coexist with a commercial market, thus developing a "dual track allocation of resources" under a decentralized command economy.[89] Chen's study also suggests that economic marketization has been developed in the context of a socialist sociopolitical structure and systemic culture—the two bases of China's planning economy have remained: the organizational structure of the giant party–state apparatus and the monopolistic state economy has not disintegrated but only been rearranged or renamed, and its potential power of intervening in daily economic activities has never been abolished; more than 10 million party–state cadres and 20 million employees in a monopolistic state economy continue to enjoy their political and social status and their capacity for manoeuvre is enormous and goes even farther than in Mao's era.[90]

Zhang Haoluo, Vice Director of the State Restructuring Commission, admitted that the "dual track" system was the major barrier to marketizing reform in China.[91] The combination of state socialism and a commercial market economy has randomized local administration intervention in daily economic activities and greatly expanded the area of "rent-seeking" in the form of "money–power exchange." The "dual track" system is a combination of market and government intervention. The expansion of nonstate economic sectors has encountered various systemic barriers and heavy financial burdens, and their capacity for capital accumulation has been limited.

Administrative intervention is also extensive in business operations and bank financial activities. China's financial system is highly regulated and dominated by state-owned banking. The Chinese government has set administratively regulated top and bottom limits on depositing and lending, and allowed the interest rate to move up and down within a certain range in order to maintain financial stability and overall control over the socialist market economy. Administrative authorities also encroach upon the normal business operation of commercial banks. Commercial banks sometimes grant loans, not according to the profit-maximizing principle, but in compliance with administrative orders from government organs. This is one of the main causes for the preponderance of bad debts in state commercial banks.[92] The People's Bank of China exercises its administration over grassroots financial institutions through its branches at the provincial level, which are subject to the influence of local governments. Their financial activities are always motivated by the interests of local governments or departments, rather than governed by the economic laws of the marketplace.[93] In November 1998, branches at the provincial level were abolished and replaced by nine cross-regional branches to recentralize administrative power of the People's Bank of China.[94]

Since the shareholding reform, China has issued "H" shares for SOEs on the Hong Kong stock market. But its daily operation, including the figure of its profits and losses, is not a market behavior but rather a comprehensive consideration of the government's political and economic policies.[95] The Bureau of State Assets Administration of the State Council (BSAASC) is the highest power organ of the administration of the state assets and responsible for the following three major functions: (1) power to manage the state-controlled shareholding companies, including personnel appointment, performance assessment, and basic work management; (2) power to reallocate resources and profits; and (3) power to participate in decision making on investment of state assets.[96] State power is not weakened but enhanced.

The power of Chinese ministries to regulate economic activity goes beyond formal economic and industrial plans. For example, rather than letting demand for imports be determined by market forces, as is the case in true market economies, Chinese ministries determine demand themselves. The National Development and Reform Commission, the Ministry of Commerce, and other state ministries coordinate to jointly set import "demand." Quotas, import licenses, and other nontariff import controls are employed to ensure that the actual level of imports does not exceed "demand." Often these decisions are made behind closed doors for protectionism and discrimination against particular foreign companies.[97] Formal trade barriers, like tariffs, government procurement and subsidies, quotas, import licenses, and other restrictions, are the most visible impediment to free economic interchange with China. The entire Chinese trade regime is characterized by multiple layers of duplicative trade barriers. China claims that most of its direct export subsidies have been phased out. In late 1995 China even suspended the practice of rebating taxes paid on products that are exported. However, Chinese government subsidies go far beyond the government's narrow definition of export subsidy. SOEs are still responsible for a substantial share of the GDP and dominate foreign trade, though other sectors have begun to receive foreign trade rights. SOEs enjoy many benefits from the state, including loans at interest rates far below market rates and other financial subsidies, both direct and indirect. Moreover, subsidies are not limited to SOEs.

Market price formation in market socialism

The prices of energy, raw materials, and labor, in most sectors, are set by the government at much less than world market rates. The National Development and Reform Commission is in charge of not only national planning but also price control. The Commission has often made amendments to the Price Law of China—"The Measures for the Implementation of Administrative Punishments on Price-related Violations." The price departments of the governments at or above the county level have to supervise and examine price-related activities in accordance with the law and determine the administrative punishment for price violation activity. The administrative punishment on any price violation act shall be determined by the price department of the local government at the place where such price violation act taken place.[98] Since the prices of so many basic inputs are set by the government, all prices would be at least partly influenced by the government and partly determined by the market.

Most of the transportation, energy, and electricity industries are owned and managed by the government, and their prices are decided by the government. Prices of key commodities and materials, such as energy and construction materials, are decided by the government. Prices of many commodities directly affecting residents' lives, such as grains and meat, are closely supervised by the government. Prices of basic inputs of production of SOEs set by the government have affected the market price formation.

In the financial market, despite the establishment of some commercial banks, the four state banks specializing in agriculture, construction, commerce, and international business still hold more than 80 percent of total business capital. State-owned banks are not market oriented but follow government directives. Many favorable loans for agricultural production, infrastructure construction, export ventures, and SOEs are granted at rates decided by government policy. These measures have become a frequent practice that has been institutionalized at all levels in China. One example is the financing of the various economic sectors by the state banks to ensure the actualization of the goal of 8 percent economic growth rate established at the 15th Party Congress and the 9th NPC. China People's Bank issued "Guidelines for Improving Financial Service to Support the Development of National Economy" and all financial institutions were required to carry out the financial policy. For example, industrial banks provided direct loans of 75 billion *yuan* to major state projects as well as 30 billion *yuan* to small and medium-sized enterprises. Agricultural banks provided loans of 25 billion yuan to TVEs to encourage their development. Bank of China undertook some special measures in financing small and medium-sized business firms as well as major state programs in foreign trade. Construction banks increased credit lines to 450 large and medium-sized enterprises in the basic construction investment. Transportation banks also took financial measures to support the major state enterprises and projects.[99] In the 2008 world financial crisis, the Chinese government also took similar measures to stabilize and boost the economy. Such financial support is provided according to the party's policy and administrative order, rather than the law of supply and demand of the market or based on the economic returns of business firms.

National industrial production of the 300 largest SOEs still follows directives from the State Planning Commission while the remaining SOEs are controlled by local government. As their production and prices would influence market price formation, the government can directly and indirectly influence the operation of the Chinese economy, and the cost of production in China often bears little resemblance to their actual market cost of production. In addition, as the World Bank has noted, China has often directed state trading companies, which export most Chinese-made goods, to export regardless of price to fill hard currency quotas.[100] Many China analysts take China's openness to foreign investment as a sign that it is pursuing a liberal trade strategy. However, the post-Mao leadership's idea is to simply attract foreign capital and technology to achieve the goal of modernization. The post-Mao leadership recognizes that foreign firms can provide a jump start for Chinese industry through capital, technology, and know-how gained in direct investment or joint ventures.[101]

Therefore, it is really hard to assess what percentage of the economy is truly adjusted by the market force, since all the key aspects, industries, resources, production factors, and "commanding heights" of the national economy, which seriously affect the market formation process, are still determined by the government and SOEs. From this perspective, talk of a free market economy in post-Mao China is premature and misleading because so many of the essential elements of the administrative command system and the governance structure of state socialism remain commonplace in post-Mao China. Post-Mao economic reforms have maintained the public ownership system which is declared by all communist states as the fundamental principles and norms of communist ideology and the core of a socialist economic system. SOEs and other public-sector enterprises have continued to dominate the economy and control all the key aspects, industries, resources, production factors, and "commanding heights" of the national economy. The administrative command system has remained effective and powerful, and state intervention has been extensive and commonplace in post-Mao policy and performance. Therefore, the Chinese economy is a type of market socialism that combines the basic socialist principle of public ownership and the basic principle of the market economy, with public ownership predominant in those areas deemed critical to the implementation of socialist principles and social policy.

Questions for discussion

1. What are the key features of state socialism and market socialism, and to what degree does market socialism retain the core of socialism while incorporating market and capitalist elements? Can we use market socialism as a conceptual framework in comparative studies of Vietnam and North Korea?
2. As a socialist economy has tried to decentralize and marketize, some questions have been raised: What is "capitalism?" What is "market socialism?" What is the most fundamental element that distinguishes between capitalist economy and other economies? Has the post-Mao Chinese economy moved toward capitalism?

Further reading

Dic Lo, *Market and Institutional Regulation in Chinese Industrialization, 1978–1994* (London: Macmillan Press, 1997).

Sujian Guo, *The Political Economy of Asian Transitions from Communism* (Aldershot: Ashgate Publishing, 2006).

Barry Naughton, *The Chinese Economy: Transitions and Growth* (Cambridge, MA: The MIT Press, 2007).

Part IX
Chinese foreign policy

17 Chinese foreign policy making

China's reform and opening also have an impact on Chinese foreign policy making because China has increasingly integrated into the world, the economy is more market and outward oriented, society is more pluralistic, and the political structure is more professionalized and specialized. Most significantly, with China transitioning from the older generation to the younger generation leadership—moving through the eras of Mao Zedong, Deng Xiaoping, Jiang Zemin, and Hu Jintao, some changes have taken place in the foreign policy-making process. The most significant change is the shift from the "strong man" model to the "collective leadership" in which foreign policy issues are handled differently. The second trend is an increased role and influence of the bureaucracy, institutions, and organizations as well as an increased informal influence of individuals (e.g., experts and scholars), groups (e.g., NGOs and think-tanks), and localities (e.g., provincial and corporate influence) in the Chinese foreign policy-making process. With China's integration into the world, some decisions in the arenas of foreign trade and international cooperation have been decentralized to lower level party–state institutions. However, as David M. Lampton points out, on the other hand, foreign policy making also shows continuity with the era of Mao, with important and strategic decisions made only by the few top leaders of the Politburo,[1] and major decisions in foreign affairs and foreign and security strategy and policy issues are still highly centralized.

How best to understand Chinese foreign policy making? There are many different approaches to the study of Chinese foreign policy making, such as historical or traditionalist approaches, ideological approaches, realist approaches, strategic triangle model, factional politics, bureaucratic politics, institutional approaches, and perceptual/cognitive approaches.[2] Although studies that focus on the international system and external relations are important to understand the input of China's international environment and China's response to it, it is essential to understand the domestic dynamics, constraints, and determinants, because the study of foreign policy making is different from the study of foreign relations with other countries, such as Sino–U.S., Sino–Japan, and Sino–Russian relations, which involve a multitude of complex, multilevel variables, including international, regional, state, transnational, and many others. It is also because there is close and direct interplay between foreign policy and domestic politics and the two processes are intertwined and constrained in the interlocking political context of power structure, ideology, and organization. As David M. Lampton puts it, to understand how major decisions are made, "it is essential to know the arena in which decisions are made and who sits at the table."[3]

Chinese foreign policy-making structure and process

Foreign policy making in the PRC can be generally divided into two distinct periods, Mao's China and post-Mao China, with the former characterized by the revolutionary, charismatic "strong man" model and the latter by the party–state technocratic elitist model of "collective decision" (which should not be confused with "democratic") at the top of the political structure (the CPC Politburo Standing Committee).

In Mao's China, foreign policy strategies, major foreign policy making, and high-level appointments in foreign affairs were determined by Mao Zedong, with a limited degree of top leadership involvement in some key policy making. Zhou Enlai and a few top leaders were mainly implementers of his ideological visions in foreign policy strategies and policies—from the "leaning to one side" with the Soviet Union, intervention in the Korean War and the Vietnam War, which was highly ideologically motivated and oriented, to the rapprochement with the United States in the early 1970s, which was more realist oriented and motivated by practical concerns with China's major security threat from the Soviet Union as a result of armed border conflicts between the two countries. "Throughout the whole process Mao not only made all the major decisions but also decisions concerning the implementation of the policy change."[4]

In post-Mao China, a gradual transition has taken place from a "strong man" model (Deng Xiaoping, though he did not have the same absolute authority as Mao) to an elitist model in which any key foreign policy making is still made by the top leadership, but collectively by a small group of top leaders at the CPC Politburo Standing Committee, aided by bureaucratic institutions and organizations in foreign affairs to provide the top leaders with information, intelligence, policy consultation, analysis, and recommendation. Despite the changes, the foreign policy-making structure and process has been characterized by a highly centralized, elitist, and closed-door model, which is defined, constrained, or determined by the party–state political system, as long as such a system remains fundamentally unchanged (see Chapter 9). Therefore, the political structure and institutional setting are a starting point in understanding Chinese foreign policy making, particularly with regard to those major decisions that would affect the formation of foreign policy visions, slogans, orientation, policy priorities and objectives, and strategies and key policies to achieve them.

As we discussed in Chapter 9, the Chinese party–state consists of three major systems (*xitong* 系统)—the party, the government, and the military—and each plays a certain role in the highly centralized decision-making structure. But, all are subject to the leadership of the Politburo Standing Committee, which is the power center of the party–state. Foreign policy making has been considered as the most sensitive area of decision making, and always officially claimed "there is no trivial matter in foreign affairs" (外事无小事). The foreign policy-making agenda and deliberation are not made in public or allowed for in congressional debate. Foreign policy making has always been concentrated in the hands of a "strong man" (Mao's China) or a few top elite of the Politburo (post-Mao China). Of the top decision makers today, Hu Jintao is supreme leader as general secretary of the CPC, chairman of the Central Military Commission (CMC), and president of the PRC. He also chairs the CPC Central Committee Foreign Affairs Leading Small Group (FALSG) (中央外事工作领导小组)—also known as the National Security Leading Small Group (NSLSG)中央国家安全领导小组—which deliberates foreign and security policy. FALSG and NSLSG are the same institution with one team of staff members but two name plates (*yitaorenma, liangkuaipaizi* 套人马，两块牌子). However, with the reform and open-door policy, China has developed a closer relationship with the world, and foreign affairs are more complicated than in the time of Mao's China, which was closed to the outside world. The central decision makers began to rely on the institutions and organizations in foreign affairs of the three systems (the party, the government, and the military) for policy consultation, information collection, policy analysis, and policy research. Some key institutions in the three major systems have been involved in the major policy-making process.

The party

The CPC Central Committee Foreign Affairs Leading Small Group (the National Security Leading Small Group)—FALSG/NSSLG—is headed by Hu Jintao, general secretary of the CPC Politburo Standing Committee to deliberate foreign and security policy, exercise sectoral coordination, supervise foreign policy implementation, and oversee foreign affairs at large. FALSG/NSSLG is made up of the Politburo standing members and members who are in charge of foreign affairs in different areas, and foreign and security affairs department heads and ministers, such as the CPC International Department Head, CPC Propaganda Department Head, Minister of Foreign Affairs, Minister of Commerce, Minister of Defense, Minister of State Security, Minister of Public Security, Head of State Council Information Office, and Head of State Council Overseas Chinese Affairs Office. This central body "serves as the central processing unit (CPU) between the decisionmakers and implementing organs in the party, government, and military systems."[5] The foreign affairs sector in the party system also includes these key actors: Taiwan Affairs LSG (TALSG), Financial and Economic Affairs LSG

(FEALSG), CPC International Department, and the Central Policy Research Office, which also play a role in the foreign policy-making process.

The government

The governmental body that involves foreign affairs consists of the Ministry of Foreign Affairs, Ministry of Commerce (previously the Ministry of Foreign Trade and Economy), the National Development and Reform Commission, the Commission for External Cultural Liaison, the State Science Commission, the Ministry of Defense, and the Commission for Overseas Chinese Affairs, Xinhua News Agency. Their main role is to provide information, recommendation, and implementation of foreign policies decided by the CPC Politburo or FALSG/NSSLG. But, there is a "division of labor" in issue areas related to their administrative jurisdiction and responsibility.

The military

In the military system there are the Second Directorate and the Third Directorate of the PLA General Staff Department, the PLA General Political Department, and the Commission of Science, Technology and Industry for National Defense. The PLA has greater influence in decision making related to defense and security policies, such as arms control and nonproliferation, military R&D, strategic arms, territorial disputes, military overseas operation, and national security towards countries such as the United States, Russia, Japan, North Korea, India, and Pakistan.[6]

The aforementioned institutions and organizations are major actors in foreign and security policy making by providing policy consultation, information, and policy analysis in their areas of administrative jurisdiction to influence top elite perceptions, objectives, and policy alternatives, although the Politburo Standing Committee is the power center that makes all crucial or important decisions in foreign and security policy areas. Moreover, these bureaucratic institutions, such as the Ministry of Foreign Affairs and the Ministry of Commerce, could play a more significant role in areas of foreign affairs that are considered less crucial or important, such as economic and cultural exchange with less political sensitivity and significance. However, as each of these foreign policy establishments attempts to influence the decision-making process—they actually often compete to exert influence over policy formulation—by offering their policy advice and alternatives or by influencing any Politburo standing member, "consequently, foreign policy decision making can be 'unwieldy, messy and inefficient.'"[7]

Factors influencing Chinese foreign policy making

Some Chinese foreign policy analysts have focused on the external factors, such as international system and structure, in shaping the Chinese foreign policy making, while others have focused on the domestic factors and contended that domestic factors profoundly shape China's foreign policy from the late Mao era to the reform era. Hongyi Lai, based on his empirical analysis of some major cases of Chinese foreign policy making, demonstrates how China's foreign policy is determined by the preservation of political and economic regimes; the political survival of the top leader; the top leader's vision for, and skills in, managing external affairs; the leader's policy priorities; dramatic events and the process of policy making.[8]

There are a number of important factors that interact to influence Chinese foreign policy making. The most important factors are ideological orientation, national identity, policy priorities and primary objectives (influenced by internal and external factors), strategies to achieve objectives, consensus-driven decision making influenced by formal and informal channels.

Ideology

Many foreign policy analysts have found a decline or irrelevance of ideology in Chinese foreign policy making. However, ideology continues to play an important role in the foreign policy-making process, setting out the principles and policy guidelines. Concepts and slogans are often symbols of ideological orientation and representation of those principles and guidelines. These concepts and slogans are also used by the Chinese government to educate the public and the world, establish its foreign policy images, and justify its policies and actions in foreign affairs. China always declaims to the world that its foreign policy decisions are based on the "Five Principles of Peaceful Coexistence" (和平共处五项原则)—mutual respect for sovereignty and territorial integrity, mutual nonaggression, noninterference in each other's internal affairs, equality and mutual benefit, and peaceful coexistence. These principles were originally adopted in 1954 in Mao's China, but have continued to serve the guiding principle of Chinese foreign policy and behavior and show its commitment to its ideological distinctiveness. More recently, "peaceful development" (和平发展) and "harmonious world" (和谐世界) have become slogans under Hu Jintao to guide Chinese foreign policy and project its image to the world, as well as offer the world an alternative for a new world order in which all nation-states perceive the value of peaceful development, respect the internal affairs of other nations, and cooperate to create a harmonious relationship with one another.

National pride and national humiliation

As William A. Callahan described in his book *China: The Pessoptimist Nation,*[9] there is a combination of national pride and national humiliation in the Chinese dual identity that has affected the mindset of Chinese people and decision makers. With China's rise, the Chinese government has boosted its national pride, but national humiliation has always affected its foreign policy making. As Callahan argues, China's pride and humiliation are interwoven. While China does promote a positive and proud image of itself, it also presents a very negative view of China's relationship with the world based on the history of national humiliation. National humiliation has been part of patriotic education and propaganda campaigns for public edification in the past and present, and as a major driving force to achieve their future success and pride. China's view of the world and dealings with its neighboring states presents two images of China: China as a victim state and China as a victorious great power. China's national security is thus closely linked to its nationalist insecurities. China's pessoptimism is Beijing's way of hedging against the possibility of being humiliated again.[10] Some China scholars look at the dual identity as contradictions constraining Chinese foreign policy making. Beijing's foreign policy making has been constrained by a set of contradicting variables. China views itself as a major power and wants to play a role accordingly in the world, while lacking adequate power to do so. China wants to be fully integrated into international society, while strong concern over sovereignty makes it difficult for Beijing to embrace some of the mainstream international values. China agrees on a set of principles in international affairs, while consideration of its national interests causes Beijing to make a pragmatic compromise from time to time. Beijing has long been accustomed to dealing with others in bilateral settings while the post-Cold War era is witnessing a rise of mulilateralism in international politics, which is putting more and more pressure on China's traditional diplomacy.[11]

Influence by actors through formal and informal channels

As China is transitioning away from "strong man" politics to "collective leadership," Chinese foreign policy making has also been influenced by both formal and informal channels. Bureaucratic institutions are formal channels by which officials in different foreign affairs sectors within the government, party, and PLA have striven to influence the top leadership's policy making; at the same time, other emerging actors since China's reform and opening up in past decades have also maneuvered to influence the policy-making process through informal channels. "These new actors operate outside the official realm of the foreign policy establishment and include Chinese state-owned enterprises, financial institutions and energy companies, local governments, research institutions, and media and netizens."[12] These new actors have emerged from the process of professionalization of the expert-based bureaucratic elite with a higher level of specialized knowledge in foreign affairs; corporate pluralization with the proliferation of social organizations, NGOs, groups, and individuals; decentralization of the authority to local authority and local actors in foreign economic and cultural exchange; and economic and information globalization with increased interdependence and pressure on Chinese people's cooperation and conformity with international norms. All these actors seek to exert their influence on decisions in foreign affairs, which increases the diversity of views in the policy-making process and makes for an increasing amount of coordination in policy implementation. As a result, the central leadership has been forced to consult more broadly, and consider different views, which puts the formal policy-making process in a position of often reacting to issues and challenges imposed on it by the bureaucratic elite, local governments, society, and global actors, particularly in dealing with those issues and challenges in the arenas of foreign economic relations, cultural exchange, and environment, and multilateral international organizations.[13] However, given the power structure, ideology, and organizational principles of the CPC and the party–state, their influence in major foreign and security policy strategies and issue areas is very limited.

As "collective leadership" at the top decision-making level, the CPC Politburo, requires consensus building, and even Hu Jintao needs to seek support for his policy preferences, despite his position as supreme leader, some Chinese foreign policy analysts have begun to describe the process as "consensus-driven" and argue that

> Chinese decision making requires an enormous amount of discussion and bargaining to reach a compromise acceptable to all parties concerned ... A failure to reach consensus often means agreeing to postpone a decision to enable further study of the matter ... As a result, decision-making processes on sensitive issues are lengthy and complicated. Sometimes they end in deadlock.[14]

This research, primarily based on interviews with foreign policy researchers and scholars, suggests that some emerging actors have attempted to influence the foreign policy-making process beyond formal government establishments while the top decision makers have sought advice and suggestions from foreign affairs bureaucrats, think-tank researchers, and scholars, and this may become a trend in the future.[15] However, the degree of such influence cannot be certain because Chinese foreign policy making in general and in principle remains opaque, restricted within the small circle of the top leadership. The foreign policy-making agenda is neither publicized nor subject to congressional and public debate in the Chinese party–state political and ideological context.

Domestic policy priorities, objectives, and foreign policy strategy

In order to understand how the Chinese government would respond to international events and potential crises around the world, we must first understand the political elite, their policy priorities and objectives, and their grand foreign policy strategy by which foreign policy is framed and determined. The politburo of the 17th Party Central Committee demonstrated a continuity of leadership under Hu Jintao and in its domestic and foreign policies in the past five years. The political report is a summary of what they have done and provides guidelines for what they will do in the next five years to come. The leaders under Hu Jintao have continued to focus on their domestic priorities—promoting economic development and maintaining political stability, which includes their vision of how to maintain continued growth and sustainable development in the economy, how to build a "harmonious society" to resolve the serious problems and daunting challenges facing China today, and how to strengthen the party's governing capacity and move at a gradualist pace toward intra-party democracy while sustaining the CPC one-party rule. This set of macro-strategies is framed as peaceful development toward a harmonious society. Their foreign policy strategies to achieve the priorities and objectives are essential for them to achieve the above priorities and objectives. According to the new leadership, this new foreign strategy is formulated as "peaceful development" to build a "harmonious world" that would be conducive to fostering a peaceful international environment that can serve the party's objectives and priorities.

The new thinking in Chinese foreign policy

Despite the continuity between Deng, Jiang, and Hu's foreign policy, we can also observe the "new" thinking in its grand foreign policy strategy. Although the concept "peaceful development" foreign policy strategy is a continuity of Deng Xiaoping's concept "*taoguang yanghui*" (韬光养晦 keep a low profile and never take the lead), it is a break away from Jiang Zemin's "*duoji shijie*" (多极世界 multipolar world). Under Jiang, building a multipolar world implies to "multipolarize" the American unipolarity and counterbalance U.S. hegemony. This "peaceful development" foreign policy strategy is, in fact, to accept the unipolar structure dominated by U.S. hegemony. It proposes that China must avoid direct confrontation with the United States in order to secure a favorable external environment for its rise.

Second, "peaceful development" seeks to reassure the United States and other countries that China's rise will not be a threat to peace and stability in the region and the world and that the United States and other countries can benefit from China's peaceful development. China's development is mutually beneficial to China and the world in the process of globalization. Therefore, the new foreign policy stresses that China is a people-based (*yiren weiben*), cooperative, tolerant, confident, and responsible power. However, China also should seek to utilize its "soft power" to enhance its role as a rising power in regional and world affairs and to facilitate its economic development and modernization. Specific foreign policies and diplomatic measures have been used to enhance a good neighbor relationship, negotiated settlements on territory disputes, and cooperation with ASEAN, Oceania, EU, Latin America, Africa, Central Asia, and the United States on the Korean peninsula, etc.

Third, Chinese foreign policy has therefore put great emphasis on economic integration with the world economy and the importance of China's international economic exchange that would benefit its economic development and the mutual dependence that would help create a peaceful international environment for China's economic development and political stability. China's domestic priority has put itself in a position that seeks to set aside areas of disagreement with other nations, promote economic ties, and reassure others about its peaceful rise.[16] China is the destination of the largest FDI in the world, the second largest consumer of oil and raw materials, the third largest trading nation, and it is in the fundamental interests of China to maintain a peaceful international environment for its domestic economic development, political stability, and resolution of social problems.

Taking Beijing's Taiwan policy as an example, the "peaceful development" strategy also impacts Beijing's Taiwan policy. Beijing has quietly shifted its Taiwan policy to "*budu buwu*" (不独不武 no independence, no war)—aimed at maintaining the status quo and putting aside "*tongyi*" (统 unification) for the time being. Deng Xiaoping made the unification one of the central tasks for the Chinese government, and Jiang Zemin pressed Taiwan for unification by declaring that the resolution of the "Taiwan issue" would not be delayed indefinitely. However, Hu Jingtao declared during his visit to Canada in September 2005 that the resolution of the Taiwan issue is complicated and would take a long time, and that "*fangtaidu*" (反台独 struggle against the "Taiwan independence") would be a long fight—without setting a time table for the unification. This is a departure from Jiang's "*jitong*" (急统 hasty unification) to a new thinking that seeks "peace," "reconciliation," "cooperation," and a "win–win situation" (和平 *heping*, 和谐 *hejie*, 合作 *hezuo*, 双赢 *shuangying*) across the Taiwan Strait that could lead to a future of "peaceful development" and "common prosperity." In 2005, Beijing invited Taiwan's top two opposition leaders, Lien Chan (KMT) and James Soong (PFP), to visit mainland China, accompanied by Taiwanese legislators, politicians, businessmen, and media leaders, and embarked on the first dialogue and political interaction across the Taiwan Straits since 1949. At the 17th Party Congress Political Report, Hu Jintao declared that the new leaders seek to negotiate with Taiwan and sign a peace treaty across the Strait despite the challenges from Chen Shuibien and DPP's effort to resort to a referendum for joining the UN as the Taiwan state. With Ma Yingjeou becoming the president of Taiwan, the cross-Taiwan Strait relationship has indeed been "harmonized." The new shift in the Taiwan policy is an integral part of Beijing's "peaceful development" strategy.

Apparently, the Chinese leaders have made clear to the world that China has no interest in seeking regional hegemony or a change in the existing world order and China is committed to "peaceful development." This is mainly because the Chinese leadership is preoccupied with domestic priorities and objectives—economic development and political stability. As Robert Sutter argues, the Chinese leadership will probably remain focused on promoting China's economic development and maintaining domestic political and social stability while China's military ambitions and aspirations for enhanced regional and global leadership will also likely grow along with growing national power.[17] Therefore, is "peaceful development" possible given the existing domestic and international conditions and challenges China faces in the twenty-first century? This is the question that remains to be discussed and answered.

Questions for discussion

1. What are the changes and continuities in China's foreign policy-making process?
2. What is the relationship between the political structure and the bureaucratic behavior in the foreign policy-making process in China?
3. How do various international and domestic factors affect China's foreign policy making today? What is the relationship between domestic politics and international relations in the Chinese foreign policy-making process?
4. Is "peaceful development" possible given the existing domestic and international conditions and challenges China faces in the twenty-first century?

Further reading

Lu Ning, *The Dynamics of Foreign-Policy Decisionmaking in China* (Boulder, CO: Westview, 1997).

David M. Lampton, ed., *The Making of Chinese Foreign and Security Policy in the Era of Reform*, 1978–2000 (Stanford: Stanford University Press, 2001).

Robert G. Sutter. *Chinese Foreign Relations – Power and Policy Since the Cold War* (Lanham, MD: Rowman & Littlefield, 2010).

What will be the future directions of Sino–U.S. relations? Former Secretary of State Henry Kissinger suggested that the United States and China could raise their relations to a "life community," similar to United States relations with the Atlantic community. He believed that the two countries could cooperate with each other to build a "new global order."[12] Zbigniew Brzezinski, a former national security adviser under the Carter administration, also proposed raising bilateral relations to a special relation, equivalent to the U.S.–EU relations or U.S.–Japan relations. C. Fred Bergsten, the Director of the Peterson Institute for International Economics in Washington, DC, suggested that the United States and China had already formed a *de facto* Group of Two (G2), and this is poised to replace Group of Seven (G7) or Group of Twenty (G20) as a main player in global affairs.[13] Niall Ferguson, Dean of Harvard Business School, even gave a new name to the G2 concept: "Chimerica."[14] So far, the Chinese side has remained cool to these ideas,[15] and some even consider these proposals to be politically motivated aimed at dragging China's feet into an unfriendly trap.[16]

The nature of U.S–China relations has been transformed and thus redefined a number of times in recent years. The Clinton administration described the relations as a "strategic partnership." The Bush administration in its earlier years changed it to a "strategic competitor," but later modified its position and called China a "stakeholder" and a "strategic collaborator." The Obama administration has called for "active, cooperative, and comprehensive" relations with China while sometimes describing the bilateral relationship as "complex and multi-faceted."

There is no doubt that relations between the two countries are among the most important of the twenty-first century. But, how to define the relationship and what direction it is headed remains to be seen. In my view, it will continue to be neither "friend" nor "foe" in the near future, because of mutual strategic mistrust, and different political ideologies and political systems. To many, the Americans and the Chinese play chess games on the same chess board, but they are different chess games with different rules defined and shaped by different political principles, norms, and politics (Figure 18.1). However, to many others, a variety of factors could shape the long-term relationship between the two countries. We will examine these factors in the next section.

Factors shaping U.S.–China relations

There are a number of favorable and unfavorable factors shaping U.S.–China relations in the long run and working in the opposite directions that are pushing the U.S.–China relationship toward conflict or peace, competition or cooperation, foe or friend not only in the present but also in the future.

First of all, some unfavorable factors are observable—different political regimes and ideologies, disputes over human rights, trade conflicts, interest conflicts and clashing political objectives in regional and global affairs, rising

Figure 18.1 Political cartoon: "Different chess games".
Source: Courtesy of Luo Jie,www.chinadaily.com.cn/opinion/2011–01/11/content_11823292.htm

power of China and its implications for U.S. domination, and so forth. As Robert Sutter pointed out,

> China and the USA have conflicting interests over the international balance of power, NATO expansion, the US role in East Asia (especially its increasingly close alliance with Japan), the USA's growing military ties to Taiwan, US hostility to Iraq, Iran, Palestine, Sudan, Serbia, Myanmar, Venezuela, Zimbabwe and Cuba, and US deployment of its missile 'defense' system. China opposes the sanctions and other coercive measures that the US state routinely imposes.[17]

David A. Lampton pointed out that the bilateral relationship has been plagued with "mutual strategic mistrust" derived from their differences in defining the challenges of U.S.–China relations, miscalculating powers, Chinese desire to change the game, and challenge and response dynamics.[18] These factors are the primary sources of strategic mistrust and interest conflict between the United States and China, leading to tension, friction, and even confrontation between the two countries in recent years.

However, some factors also pull the two countries together—common interests in global issues (terrorism, nuclear proliferation, energy, environmental protection, stabilizing the world economy, and public health), regional security issues (the nuclear crisis on the Korean peninsula and peace across the Taiwan Strait), and growing integration of the two largest economies in the world in which both countries recognize the bilateral economic, business, and market benefits of cooperation rather than confrontation. It can be observed that there are two opposing sets of causal forces at work that are pushing the U.S.–China relationship toward conflict or peace, competition or cooperation, foe or friend.[19]

First of all, we need to put our understanding of the nature and changes in U.S.–China relations in a broader, long-term perspective and in the context of China's rising and changing world characterized by globalization, with new emerging powers coming to the fore. China's rapid development and the implications of China's rise, from its expanding influence and military muscle to its growing demand for energy supplies and increasing concerns about China's unfair trade and currency regimes, are being heatedly debated in the United States. Faced with a rising China, there has been increasing wariness, fear, and suspicion from the United States. The U.S. Administration has been advised to adopt a new containment strategy to counterbalance the "China Threat."[20]

In response to the "China Threat" and U.S. pressure, the Chinese government proposed "peaceful development," which has become a new way of thinking in Chinese foreign policy under the Fourth Generation Leadership as we discussed in Chapter 17. However, the question is whether China will rise peacefully, which will affect the U.S.–China relationship in different directions.

In world history, no major power has risen "peacefully." From the early colonial powers, Spain and Britain, to late industrializers, Germany and Japan, all new powers have fought their way to their power status. "The history of the United States is the history of confrontation, even conflict, with the other great powers of the earth," first with Britain and France in the nineteenth century and then with Germany, Japan, and then Russia in the twentieth century, not to mention many wars fought by proxy.[21] Moreover, past experience of great powers suggests that dominant powers have typically seen rising powers as potential threats and have sought to thwart their rise. Containment, however, has often produced a nationalist backlash in the rising power that has intensified its desire to revise the status quo. As Aaron L. Friedberg put it,

> throughout history, relations between dominant and rising states have been uneasy—and often violent. Established powers tend to regard themselves as the defenders of an international order that they helped to create and from which they continue to benefit; rising powers feel constrained, even cheated, by the status quo and struggle against it to take what they think is rightfully theirs.[22]

The rapid economic development associated with rising power also tends to produce complex domestic political pressures that can prove destabilizing. The pre- and post-WWII experiences of Germany and Japan have provided both positive and negative lessons for the world. Globalization, economic interdependence, and changes in the post-Cold War international system have brought new opportunities and challenges for China, and have also become an important force shaping the U.S.–China long-term relationship.

There have been three major theoretical perspectives in shaping our understanding of China's rise and its implications for the United States. The rise of past great powers has led the realists or realpolitik pessimists to believe that China's rise will inevitably collide with existing great powers and China and the United States are likely to engage in an intense security competition with considerable potential for war.[23] Liberal theorists, however, argue that in an era of deepening globalization, integration, and democratization, peaceful development may be possible, but only if China can overcome the challenges and leverage the opportunities on both the domestic and the international fronts.

The realist assumption, however, seems to be contradicted by the peaceful rise of Japan, Germany, and Europe after WWII. Because they were fully integrated into the international system and economy, these "new" powers did not emerge as anti-status quo revisionist power, but instead they emerged as status quo powers and key supporters of the established world order and contributed heavily to the stability of international financial, monetary, trade, and security systems. China could also become a status quo power and play a similar role in the international system if it is allowed to be fully integrated into the established international system and economy.

From a constructivist perspective, the Chinese leaders have moved toward a more comfortable embrace of liberal values, norms, and institutions in their contact with Western countries since China's reform and open-door policy, and shifted away from cognitive rigidity and dogmatism to flexibility and pragmatism in Beijing's foreign policy thinking and behavior. China's embracing of the "peaceful development" policy suggests that its leaders have learned from historical lessons that China must avoid the path of pre-WWII Germany and Japan and the Soviet Union in the Cold War and seek to proceed on the path of peaceful development.[24] "Peaceful development" defines a rising China as a status quo power, not a threat to the status quo. As Avery Goldstein points out, "China's foreign policy behavior continues to conform closely to that typical of a status quo state."[25]

However, although the Chinese leadership may believe that it is possible for China to rise peacefully, in reality China faces a series of challenges, both at home and in the international system, that if not properly and skillfully handled could lead China down the revisionist path associated with previous rising powers. China does not, of course, entirely control the fate of peaceful development and even if it embraces peaceful development, a containment policy directed by the dominant powers against China could derail even the best intentions.

Recognizing the growing threat to their position, dominant powers (or a coalition of status quo states) have occasionally tried to attack and destroy a competitor before it can grow strong enough to become a threat. Others— hoping to avoid war—have taken the opposite approach: attempting to appease potential challengers, they look for ways to satisfy their demands and ambitions and seek to incorporate them peacefully into the existing international order.[26]

Although China is unlikely to challenge U.S. dominance for the foreseeable future, the rising power of China may pose economic challenges to the United States and influence U.S. strategic relationships with other countries and even allies around the world.[27] Therefore, how the dominant powers respond to the challenges of China's rise also determines the fate of China's peaceful rise and thus the changes in U.S.–China relations in the long run.

The aforementioned discussion has placed U.S.–China relations in a long-term theoretical perspective and in the context of China's rise and its implications for the United States. In what follows, we will examine some important factors that tend to shape U.S–China relations in opposing directions, which would suggest that the U.S.–China relationship is the most important but complicated one in the twenty-first century.

The Taiwan issue has been and will continue to be a difficult challenge facing political leaders in two countries. The United States has maintained a "One China Policy" toward Taiwan since the Sino-American normalization while it has continued to sell arms to Taiwan, which has generated many grievances and protests from China, and created many twists and turns in U.S.–China relations over the past 30 years. The United States considers Taiwan as its traditional sphere of influence in Asia and uses it as strategic leverage to deal with China while China views Taiwan as its internal affairs and core national interest that should be free from U.S. interference. The United States would like to see a peaceful Taiwan Strait but does not want to see the cross-Taiwan Strait relationship getting too close to expel the United States from the game. In the short term, the U.S. role in the Taiwan Strait continues to be prominent. However, the United States is also concerned that, when the "time" factor weighs in, China can develop a formidable military force that would effectively deter the American leadership from risking a war with China in defending Taiwan. Therefore, the United States has an interest in a democratic and strong Taiwan to counterbalance the rising power of China, which in the same vein sees the United States as the most disturbing force behind Taiwan and the most serious barrier to unification.

China's border and maritime territorial disputes with neighboring states could be another flashpoint in the East and Southeast region that would challenge the U.S.–China leadership in dealing with those disputes. China views those issues as threats to China's national security and sovereignty, particularly Sino-Japanese tension over gas and oil reserves beneath the East China Sea and territorial quarrel over the Diaoyu/Senkaku Islands as well as the South China Sea dispute between China and some Southeast Asian countries. The presence of these disputes between China and its neighboring states has the potential to worsen. Beijing understands that escalation is not favorable for China because it would face the combined forces of the United States and Japan, or other states involved, hence there is a high probability of significant geopolitical turbulence if the tensions and conflicts cannot be resolved but escalate into armed conflict. Therefore, China is always suspicious about the U.S. role and military cooperation with these countries in the region, and has seen the United States as a key factor that may hinder the resolution of these disputes and conflicts in its favor. However, after WWII the United States views the region as its traditional sphere of influence and domination and sees its military presence and maintaining the status quo of regional security arrangements established by the United States in the post-WWII era as its long-term strategic interest and a serious responsibility.

Moreover, China has recognized that the United States has in fact maintained a security circle or a strategic hedge against China not only along the Asian Pacific rim through bilateral military agreements with Japan, South Korea, and other Asian Pacific countries. More recently the United States has begun building a new network of military partnerships in South Asia and Central Asia. To many Chinese, the United States has already begun constructing a new containment structure whose purpose is to block China's rise. To some Americans, however, China's military modernization is viewed as a harbinger of a more aggressive China, leading American policy makers to adopt policies aimed at containing the potential threat from China. Thus, mutual suspicion and mistrust have continued to plague the bilateral relationship between the two countries.

However, at the same time, bilateral trade and economic ties between the United States and China have deepened, thus creating a situation of complex interdependence that has, on the one hand, drawn the two economies together while at the same time creating new friction over trade. Competition for access to energy has also increased in recent years as China's military upgrading efforts and global search for oil and resources are perceived to be assertive and threatening to U.S. interests in the region and around the globe. Mutual suspicion and misperception could, therefore, destabilize U.S.–China relations and jeopardize China's "peaceful development."

Despite mutual suspicion and conflicts in the region, the United States and China also have significant common interests, and most of these shared interests actually correspond with China's interest in maintaining a peaceful international environment for achieving its domestic priorities. Both countries have a lot of shared interests in many global issues (terrorism, nuclear proliferation, energy, environmental protection, and public health), regional security issues (nuclear crisis on the Korean peninsula and peace across the Taiwan Strait), and bilateral economic, business and market benefits. Thus, challenges and opportunities coexist in the development of U.S.–China relations. Aaron L. Friedberg points out, "the contemporary U.S.–China relationship is clearly mixed, consisting of an array of cooperative and competitive elements."[28]

Clearly, there are two opposing sets of causal forces at work that are pushing the relationship toward conflict and peace, competition and cooperation, foe and friend. But, the two opposing causal forces tend to be "mutually offsetting," and the forces tending toward cooperation appear stronger than those pointing toward competition.[29] In fact, there is ample evidence of increasing cooperation between the United States and China. As the United States has adopted policies aimed at military deterrence and prevention, there exists a nonconfrontational dimension to Sino–U.S. military relations that has provided opportunities for bilateral military exchanges and cooperation.

The coexistence of challenges and opportunities for cooperation are also evident in regional and bilateral hot issues. Even though Taiwan poses a most serious challenge to U.S.–China relations, both countries have sought to avoid conflict across the Taiwan Strait, and have made clear that both oppose a change in the status quo across the Taiwan Strait. The nuclear crisis on the Korean peninsula could be potentially an explosive security issue for China and the United States, but once again we have found the two countries have worked together for years to manage the crisis and bring all parties to the negotiating table. Economic and trade conflicts have recently increased between the two countries. Nonetheless, both sides have sought to avoid a trade war, looking instead to negotiations to resolve bilateral economic conflicts. The U.S.–Japan security alliance poses a threat to China, and to Chinese people, it encourages Japan to adopt a tougher position toward China. Yet at the same time, a stable and constructive Sino–U.S. relationship would provide opportunities for maintaining stable Sino–Japanese relations because postwar Japan has maintained strong security ties with the United States and become dependent upon the United States for its security shield, which places constraints on Japanese foreign policy making. In fact, the United States has historically played a vital balancing role in this region, and will likely continue to play such a role. The extensive mutual dependence of Sino-American and Sino-Japanese commercial relations and interests has created common interests which could shield each of them from excessive offensive actions and military adventurism that could put peace and economic growth at risk, particularly in the nuclear age in which each major actor has a significant nuclear deterrent. As Zbigniew Brzezinski put it, "the nuclear age has altered power politics in a way that was already evident in the U.S.–Soviet competition."[30]

The United States, which would continue to play a role of balancer, could be an important stabilizing factor in maintaining peace in Asia. China itself can also be a stabilizing factor in the region since it is also in China's fundamental interests to maintain stability and prosperity in Asia. In a fundamental sense, in fact, China's adoption of a new "peaceful development" foreign policy strategy suggests that the new Chinese leadership already recognizes the importance of maintaining peace with all actors involved in this region for China's further development and modernization. The new foreign policy strategy is defensive in nature, aimed at decreasing the fear of a "China Threat," promoting good neighbor relations and multilateral relations in the region and around the globe, and creating a peaceful and stable external environment for its economic development. However, China's rise would intensify fears and suspicions of a "China Threat" and fuel efforts to contain and constrain it. "Peaceful development" could degenerate into wishful thinking if China cannot dispel suspicion and concerns about the rise of China in an undemocratic political context and thus about the kind of role a more powerful China would play in the region and in the world affairs. As Evan S. Medeiros put it,

> the future evolution of China's new external strategy of peaceful rise is unclear . . . Regardless of how peace-loving the Chinese people feel they are, Chinese leaders need to take into account the legitimate concerns of its Asian neighbors and major powers in the region. Whether Chinese leaders can translate this new expression into tangible policies and deeds of reassurance remains an open question.[31]

Questions for discussion

1. Is China a revisionist power or a status quo power from the perspectives of world history and Chinese history?
2. What are the major challenges and opportunities of cooperation in U.S.–China relations? Will China be a potential threat to the United States or form a strategic partnership with the United States in the twenty-first century?

Further reading

Avery Goldstein, *Rising to the Challenge: China's Grand Strategy and International Security* (Stanford, CA: Stanford University Press, 2005).

C. Fred Bergsten, Bates Gill, Nicholas R. Lardy, and Derek Mitchell, *China: The Balance Sheet—What the World Needs to Know Now About the Emerging Superpower* (New York: Public Affairs, 2006).

Robert G. Sutter, *U.S.–Chinese Relations: Perilous Past, Pragmatic Present* (Lanham, MD: Rowman & Littlefield Publishers, 2010).

Notes

1 Chinese politics in comparative communist systems

1 National Bureau of Statistics of China, *China Statistical Yearbook 2010* (中国统计年鉴 Beijing, National Bureau of Statistics of China, 2010, http://ishare.iask.sinxa.com.cn/f/10462582.html); International Monetary Fund, *World Economic Outlook Database*, October 2010 (www.imf.org/external/pubs/ft/weo/2010/02/weodata/index.aspx).
2 Sujian Guo, "Challenges and Opportunities for China's 'Peaceful Rise'," in Sujian Guo, ed., *China's Peaceful Rise in the 21st Century: Domestic and International Conditions* (Ashgate Publishing, 2006).
3 U.S. Census Bureau, "Foreign Trade Statistics," www.census.gov/foreign-trade/statistics/highlights/toppartners.html.
4 U.S. Census Bureau, "Foreign Trade Statistics," www.census.gov/foreign-trade/balance/c5700.html.
5 U.S. Treasury, "Major Foreign Holdings of Treasury Securities," www.treasury.gov/resource-center/data-chart-center/tic/Documents/mfh.txt.
6 The US–China Business Council, "US-China Trade Statistics and China's World Trade Statistics," www.uschina.org/statistics/tradetable.html.
7 John J. Mearsheimer, "The Gathering Storm: China's Challenge to US Power in Asia," *The Chinese Journal of International Politics*, vol. 3, no. 4, Winter 2010; John J. Mearsheimer, "China's Unpeaceful Rise," *Current History*, vol. 105, no. 690, April 2006, pp. 160–62; Robert D. Kaplan, "How We Would Fight China," *The Atlantic Monthly*, vol. 295, no. 5, June 2005, pp. 49–64.
8 Howard J. Wiarda, *Introduction to Comparative Politics: Concepts and Processes* (Harcourt Brace & Company, 2000), pp. 7–8.
9 Stephen White, John Gardner, George Schopflin, and Tony Saich, *Communist and Postcommunist Political Systems: An Introduction* (Palgrave Macmillan, 1990).
10 Janos Kornai, *The Socialist System: The Political Economy of Communism* (Princeton: Princeton University Press, 1992), pp. 37–39.
11 Ibid., Chapter 3.
12 Ibid., Chapter 4.
13 Ibid., pp. 37–39.
14 Ibid., pp. 46–48.
15 http://en.wikipedia.org/wiki/File:Communist_countries.svg.

2 Theoretical models for studying Chinese politics

1 See David Adger, "Why Theory is Essential: the Relationship between Theory, Analysis and Data," accessed from www.llas.ac.uk/resources/gpg/405.

2 "Sinology assumes that China is sufficiently different from the 'west' that it cannot be understood in terms assumed in the west." Cited from Peter Moody, "Political Culture and the Study of Chinese Politics," *Journal of Chinese Political Science*, vol. 14, no. 3, 2009.

3 Sujian Guo and Jean-Marc F. Blanchard, "The State of the Field: Political Science and Chinese Political Studies," *Journal of Chinese Political Science*, vol. 14, no. 4, 2009.

4 Carl Friedrich and Zbigniew Brzezinski identified six essential institutional features of totalitarianism in the mid-1950s. See Carl J. Friedrich and Zbigniew K. Brzezinski, *Totalitarian Dictatorship and Autocracy* (MA: Harvard University Press, 1956). On China, see Tang Tsou, *The Cultural Revolution and Post-Mao Reforms: A Historical Perspective* (The University of Chicago Press, 1986).

5 Stephen White, John Gardner, and George Schopflin, *Communist Political Systems: An Introduction* (New York: St. Martin's Press, 1987), pp. 14–16; Chalmers Johnson, ed., *Change in Communist Systems* (Stanford: Stanford University Press, 1970), pp. 2–3, 117, 135–36, 314, 347–51; Andrew C. Janos, "Social Science, Communism, and The Dynamics of Political Change," *World Politics*, vol. 44, no. 1, 1991, p. 82; Christopher Hitchens, "How Neoconservatives Perish: Goodbye to Totalitarianism and All That," *Harper's*, July 1990, pp. 65–70.

6 For more recent efforts to resurrect the totalitarian model, see Donald W. Treadgold, *Twentieth Century Russia* (Boulder, CO: Westview Press, 1990); Giovanni Sartori, "Totalitarianism, Model Mania, and Learning From Error," *Journal of Theoretical Politics*, vol. 5, 1993; Richard Pipes, *Russia Under the Bolshevik Regime* (New York: Alfred Knopf, 1993); William E. Odom, "Soviet Politics and After: Old and New Concepts," *World Politics*, vol. 45, no. 1, 1992; Stephen E. Hanson, "Social Theory and the Post-Soviet Crisis: Sovietology and the Problem of Regime Identity," *Communist and Post-Communist Studies*, vol. 28, no. 1, 1995; Sujian Guo, *Post-Mao China: From Totalitarianism to Authoritarianism?* (Praeger, 2000). For the earlier works, see Allen Kassof, "The Administered Society: Totalitarianism Without Terror," *World Politics*, vol. 16, no. 4, July 1964; Hannah Arendt, *The Origins of Totalitarianism* (New York: Harcourt, Brace, 1966); Carl J. Friedrich, ed., *Totalitarianism in Perspectives* (New York: Praeger, 1969); Robert Orr, "Reflections on Totalitarianism, Leading to Reflections on Two Ways of Theorizing," *Political Studies*, vol. 21, no. 4, December 1973; George Breslauer, *Five Images of the Soviet Future* (Berkeley, CA: Institute of International Studies, 1978); Stephen J. Whitefield, *Into the Dark: Hannah Arendt and Totalitarianism* (Philadelphia, PA: Temple University Press, 1980); Ernest A. Menze, ed., *Totalitarianism Reconsidered* (Port Washington, NY: Kennikat Press, 1981); Abbott Gleason, "Totalitarianism in 1984," *Russian Review*, vol. 43, no. 1, April 1984.

7 William E. Odom, p. 77.

8 Ibid., p. 72.

9 Ibid., p. 67.

10 Stephen E. Hanson, p. 126.

11 Donald W. Treadgold, *Twentieth Century Russia*, (Boulder: Westview Press, 1990), p. 12.

12 Seymour Martin Lipset, "Some Social Requisites of Democracy," *American Political Science Review*, 53, March 1959; Dankwart A. Rustow, "Transitions to Democracy: Toward a Dynamic Model," *Comparative Politics*, vol. 2, April 1970; Ronald Inglehart and Christian Welzel, *Modernization, Cultural Change, and Democracy: The Human Development Sequence* (New York, NY: Cambridge University Press, 2005).

13 Stephen White, pp. 16–17.
14 Allison, Graham, *Essence of Decision: Explaining the Cuban Missile Crisis* (Boston: Little Brown, 1971); A. Doak Barnett, *Cadres, Bureaucracy, and Political Power in Communist China* (New York: Columbia University Press, 1967); David Buchman, *Bureaucracy, Economy and Leadership in China: the Institutional Origins of the Great Leap Forward* (New York: Cambridge University Press, 1991); Kenneth G. Lieberthal and David M. Lampton, eds., *Bureaucracy, Politics, and Decision Making in Post-Mao China* (Berkeley: University of California Press, 1992).
15 Stephen White, pp. 21–23.
16 David Easton, *A Systems Analysis of Political Life* (New York: Wiley, 1965).
17 Lianjiang Li, "Political Trust in Rural China," *Modern China*, Vol. 30, No. 2, 2004, pp. 228–58; Bruce Gilley, "Legitimacy and Institutional Change: The Case of China," *Comparative Political Studies*, vol. 41, No. 3, 2008, pp. 259–84; John James Kennedy, "Supply and Support for Grassroots Political Reform in Rural China," *Journal of Chinese Political Science*, Vol. 15, No. 2, pp. 169–90; Gunter Schubert and Anna L. Ahlers, "'Constructing a New Socialist Countryside' and Beyond: An Analytical Framework for Studying Policy Implementation and Political Stability in Contemporary China," *Journal of Chinese Political Science*, Vol. 16, No. 1, 2011, pp. 19–46.
18 Andrew J. Nathan, "A factionalism model for CCP politics," *The China Quarterly* 53, (January–March. 1973), pp. 34–66; Harry Harding, *China's Second Revolution: Reform After Mao* (Washington, DC: Brookings Institution Press, 1987).
19 See more works: Lowell Dittmer and Yu-Shan Wu, "The Modernization of Factionalism in Chinese Politics," *World Politics*, 1995, vol. 47, no. 4, 467–94; W. Lucien Pye, "Factions and the Politics of Guanxi: Paradoxes in Chinese Administrative and Political Behaviour," *The China Journal*, 1995, vol. 34, 35–54; Andrew J. Nathan and Kellee S. Tsai, "Factionalism: A New Institutionalist Restatement," *The China Journal*, 1995, vol. 34, 157–92.
20 Ziyue Bo, *China's Elite Politics: Political Transition and Power Balancing* (Singapore: World Scientific publishing, 2007); Ziyue Bo, *China's Elite Politics: Governance and Democratization* (Singapore: World Scientific, 2010); Zheng Yongnian and Lye Liang Fook, "Elite Politics and the Fourth Generation of Chinese Leadership," *Journal of Chinese Political Science*, vol. 8, nos 1–2, 2003.
21 Joseph Fewsmith, *Elite Politics in Contemporary China* (Armonk, NY: M.E. Sharpe, 2000).
22 David Shambaugh, "The Dynamics of Elite Politics During the Jiang Era," *The China Journal*, No. 45, 2001, pp. 101–12.
23 Lucian W. Pye, *The Dynamics of Chinese Politics* (Cambridge, MA: Oelgeschlager Gunn & Hain, 1982); Lucian W. Pye, "Factions and the Politics of Guanxi: Paradoxes in Chinese Administrative and Political Behaviour," *The China Journal*, No. 34, 1995, pp. 35–53; Lowell Dittmer, "Chinese Informal Politics," *The China Journal*, No. 34, 1995; Xuezhi Guo, "Dimensions of Guanxi in Chinese Elite Politics," *The China Journal,* No. 46, 2001, pp. 69–90.
24 Tang Tsou, "Chinese politics at the top: factionalism or informal politics? Balance-of-power politics or a game to win all," in Jonathan Unger, ed., *The Nature of Chinese Politics: From Mao to Jiang* (Armonk, NY: M.E. Sharpe, 2002), pp. 98–159; Joseph Fewsmith, "Institutions, Informal Politics, and Political Transition in China," *Asian Survey*, vol. 36. no. 3, 1996; Lily L. Tsai, *Accountability without Democracy: Solidary Groups and Public Goods Provision in Rural China* (New York: Cambridge University Press, 2007).

25 David S. G. Goodman, *Centre and Province in the People's Republic of China* (Cambridge University Press, 1986), p. 257; David S. G. Goodman, *Groups and Politics in the People's Republic of China* (New York: M.E. Sharpe, 1984); Victor Falkenheim, ed., *Citizens and Groups in Contemporary China*, (Ann Arbor: The University of Michigan Center for Chinese Studies, 1987).

26 Zheng Yongnian, *De facto Federalism in China: Reforms and Dynamics of Central-Local Relations* (Singapore: World Scientific Publishing, 2007), p. 11.

27 Michael Oksenberg, "Chinese Political System: Challenges of the Twenty-First Century," in Jonathan Unger, ed., *The Nature of Chinese Politics. From Mao to Jiang* (New York: M. E. Sharpe, 2002); Kenneth Lieberthal and Michael Oksenberg, *Policy Making in China: Leaders, Structures, Processes* (Princeton: Princeton University Press, 1988); Kenneth Lieberthal and David Lampton, eds., *Bureaucracy, Politics and Decision Making in Post-Mao China* (Berkeley: University of California Press, 1992).

28 Michael Oksenberg, 2002.

29 Elizabeth J. Perry, "Trends in the Study of Contemporary Chinese Politics: State-Society Relations," *China Quarterly*, No. 139 (September 1994), pp. 704–13.

30 Victor Nee and David Mozingo, eds., *State and Society in Contemporary China* (Ithaca: Cornell University Press, 1983).

31 Kuotsai Tom Liou, "State-Society Relations in Post-Mao Chinese Economic Reforms: Changes and Challenges," *International Journal of Economic Development*, vol. 2, no. 1, 2000, pp. 132–54.

32 Vivienne Shue, *The Reach of the State: Sketches of the Chinese Body Politic* (Stanford: Stanford University Press, 1988); Merle Goldman, *Sowing the Seeds of Democracy in China: Political Reform in the Deng Xiaoping Era* (Cambridge, MA: Harvard University Press, 1994); Vivienne Shue and Marc Blecher, *Tethered Deer: Government and Economy in a Chinese County* (Stanford, Stanford University Press, 1996); Elizabeth J. Perry and Mark Selden, eds., *Chinese Society: Change, Conflict, and Resistance* (New York: Routledge, 2000); Tianjian Shi, *Political Participation in Beijing* (Cambridge, MA: Harvard University Press, 1997).

33 Minxin Pei, "Societal Takeover in China and the USSR," *Journal of Democracy*, vol. 3, no. 1, 1992, pp. 108–18.

34 Peter J. Williamson, *Varieties of Corporatism: A Conceptual Discussion* (Cambridge, Cambridge University Press, 1985).

35 Howard J. Wiarda, *Corporatism and Comparative Politics* (Armonk, NY: M.E. Sharpe, 1996), Ch. 2, pp. 28–31; Jean C. Oi, "Fiscal Reform and the Economic Foundations of Local State Corporatism in China," *World Politics*, vol. 45, no. 1, 1992; Jonathan Unger and Anita Chan, "China, Corporatism, and the East Asian Model," *The Australian Journal of Chinese Affairs*, No. 33 (January 1995), pp. 29–53.

36 Jonathan Unger and Anita Chan, "China, Corporatism, and the East Asian Model," *Australian Journal of Chinese Affairs*, no. 33, 1995.

37 David Yang Da-hua, "Civil Society as an Analytic Lens for Contemporary China," *China: an International Journal*, vol. 2, no. 1, 2004, pp. 1–27.

38 Peter Moody, "Political Culture and the Study of Chinese Politics," *Journal of Chinese Political Science*, vol. 14, no. 3, 2009, pp. 253–74.

39 Ibid. For more examples, see Jeffrey N. Wasserstrom, *China in the 21st Century: What Everyone Needs to Know* (New York: Oxford University Press, 2010); Shiping Hua, ed., *Chinese Political Culture from 1989–2000* (Armonk, NY: M.E. Sharpe, 2001).

40 Lynn T. White III, "Chinese Political Studies: Overview of the State of the Field," *Journal of Chinese Political Science*, vol. 14, no. 3, 2009, pp. 229–51.

41 Douglass C. North, *Institutions, Institutional Change and Economic Performance* (Cambridge: Cambridge University Press, 1990); Jonathan Turner, *The Institutional Order* (New York: Longman, 1997); Mayntz, Renate, "Mechanisms in the Analysis of Social Macro-Phenomena," *Philosophy of the Social Sciences*, vol. 34, no. 2, 2004, pp. 237–59; Ha-Joon Chang, ed., *Institutional Change and Economic Development* (London: Anthem Press, 2007).

42 Colin Hay, "Structure, Agency, and Historical Institutionalism," *Political Studies*, vol. 46, no. 5, 1998, pp. 951–57; Peter A. Hall, and Rosemary C. R. Taylor, "Political Science and the Three New Institutionalism," *Political Studies*, vol. 44, no. 4, 1996, pp. 936–57.

43 Xiaoming Huang, ed., *The Institutional Dynamics of China's Great Transformation* (Routledge, 2010); Ming Xia, *The Dual Developmental State: Development Strategy and Institutional Arrangements for China's Transition* (Ashgate, 2000); Jean C. Oi, *Rural China Takes Off: Institutional Foundations of Economic Reform* (Berkeley: University of California Press, 1999); Dali Yang, *Calamity and Reform: State, Rural Society, and Institutional Change since the Great Leap Forward* (Stanford, Stanford University Press, 1998).

44 David Collier and James E. Mahon, "Conceptual Stretching Revisited: Adapting Categories in Comparative Analysis," *American Political Science Review*, vol. 87, no. 4, 1993, pp. 845–55.

45 Samuel Huntington, "Paradigms of American Politics: Beyond the One, the Two, and the Many," *Political Science Quarterly*, vol. 89, March 1974, p. 7.

46 Previous depictions of China as "Leninist" are works by some American scholars. For example, Barrett McCormick, *Political Reform in Post-Mao China: Democracy and Bureaucracy in a Leninist State* (Berkeley, University of California Press, 1990); Bruce Dickson, *Democratization in China and Taiwan: The Adaptability of Leninist Parties* (New York: Oxford University Press, 1997).

47 Pierre F. Landry, *Decentralized Authoritarianism in the Post-Mao Era* (Cambridge: Cambridge University Press, 2008); Kalpana Misra, *From Post-Maoism to Post-Marxism: The Erosion of Official Ideology in Deng's China* (London: Routledge, 1998); Steven I. Levine, "China's Fuzzy Transition: Leninism to post-Leninism," *The China Quarterly*, 136: 972–83, 1993; Lieberthal and David Lampton, eds., *Bureaucracy, Politics and Decision Making in Post-Mao China* (Berkeley: University of California Press, 1992).

48 Deng Xiaoping, "Uphold the Four Cardinal Principles," *Selected Works*, Vol. 2 (Beijing: Foreign Language Press, 1995); Jiang Zemin, "Uphold the Four Cardinal Principles," *Selected Works*, Vol. III, Chinese edition (Beijing: People's Publishing House, 2006).

49 Josef Gregory Mahoney, "Legitimizing Leninism," in Zhenglai Deng and Sujian Guo, ed., *Reviving Legitimacy: Lessons for and from China* (Lanham, MD: Rowman & Littlefield-Lexington, 2011)

50 Vladimir Ilyich Lenin, "What Is To Be Done?" (1901) in *Lenin's Collected Works*, Vol. 5 (Foreign Languages Publishing House, 1961, Moscow), pp. 347–530; Joseph Stalin, "Foundations of Leninism," *Works*, Vol. 6 (Foreign Language Publishing House, Moscow, 1953).

51 Philosophical absolutism, ideological monopoly, and party–state are in a fundamental sense interrelated and intertwined with one another—one overlaps and reinforces another. However, it is useful to deconstruct and reorganize them for analytic purposes.

52 The term "regime" here is employed as a label to characterize the structure of government or the nature of policy under the leadership of an individual political elite or as a name usually given to a sequence of governments formed and led by

the same party or in which power remains essentially in the hands of the same elite group, This is a fairly common usage of regime, such as "Thatcher regime," "Marcos regime," and "Stalin regime," see Lawson, p. 202 fn. 17; Calvert, p. 18.

53 Maria H. Chang, "Totalitarianism and China: The Limits of Reform," *Global Affairs*, (fall, 1987), pp. 150–53; 157.

54 This figure is based on the diagram presented by Collier and Mahon, p. 849.

55 Karl Marx, "Preface to A Critique of Political Economy," in David McLellan, ed., *Karl Marx, Selected Writings* (London: Oxford University Press, 1977), pp. 389–90; Roger Garaudy, *Karl Marx: The Evolution of His Thought* (New York: International Publishers, 1967), pp. 68–77, 89–98; Iain McLean, ed., *The Concise Oxford Dictionary of Politics* (Oxford, Oxford University Press, 1996), p. 139.

56 Richard Lowenthal, "Development vs. Utopia in Communist Policy," in Chalmers Johnson, ed., *Change in Communist Systems* (Stanford: Stanford University Press, 1970), p. 51.

57 Ibid., p. 53.

58 Thomas Sowell, *A Conflict of Visions: Ideological Origins of Political Struggles* (New York: William Morrow, 1987), pp. 1–39.

59 Maria H. Chang, "What Is Left of Mao Tse-tung Thought?" *Issues and Studies*, vol. 28, no. 1 (January 1992), pp. 18–38.

60 Paul Cocks, "The Rationalization of Party Control," in Chalmers Johnson, p. 153.

61 Karl A. Wittfogel, *Oriental Despotism: A Comparative Study of Total Power* (New Haven, CT: Yale University Press, 1967), Chapters 1–5.

3 Shaping forces of Chinese state-making, political culture, and political tradition

1 Although some may criticize this explanation as "environmental determinism," which believes that a land's physical characteristics, such as environmental, climatic, and geographical factors, determine the patterns of human culture and socioeconomic and political development, it does provide good insights for an explanation of the creation and development of a human society.

2 http://en.wikipedia.org/wiki/Yellow_River.

3 http://afe.easia.columbia.edu/china/geog/maps.htm.

4 Barry Naughton, *The Chinese Economy: Transitions and Growth* (Cambridge: The MIT Press, 2007), p. 20.

5 John M. Laflen, Junliang Tian and Chi-Hua Huang, eds., *Soil Erosion and Dryland Farming* (Florida: CRC Press, 2000). http://en.wikipedia.org/wiki/Loess_Plateau.

6 www.eosnap.com/tag/yellow-river.

7 Hong-key Yoong, "Loess Cave Dwellings in Shaanxi Province, China." *Geojournal*, vol. 21, no. 1/2, 1990, pp. 95–102. www.angelfire.com/nc/prannn/loess. html.

8 Xin-min Meng and Edward Derbyshire, "Landslides and Their Control in the Chinese Loess Plateau: Models and Case Studies From Gansu Province, China," *Geohazards in Engineering Geology*, vol. 15, no. 1, 1998, pp. 141–53. www. angelfire.com/nc/prannn/loess.html.

9 http://en.wikipedia.org/wiki/Loess_Plateau.

10 Hong Jiang, *The Ordos Plateau of China: An Endangered Environment* (New York: United Nations UP, 1999), p. 18. www.angelfire.com/nc/prannn/loess.html.

11 Doug Kleine, "Who Will Feed China?" *Journal of Soil and Water Conservation* vol. 52, no. 1, 1997, pp. 398–99. www.angelfire.com/nc/prannn/loess.html

12 Jingneng Li, "Comment: Population Effects on Deforestation and Soil Erosion in China," *Population and Development Review* vol. 16, suppl., 1990, p. 257. www.angelfire.com/nc/prannn/loess.html.

13 Ian J. Smalley, ed., *Loess: Lithology and Genesis* (Stroudsburg: Dowden, 1975), p. 362. www.angelfire.com/nc/prannn/loess.html.

14 Xin-min Meng and Edward Derbyshire, "Landslides and Their Control in the Chinese Loess Plateau: Models and Case Studies From Gansu Province, China," *Geohazards in Engineering Geology*, vol. 15, no. 1, 1998, p. 141. www.angelfire.com/nc/prannn/loess.html.

15 Shiuhung Luk, "Soil Erosion and Land Management in the Loess Plateau Region, North China," *Chinese Geography and Environment: A Journal of Translations*, vol. 3, no. 4, 1990–91, p. 10. www.angelfire.com/nc/prannn/loess.html.

16 Junhu Dai, *et al.*, "Wet-Dry Changes in the Borderland of Shaanxi, Gansu and Ningxia from 1208 to 1369 Based on Historical Records," *Journal of Geographical Sciences*, Vol. 19, No. 6, 2009, pp. 750–64.

17 Edwin O. Reischauser and John K. Fairbank, *East Asia: The Great Tradition* (Boston: Houghton Mifflin Company, 1962), p. 20.

18 *Zhan Guo Ce*, Volume 1, "Eastern Chou," Chapter 4, "Eastern Chou Wished to Plant Rice," translated by B.S. Bonsall, http://lib.hku.hk/bonsall/zhanguoce/index1.html.

19 Edwin O. Reischauser and John K. Fairbank, p. 19.

20 Zhao Songqiao, *Geography of China: Environment, Resources, Population, and Development* (New York: John Wiley, 1994), p. 15; Gregory Veeck, *et al.*, *China's Geography: Globalization and the Dynamics of Political, Economic, and Social Change* (Lanham: Rowman & Littlefield, 2007).

21 Barry Naughton, pp. 20–21.

22 James C. F. Wang, *Contemporary Chinese Politics: An Introduction* (Upper Saddle River, New Jersey: Prentice Hall, 2002), p. 2.

23 Edwin O. Reischauser and John K. Fairbank, pp. 21–23.

24 Shan-yu Yao, "The Chronological and Seasonal Distribution of Flood and Droughts in Chinese History, 206 B.C.–A.D. 1911," *Harvard Journal of Asiatic Studies*, vol. 7, 1942, p. 275. James C. F. Wang, *Contemporary Chinese Politics: An Introduction* (Upper Saddle River, New Jersey: Prentice Hall, 2002), p. 2.

25 Cormac Ó Gráda, *Famine: A Short History* (Princeton: Princeton University Press, 2009). Cite from http://press.princeton.edu/chapters/s8857.html; Walter H. Mallory, *China: Land of Famine* (New York: American Geographical Society, 1926, special publication, no. 6); See a book review essay published by *Journal of the Royal Institute of International Affairs*, vol. 6, no. 3 (1927), pp. 185–87.

26 David E. Mungello, *The Great Encounter of China and the West, 1500–1800* (Lanham, MD: Rowman & Littlefield, 2009), p. 97; Xing Lu, *Rhetoric in Ancient China, Fifth to Third Century, B.C.E.: A Comparison with Classical Greek Rhetoric* (Columbia, SC: University of South Carolina Press, 1998), p 46–47.

27 Deng Yunte. "(邓云特), 中国救荒史 [History of Disaster Relief in China]", (北京出版社, 1998).

28 John King Fairbank, *The United States and China* (New York: Viking Press, 1962), p. 48. James C. F. Wang, *Contemporary Chinese Politics: An Introduction* (Upper Saddle River, New Jersey: Prentice Hall, 2002), p. 2.

29 Karl A. Wittfogel, *Oriental Despotism: A Comparative Study of Total Power* (New Haven, Yale University Press, 1957).

30 Michael Curtis, "Asiatic Mode of Production and Oriental Despotism," in Michael Curtis, ed., *Marxism: The Inner Dialogues* (Transaction Publisher, 1997), pp. 326–75; Craig Calhoun, ed. *Dictionary of the Social Sciences* (Oxford University Press, 2002).

31 http://social.jrank.org/pages/2584/Oriental-despotism.html.

32 John King Fairbank, *China: A New History* (Cambridge: Harvard University Press, 1992), p. 16.

33 Peter R. Moody, 1995, pp. 59, 78–81.
34 Ibid. p. 79.
35 James C. F. Wang, p. 8.
36 James C. F. Wang, p. 7–8. John King Fairbank, *The United States and China* (New York: Viking Press, 1962), pp. 90–95.

4 Traditional Chinese culture and Confucianism

1 Peter R. Moody, Jr., *Tradition and Modernization in China and Japan* (Belmont, CA: Wadsworth Publishing Company, 1995), p. 41.
2 Ibid., pp. 42–45.
3 Ibid., pp. 44–49.
4 Robert L. Worden, Andrea Matles Savada, and Ronald E. Dolan, eds., *China: A Country Study* (Washington, DC: The Federal Research Division of the Library of Congress, 1988), pp. 102–3.
5 James C. F. Wang, *Comparative Asian Politics* (Englewood Cliffs, NJ: Prentice-Hall, 1994), p. 21; Debra E. Soled, ed., *China: A Nation in Transition* (Washington, DC: CQ, 1995), p. 7.
6 James C. F. Wang, pp. 20–21.
7 John King Fairbank, *China: A New History* (Cambridge: Harvard University Press, 1992), p. 52.
8 Confucius, *The Analects* (London: The Penguin Group, 1979), Book 12, Verse 19.
9 Ibid., p. 21.
10 Ibid. pp. 21–22.
11 Robert J. Lifton, p. 11.
12 http://en.wikipedia.org/wiki/Robert_Jay_Lifton.
13 John King Fairbank, p. 55.
14 Zhengyuan Fu, *China's Legalists: The Earliest Totalitarians and Their Art of Ruling* (Armonk, NY: Sharpe, 1996); Han Fei-tzu: *Basic Writings*, Translated by Burton Watson (New York: Columbia University Press, 2003).
15 John King Fairbank, p. 53.
16 Peter R. Moody, pp. 49–52.
17 Dennis Twitchett and Michael Loewe, *The Cambridge History of China* (Cambridge: Cambridge University Press, 1986), p. 767.
18 Fritjof Capra, "Chinese Thought," in Fritjof Capra, *The Tao of Physics: An Exploration of the Parallels between Modern Physics and Eastern Mysticism* (Boston: Shambhala Publications, Inc., 2000), pp. 101–12.
19 Dennis Twitchett and Michael Loewe, p. 766.
20 Robert J. Lifton, *Thought Reform and the Psychology of Totalitarianism: A Study of Brainwashing in China* (NY: W. W. Norton & Company, 1961), p. 11.
21 Lucian W. Pye, "The State and the Individual: An Overview Interpretation," *The China Quarterly*, no. 127, 1991, pp. 443–66.
22 R. Randle Edwards, Louis Henkin, Andrew J. Nathan, *Human Rights in Contemporary China* (New York: Columbia University Press, 1986), p. 21.
23 Ibid., pp. 137–38.
24 Ibid., p. 21.
25 Ibid., p. 21.

5 The collapse of the imperial state and the communist road to power

1 See Susan Williams' one of four PBS documentaries on China, *China—A Century of Revolution, Part I: China in Revolution 1911–1949* (1989).

2 Frederica M. Bunge and Rinn-Sup Shinn, eds., *China: A Country Study* (Washington, D.C.: Government Printing Office, 1981), pp. 21–23. The following website provides a good outline of Chinese history over thousands of years: www.mongabay.com/reference/country_studies/ china/all.html.

3 Ibid.

4 Ibid., pp. 23–30.

5 Robert J. Lifton, "Death and History", in Ernest A. Menze, ed., *Totalitarianism Reconsidered* (Port Washington, NY: Kennikat Press Corp., 1981), pp. 206–30.

6 Xiaqun Hao *et al.*, *Comparison of China and the West: 500 Years* (Beijing, China: The Worker's Publishing House, 1989), p. 389.

7 http://orpheus.ucsd.edu/chinesehistory/pgp/index.html.

8 Jonathan D. Spence, *The Search for Modern China* (NY: W. W. Norton & Company, 1990), pp. 224–99.

9 Frederica M. Bunge and Rinn-Sup Shinn, pp. 23–30; Jonathan D. Spence, pp. 224–99.

10 Jonathan D. Spence, p. 318.

11 Ibid., p. 312.

12 Lucien Bianco, *Origins of the Chinese Revolution, 1915–1949* (Stanford, CA: Stanford University Press, 1971).

13 Chunhou Zhang, et al., *Mao Zedong as Poet and Revolutionary Leader: Social and Historical Perspectives* (Lanham, MD: Lexington books, 2002), pp. 58, 65.

14 Frederica M. Bunge and Rinn-Sup Shinn, pp. 35–39.

15 Mark Selden, *The Yenan Way in Revolutionary China* (Cambridge: Harvard University Press, 1971).

16 Yinghong Cheng, "The Yan'an Period: Beginning the Systematic Remolding of Human Minds," in *Creating the "New Man": From Enlightenment Ideals to Socialist Realities* (University of Hawaii Press, 2009).

17 See a complete list of Mao's works online: www.marxists.org/reference/archive/ mao/selected-works/date-index.htm.

18 The Xi'an Incident was a coup staged by General Zhang Xueliang and General Yang Hucheng, whose Northeastern Army and Northwestern Armies had been dissatisfied with Chiang Kai-shek's policy that focused on eliminating communists rather than stopping the Japanese aggression. On December 12, 1936, Chiang Kai-shek, who visited General Zhang Xueliang's headquarters in Xi'an, was abducted in order to force Chiang Kai-shek into stopping the civil war against the communists and from forming an alliance (i.e., the Second United Front) with the CPC to fight against the Japanese aggression.

19 Frederica M. Bunge and Rinn-Sup Shinn, pp. 35–39.

20 Odd Arne Westad, *Decisive Encounters: The Chinese Civil War, 1946–1950* (Stanford University Press, 2003).

6 The making of the new communist state and the post-Mao transition

1 http://orpheus.ucsd.edu/chinesehistory/pgp/index.html.

2 Robert L. Worden, Andrea Matles Savada and Ronald E. Dolan, eds., *China: A Country Study*. (Washington: GPO for the Library of Congress, 1987), pp. 213.

3 Ibid.

4 Julia C. Strauss, "Paternalist Terror: The Campaign to Suppress Counter-revolutionaries and Regime Consolidation in the People's Republic of China, 1950–53," *Comparative Studies in Society and History*, vol. 44, no. 1 (2002); Marie-Claire Bergère, "China in the Wake of the Communist Revolution: Social

Transformations, 1949–66," in Werner Draguhn and David S.G. Goodman, eds., *China's Communist Revolutions—Fifty Years of The People's Republic of China* (London, etc.: Routledge, 2002); Charles P. Cell, *Revolution at Work—Mobilization Campaigns in China* (New York: Academic Press, 1977).

5 Roderick MacFarquhar and John K. Fairbank, eds., *The People's Republic of China, Vol. 14, Part 1: The Emergence of Revolutionary China 1949–1965* (Cambridge: Cambridge University Press, 1987), p. 87.

6 Robert L. Worden, Andrea Matles Savada and Ronald E. Dolan, pp. 41–43; "The People's Republic of China: The Transition to Socialism, 1953–57," accessed from www-chaos.umd.edu/history/prc.html#transition.

7 Barry Naughton, *The Chinese Economy: Transitions and Growth* (Cambridge, MA: The MIT Press, 2007), p. 67.

8 Ibid.

9 Ibid., pp. 43–46.

10 Robert L. Worden, et al., *China: A Country Study* (Washington: GPO for the Library of Congress, 1987), pp. 216; www.mongabay.com/reference/country _ studies/china/ HISTORY.html; James C. F. Wang, *Contemporary Chinese Politics: An Introduction* (Upper Saddle River, New Jersey: Prentice Hall, 2002), p. 23.

11 Nicholas R. Lardy and John K. Fairbank, "The Chinese Economy under Stress, 1958–65," In Roderick MacFarquhar and John K. Fairbank, eds., *The People's Republic of China, Vol. 14, Part 1: The Emergence of Revolutionary China 1949–1965* (Cambridge: Cambridge University Press, 1987), p. 367.

12 The University of Chicago Chronicle: "China's Great Leap Forward." March 14, 1996, Vol. 15, No. 13. http://chronicle.uchicago.edu/960314/china.shtml.

13 Yang Jisheng, *Tombstone—A Record of the Great Chinese Famine in 1960s* (Hong Kong: Cosmos Books, 2008).

14 Frank Dikötter, *Mao's Great Famine: The History of China's Most Devastating Catastrophe, 1958–62* (New York: Walker & Company, 2010); Dali Yang, *Calamity and Reform in China: State, Rural Society and Institutional Change Since the Great Leap Famine* (Stanford: Stanford University Press, 1998); MacFarquhar, Roderick, *The Origins of the Cultural Revolution: Contradictions Among the People, 1956–1957* (New York: Columbia University Press, 1973).

15 Robert L. Worden, Andrea Matles Savada and Ronald E. Dolan, pp. 46–47.

16 Ibid., pp. 47–53; p. 220.

17 Guo Jian, Yongyi Song and Yuan Zhou, *Historical Dictionary of the Chinese Cultural Revolution* (Lanham, MD: The Scarecrow Press, Inc., 2006); Michael Schoenhals, ed., *China's Cultural Revolution, 1966–1969—Not A Dinner Party* (Armonk NY: M.E. Sharpe, 1996).

18 China Online; Discovering China. "The Middle Kingdom." http://chinese culture.about.com/gi/dynamic/offsite.htm?site=http%3A%2F%2Flibrary.thinkques t.org%2F26469%2Fcultural-revolution%2F; Roderick MacFarquhar, *The Origins of the Cultural Revolution: Contradictions Among the People, 1956–1957* (New York: Columbia University Press, 1973).

19 Robert L. Worden, Andrea Matles Savada and Ronald E. Dolan, pp. 53–58.

20 The four basic principles that were formally codified into the Constitution are (1) the socialist path, (2) the dictatorship of the proletariat, (3) Party leadership, and (4) Marxism-Leninism-Mao Zedong Thought.

21 Robert L. Worden, Andrea Matles Savada and Ronald E. Dolan, pp. 222–23.

22 The following discussion incorporates some material from Sujian Guo, *The Political Economy of Asian Transition from Communism* (Ashgate Publishing, 2006), pp. 56–59.

23 Harry Harding, *China's Second Revolution: Reform after Mao* (Washington, DC: The Brookings Institute, 1987), p. 77.
24 Ibid., p. 46.
25 Ibid., pp. 78–83.
26 Wing Thye Woo, "The Economics and Politics of Transition to an Open Market Economy: China," *Technical Papers*, no. 153, OECD Development Centre, October 1999, p. 34.
27 Harry Harding, p. 83.
28 Wing Thye Woo, p. 34.
29 Harry Harding, pp. 83–85.
30 Wing Thye Woo, p. 37.
31 Harry Harding, pp. 86–90.
32 Gao Shangquan, *Two Decades of Reform in China* (Singapore: World Scientific, 1999), p. 34.
33 Wing Thye Woo, p. 54.

7 Marxism–Leninism and Chinese political ideology

1 David McLellan, *Karl Marx* (New York: The Viking Press, 1975), pp. 1–17.
2 Angus Walker, *Marx: His Theory and Its Context* (Winchester, MA: Unwin Hyman Inc., 1979), pp. 71–85.
3 McLellan, 1975, pp. 36–37; "Karl Marx, Theories of Surplus Value," in David McLellan, ed., *Karl Marx, Selected Writing* (London: Oxford University Press, 1977), pp. 398–394.
4 McLellan, 1975, p. 42.
5 Karl Marx, "The Eighteenth Brumaire of Louis Bonaparte," in K. Marx and F. Engels, *Selected Works* (Moscow, 1962), vol. I, p. 247.
6 Roger Garaudy, *Karl Marx: The Evolution of His Thought* (New York: International Publishers, 1967), pp. 68–77.
7 Ibid.
8 Karl Marx, "Preface to A Critique of Political Economy," in David McLellan, ed., *Karl Marx, Selected Writings* (London: Oxford University Press, 1977), pp. 389–90.
9 Iain Mclean, ed., *The Concise Oxford Dictionary of Politics* (Oxford, Oxford University Press, 1996), p. 139.
10 John P. Burke, Lawrence Crocker, Lyman Howard Legters, *Marxism and the Good Society* (New York: Cambridge University Press, 1981), p. 114.
11 Nicholas Churchich, *Marxism and Alienation* (Cranbury, NJ: The Associated University Press, 1990), p. 77.
12 Ibid.
13 A. D. Lindsay, *Karl Marx's Capital: An Introductory Essay* (London: Oxford University Press, 1925), pp. 81–82
14 Angus Walker, *Marx: His Theory and Its Context* (Winchester, MA: Unwin Hyman Inc., 1979), pp. 130–34.
15 Ibid.
16 Karl Marx, *Selected Writings*, in McLellan, 1977, p. 487.
17 Ibid., p. 89.
18 Ibid., p. 238.
19 Angus Walker, pp. 130–34.
20 Richard Schmitt, *Introduction to Marx and Engels: A Critical Reconstruction* (Boulder: Westview Press, 1987), pp. 189–91; Jon Elster, ed., *Karl Marx: A Reader* (New York: Cambridge University Press, 1986), pp. 257–93.

21 Karl Marx, *Selected Writings*, in McLellan, 1977, p. 568
22 V. I. Lenin, "State and Revolution," *Selected Works* (Moscow: Progress Publishers, 1967), pp. 322–37, especially Chapters 2–3.
23 Ibid., p. 569.
24 Karl Marx, p. 570.
25 The Paris Commune (*La Commune de Paris*) was the result of an uprising of workers and the lower-middle classes in Paris after the French military defeat in the Franco-Prussian War in 1871. It was the first time the working class exercised power and ruled Paris for two months from March 28 to May 28, 1871.
26 Jon Elster, ed., *Karl Marx: A Reader* (New York: Cambridge University Press, 1986), pp. 257–93.
27 James E. Dougherty and Robert L Pfaltzgraff, eds., *Contending Theories of International Relations* (New York: Harper & Row Publishers, 1990); Albert Szymanski, *The Logic of Imperialism* (New York: Praeger, 1981).
28 Karl Marx and Friedrich Engels, *The Communist Manifesto* (New York: Signet Classics, 1998), p. 1.
29 C. R. Mitchell, *The Structure of International Conflict* (New York, St. Martin's Press, 1980); Karl Marx and Friedrich Engels, "The German Ideology" (1846), in R. Pascal, ed., (New York: International Publishers, 1947); Karl Marx and Friedrich Engels, "Manifesto of the Communist Party" (1848), in Robert C. Tucker, ed., *The Marx-Engels Reader* (New York: Norton, 1972).
30 Philip Siegleman, *Introduction to J. A. Hobson: Imperialism, A Study* (Ann Arbor: University of Michigan Press, 1965); V. I. Lenin, *Imperialism, the Highest Stage of Capitalism* (New York: International Publishers, 1977).
31 Ibid.
32 Ibid.
33 Maurice Meisner, *Mao's China and After* (New York: Free Press, 1999), pp.12–16.
34 Mao Tse Tung, *"On contradiction"*, *Selected Readings from the Works of Mao Tse-Tung* (Beijing: Foreign Language Press, 1967), p. 75
35 Ibid., p. 89.
36 Ibid., p. 55
37 Maurice Meisner, pp.41–45.
38 http://en.wikipedia.org/wiki/Maoism
39 Peter R. Moody, Jr., *Tradition and Modernization in China and Japan* (Belmont, CA: Wadsworth Publising Company, 1995), p. 178.
40 Ibid.
41 Ibid., 179.
42 Ibid., 182.
43 Karl Marx, *Selected Writings*, in McLellan, 1977, p. 568
44 http://en.wikipedia.org/wiki/Jiang_Zemin
45 Ibid.
46 Li, Peilin, "The Development of the Ideas of Building a Socialist Harmonious Society" (Goujian Shehui zhuyi hexie shehui tichu de guocheng), on-line, accessed on Jan. 25, 2008, www.southcn.com/nflr/llzhuanti/hexie/hxlw/200504150397.htm
47 Boagang Guo and Sujian Guo, "China in Search of a Harmonious Society," in Sujian Guo and Baogang Guo, eds., *China in Search of a Harmonious Society* (Rowman & Littlefield–Lexington, 2008), pp. 2–3
48 CPC Central Committee, *The Decision on a Number of Important Issues Regarding the Building of a Socialist Harmonious Society,* Oct. 8–11, 2006, on-line, accessed on Dec. 12, 2007, http://cpc.people.com.cn/GB/64093/64094/4932424.html; *Communiqué of the Sixth Plenum of the 16th CPC Central Committee*, http://news.xinhuanet.com/english/ 2006–10/11/content_5191071.htm

49 See Boagang Guo and Sujian Guo, 2008.
50 Baogang Guo, "Political Legitimacy and China's Transition," *Journal of Chinese Political Studies* vol. 8, nos. 1–2, 2003, pp. 1–16.
51 Arthur M. Okun, *Equity and Efficiency: the Big Tradeoff* (Washington D.C.: Brookings Institution, 1975).
52 See Boagang Guo and Sujian Guo, 2008.

8 Ideological modifications in post-Mao China

1 The discussion in this Chapter incorporates some material from Sujian Guo, *Post-Mao China: From Totalitarianism to Authoritarianism* (Westport, CT: Praeger Publishers, 2000), pp. 33–63.
2 Gordon White, "The Decline of Ideocracy," in Robert Benewick and Paul Wingrove, eds., *China in the 1990s* (London: Macmillan, 1995), pp. 23–24; for more sources of such critics, also see Wei-wei Zhang, *Ideology and Economic Reform under Deng Xiaoping 1978–1993* (London and New York: Kegan Paul International, 1996), p. 7.
3 Cheng Li, *Rediscovering China: Dynamics and Dilemmas of Reform* (Lanham, Maryland: Rowman & Littlefield Publishers, 1997), pp. 305–7.
4 Guoguang Wu, "China in 2010: Dilemmas of 'Scientific Development'," *Asian Survey* 51:1 (January–February 2011), pp. 18–32; Wei-wei Zhang, pp. 1–10; Feng Chen, *Economic Transition and Political Legitimacy in Post-Mao China: Ideology and Reform* (New York: State University of New York Press, 1995), pp. 2–6.
5 Terry Eagleton, *Ideology—An Introduction* (London: Verso, 1991), p. 1.
6 Zbigniev Brzezinski, *Ideology and Power in Soviet Politics* (Westport, CT.: Greenwood Press, 1976), p. 98.
7 Martin Seliger, *Ideology and Politics* (New York: The Free Press, 1976), p. 14.
8 Gordon White, p. 21.
9 Wei-wei Zhang, p. 5.
10 Seliger, p. 109.
11 Barrington Moore, *Soviet Politics—The Dilemma of Power, the Role of Ideas in Social Change* (Cambridge, MA, Harvard University Press, 1950), pp. 402–3.
12 Franz Schurmann, *Ideology and Organization in Communist China* (Berkeley: University of California Press, 1966), pp. 21–45.
13 Richard Lowenthal, "Development vs. Utopia in Communist Policy," in Chalmers Johnson, ed., *Change in Communist Systems* (Stanford, CA: Stanford University Press, 1970); "The Ruling Party in a Mature Society," in Mark Field, ed., *Social Consequences of Modernization in Communist Societies* (Baltimore: Johns Hopkins University Press, 1976).
14 Lowenthal, pp. 51, 53; for a more detailed discussion, see Feng Chen, pp. 5, 13–20.
15 Giovanni Sartori, "Politics, Ideology, and Belief Systems," *American Political Science Review*, vol. 63, 1969, pp. 398–411; Feng Chen, pp. 10–13.
16 Daniel Bell, "Ideology and Soviet Politics," *Slavic Review*, vol. 24, no. 4, 1965, p. 602 [emphasis in original].
17 Zhang, pp. 5–6.
18 Anthony Wallace, *Culture and Personality* (New York, 1961), p. 148.
19 Chalmers Johnson, ed., *Change in Communist Systems* (Stanford: Stanford University Press, 1970), p. 7.
20 Johnson, pp. 6, 25.
21 Johnson, p. 12.
22 Johnson, p. 8.

23 Cal Clark, "The Nature of Chinese Communism and the Prospects for Teng's Reforms," in Yu-ming Shaw, ed., *Mainland China: Politics, Economics, and Reform* (Boulder: Westview Press, 1986), p. 41.

24 *Selected Works of Mao Tse-tung* 5:20, quoted in Alan P. L. Liu, "How Can We Evaluate Communist China's Political System Performance?" in Yu-ming Shaw, ed., *Changes and Continuities in Chinese Communism* (Boulder: Westview Press, 1988), p. 28, fn. 90.

25 See Liu, p. 30, fn. 101–3.

26 Wei-wei Zhang, p. 2.

27 Feng Chen, pp. 2–3.

28 Alan R. Kluver, *Legitimating the Chinese Economic Reforms: A Rhetoric of Myth and Orthodoxy* (New York: State University of New York Press, 1996), p. 77.

29 Ibid., p. 78.

30 Ibid., p. 80.

31 Ibid., p. 84.

32 Zhao Ziyang, "Advance along the Road of Socialism with Chinese Characteristics," *Documents of the Thirteenth National Congress of the Chinese Communist Party* (Beijing: Foreign Languages Press, 1987), p. 69.

33 Jiang Zemin, "Accelerating Reform and Opening-up," *Beijing Review*, October 26 to November 1, 1992, pp. 10–11.

34 Jiang, p. 33.

35 Kluver, p. 109.

36 The Central Propaganda Department of the CPC, "The Party Central Committee Resolution on Several Important Problems in Strengthening the Construction of Socialist Spiritual Civilization" (issued at the Sixth Plenary Session of the Fourteenth Central Committee), in *Study Brochure of Building Socialist Spiritual Civilization* (Beijing: The CPC Party History Press, 1997), p. 164.

37 *People's Daily*, October 16, 1998, pp. 1–2.

38 Ibid., p. 2.

39 "不搞多党轮流执政，不搞指导思想多元化，不搞"三权鼎立"和两院制，不搞联邦制，不搞私有化" www.theaustralian.com.au/news/world/china-rules-out-political-reform/story-e6frg6so-1226020720813

40 *Singtao Daily*, March 30, 2011.

41 *The Constitution of the Chinese Communist Party* (Beijing: People's Publishers, 1997), pp. 1–2.

42 Deng Xiaoping, "Uphold the Four Cardinal Principles," *A Selection of Important Documents Since the Third Plenary Session* (Beijing: People's Publishing House, August 1982), p. 87.

43 Guoguang Wu, "China in 2010: Dilemmas of 'Scientific Development'," *Asian Survey* vol. 51, no. 1, 2011, pp. 18–32.

44 Xinhua News Agency, "CPC Central Committee plenum ends with cultural development guideline," http://news.xinhuanet.com/english2010/china/2011–10/18/c_131198658.htm

45 An-chia Wu, "Whither Mainland China: On the Theoretical Study Campaign," in Yu-ming Shaw, ed., *Changes and Continuities in Chinese Communism* (Boulder: Westview Press, 1988), pp. 153–54.

46 Teng Teng, "Wenke jiaogai tixi jianchi Makesi zhuyi zhidao he lilun lianxi shiji" [The education reform system in humanities and social sciences must adhere to Marxism and the connection of theory with practice], *Zhongguo Gaodeng Jiaoyu*, no. 6, 1991, pp. 2–7.

47 *People's Daily*, April 21, 1998, p. 1.

48 Hannah Arendt, *The Origins of Totalitarianism* (New York: Harcourt, Brace and Co., 1951); Zbigniew Brezinski, *Ideology and Power in Soviet Politics* (New York: Praeger University Press, 1967); Michael Curtis, *Totalitarianism* (New Brunswick, NJ: Transaction Books, 1980); Carl Friedrich and Zbigniew Brezinski, *Totalitarian Dictatorship and Autocracy*, 2nd ed., rev. (New York: Praeger, 1966); Carl Friedrich, et al., *Totalitarianism in Perspectives* (New York: Praeger, 1969); George Kennan, "Totalitarianism in the Modern World," in Carl Friedrich, ed., Totalitarianism (Cambridge: Harvard University Press, 1954); Ernest Menze, ed., *Totalitarianism Reconsidered* (Port Washington, NY: Kennikat, 1981); Juan Linz, "Totalitarian and Authoritarian Regimes," in Volume 2 of Fred Greenstein and Nelson Polsby, eds., *Handbook of Political Science* (Reading, MA: Addison Wesley, 1975).
49 Heller, chapter 11; Dujmovic, p. 142.
50 Brantly Womack, "The Problems of Isms: Pragmatic Orthodoxy and Liberalization in Mainland China," in Bih-jaw Lin and James T. Myers, eds., *Contemporary China in the Post-Cold War Era* (Columbia: University of South Carolina Press, 1996), pp. 4–11.
51 Ibid., October 3, 1996, p. 1.
52 *Ming Po* (Hong Kong), May 12, 1994.
53 Anne S. Y. Cheung, "Public Opinion Supervision: A Case Study of Media Freedom in China," *Columbia Journal of Asian Law*, No. 20, 2007, pp. 357–84.
54 *Press Freedom Guardian*, May 23, 1998, p. 1, June 18, 1999, p. 2; September 24, 1999, p. 1.
55 Anne S. Y. Cheung, pp. 357–84.
56 Milton Mueller and Zixiang Tan, *China in the Information Age: Telecommunications and the Dilemmas of Reform* (Westport, CT: Praeger Publishers, 1997), pp. 81–99.
57 A example of email blockage would be shown as "undeliverable" in the subject line of returning message and in the returning message: "XFORWARD rejected your message to the following e-mail addresses: xxx XFORWARD gave this error: mail rejected by keyword."
58 http://online.wsj.com/article/SB10001424052748704443045756284106700226430.html
59 Milton Mueller and Zixiang Tan, 1997, pp. 91–94; note 20 of Chapter 5, p. 148.

9 The party–state structure of Chinese government

1 John Bryan Starr, *Understanding China: A Guide to China's Economy, History, and Political Culture* (Hill and Wang, 2001), p. 54.
2 Deng Xiaoping, "Uphold the Four Cardinal Principles," *Selected Works*, Vol. 2. (Beijing, China: Foreign Language Press, 1995), p. 168.
3 Josef Gregory Mahoney, "Legitimizing Leninism," in Deng Zhenglai and Sujian Guo, *Reviving Legitimacy: Lessons for and from China* (Lanham, MD: Rowman & Littlefield-Lexington, 2011).
4 This new policy adopted in the post-Mao era refers to the four criteria for choosing and promoting party-state cadres: younger, better educated, revolutionary, and modernized.
5 Jiang Zemin's political report at the 16th CPC Congress, November 2002.
6 *Dangjian Yanjiu* [*Party construction studies*], no. 4, 1998.
7 Jiang Zemin, "Uphold the Four Cardinal Principles," *Selected Works*, Vol. III (Beijing: Foreign Language Press, 2010), pp. 224–25.
8 *People's Daily*, April 2, 1998, p. 4.

9 *Beijing Review*, no. 42, 1993, p. v.
10 Graham Young, "Party Reforms," in Joseph Y. S. Cheng, ed., *China: Modernization in the 1980s* (New York: St. Martin's Press, 1990), pp. 75–86.
11 *People's Daily*, March 13, 1985, p. 4.
12 Ibid., June 25, 1991.
13 Lam, pp. 155–56.
14 *People's Daily*, April 2, 1998, p. 4.
15 Graham Young, pp. 83–85.
16 Ming Xia, "The Communist Party of China and the 'Party-State'," www.nytimes.com/ref/college/coll-china-politics-002.html.
17 See Chinese central government official website: http://english.gov.cn/links/statecouncil.htm.
18 James V. Feinerman, "Economic and Legal Reform in China, 1978–91," *Problems of Communism*, vol. 40, September—October 1991, pp. 69–70.
19 Kevin J. O'Brien, "Chinese People's Congresses and Legislative Embeddedness," *Comparative Political Studies*, vol. 27, no. 1, 1994, p. 85.
20 Yu Shi, "Establishing county-level people's congress standing committees is an important reform" (She xianji renda changweihui shi yixiang zhongyao gaige), *Neibu Wengao* (Beijing), vol. 23, 1988, pp. 12–14.
21 China Renmin University, *Research Report on Chinese Social Development (1994–1995): Chinese Society in Fast Transformation from Traditional to Modern Modes* (Beijing: China Renmin University Press, 1996), p. 65.
22 Yan Jiaqi, "The NPC's 'Honeycomb Structure' and 'Mute Congress'," p. 2.
23 O'Brien, pp. 86–90.
24 Ibid., pp. 90–91.
25 Starr, p. 60.
26 Feinerman, p. 70.
27 *China: Facts and Figures—Legal System* (Beijing: Foreign Languages Press, 1982), p. 3; Colin Mackerras, *The Cambridge Handbook of Contemporary China* (Cambridge: Cambridge University Press, 1990), p. 68.
28 *South China Morning Post*, December 16, 1992.
29 Lam, p. 269–70.
30 Zhou Hairong, "The Re-establishment of the Chinese Legal System: Achievements and Disappointments," *Civil Justice Quarterly* (London), vol. 10, 1991, pp. 44, 54–55.
31 Jiang Zemin speech on the CPC's absolute leadership over the PLA and the nature of the PLA as "the strong pillar of the People's Democratic Dictatorship," in *People's Daily*, March 13, 1999, p. 1.
32 *People's Daily*, July 30, 1997, p. 1.
33 *China Daily*, March 11, 1998, p. 1.
34 *People's Daily*, January 8, 1999, p. 1.
35 Mackerras, p. 59.
36 Starr, p. 61.
37 *New China News Agency*, February 7, 1990, quoted from Willy Wo-Lap Lam, p. 297.
38 *People's Daily*, February 8, 1990.
39 Ibid., March 31, 1998, p. 1.
40 *China News Service*, June 14, 1990, quoted from Willy Wo-Lap Lam, p. 297.
41 *South China Morning Post*, January 5, 1990, quoted from Willy Wo-lap Lam, p. 298.
42 *China News Service*, June 1, 1991, quoted from Willy Wo-Lap Lam, p. 298.
43 *People's Daily*, January 1, 1998, p. 2.

44 *Wen Hui Bao*, June 23, 1993, February 14, 1994; *China News Service*, February 2, February 6, 1993, in Willy Wo-Lap Lam, pp. 300–301.
45 *New China News Agency*, May 17, 1993, in Willy Wo-Lap Lam, pp. 300–301.
46 *Shenzhen Special Zone Daily*, January 31, 1993, in Willy Wo-Lap Lam, p. 301.
47 *New China News Agency*, May 17, 1993, in Willy Wo-Lap Lam, p. 302.
48 *People's Daily*, March 31, 1998, p. 1.
49 Ibid., March 2, 1998, p. 1; March 4, 1998, p. 1, 2, 4. "Hold high one banner" refers to Deng Xiaoping Theory; "uphold one goal" refers to the establishment of a socialist market economy; "promote one style" refers to socialist spiritual civilization; "master one method" refers to the party's seeking truth and mass line; "create one environment" refers to stability, unity, forging ahead and initiative; "adopt one strategy" refers to the strategy of economic modernization laid down by Deng Xiaoping; "improve one system" refers to the multiparty cooperation and political consultative system under the leadership of the CPC.
50 Kenneth G. Lieberthal, "Introduction: The 'Fragmented Authoritarianism' Model and Its Limitations," in Lieberthal and David M. Lampton, eds., *Bureaucracy, Politics, and Decision Making in Post-Mao China* (Berkeley, CA: University of California Press, 1992).
51 Jean Oi, "The Evolution of Local State Corporatism," in Andrew Walder, ed., *Zouping in Transition: The Process of Reform in Rural North China* (Cambridge, MA: Harvard University Press, 1998), pp. 35–61.
52 Bruce Gilley, "From Decay to Democracy", *Foreign Policy* (May/June 2006); "The Limits of Authoritarian Resilience," *Journal of Democracy*, vol. 14, no. 1, 2003.

10 Political development in post-Mao China

1 The discussion in this section incorporates some material from Sujian Guo, *Post-Mao China: From Totalitarianism to Authoritarianism* (Westport, CT: Praeger Publishers, 2000), pp. 70–92.
2 Joseph Fewsmith, "The Logic and Limits of Political Reform in China," http://chinastudygrouplondon.wordpress.com/tag/joseph-fewsmith.
3 H. H. Gerth and C. Wright Mills, "Introduction: The Man and His Work," in Gerth and Mills, eds., *From Max Weber: Essays in Sociology* (New York: Oxford University Press, 1958), pp. 3–74.
4 Maurice J. Meisner, *The Deng Xiaoping Era: an Inquiry into the Fate of Chinese Socialism, 1978–1994* (New York: Hill and Wang, 1996), p. 481.
5 Deng Xiaoping, *Selected Works of Deng Xiaoping* (Beijing: People's Publishing House, 1993), vol. III, pp. 177–78.
6 www.theaustralian.com.au/news/world/china-rules-out-political-reform/story-e6frg6so-1226020720813.
7 For a detailed discussion on the actual practices and political/ideological campaigns to enforce these principles, see Chapter 8.
8 Zaijun Yuan, *The Failure of China's "Democratic" Reforms* (Lanham, MD: Rowman & Littlefield-Lexington, 2011); Xiaoling Zhang, "From Totalitarianism to Hegemony: The Reconfiguration of the Party-State and the Transformation of Chinese Communication", *Journal of Contemporary China*, Vol. 20, No. 68 (January 2011), pp. 103–15.
9 We will define the concept "privatization" and discuss its relevance in the post-Mao economic reform in Chapter 16 on economic change.
10 CNN's interview with Wen Jiabao, http://transcripts.cnn.com/TRANSCRIPTS/1010/03/ fzgps.01.html; www.telegraph.co.uk/news/worldnews/asia/china/8040534/Wen-Jiabao-promises-political-reform-for-China.html.

11 Tatsumi Okabe, "China: The Process of Reform," in Gilbert Rozman, Seizaburo Sato and Gerald Segal, eds., *Dismantling Communism: Common Causes and Regional Variations* (Washington, DC: The Woodrow Wilson Center Press, 1992), p. 190.

12 Andrew Nathan, *China's Crisis: Dilemmas of Reform and Prospects for Democracy* (New York: Columbia University Press, 1990) pp. 178–79.

13 Xie Qingkui, "Retrospect and Prospect of Restructuring China's Administrative Institutions" [*Zhongguo xingzheng gaige de huigu yu zhanwan*], *XinHua Wenzhai* [New China Digest], no. 3, 1998, p. 4.

14 *People's Daily*, October 17, 1995, p. 1.

15 Xie Qingkui, p. 5.

16 www.gov.cn/gjjg/2005–8/01/content_18608.htm; www.gov.cn/gjjg/2005–8/28/content_27083.htm.

17 Starr, pp. 64–65.

18 *People's Daily*, May 7, 1998, p. 1.

19 *Press Freedom Guardian*, November 21, 1997, p. 4.

20 Boagang Guo and Sujian Guo, "Challenges Facing Chinese Political Development," in Sujian Guo and Baogang Guo, eds., *Challenges Facing Chinese Political Development* (Lanham, MD: Rowman & Littlefield-Lexington, 2008), p. 3

21 Daniel Kaufmann, Kraay Aart, and Massimo Mastruzzu, *Governance Matter IV: Aggregate and Individual Governance Indicators (1996–2006)*, World Bank Policy Research Paper 4280, July 2007 (Washington, DC: World Bank).

22 "National poverty does not affect political stability in China," *Pravda*, Aug. 15, 2005, http://english.pravda.ru/ world/20/91/366/15985_China.html.

23 John Less, "China Won't Revalue the Yuan," *Foreign Policy*, September 24, 2010. (www.foreignpolicy.com/articles/2010/09/24/china_won_t_revalue_the_yuan?page = 0,1).

24 Minxin Pei, "Is China unstable?" *American Diplomacy*, on-line, accessed on Jan. 21, 2008, www. unc.edu/depts/diplomat/AD_Issues/amdipl_13/china_pei.html.

25 "The Survivors Take Over," *Economist* 366 (March 22, 2003): 37–38.

26 Boagang Guo and Sujian Guo, p. 3

27 Ibid.

28 Qin Xiaoying, "Harmonious Society To Be a Model for the World," *China Daily*, Oct. 13, 2006.

29 Hu Jintao's speech at the meeting marking the 30th anniversary of reform and opening up, accessed from www.china.org.cn/archive/2009–05/11/content_17753659_9.htm

30 Pan Wei, "China's Party-Government System—The Origins of the Current Political Regime" (in Chinese), accessed from www.chinaelections.org/NewsInfo.asp?NewsID=111152.

31 Mao Zedong, "War and Problems of Strategy," *Selected Works*, Vol. 2 (Beijing: People's Publishing House, 1991); http://baike.baidu.com/view/139621.htm.

32 "China military still under Communist Party control," Victoria Advocate Publishing Co., www.victoriaadvocate.com/news/2009/apr/01/bc-as-china-communist-party-military.

33 Paul Charles Sondrol, *Castro's Cuba and Stroessner's Paraguay: A Comparison of the Totalitarian/authoritarian taxonomy*, Doctoral Dissertation in Political Science, The University of Arizona, 1990, p. 14.

11 The Chinese legal and legislative systems

1 Thomas Chiu, Ian Dobinson and Mark Findlay, *Legal System of the PRC* (Hong Kong: Longman, 1991); Pitman B. Potter, "The Chinese Legal System: Continuing

Commitment to the Primacy of the State Power," *China Quarterly*, No. 159, September 1999. Daniel C. K. Chow, *The Legal System of the People's Republic of China in a Nutshell* (St. Paul, MN: Thomson/West, 2009).

2 China administers 33 province-level regions, 333 prefecture-level regions, 2,862 county-level regions, 41,636 township-level regions.

3 Daniel C. K. Chow, pp. 199–209.

4 www.lawinfochina.com/Legal/index.asp.

5 Yuwen Li, "Court Reform in China: Problems, Progress and Prospects," in Jianfu Chen, Yuwen Li, Jan Michiel Otto, eds., *Implementation of Law in the People's Republic of China* (Hague, Netherlands: Kluwer Law International, 2002), pp. 63–69.

6 Chinese Government's Official Web Portal. www.gov.cn/english/2005–10/02/content_74192.htm.

7 www.mps.gov.cn/English/index.htm.

8 Chinese Government's Official Web Portal. www.gov.cn/english/2005–10/02/content_74192.htm.

9 Tao-tai Hsia and Wendy I. Zeldin, "Sheltering for Examination (Shourong Shencha) in the Legal System of the People's Republic of China," *Maryland Series in Contemporary Asian Studies*: Vol. 1993: No. 3, 2010; Kam C. Wong, "Sheltering for Examination (Shoushen) in the People's Republic of China: Law, Policy, and Practices," *Maryland Series in Contemporary Asian Studies*: Vol. 1997: No. 3, 2010.

10 Klaus Mühlhahn, *Criminal Justice in China: A History* (Harvard University Press, 2009).

11 Fu Hualing, "Sarah Biddulph, Legal Reform and Administrative Detention Powers in China," *China Perspectives*, 2008/4 http://chinaperspectives.revues.org/4758.

12 Hualing Fu, "A Case for Abolishing Shelter for Examination: Judicial Review and Police Powers in China," *Police Studies*, vol. 17, no. 4, 1994, p. 41–60.

13 Hualing Fu, "Criminal Defence in China: The Possible Impact of the 1996 Criminal Procedure Law Reform," *The China Quarterly* 153 (1998): 31–48.

14 Chen Jianfu, *Chinese Law, Towards an Understanding of Chinese Law, Its Nature and Development* (Boston: Kluwer Law International, 1999).

15 Yan Jiaqi, "The Relations between the NPC and the Politburo," *China Spring*, no. 174, 1998, p. 20.

16 *People's Daily*, March 11, 1998, p. 1.

17 Yan Jiaqi, "Abandoning the Official Slate System," *Press Freedom Guardian*, January 16, 1998, p. 3.

18 Yan Jiaqi, "The NPC's 'Honeycomb Structure' and 'Mute Congress,'" *Press Freedom Guardian*, March 13, 1998, p. 2.

12 Legal and legislative reforms in post-Mao China

1 At the press conference sponsored by the State Council Information Office on September 22, 2009, Ms. Xin Chunying, Vice-Chairwoman of the Legislative Affairs Commission of the Standing Committee of the National People's Congress briefed the press on "Sixty Years of Achievements in Building China into a State of Rule of Law." Cited from www.kouyi.org/press/798.html.

2 *People's Daily*, July 8, 1996, p. 4.

3 www.148-law.com/actuality/official.htm.

4 www.moj.gov.cn/2008zwgg/2009–01/14/content_1019840.htm.

5 See "The Regulations on the Management of Representative Offices Set up by Foreign Law Firms in China," Chapter 3, Order No. 338 of the State Council,

December 19, 2001. Cited from http://news.xinhuanet.com/ chanjing/2001–12/30/ content_18900.htm.

6 Peter H. Solomon Jr., "Authoritarian Legality and Informal Practices: Judges, Lawyers and the State in Russia and China," *Communist and Post-Communist Studies*, vol. 43, no. 4, 2010, pp. 351–62.

7 Kevin J. O'Brien, "Chinese People's Congresses and Legislative Embeddedness" *Comparative Political Studies*, vol. 27, no. 1, 1994, pp. 96–97; for some specific cases, see Chai Dingjian, *The People's Congress System of China* (Beijing: Law Press, 1998), p. 359 (table footnote).

8 Kevin J. O'Brien, *Reform without Liberalization: China's National People's Congress and the Politics of Institutional Change* (Cambridge: Cambridge University Press, 1990), pp. 6–7.

9 Liu Jui-shao, "Beijing Keen on Improving Quality of NPC Sessions," *FBIS–Daily Report, China* 39 (February 29, 1988).

10 *The Constitution of the People's Republic of China* (Beijing: Law Press, 1998), p. 26.

11 Ibid., pp. 25–26.

12 Wang Dexiang, "Zhixunquan jianlun" [A Brief Explanation of the Right to Address Inquiries], in Zhongguo Faxuehui, ed., *Xianfalun Wenxuan* (Beijing: Law Press, 1983), pp. 198–99.

13 "Progress Made in Legal System," *Beijing Review* 31, April 18–24, 1988, p. 11.

14 Minxin Pei, " 'Creeping Democratization' in China," in Larry Diamond, *et al.*, eds., *Consolidating the Third Wave Democracies: Regional Challenges* (Baltimore and London: The Johns Hopkins University Press, 1997), pp. 213–27.

15 The following discussion incorporates some material from Sujian Guo, *Post-Mao China: From Totalitarianism to Authoritarianism* (Westport, CT: Praeger Publishers, 2000), pp. 99–120.

16 Ralf Dahrendorf, "A Confusion of Powers: Politics and the Rule of Law," *Modern Law Review*, no. 40, 1977, p. 9.

17 Ronald Dworkin, "Political Judges and the Rule of Law," in Ronald Dworkin, *A Matter of Principle* (Cambridge: Harvard University Press, 1985), pp. 9–32; Ronald Dworkin, *Law's Empire* (Cambridge: Harvard University Press, 1986), p. 93; Allan C. Hutchinson and Patrick Monahan, eds., *The Rule of Law: Ideal or Ideology* (Toronto: Carswell, 1987a), p. ix; Geoffrey Walker, *The Rule of Law* (Melbourne, Australia: Melbourne University Press, 1988), pp. 23–42; Andrew Altman, *Critical Legal Studies: A Liberal Critique* (Princeton: Princeton University Press, 1990); Thomas Buergenthal, "The CSCE Rights System," *George Washington Journal of International Law and Economics*, no. 77, 1991, p. 356.

18 John Reitz, "Constitutionalism and the Rule of Law: Theoretical Perspectives," in Robert D. Grey, ed., *Democratic Theory and Post-Communist Change* (New Jersey: Prentice Hall, 1997), p. 114.

19 Ibid., pp. 118–19.

20 Ibid., p. 135.

21 China Renmin University, *Research Report on Chinese Social Development (1994–1995): Chinese Society in Fast Transformation from Traditional to Modern Modes* (Beijing: China Renmin University Press, 1996), p. 50.

22 *People's Daily*, March 14, 1998, p. 4.

23 Donald C. Clarke, "Justice and the Legal System in China," in Robert Benewick and Paul Wingrove, eds., *China in the 1990s* (London: Macmillan, 1995), pp. 86–89.

24 *Black's Law Dictionary* (St. Paul, MN: West Publishing Co., 1979), p. 282.

25 Clarke, p. 86.

26 W. C. Jones, "The Constitution of the People's Republic of China," *Washington University Law Quarterly*, LXIII, 1985, p. 710.

27 Clarke, p. 86.

28 Ibid., p. 87.

29 John Bryan Starr, *Understanding China* (New York: Hill and Wang, 1997), p. 60.

30 Clarke, p. 87.

31 Starr, p. 60; Clarke, p. 87.

32 James V. Feinerman, "Economic and Legal Reform in China, 1978–91," *Problems of Communism*, vol. 40, September–October 1991, p. 63.

33 Mu Rui, "New Developments in China's Economic Legislation," *Columbia Journal of Transnational Law* (New York), No. 1, 1983, pp. 61–76.

34 Feinerman, p. 64.

35 For the discussion on the extensive state intervention and the fledging market in post-Mao China, refer to Chapter 16 on economic change.

36 Feinerman, p. 68.

37 Feinerman, p. 62.

38 Gary Watson, "Business Law in the People's Republic of China: 1978–88," *American Business Law Journal* (Athens, GA), fall 1989, pp. 315–75.

39 *People's Daily*, October 17, 1995, p. 4.

40 China Renmin University, 1996, pp. 22–23, 49, 61, 65, 67.

41 *People's Daily*, October 17, 1995, p. 4.

42 Feinerman, p. 69.

43 Ibid., p. 70.

44 Ibid.

45 Ibid., p. 70.

46 Barrett McCormick, *Political Reform in Post-Mao China: Democracy and Bureaucracy in a Leninist State* (Berkeley: University of California Press, 1990), p. 126.

47 Clarke, p. 91.

48 *Constitution of the People's Republic of China* (Beijing: Law Press, 1998), Articles 127 and 132, pp. 39–40.

49 For a more detailed discussion of the problems of the Chinese judicial system, see *Xinhua Wenzhai*, no. 3, 1998, pp. 8–12.

50 Clarke, pp. 92–93.

51 Hongming Xiao, "The Internationalization of China's Legal Services Market," *Perspectives*, vol. 1, no. 6, 2000, an online journal website: www.oycf.org/Perspectives2/6_063000/Contents.htm

52 Randall Peerenboom, *Lawyers in China: Obstacles to Independence and the Defense of Rights* (New York: Lawyers' Committee on Human Rights, 1998), pp. 61–62.

53 Interviews with Xie Xiuru, managing partner of Allied Law Firm, Beijing, November 5–6, 2002

54 Randall Peerenboom, "Law Enforcement and the Legal Profession in China," in Jianfu Chen, Yuwen Li, Jan Michiel Otto, eds., *Implementation of Law in the People's Republic of China* (Hague, Netherlands: Kluwer Law International, 2002), pp. 130–36.

55 Ethan Michelson, "Lawyers, Political Embeddedness, and Institutional Continuity in China's Transition from Socialism," *American Journal of Sociology*, vol. 113, no. 2, 2007, pp. 352–414.

56 O'Brien, 1990, pp. 4–5.

57 Ibid., pp. 6–7, 130.

58 These four aspects are functional to the post-Mao legislative system and discussed in Kevin J. O'Brien's work which I shall refer to most in the following discussion.

59 Pi Chunxie and Nian Xinyong, "Zhengzhi tizhi gaige de yixie zhongyao renwu— tantan jianquan renmin daibia dahui zhidu" [Some Important Tasks in the Reform of Political System—Discussing Perfecting the NPC System], *Zhongguo Zhengzhi*, no. 1 (January 1987), p. 28.

60 O'Brien, 1990, pp. 131–32.

61 Ibid.

62 For a more detailed discussion of "electoral units," refer to Chapter 3 on political change.

63 Chai Dingjian, *The People's Congress System of China* (Beijing: Law Press, 1998), p. 158.

64 O'Brien, 1990, p. 143.

65 Ibid.

66 Du Xichuan, "Renda daibiao ying daibiao shui de liyi?" [Whose Interests should People's Deputies Represent?] *Faxue Zazhi*, no. 1 (January 1989), pp. 19–20.

67 Zhang Youyu, "Lun renmin daibiao dahui daibiao de renwu, zhiquan he huodong fangshi wenti" [On the Tasks, Powers, Functions, and Activities of NPC Deputies], *Faxue Yanjiu*, no. 2 (April 1985), p. 7, cited in Kevin J. O'Brien, p. 170.

68 O'Brien, 1990, p. 145.

69 Ibid., p. 14; Zhang Yu-an, "Less Deputy Fanfare—Start of a Trend?" *China Daily*, April 5, 1989, p. 4.

70 O'Brien, p. 141.

71 Ibid., p. 148.

72 Ibid., p. 148; Wang Shuwen, "Jiaqiang shehuizhuyi he fazhi de liangzhong zhongda cuoshi" [Two Important Measures to Strengthen Socialist Democracy and Legal System], *Minzhu yu Fazhi*, no. 7 (July 1982), pp. 7–8.

73 See O'Brien, 1990, pp. 159–64 for a more detailed discussion.

74 Ibid., p. 159.

75 Ibid., p. 160; Zhang Youyu, "Guanyu woguo falu de lifa changxu he qicao gongzuo" [On Our Country's Legislative Procedures and Legal Drafting Work], *Zhengzhixue Yanjiu*, no. 3 (August 1985), p. 3; Yao Dengkui and Deng Quangan, "Qianlun woguo lifa tizhi de tedian" [Discussing the Features of Our Country's Legislative System], *Faxue Jikan*, no. 2 (April 1985), p. 7; Huang Shuhai and Zhu Weijiu, "Shilun shouquan lifa" [On Empowered Legislation], *Faxue Yanjiu*, no. 1 (February 1986), p. 9.

76 China Renmin University, 1996, p. 50.

77 O'Brien, 1990, pp. 161–62; Luo Yapei, "Shehuizhuyi minzhu zhengzhi jian she chutan" [Research on Socialist Democratic Politics], Faxue Yanjiu, no. 3 (June 1988), p. 12; Li Maoguan, "Why Laws Go Unenforced," *Beijing Review*, vol. 32 (September 11–17, 1989), p. 17.

78 O'Brien, p. 161; "NPC Standing Committee's Work Outline Adopted," *FBIS–Daily Report, China* 132 (July 11, 1988), pp. 35–36.

79 O'Brien, 1990, pp. 163–64.

80 See O'Brien, 1990, pp. 164–68 for a more detailed discussion.

81 Ibid., p. 167.

82 Starr, p. 68.

83 O'Brien, 1990, pp. 154–55.

84 O'Brien, 1990, pp. 177–78.

85 *Constitution of the People's Republic of China*, Articles 1, 28, 51, and 54, as cited in Maria H. Chang, "What is Left of Mao Tse-tung Thought?" *Issues and Studies*, 28:1, January 1992, p. 38.

13 Chinese social structure and state–society relations

1 Talcott Parsons, "An Analytical Approach to the Theory of Social Stratification," in Talcott Parsons, *Essays in Sociological Theory* (Glencoe: Free Press, 1954), p. 69.
2 Ibid., 77–78.
3 Edwin O. Reischauer and John K. Fairbank, *East Asia: The Great Tradition* (Boston: Houghton Mifflin Company, 1962), p. 48.
4 Ibid., p. 51.
5 John K. Fairbank and Albert Feuerwerker, eds., *The Cambridge History of China* (New York: Cambridge University Press, 1986), Vol. 13, Part 2, p. 30.
6 Yi Li, *The Structure and Evolution of Chinese Social Stratification* (The University Press of America, 2005), p. 33.
7 John K. Fairbank and Albert Feuerwerker, eds., *The Cambridge History of China* (New York: Cambridge University Press, 1986), Vol. 13, Part 2, p. 30.
8 Peter R. Moody, Jr., *Tradition and Modernization in China and Japan* (Belmont, CA: Wadsworth Publishing Company, 1995), p. 78.
9 Ibid., p. 81.
10 Ibid., p. 79.
11 Yi Li, chapter 2.
12 Qiusha Ma, *Non-governmental Organizations in Contemporary China: Paving the Way to Civil Society?* (London and New York: Routledge, 2006), pp. 33–47.
13 Qiusha Ma, pp. 33–47.
14 Yi Li, chapter 2.
15 Barry Naughton, *The Chinese Economy: Transitions and Growth* (Cambridge: The MIT Press, 2007), pp. 43–44.
16 Yi Li, chapter 2.
17 Ibid.
18 Li Qiang, "Modernization and Evolution of China's Social Stratification and Structure," www.china001.com/show_hdr.php?xname = PPDDMV0&dname = DSGGF41 &xpos = 30.
19 Robert L. Worden, *et al.*, *China: A Country Study* (Washington: GPO for the Library of Congress, 1987), pp. 216; www.mongabay.com/reference/country _studies/china/ HISTORY.html; James C. F. Wang, *Contemporary Chinese Politics: An Introduction* (Upper Saddle River, New Jersey: Prentice Hall, 2002), p. 23.
20 Andrew G. Walder, *Communist Neo-traditionalism: Work and Authority in Chinese Industry* (Berkeley: University of California Press, 1984), p. 85.
21 Wang Ying, "Stratification of Social Structure in Social Transition," in Lu Xueyi and Jing Tiankui, eds., *Chinese Society in Transition* (Haerbin: Heilongjiang People's Publishing House, 1994), pp. 140–74.
22 Zhang Qing, "From Identity to Contract: China Structural Change of Social Stratum," *Jiangsu Social Sciences*, No. 3, 2002, pp. 187–92.
23 Lu Xueyi, ed., *Research Report on Contemporary China's Social Stratums* (Beijing: Social Science Literature Press, 2002), pp. 4, 7–8, 43–61.

14 Social changes and state–society relations in post-Mao China

1 Elizabeth J. Perry and Mark Selden, eds., *Chinese Society: Change, Conflict and Resistance*, 3rd Edition (NY: Routledge, 2010); Peter Hays Gries and Stanley Rosen, eds., *Chinese Politics: State, Society and the Market* (NY: Routledge, 2010).
2 http://news.cntv.cn/china/20110308/108526.shtml.

3 Jean C. Oi, "The Fate of the Commune after the Collective," in Deborah S. Davis and Ezra F. Vogel, eds., *Chinese Society on the Eve of Tiananmen: The Impact of Reform* (Cambridge, MA: Harvard University Press for the Council on East Asian Studies, 1990).

4 Zbigniew Brzezinski, *The Grand Failure: the Birth and Death of Communism in the Twentieth Century* (New York: Collier Books, 1990), pp. 256–57.

5 Larry Diamond, *et al.*, *Consolidating the Third Wave Democracies: Regional Challenges* (Baltimore and London: The Johns Hopkins University Press, 1997), p. xxx.

6 Jude Howell, "Civil Society," in Robert Benewick and Paul Wingrove, eds., *China in the 1990s* (London: Macmillan, 1995), p. 76–77.

7 Gordon White, "Democratization and Economic Reform in China," *Australian Journal of Chinese Affairs*, January 1994.

8 This table and the following discussion will use the main idea of Jude Howell's classification scheme, which includes four broad categories of social organization in terms of their autonomy, voluntariness, and spontaneity. See Jude Howell, p. 77.

9 Ibid.

10 Kristen Parris, "Local Initiative and National Reform: The Wenzhou Model of Development," *The China Quarterly*, no. 134, June 1993, p. 260–61.

11 For a more detailed discussion on all the four categories, see Jude Howell, pp. 77–80.

12 Bart van Steenbergen, "Transition from Authoritarian/Totalitarian Systems: Recent Developments in Central and Eastern Europe in a Comparative Perspective," *Futures*, March 1992, p. 164.

13 Terry Lynn Karl and Philippe C. Schmitter, "Modes of Transition in Latin America, Southern and Eastern Europe," *International Social Science Journal*, vol. 43, no. 2, 1991, p. 272.

14 William Kornhauser, *The Politics of Mass Society* (Glencoe, IL: The Free Press, 1959), p. 32.

15 Yu Jianxing, *Chinese Civil Society Growing out of Participation* (Hangzhou, China: Zhejiang University Press, 2008).

16 *People's Daily*, November 5, 1998, p. 1; November 6, 1998, p. 1.

17 *Rules of Registration and Regulations of Mass Organizations* (Beijing: People's Publishing House, 1989).

18 Such cases have been widely reported. For full news coverage on such cases, see reports carried in almost every issue of the California-based Chinese newspaper *Press Freedom Guardian*.

19 Chalmers Johnson, "Comparing Communist Nations," in Chalmers Johnson, ed., *Change in Communist Systems* (Stanford, CA: Stanford University Press, 1970), pp. 23–24.

20 *Press Freedom Guardian*, August 28, 1997, p. 2.

21 *South China Morning Post*, November 6, 1991, cited from Willy Wo-Lap Lam, p. 257.

22 *Reuters*, September 17, 1991, cited from Willy Wo-Lap Lam, pp. 257–58.

23 *People's Daily*, December 15, 1993, p. 1.

24 "China's internal security spending tops army budget," www.chinapost.com.tw/china/national-news/2011/03/06/293553/Chinas-internal.htm

25 *People's Daily*, February 4, 1990.

26 Ibid., February 4, 1990.

27 Ibid., November 12, 1991.

28 Lu Xueyi, ed., *Research Report on Contemporary China's Social Stratums* (Beijing: Social Science Literature Press, 2002), pp. 4, 7–8, 43–61.

29 *Dong Fang Daily* (东方早报), www.dfdaily.com, Friday, 2010.12.24, p. A19.

30 Kam Wing Chan and Will Buckingham, "Is China Abolishing the Hukou System?" *The China Quarterly*, No. 195, 2008, pp. 582–606.

31 Wang Feiling, "A Success Tough to Duplicate: China's Hokou System," accessed from http://fairobserver.com/article/success-tough-duplicate-chinese-hukou-system.

32 Li Qiang, "Modernization and Evolution of China's Social Stratification and Structure," accessed from www.china001.com/show_hdr.php?xname = PPDDMV0& dname = DSGGF41&xpos = 30.

33 John Bryan Starr, *Understanding China* (New York: Hill and Wang, 1997), p. 71; Martin K. Whyte and William L. Parish, *Urban Life in Contemporary China* (Chicago: University of Chicago Press, 1984), p. 25; Andrew G. Walder, "Organized Dependency and Cultures of Authority in Chinese Industry," *Journal of Asian Studies*, vol. 43, no. 1, pp. 51–76; Andrew G. Walder, *Communist Neo-Traditionalism: Work and Authority in Chinese Industry* (Berkeley: University of California Press, 1986).

34 Walder, p. 85.

35 Party Central Committee, "Guoying gongye qiye gongzuo tiaoli" [Work regulations for state industrial enterprises], in *Zhongguo gongye guanli bufen tiaoli huibian* [A partial compendium of Chinese industrial management regulations], ed. by Industrial Economics Research Institute, Chinese Academy of Social Sciences, pp. 216–43 (Beijing: Dizhi Chubanshe, 1980), p. 240.

36 *People's Daily*, June 3, 1996, p. 4.

37 *People's Daily*, September 27, p. 2.

38 Walder, 1986, pp. 235–39, 246–47, 250.

39 *Ming Bao,* June 13, 1991, cited from Lam, p. 246.

40 *People's Daily*, October 23, 1998, p. 2.

41 http://www.ihlo.org/LRC/ACFTU/0010309.html.

42 Melanie Manion, "The Electoral Connection in the Chinese Countryside," *American Political Science Review*, vol. 90, no. 4 (1996); Tianjian Shi, "Village Committee Elections in China: Institutionalist Tactics for Democracy," *World Politics*, vol. 51, no. 3 (1999); Tianjian Shi, "Voting and Non-Voting in China: Voting Behavior in Plebiscitary and Limited Choice Elections," *The Journal of Politics*, vol. 61, no. 4 (1999); Yang Zhong and Jie Chen, "To Vote or Not to Vote," *Comparative Political Studies*, vol. 35, no. 6 (2002); Lianjiang Li, "The Empowering Effect of Village Elections in China," *Asian Survey*, vol. 43, no. 4 (2003); Fubing Su and Dali Yang, "Elections, Governance, and Accountability in Rural China," *Asian Perspective*, vol. 29, no. 4 (2005); Pierre F. Landry, Deborah Davis and Shiru Wang, "Elections in Rural China: Competition without Parties," *Comparative Political Studies*, vol. 43, no. 6 (2010); Qingshan Tan, "Why Village Election Has Not Much Improved Village Governance," *Journal of Chinese Political Science*, vol. 15, no. 2 (2010).

43 John Dearlove, "Village Politics," in Robert Benewick and Paul Wingrove, eds., *China in the 1990s* (London: Macmillan Press, 1995), pp. 122–24.

44 *Constitution of the People's Republic of China* (Beijing: Legal Press, 1998), p. 36.

45 The Party Central Committee, "Circular of the CPC Central Committee and the State Council on Strengthening the Construction of Rural Grassroots Government" [Documents of the Party Central Committee (*Zhongfa*), no. 22, 1986], in The Department of Civil Affairs of Jiangsu Province, ed., *Guideline in the Electoral*

Work of Villagers' Committees (*Cunweihui xuanju gongzuo zhinan*), 1995, pp. 29, 30.

46 The Ministry of Civil Affairs, "Circular of Further strengthening the Construction of the Villagers' Committees" [The Ministry of Civil Affairs, February 27, 1995], in The Department of Civil Affairs of Jiangsu Province, ed., *Guideline in the Electoral Work of Villagers' Committees* (*Cunweihui xuanju gongzuo zhinan*), 1995, p. 45.

47 Dearlove, p. 123–24.

48 *The Organic Law of Villagers' Committees in the People's Republic of China* (Beijing, Legal Press, 1987), Articles 2, 3, 4, and 5.

49 Ibid., Article 2; Dearlove, p. 124.

50 *People's Daily*, April 10, 1998, p. 1.

51 *The Organic Law of the Villagers Committees*, Articles 2 and 3.

52 Dearlove, p. 125.

53 *People's Daily*, February 28, 1998, p. 6.

54 The Ministry of Civil Affairs, "Circular of Further Strengthening the Construction of the Villagers' Committees" [The Ministry of Civil Affairs, February 27, 1995], in The Department of Civil Affairs of Jiangsu Province, ed., *Guideline in the Electoral Work of Villagers' Committees* (*Cunweihui xuanju gongzuo zhinan*), 1995, p. 47.

55 The Party Central Committee, "Circular of the CPC Central Committee on Strengthening the Construction of Rural Grassroots Organizations" [Documents of the Party Central Committee (*Zhongfa*), no. 10, 1994], in The Department of Civil Affairs of Jiangsu Province, ed., *Guideline in the Electoral Work of Villagers' Committees* (*Cunweihui xuanju gongzuo zhinan*), 1995, p. 32.

56 The Department of Civil Affairs of Jiangsu Province, pp. 156, 132.

57 Ibid., pp. 109–63.

58 M. Kent Jennings, "Political Participation in the Chinese Countryside," *American Political Science Review*, vol. 91, no. 1, June 1997, p. 361.

59 S. H. Potter and J. M. Potter, *China's Peasants* (Cambridge: Cambridge University Press, 1990), pp. 280, 271.

60 *Press Freedom Guardian*, October 11, 1997, p. 4. A. Chan, R. Madsen, and J. Unger, *Chen Village Under Mao and Deng* (Berkeley, University of California Press, 1992) p. 318.

61 Kelliher D. Kelliher, "Privatization and Politics in Rural China," in G. White, ed., *The Chinese State in the Era of Economic Reform* (London: Macmillan, 1991) p. 333.

62 Yang Zhong, "Withering Governmental Power in China? A View from Below" *Communist and Post-Communist Studies*, vol. 29, no. 4, 1996, pp. 363–75; for another recent field study in China which supports the same view, see Weixing Chen, "The Political Economy of Rural Industrialization in China: Village Conglomerates in Shangdong Province," *Modern China*, vol. 24, no. 1, 1998, pp. 73–100.

63 *Xinhua Wenzhai*, no. 8, 1998, p. 23.

64 Ibid., p. 21.

65 Dearlove, p. 131.

66 "Report on Our Implementation of 'Organic Law of Villagers' Committees and Promotion of Villagers' Self-Management Activities," in Department of Civil Affairs of Jiangsu Province, pp. 2–3.

67 *People's Daily,* September 1, 1997, p. 4.

68 Xu Yong, *Rural Governance and Chinese Politics* (Beijing: China Social Sciences Publishing House, 2003), p. 154.

15 State socialism and the Chinese communist economy

1 James N. Danziger, *Understanding the Political World: A Comparative Introduction to Political Science* (New York: Longman, 1998), p. 195.
2 Ibid.
3 Mark N. Hagopian, *Regimes, Movements, and Ideologies* (New York and London: Longman, 1978), pp. 436–37.
4 Thomas M. Magstadt and Peter M. Schotten, p. 367; Robert J. Jackson and Doreen Jackson, *A Comparative Introduction to Political Science* (New Jersey: Prentice Hall, 1997), p. 160; For a detailed discussion, see Yu-Shan Wu, *Comparative Economic Transformations: Mainland China, Hungary, the Soviet Union, and Taiwan* (Stanford, CA: Stanford University Press, 1994), pp. 7–9.
5 David Lane, ed., *The Legacy of State Socialism and the Future of Transformation* (Rowman & Littlefield Publishers, 2002); Andrew G. Walder, Denise O'Leary and Kent Thiry, "Transitions from State Socialism: A Property Rights Perspective," in Mark Granovetter and Richard Swedberg, eds., *The Sociology of Economic Life* (Westview Press, 2011).
6 Janos Kornai, *The Socialist System: The Political Economy of Communism* (Princeton, Princeton University Press, 1992); David Lane, 2002; Andrew G. Walder, *et al.*, 2011.
7 Ibid.
8 Gregory C. Chow, *The Chinese Economy* (Singapore: World Scientific Publishing, 1987), p. 41.
9 Ibid., p. 135. Also see Chinese State Statistics Bureau, Statistical Yearbook of China (Hong Kong: Hong Kong Economic Review Publishing House, 1981), pp. 207 and 212.
10 Ibid., pp. 69–71.
11 Barry Naughton, *The Chinese Economy: Transitions and Growth* (Cambridge, MA: The MIT Press, 2007), p. 61.
12 Janos Kornai, 1992.
13 Susan L. Shirk, "The Politics of Industrial Reform," in Elizabeth J. Perry and Christine Wong, *The Political Economy of Reform in Post-Mao China* (Cambridge, MA: Harvard University Press, 1985), pp. 197–98.
14 Barry Naughton, pp. 73–74.
15 Ibid., pp. 80.
16 Gregory C. Chow, pp. 97–98.
17 Gregory C. Chow, p. 97.
18 Barry Naughton, pp. 235–36.
19 For more details on a list of campaigns and movements, see Chinese and English websites: http://hi.baidu.com/xh9831/blog/item/3a273912f370f05bf819b8a2.html; http://en.wikipedia.org/wiki/List_of_campaigns_of_the_Communist_Party_of_China
20 Barry Naughton, pp. 63–76.
21 L. Ch. Schenk-Sandbergen, "Some Aspects of Political Mobilization in China," *Modern Asian Studies*, vol. 7, no. 4, 1973, pp. 679–80.
22 Barry Naughton, p. 56.
23 People's Republic of China: "Reforms, 1980–88." www.chaos.umd.edu/history/prc5.html

16 Market socialism and economic transition in Post-Mao China

1 C. Fred Bergsten, Bates Gill, Nicholas R. Lardy, and Derek Mitchell, *China: The Balance Sheet—What the World Needs to Know Now About the Emerging Superpower* (New York: Public Affairs, 2006), pp. 18–19.

2 Tien-tung Hsueh and Tun-oy Woo, "Reforms of the Economic Structure in the People's Republic of China," in Joseph Y. S. Cheng, ed., *China: Modernization in the 1980s* (New York: St. Martin's Press, 1990), p. 231.

3 Harry Harding, *China's Second Revolution: Reform after Mao* (Washington, DC: The Brookings Institution, 1987), pp. 99–171.

4 Wanda Tseng, *et al.*, *Economic Reform in China: A New Phase* (Washington, DC: International Monetary Fund, 1994), pp. 43–45.

5 *New York Times*, September 6, 1993, p. 5.

6 Cheng Li, *Rediscovering China: Dynamics and Dilemmas of Reform* (Lanham, Maryland: Rowman & Littlefield Publishers, 1997), p. 53.

7 Ibid., p. 54.

8 See the figure in Table X in Minxin Pei, 1994.

9 Dic Lo, *Market and Institutional Regulation in Chinese Industrialization, 1978–1994* (London: Macmillan Press, 1997), p. 90.

10 Janos Kornai, *The Socialist System: The Political Economy of Communism* (Princeton, Princeton University Press, 1992), p. 91.

11 Sujian Guo, *The Political Economy of Asian Transitions from Communism* (Ashgate, 2006), p. 172.

12 Pranab K. Bardhan and John E. Roemer, eds., *Market Socialism: The Current Debate* (New York: Oxford University Press, 1993), p. 3.

13 An-chia Wu, "Whither Mainland China: On the Theoretical Study Campaign," in Yu-ming Shaw, ed., *Changes and Continuities in Chinese Communism* (Boulder and London: Westview Press, 1988), p. 163.

14 V. I. Lenin, *Selected Works*, vol. III (Moscow, 1975), p. 585.

15 *People's Daily*, August 12, 1997, p. 1.

16 Wu, p. 163.

17 Ibid., pp. 163–64.

18 *People's Daily*, September 23, 1999, pp. 1–2; September 27, 1999, p. 1.

19 Mark N. Hagopian, *Regimes, Movements, and Ideologies* (New York and London: Longman, 1978), pp. 436–37. According to Hagopian, the means of production include such things as energy resources, land, raw materials, tools, machines, and factories. The means of exchange include transportation and communication facilities, wholesale and retail outlets, banking and credit institutions, and so forth.

20 Thomas M. Magstadt and Peter M. Schotten, *Understanding Politics: Ideas, Institutions, and Issues* (New York: St. Martin's Press, 1996), p. 367; Robert J. Jackson and Doreen Jackson, *A Comparative Introduction to Political Science* (New Jersey: Prentice Hall, 1997), p. 160; Jack C. Plato and Roy Olton, *The International Relations Dictionary* (Santa Barbara, CA: ABC, 1982), p. 81.

21 Leon P. Baradat, *Political Ideologies: Their Origins and Impact* (New Jersey: Prentice Hall, 1979), p. 186.

22 *Press Freedom Guardian* (USA), May 22, 1998, p. 4.

23 John Bryan Starr, *Understanding China: A Guide to China's Economy, History, and Political Structure* (New York: Hill and Wang, A Division of Farrar, Straus and Giroux, 1997), p. 81.

24 Michael W. Bell, p. 13.

25 National Statistics Bureau of China, *China's Statistical Yearbook* (Beijing: China Statistics Press, 2001). See section 13.5: "Main Indicators of All State-owned and Non-state-owned Above Designed Size Industrial Enterprises."

26 Lo, p. 6.

27 Rupert Hodder, "State, Collective and Private Industry in China's Evolving Economy," in Denis Dwyer, ed., *China: The Next Decades* (Essex, UK: Longman Group, 1994), p. 120.

28 Xu Yuanmin, *et al.*, *New Explorations of Jiangsu TVEs* (Nanking: Jiangsu People's Publisher, 1997), pp. 1–5; C. Riskin, *China's Political Economy: The Quest for Development Since 1949* (New York: Oxford University Press, 1987), pp. 213–18; Joseph C. H. Chai, *China: Transition to a Market Economy* (New York: Oxford University Press, 1997), p. 168.

29 William Byrd and Qingshong Lin, eds., *China's Rural Industry: Structure, Development, and Reform* (London and New York: Oxford University Press, 1990); Martin Weitzman and Chenggang Xu, "Chinese Township Village Enterprises as Vaguely Defined Cooperatives," *Journal of Comparative Economics*, vol. 18, 1994, pp. 121–45; Chun Chang and Yijiang Wang, "The Nature of the Township-Village Enterprise," *Journal of Comparative Economics*, vol. 19, 1994, pp. 434–52; Xun Wang and Douglas Hechathorn, "Tigers are Bound and Monkeys are Free: A Comparative Study of State-Owned and Township/Village-Owned Enterprises in China," *Chinese Journal of Political Science*, vol. 1, no. 1, Spring 1995, pp. 7–42.

30 Chun Chang and Yijiang Wang, "The Nature of the Township-Village Enterprise," *Journal of Comparative Economics*, vol. 19, 1994, pp. 434–52.

31 Chang and Wang, p. 450.

32 Yang Zhong, "Withering Governmental Power in China? A View from Below" *Communist and Post-Communist Studies*, vol. 29, no. 4, 1996, pp. 363–75; for another recent field study in China which supports this view, see Weixing Chen, "The Political Economy of Rural Industrialization in China: Village Conglomerates in Shangdong Province," *Modern China*, vol. 24, no. 1, 1998, pp. 73–100.

33 Kevin Lee, *Chinese Firms and the State in Transition: Property Rights and Agency Problems in the Reform Era* (New York: M. E. Sharpe, 1991); Victor Nee, "Organizational Dynamics of Market Transition: Hybrid Forms, Property Rights, and Mixed Economy in China," *Administration Science Quarterly*, vol. 37, no. 1; David S. G. Goodman, "Collectives and Connectives, Capitalism and Corporatism: Structural Change in China," *The Journal of Communist Studies and Transition Politics*, vol. 11, no. 1, March 1995, p. 12.

34 *People's Daily*, February 6, 1997, p. 2.

35 *Xinhua Daily*, May 10, 1998, 2.

36 Wei-wei Zhang, *Ideology and Economic Reform under Deng Xiaoping 1978–1993* (London and New York: Kegan Paul International, 1996), p. 216.

37 Michael W. Bell, pp. 13, 15.

38 Ibid., p. 15.

39 Feng Chen, *Economic Transition and Political Legitimacy in Post-Mao China* (New York: State University of New York Press, 1995), p. 82.

40 Ibid., p. 82–83, 87–88.

41 Feng Chen, p. 89.

42 Michael W. Bell, p. 15.

43 *People's Daily*, June 18, 1999, p. 2.

44 Janos Kornai, p. 71.

45 *People's Daily*, August 14, 1995, p. 1; May 27, 1997, p. 2.

46 Greg Mastel, *The Rise of the Chinese Economy: The Middle Kingdom Emerges* (New York: M. E. Sharpe, 1997), p. 71.

47 *People's Daily*, August 12, 1997, p. 4.

48 Lo, pp. 6, 89.

49 Ibid., p. 90.

50 For a detailed discussion of this policy, see also Chapters 2 and 6.

51 *People's Daily*, January 3, 1998, p. 1.

52 *Xinhua Wenzhai*, no. 4, 1998, pp. 52–53.

53 *People's Daily*, August 26, 1997, p. 4.

54 Ibid., October 16, 1998, pp. 1–2.

55 Wanda Tseng, et al., *Economic Reform in China: A New Phase* (Washington, DC: International Monetary Fund, 1994), pp. 43–45.

56 Qi Guizhen and Wang Peirong, *Answers to Questions in the Economic Restructuring* (Beijing: Tongxin Chubanshe, 1997), p. 97.

57 Ibid., pp. 124–25.

58 *People's Daily*, August 7, 1997, p. 1; October 13, 1997, p. 2.

59 *China Daily*, March 10, 1998, p. 4.

60 *People's Daily*, August 18, 1997, p. 1.

61 Feng Chen, p. 121.

62 Ibid.; Guo Zhengying, *Questions and Answers Regarding the Shareholding Economy under Socialism* (Beijing: Beijing Aeronautical Institute Press, 1986); Zhao Ziyang, *Political Report to the 13th National Congress of the Chinese Communist Party* (Beijing: People's Publisher, 1987).

63 *People's Daily*, August 12, 1997, p. 4.

64 Starr, pp. 83, 85.

65 Kristen Parris, "Local Initiative and National Reform: The Wenzhou Model of Development," *The China Quarterly*, no. 134, June 1993, pp. 245–46; pp. 258–59.

66 Jean Oi, "Private and Local State Entrepreneurship: The Shangdong Case," presented at the conference of the Association for Asian Studies, April 2–5,1992, Washington, D.C.

67 *China Daily*, March 10, 1998, p. 4.

68 Jialin Zhang, "The Advance of China's State Sector: Some Implications for the China's Economy," August 1, 2010, www.chinausfriendship.com/article1.asp?mn=222

69 Ibid.

70 *Southern Weekend*, November 3, 2011, www.infzm.com/content/64481

71 Thomas Rawski, "Chinese Industrial Reform: Accomplishments, Prospects, and Implications," *American Economic Review*, vol. 84, no. 2, 1994, pp. 271–75.

72 E. Borensztein and M. Kumar, "Proposals for Privatization in Eastern Europe," *IMF Staff Papers*, vol. 38, no. 2, 1991, p. 302.

73 Janos Kornai, *The Road to a Free Economy: Shifting from a Socialist System, the Example of Hungary* (New York: W. W. Norton and Company, 1990), p. 57.

74 Lo, pp. 47, 49.

75 *Beijing Review*, 24–30 May 1993, p. 14.

76 *Economist*, "Asia's emerging economies," 30 November, 1991, p. 67.

77 *International Herald Tribune*, 13 October 1992.

78 Michael W. Bell, p. 11.

79 *Almanac of Socialism with the Chinese Characteristics 1997* (Beijing: China Legal Press, 1998), p. 367.

80 Deng Xiaoping, *Selected Works of Deng Xiaoping* (Beijing: People's Publishing House, 1993), vol. III, p. 306.

81 Mastel, pp. 71–73.
82 Ibid., pp. 71–72.
83 Michael W. Bell, p. 2.
84 *People's Daily*, October 21, 1993; Zhang, p. 215.
85 *People's Daily*, May 1, 1998, p. 1.
86 Hodder, pp. 117–18.
87 Ibid., p. 118.
88 *China Daily,* April 4, 1998, p. 4.
89 Cheng Xiaonong, "Where does Prosperity come from?" *China Spring*, vol. 165, 1997, p. 12–13.
90 Ibid., p. 12.
91 *People's Daily*, October 13, 1997, p. 2.
92 *China Daily*, April 4, 1998, p. 4.
93 *China Daily–Business Weekly*, March 30, 1998, p. 3.
94 *People's Daily*, November 16, 1998, p. 1.
95 *The China Times Magazine* (Hong Kong), vol. 196, October 1–7, 1995, p. 51.
96 *People's Daily*, October 7, 1995, p. 2.
97 World Bank, *China: Foreign Trade Reform* (Washington, DC: The World Bank, 1994), pp. 75–76.
98 www.chinanews.com/cj/2010/12–10/2713868.shtml; *China Daily*, December 24, 2010, p. 8
99 *People's Daily*, June 30, 1998, p. 2.
100 World Bank, pp. 103–15.
101 Ibid., pp. 120–21.

17 Chinese foreign policy making

1 David M. Lampton, ed., *The Making of Chinese Foreign and Security Policy in the Era of Reform, 1978–2000* (Stanford: Stanford University Press, 2001), p. 2.
2 Bin Yu, "The Study of Chinese Foreign Policy: Problems and Prospect," *World Politics*, vol. 46, no. 2, 1994, pp. 235–61.
3 David M. Lampton, p. 2.
4 Lu Ning, *The Dynamics of Foreign-Policy Decisionmaking in China* (Boulder, CO: Westview, 1997), p. 86.
5 Ibid., p. 12.
6 Linda Jakobson and Dean Knox, *New Foreign Policy Actors in China*, SIPRI Policy Paper No. 26, September 2010, pp. 12–13.
7 Ibid., p. 5.
8 Lai Hongyi, *The Domestic Sources of China's Foreign Policy: Regimes, Leadership, Priorities and Process* (Routledge, 2010).
9 William A. Callahan, *China: The Pessoptimist Nation* (Oxford: Oxford University Press, 2010).
10 See Yitan Li's book review essay on William A. Callahan, *China: The Pessoptimist Nation* (Oxford: Oxford University Press, 2010), *Journal of Chinese Political Science*, vol. 16, no. 4, 2011.
11 Wu Xinbo, "Four Contradictions Constraining China's Foreign Policy Behavior," *Journal of Contemporary China* (2001), 10 (27), 293–301.
12 Linda Jakobson and Dean Knox, p. 18.
13 David M. Lampton, p. 2–31.
14 Ibid., p. 17.
15 Ibid., p. 51.

16 C. Fred Bergsten, Bates Gill, Nicholas R. Lardy, and Derek Mitchell, *China: The Balance Sheet—What the World Needs to Know Now About the Emerging Superpower* (New York: Public Affairs, 2006), p. 13.
17 Robert G. Sutter. *Chinese Foreign Relations—Power and Policy Since the Cold War* (Lanham, MD: Rowman & Littlefield, 2010).

18 U.S.–China relations in transformation

1 www.usatoday.com/news/washington/2009-07-27-obama-china_N.htm
2 Ezra F. Vogel, ed., *Living with China: U.S.–China Relations in the Twenty-First Century* (New York: W.W. Norton & Company, 1997); Bill Gertz, *The China Threat* (Washington, DC: Regnery Publishing, 2000); C. Fred Bergsten, Bates Gill, Nicholas R. Lardy, and Derek Mitchell, *China: The Balance Sheet—What the World Needs to Know Now About the Emerging Superpower* (New York: PublicAffairs, 2006); Sujian Guo, ed., *China's Peaceful Rise in the 21st Century: Domestic and International Conditions* (Hampshire, UK: Ashgate Publishing, 2006).
3 C. Fred Bergsten, Bates Gill, Nicholas R. Lardy, and Derek Mitchell, p. 1.
4 Robert L. Worden, Andrea Matles Savada and Ronald E. Dolan, eds., *China: A Country Study.* (Washington: GPO for the Library of Congress, 1987), p. 492.
5 Ibid., pp. 492–94.
6 The discussion on the nature of the U.S.–China relationship in the following pages incorporates some material from Baogang Guo and Sujian Guo, "Thirty Years of China–U.S. Relations: Reappraisal and Reassessment," in Sujian Guo and Baogang Guo, eds., *Thirty Years of China–U.S. Relations: Analytical Approaches and Contemporary Issues* (Lanham: Rowman & Littlefield-Lexington, 2010), pp. 1–7.
7 Kerry Daubaugh, *China–U.S. Relations in the 110th Congress: Issues and Implications for U.S. Policy*, CRS Report RL33877, February 10, 2009. www.crs.gov.
8 Bill Gertz, *China Threat: How the People's Republic Targets America* (Washington, DC: Regnery Publishing, Inc., 2000); Constaine C. Menges, *China: the Gathering Threat* (Nashville, TN: Thomas Nelson, 2005), 5th ed.
9 Al Pressiin, "U.S. Moves to Counter Chinese Military Modernization," VOA News, January 27, 2009; Ivan Eland, "Is Chinese Military Modernization a Threat to the United States?" *Policy Analysis*, No. 465, January 23, 2003, Cato Institute, www.cato.org/pubs/pas/pa465.pdf (accessed on December 15, 2009).
10 David W. Moore, "American Divided in Feelings about China," Gallup Poll, April 3, 2001, www.gallup.com/poll/1837/Americans-Divided-Feelings-About-China.aspx.
11 Reuter, "China Seen as a Key U.S. Relations, also a Foe," www.reuters.com/article/oU.Sl.ivMolt/idU.SL.TRE5A308C20091104 (accessed on November 12, 2009).
12 "Kissinger: U.S. China Can Form 'New Global Order,'" Newsmax.com, http://archive.newsmax.com/archives/ic/2007/4/3/73126.shtml?s = ic.
13 C. Fred Bergsten, "Pacific and Asia Pacific: the Choices for APEC," *Policy Brief*, July 2009, Peterson Institute of International Economics, Number PB09–16.
14 Niall Ferguson, "Team Chimerica," *Washington Post*, Nov. 17, 2008.
15 CCTV, "Wen Rules out 'G2' Proposal," http://english.cctv.com/20090525/101054shtml.
16 Guo Wang, "G2: Untold Truth about Sino-U.S. Relations," *Lianhe Zaobao* (Singapore), July 14, 2009.

17 Robert G. Sutter, *Chinese Foreign Relations: Power and Policy since the Cold War* (Rowman & Littlefield Publishers, 2007).

18 David M. Lampton, "Power Constrained: Sources of Mutual Strategic Suspicion in U.S.–China Relations," *NBA Analysis*, June 2010, accessed from www.nbr.org/publications/element.aspx?id=455.

19 See Sujian Guo, "Introduction: Challenges and Opportunities for China's 'Peaceful Rise'," in Sujian Guo, ed., *China's Peaceful Rise in the 21st Century: Domestic and International Conditions* (Hampshire, UK: Ashgate Publishing, 2006).

20 Robert D. Kaplan, "How We Would Fight China," *The Atlantic Monthly*, vol. 295, no. 5, June 2005, pp. 49–64, www.theatlantic.com/doc/prem/200506/kaplan.

21 James P. Pinkerton, "Superpower Showdown," *The American Conservative,* November 7, 2005.

22 Aaron L. Friedberg, "Hegemony with Chinese Characteristics," *The National Interest*, July–August 2011.

23 John Mearsheimer, "Better to Be Godzilla than Bambi," *Foreign Policy* (FP), January/February 2005, www.foreignpolicy.com/story/cms.php?story_id = 2740 &page = 2.

24 Huang Renwei, "Zhongguo heping jueqide daolu xuanze he zhanlue guannian," *Jiefang Ribao* (Liberation Daily), April 26, 2004.

25 Avery Goldstein, *Rising to the Challenge: China's Grand Strategy and International Security* (Stanford, CA: Stanford University Press, 2005), p. 213.

26 Aaron L. Friedberg, 2011.

27 C. Fred Bergsten, Bates Gill, Nicholas R. Lardy, and Derek Mitchell, p. 16.

28 Aaron L. Friedberg, "The Future of U.S.–China Relations: Is Conflict Inevitable?" *International Security*, vol. 30, no. 2, Fall 2005, p. 40.

29 Ibid., pp. 40–45.

30 Zbigniew Brzezinski, "Nukes Change Everything," *Foreign Policy* (FP), January/February 2005.

31 Evan S. Medeiros, "China Debates Its 'Peaceful Rise' Strategy" *YaleGlobal*, June 22, 2004, http://yaleglobal.yale.edu/display.article?id=4118.

Index